Waffen-SS
Encyclopedia

Waffen-SS Encyclopedia

Marc J. Rikmenspoel

THE ABERJONA PRESS
Bedford, PA

Editor: Keith E. Bonn
Production: Aegis Consulting Group, Inc.
Printer: Mercersburg Printing, Mercersburg, PA

The Aberjona Press is an imprint of Aegis Consulting Group Inc.
    Bedford, Pennsylvania 15522
© 2004 Marc J. Rikmenspoel
All rights reserved.
Printed in the United States of America
13 12 11 10 09   7 6 5 4 3

ISBN 13: 978-0-9717650-8-5
ISBN 10: 0-9717650-8-1

Originally published by The Military Book Club as *Waffen-SS: The Encyclopedia*
Visit us at www.militarybookclub.com
This edition published in cooperation with BOOKSPAN

The photographs in this book are predominantly from the author's private collection or are used with the permission and by the courtesy of those individuals recognized in the Introduction. Other photos are from the US National Archives and are designated by "(NA)" in the caption.

On the front cover: top row, left: Typical *Waffen-SS* soldier, summer 1942 (author's collection)
Top row, right: Soldiers of the *SS*-Estonian Legion, circa 1943 (Erik Rundkvist collection)
Middle row, left: Volunteers of the Flemish Legion, spring 1942 (Geert De Vos collection)
Middle row, right: *Untersturmführer* Gerhard Stiller with a Panzer III at the training center in Bitsh (Bitche), 1942 (Martin Månsson collection)
Bottom row, left: An *SS-Totenkopf* infantry regiment, 1941 (author's collection)
Bottom row, right: Soldier of *SS-Nord*, 1942 (Richard Warfield collection)

To the memory of Terry C. Johnston,
who taught me what it truly means
to be an author.
Ake wancinyankin ktelo, mitakola.
Mitakuye oyasin.

This new edition is dedicated to the
memory of Tomas "Quorthon" Forsberg and
Terje "Valfar" Bakken, who now make their
music in Valhalla.

It is further dedicated to the memory of Kit
Bonn, Erik Rundkvist, and Adrian Bromley,
all of whom were far too young....

Contents

Introduction *x*
About the Author *xii*
Rank Equivalences *xiii*
A Guide to Tactical Unit Symbols *xiv*

Formations of the *Waffen-SS* 1

Armies 7
Corps 8
Divisions 16
Brigades 57
Regiments 57
Battalions 57
Never Formed 58

Structure of *Waffen-SS Divisions* 59

Early War 60
Panzer Divisions 60
Panzer-Grenadier Divisions 63
Mountain Divisions 64
Cavalry Divisions 66
Grenadier (Infantry) Divisions 68

Germans in the *Waffen-SS* 69

Germanics in the *Waffen-SS* 83

The *Wiking* Division 84
SS-Volunteer Regiment *Nordwest* 89
The *SS-Nordland* and *SS-Nederland* Divisions 90

The Germanic Nations 98
Denmark 98
Finland 110
Flanders 116
Great Britain 130
Iceland 134
The Netherlands 134
Norway 147
Sweden 160
Switzerland and Liechtenstein 166
Wallonia 169
Conclusions 179

Non-Germans and Non-Germanics in the *Waffen-SS* 181

Albania 181
Armenia 182
Azerbaijan 182
Bosnia 182
Bulgaria 183
Belorussia 183
Czechia 183
Estonia 184
France 185
Georgia 186
Hungary 187
India 187
Ireland 188
Italy 188
Latvia 188
Lithuania 189
North Caucasus 189
Poland 190
Romania 190
Russia 191
Slovakia 191
Spain 192
Turkics 192
Ukraine 193
Conclusion 194

Leading Personalities of the *Waffen-SS* 195

    Paul Hausser 195
    Felix Steiner 199
    Sepp Dietrich 203
    Theodor Eicke 206
    Herbert Otto Gille 210
    Willi Bittrich 213
    Matthias Kleinheisterkamp 215
    Otto Kumm 217
    Heinz Harmel 220
    Dr. Oskar Dirlewanger 223
    Otto Weidinger 226
    Hans Dorr 228
    Walter Schmidt 231

Weapons of the *Waffen-SS* 235

    Infantry Weapons 235
    Anti-Tank Weapons (Including Tank-Destroying Vehicles) 238
    Armored Vehicles 240
    Artillery 246

Myths About the *Waffen-SS* 251

    The *Waffen-SS* Were the "Asphalt Soldiers" 251
    The *Waffen-SS* Was Atheistic 252
    The *Waffen-SS* Suffered Unnecessarily High Casualties in Battle 253
    The *Waffen-SS* Had Inferior Leadership 256
    The *Waffen-SS* Possessed Superior Weaponry to the *Heer* 257

Appendix: Weapons Tables 261
Annotated Bibliography 265

Introduction

The list of published works about the Waffen-SS grows longer every year. New accounts and information see publication in every language used by members of the Waffen-SS, meaning that many specialized details useful to historians are found in books not available in English or German. Meanwhile, the contents of various archives around the world have yet to be explored in full. These factors allow for the happy event that as a field of study, the topic of the Waffen-SS remains fresh; more remains to be said without simply rehashing what has come before.

Unfortunately, many works exist, particularly in English, which are rehashes, cutting and pasting out of published books to create a "new" volume. The result is that much misinformation has been widely spread, with the Waffen-SS order of battle suffering greatly in this regard.

Thus, this reason for being is laid out. My aim is to present readers and researchers with a handy reference on: the precise order of battle of its major formations; the manpower sources and nationalities that comprised the force, the "movers and shakers" of the Waffen-SS, and the weapons they used.

As a bonus, extended detail is provided on the history of the "Germanic" Waffen-SS, that part of it formed from Scandinavians and West Europeans. This sub-topic has suffered from shallow and sloppy research more than any other, in the realm of Waffen-SS books published in English. Luckily, diligent researchers are investigating this aspect of the Waffen-SS, and many have kindly made their findings available to me. For this I need to particularly thank Tommy Natedal, Geir Brenden, Björn Jervas, Lennart Westberg, Martin Månsson, Erik Rundkvist, Holger Thor Nielsen, Allen Brandt, Erik Linnasmägi, Leo Tammiksaar, John P. Moore, Eddy De Bruyne, Max Cuypers, Yvo Janssens, and Peter van Holsteijn. With their help, I was able to present information never before published in such a comprehensive manner. It is my hope that this section will prove useful even to those experienced researchers who find little new in the rest of the book.

The book as a whole has benefited from the writing and publishing efforts of Roger James Bender and Hugh Page Taylor, Richard Landwehr, Erik Norling, John Fedorowicz (with Michael Olive and Robert Edwards), Mark Yerger, Olli Wikberg, Munin Verlag, and the Sint Maartensfonds, among many additional researchers and publishers.

Special thanks go to Kit and Patti Bonn for bringing me this project, and for their considerate editing. The mistakes are still mine, of course.

I welcome questions and comments, and I apologize if I failed to thank anyone who assisted me. Thanks for reading my work.

Marc Rikmenspoel
Fort Collins, Colorado

About the Author

Marc Rikmenspoel was born on 26 July 1970 in Albany, New York, to a Dutch father and an American mother. He graduated Phi Beta Kappa from Colorado State University in Fort Collins in 1992 with a BA in History, and resided in Fort Collins for many years. He recently moved to Denver. This was his second book; the first, *Soldiers of the Waffen-SS: Many Nations, One Motto*, was published by J. J. Fedorowicz in 1999. Since the first edition of *Waffen-SS Encyclopedia*, he has co-authored with Eddy De Bruyne *For Rex and For Belgium: Leon Degrelle and Walloon Political & Military Collaboration, 1941–1945*, published by Helion in 2004.

Rank Equivalences

Officer

US Army	German Army	Waffen SS
General of the Army	*Generalfeldmarschall*	
General	*Generaloberst*	*Oberstgruppenführer*
Lieutenant General	*General der Infanterie, General der Panzertruppen*, etc.	*Obergruppenführer*
Major General	*Generalleutnant*	*Gruppenführer*
Brigadier General	*Generalmajor*	*Brigadeführer*
No equivalent	No equivalent	*Oberführer*
Colonel	*Oberst*	*Standartenführer*
Lieutenant Coloonel	*Oberstleutnant*	*Obersturmbannführer*
Major	*Major*	*Sturmbannführer*
Captain	*Hauptmann*	*Hauptsturmführer*
First Lieutenant	*Oberleutnant*	*Obersturmführer*
Second Lieutenant	*Leutnant*	*Untersturmführer*

Enlisted

US Army	German Army	Waffen SS
Master Sergeant First Sergeant	*Stabsfeldwebel*	*Sturmscharführer*
Technical Sergeant	*Oberfeldwebel*	*Hauptscharführer*
Staff Sergeant/ Technician 3d Grade	*Feldwebel*	*Oberscharführer*
Sergeant/ Technician 4th Grade	*Unterfeldwebel*	*Scharführer*
Corporal/ Technician 5th Grade	*Unteroffizier*	*Unterscharführer*
Private First Class	*Gefreiter/Obergefreiter*	*Rottenführer*
Private	*Soldat* (*Grenadier* in the Infantry, *Kanonier* in the field artillery, etc.)	*SS Mann*

A Guide to Tactical Unit Symbols

Types of Units

⊠	Infantry
⊠ (with triangle)	Mountain Infantry
⊠ (Füsilier)	*Füsilier* (light infantry)
⊠ (with vertical bar)	Motorized Infantry
⊠ (oval)	Panzer Grenadier
⬭	Panzer
⬭ (with slash)	Armored Recon
◸	Horse cavalry
◸ (with triangle)	Recon (in a mountain unit)
PzJg	*Panzerjäger* (Tank Destroyer/Anti-Tank)
▪	Artillery (Towed or horse-drawn)
⬭ (with dot)	Artillery (Self-Propelled)
▪ (with mark)	Artillery (Mule-packed, horse-drawn, or towed)
△	Anti-Aircraft Artillery
⊓	Engineers
⊓ (in oval)	Armored Engineers
⟋	Signal
⟋ (in oval)	Armored Signal

Sizes of Units

I	Company/Battery/Troop
II	Battalion/Squadron
III	Regiment
XX	Division

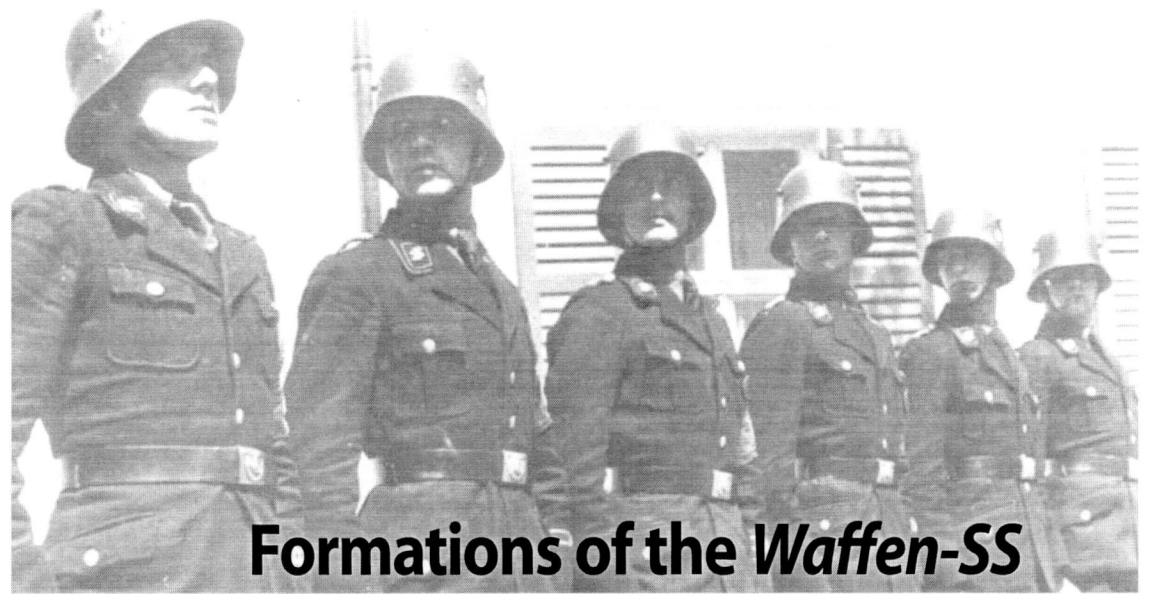

Formations of the *Waffen-SS*

To attenuate confusion which sometimes arises when studying the *Waffen-SS*, this section begins with a list of the major formations by their formal German nomenclatures. All subsequent references will be by their English language equivalents. The Germans used ordinal Arabic numerals for divisions and companies, and ordinal Roman numerals for corps and for battalions that were integral to regiments. Ordinal numbers in German military usage are designated with a period, that is, the German equivalent of the English "1st" is "1;" there is no written English equivalent of the German "I" but it would be pronounced "First." Regiments and separate battalions were designated by cardinal numbers which were place last. This means that a unit could be, "1. Company of II. Battalion of Regiment 3 of the 4. Division of V. Corps," which would be read "First Company of the Second Battalion of Regiment Three of the Fourth Division of the Fifth Corps." Honor titles, if any, are included, with a brief explanation of their respective meanings.

1. *SS-Panzer Division "Leibstandarte Schützstaffel Adolf Hitler"* (Hitler's *SS* Bodyguard)
2. *SS-Panzer Division "Das Reich"* ("The Empire")
3. *SS-Panzer Division "Totenkopf"* ("Death's Head," in reference to the symbol of the concentration camp system)
4. *SS-Polizei-Panzer-Grenadier Division*
5. *SS-Panzer Division "Wiking"* ("Viking," in reference to the non-German, Nordic volunteers in the division)
6. *SS-Gebirgs Division "Nord"* ("North," in reference to the original unit being organized for use in Norway and Finland)

7. *SS-Freiwilligen-Gebirgs Division "Prinz Eugen"* ("Prince Eugene," in reference to the Prince of Savoy who fought the Turks in the Balkans on behalf of the Habsburgs in the early eighteenth century.)
8. *SS-Kavallerie Division "Florian Geyer"* (Refers to a rebel knight from the Peasants' Revolt of 1525.)
9. *SS-Panzer Division "Hohenstaufen"* (In reference to the family of Holy Roman Emperors from the Middle Ages, including Friedrich Barbarossa.)
10. *SS-Panzer Division "Frundsberg"* (Refers to Georg von Frundsberg, founder of a band of sixteenth-century Landsknecht freebooters.)
11. *SS-Freiwilligen-Panzer-Grenadier Division "Nordland"* ("Northland," carrying on the title of the regiment that first incorporated Scandinavian volunteers in the Waffen-SS.)
12. *SS-Panzer Division "Hitlerjugend"* (Refers to the Hitler Youth organization which supplied the initial volunteers for this division.)
13. *Waffen-Gebirgs Division "Handschar"* (*kroatische nr. 1*) (In reference to the Croatian word for "scimitar," which was an Islamic symbol referring to this division's enlisted personnel's Muslim cultural roots and religion.)
14. *Waffen-Grenadier Division* (*ukrainische nr. 1*) (Ukrainians constituted this division's enlisted complement.)
15. *Waffen-Grenadier Division* (*lettische nr. 1*) (A division comprised of Latvian enlisted men)
16. *SS-Panzer-Grenadier Division "Reichsführer-SS"* (In reference to the unit's origins with Himmler's escort battalion)
17. *SS-Panzer-Grenadier Division "Götz von Berlichingen"* (Refers to another rogue knight from the Peasants' Revolt of 1525.)
18. *SS-Freiwilligen-Panzer-Grenadier Division "Horst Wessel"* (In reference to the *SA* man and Nazi "martyr," since this division was intended to include *SA* volunteers)
19. *Waffen-Grenadier Division* (*lettische nr. 2*) (Another division whose enlisted men were Latvians.)
20. *Waffen-Grenadier Division* (*estnische nr. 1*) (The enlisted men of this division were Estonians.)
21. *Waffen-Gebirgs Division "Skanderbeg"* (*albanische nr. 1*) [Refers to the fifteenth-century Albanian national hero, George Kastriotis, who fought the Turks under this nickname, which recalled Iskander (Alexander the Great). This division's enlisted complement was comprised of Albanian Muslims.]
22. *SS-Freiwilligen-Kavallerie Division "Maria Theresia"* (In reference to the Habsburg Empress and Queen of Hungary, for this cavalry division included many Hungarian citizens.)

23. *Waffen-Gebirgs Division "Kama" (kroatische nr. 2)* (Refers to another Muslim symbol, this time a knife used by shepherds. This division's enlisted complement was also comprised of Croatian Muslims.)
23. *SS-Freiwilligen-Panzer-Grenadier Division "Nederland" (niederländische nr. 1)* (Dutch for "the Netherlands," the origin of most of this division's personnel.)
24. *Waffen-Gebirgs Division "Karstjäger"* (Refers to the division's area of operations, the rocky limestone and dolomite Karst topographies of Slovenia, Croatia, and parts of Italy.)
25. *Waffen-Grenadier Division "Hunyadi" (ungarische nr. 1)* (In reference to fifteenth-century Hungarian national hero, Janos Hunyadi, who defeated the Turks. Most of this division's officers and enlisted men were Hungarians.)
26. *Waffen-Grenadier Division "Hungaria" (ungarische nr. 2)* (Most of this division's officers and enlisted men were Hungarians.)
27. *SS-Freiwilligen-Grenadier Division "Langemarck" (flämische nr. 1)* (Carried over the traditions of previous units, in reference to the Flemish town where many German student volunteers were killed during the First World War. Most of this division's enlisted men were Flemings.)
28. *SS-Freiwilligen-Grenadier Division "Wallonien" (wallonische nr. 1)* (German for Walloon, in reference to the French-speaking Walloons who were considered Germanic, and who comprised a majority of this division's enlisted complement.)
29. *Waffen-Grenadier Division (russische nr. 1).* (Division's enlisted complement consisted primarily of Russians.)
29. *Waffen-Grenadier Division (italienische nr. 1).* (Division's enlisted complement consisted primarily of Italians.)
30. *Waffen-Grenadier Division (russische nr. 2).* (Division's enlisted complement consisted primarily of Russians.)
31. *SS-Freiwilligen-Grenadier Division*
32. *SS-Freiwilligen-Grenadier Division "30. Januar"* (Refers to the date in 1933 on which the Nazis legally gained control of Germany.)
33. *SS-Freiwilligen-Grenadier Division*
33. *Waffen-Grenadier Division "Charlemagne" (französische nr. 1)* (Refers to the early medieval Emperor of the Franks, who ruled over areas which eventually became both parts of Germany and France. The division was formed from French volunteers.)
34. *SS-Freiwilligen-Grenadier Division "Landstorm Nederland" (niederländische nr. 2)* (Refers to the division's origins with a pro-Axis militia in the Netherlands.)
35. *SS-Polizei-Grenadier Division*

36. *Waffen-Grenadier Division "Dirlewanger"* (Carried over from previous units, in reference to the division's founder, Dr. Oskar Dirlewanger.)
37. *SS-Freiwilligen-Kavallerie Division "Lützow"* [Refers to Adolf Freiherr (Baron) von Lützow, who organized a force to fight behind French lines during the Napoleonic wars.]
38. *SS-Panzer-Grenadier Division "Nibelungen"* (Refers to the Rhine saga popularized by Richard Wagner, which symbolized the many Nordic volunteers in the division.)

SS-Panzer-Grenadier Regiment 1 "Leibstandarte Schützstaffel Adolf Hitler"
SS-Panzer-Grenadier Regiment 2 "Leibstandarte Schützstaffel Adolf Hitler"
SS-Panzer-Grenadier Regiment 3 "Deutschland" (Refers simply to Germany, the modern country.)
SS-Panzer-Grenadier Regiment 4 "Der Führer" (Refers to Hitler's popular title. This was originally a unit consisting primarily of Austrians, so the title symbolized Austrian loyalty to the new regime.)
SS-Panzer-Grenadier Regiment 5 "Totenkopf" (Refers to the regiment's origins with the first Totenkopf regiment.)
SS-Panzer-Grenadier Regiment 6 "Theodor Eicke" (Refers to the fallen first commander of the Totenkopf Division, the founder of the concentration camp system.)
SS-Polizei-Panzer-Grenadier Regiment 7
SS-Polizei-Panzer-Grenadier Regiment 8
SS-Panzer-Grenadier Regiment 9 "Germania" (Refers to all of the lands settled by Germans.)
SS-Panzer-Grenadier Regiment 10 "Westland" (Meaning "Western Europe," in reference to the Flemish and Dutch volunteers in the regiment.)
SS-Gebirgsjäger Regiment 11 "Reinhard Heydrich" (Refers to the assassinated founder of the *SS* Security Service, or *Sicherheitsdienst*, with whom this regiment had once served in Prague.)
SS-Gebirgsjäger Regiment 12 "Michael Gaissmair" (Refers to a Tyrolian sixteenth-century folk hero, in recognition of the presence of a significant number of Tyrolians in the regiment.)
SS-Freiwilligen-Gebirgsjäger Regiment 13 "Artur Phleps" (Refers to the fallen first commander of the *Prinz Eugen Division*)
SS-Freiwilligen-Gebirgsjäger Regiment 14 "Skanderbeg" (During 1945 took on the traditions of the disbanded Albanian 21st Waffen-Mountain Division)
SS-Kavallerie Regiment 15
SS-Kavallerie Regiment 16
SS-Kavallerie Regiment 17

SS-Kavallerie Regiment 18
SS-Panzer-Grenadier Regiment 19
SS-Panzer-Grenadier Regiment 20
SS-Panzer-Grenadier Regiment 21
SS-Panzer-Grenadier Regiment 22
SS-Freiwilligen-Panzer-Grenadier Regiment 23 "Norge" (norwegisches nr. 1) (Norwegian for "Norway," referring to the nationality of many of the regiment's enlisted men.)
SS-Freiwilligen-Panzer-Grenadier Regiment 24 "Danmark" (dänisches nr. 1) (Danish for "Denmark," referring to the nationality of many of the regiment's enlisted men.)
SS-Panzer-Grenadier Regiment 25
SS-Panzer-Grenadier Regiment 26
Waffen-Gebirgsjäger Regiment 27 (kroatisches nr. 1)
Waffen-Gebirgsjäger Regiment 28 (kroatisches nr. 2)
Waffen-Grenadier Regiment 29 (ukrainisches nr. 1)
Waffen-Grenadier Regiment 30 (ukrainisches nr. 2)
Waffen-Grenadier Regiment 31 (ukrainisches nr. 3)
Waffen-Grenadier Regiment 32 (lettisches nr. 3)
Waffen-Grenadier Regiment 33 (lettisches nr. 4)
Waffen-Grenadier Regiment 34 (lettisches nr. 5)
SS-Panzer-Grenadier Regiment 35
SS-Panzer-Grenadier Regiment 36
SS-Panzer-Grenadier Regiment 37
SS-Panzer-Grenadier Regiment 38
SS-Freiwilligen-Panzer-Grenadier Regiment 39
SS-Freiwilligen-Panzer-Grenadier Regiment 40
Waffen-Grenadier Regiment 42 "Voldemars Veiss" (lettisches nr. 1) (Refers to the former regimental commander, the first Latvian to earn the Knight's Cross)
Waffen-Grenadier Regiment 43 "Hinrich Schuldt" (lettisches nr. 2) (Refers to the fallen first commander of the 19. Waffen-Grenadier Division)
Waffen-Grenadier Regiment 44 (lettisches nr. 6)
Waffen-Grenadier Regiment 45 (estnisches nr. 1)
Waffen-Grenadier Regiment 46 (estnisches nr. 2)
Waffen-Grenadier Regiment 47 (estnisches nr. 3)
SS-Freiwilligen-Panzer-Grenadier Regiment 48 "General Seyffardt" (niederlandisches nr. 1) (In reference to the assassinated spiritual head of the Dutch SS-Legion, the former Dutch Army chief of staff, Hendrik Seyffardt)
SS-Freiwilligen-Panzer-Grenadier Regiment 49 "De Ruyter" (niederländisches nr. 2) (In reference to the seventeenth-century Dutch admiral, Michael De Ruyter, who defeated the English fleet.)
Waffen-Gebirgsjäger Regiment 50 (albanisches nr. 1)

Waffen-Gebirgsjäger Regiment 51 (albanisches nr. 2)
SS-Freiwilligen-Kavallerie Regiment 52
SS-Freiwilligen-Kavallerie Regiment 53
SS-Freiwilligen-Kavallerie Regiment 54
Waffen-Gebirgsjäger Regiment 55 (kroatisches nr. 3)
Waffen-Gebirgsjäger Regiment 56 (kroatisches nr. 4)
Waffen-Grenadier Regiment 57 (französisches nr. 1)
Waffen-Grenadier Regiment 58 (französisches nr. 2)
Waffen-Gebirgsjäger (Karstjäger) Regiment 59
Waffen-Gebirgsjäger (Karstjäger) Regiment 60
Waffen-Grenadier Regiment 61 (ungarisches nr. 1)
Waffen-Grenadier Regiment 62 (ungarisches nr. 2)
Waffen-Grenadier Regiment 63 (ungarisches nr. 3)
Waffen-Grenadier Regiment 64 (ungarisches nr. 4)
Waffen-Greandier Regiment 65 (ungarisches nr. 5)
SS-Freiwilligen-Grenadier Regiment 66 (flämisches nr. 1)
SS-Freiwilligen-Grenadier Regiment 67 (flämisches nr. 2)
SS-Freiwilligen-Grenadier Regiment 68 (flämisches nr. 3)
SS-Freiwilligen-Grenadier Regiment 69 (wallonisches nr. 1)
SS-Freiwilligen-Grenadier Regiment 70 (wallonisches nr. 2)
SS-Freiwilligen-Grenadier Regiment 71 (wallonisches nr. 3)
Waffen-Grenadier Regiment 72
Waffen-Grenadier Regiment 73
Waffen-Grenadier Regiment 74
Waffen-Grenadier Regiment 75
Waffen-Grenadier Regiment 76
Waffen-Grenadier Regiment 77
SS-Freiwilligen-Grenadier Regiment 78
SS-Freiwilligen-Grenadier Regiment 79
SS-Freiwilligen-Grenadier Regiment 80
Waffen-Grenadier Regiment 81 (italienisches nr. 1)
Waffen-Grenadier Regiment 82 (italiensches nr. 2)
SS-Freiwilligen-Grenadier Regiment 83 (niederländisches nr. 3)
SS-Freiwilligen-Grenadier Regiment 84 (niederländisches nr. 4)
Waffen-Grenadier Regiment 85 (ungarisches nr. 6)
SS-Freiwilligen-Grenadier Regiment 86 "Schill" (Refers to the code word that caused this regiment to be formed as an emergency reaction unit during the summer of 1944.)
SS-Freiwilligen-Grenadier Regiment 87 "Kurmark" (Refers to the training area where this regiment was organized for emergency service.)
SS-Freiwilligen-Grenadier Regiment 88
SS-Polizei-Grenadier Regiment 89
SS-Polizei-Grenadier Regiment 90

SS-Polizei-Grenadier Regiment 91
SS-Freiwilligen-Kavallerie Regiment 92
SS-Freiwilligen-Kavallerie Regiment 93
SS-Freiwilligen-Kavallerie Regiment 94
SS-Panzer-Grenadier Regiment 95
SS-Panzer-Grenadier Regiment 96
SS-Panzer-Grenadier Regiment 97

With the basic roster presented in "official" format, what follows is a detailed organizational description of the combat units of the *Waffen-SS* from field army to division level, with American English terminolgy used to enhance its comprehensibility. Afterwards, additional smaller combat units are listed by name only. "Volunteer-" in a unit's title implies foreign status (indicating that the preponderence of enlisted men were not of German nationality). Although it literally means "Armed," "*Waffen-*" in a unit's title implies non-Germanic origins (indicating that the preponderence of enlisted men were not of German, ethnic German, or related Nordic ancestry). *SS* and other German ranks do not correspond exactly to *Heer* (German Army) or US Army conventions, so they are portrayed in German; this is also done because many individuals often held separate commissions as officers in the *Allgemeine-SS* (the Political *SS*), *Waffen-SS*, and *Polizei* (police). (See the table of equivalent ranks on page xi) While it was common for separate commissions to be brought to equal rank, men who excelled in a particular field might attain a rank that differed from their other commission(s).

Armies

6th SS-Panzer Army

SS-Oberst-Gruppenführer und Panzergeneraloberst der Waffen-SS Josef "Sepp" Dietrich (14 September 1944–8 May 1945)

SS-Panzer Army Signal Regiment 6

Created 14 September 1944 as 6th Panzer Army to control I and II *SS*-Panzer Corps. Activated on 24 October 1944. First saw action 16 December 1944 in the Ardennes, withdrawn during late January 1945 and retitled "6th *SS*-Panzer Army." Relocated to western Hungary, major role in the *Frühlingserwachen* ("Spring Awakening") offensive, beginning 6 March 1945, followed by retrograde fighting into Austria to west of Vienna. Most survivors surrendered to American forces in May 1945, some went into Soviet captivity.

11th *SS*-Panzer Army

SS-Obergruppenführer und General der Waffen-SS Felix Steiner (5 February–early March 1945)

Created 4 February 1945 by retitling the former headquarters of Army Group *Oberrhein*, moved from Upper Rhine front to Pomerania to control the SONNENWENDE ("Solstice") offensive that began on 16 February 1945. Retitled "11th Army" in early March 1945.

Corps

I SS-Panzer Corps, 1944–45*

I *SS*-Panzer Corps *"Leibstandarte* Adolf Hitler"

SS-Obergruppenführer und General der Waffen-SS, later *SS-Oberst-Gruppenführer und Panzergeneraloberst der Waffen-SS* Josef "Sepp" Dietrich (27 July 1943–9 August 1944)

SS-Brigadeführer und Generalmajor der Waffen-SS und Oberst i.G. Fritz Kraemer (temporary, 9–16 August 1944)

SS-Obergruppenführer und General der Waffen-SS Georg Keppler (16 August–24 October 1944)

SS-Gruppenführer und Generalleutnant der Waffen-SS Hermann Priess (24 October 1944–8 May 1945)

> *SS*-Corps-Signal Battalion 501
> Heavy *SS*-Artillery Battalion 501
> Heavy *SS*-Panzer Battalion 501

Ordered into existence 27 July 1943 to control the 1st and 12th *SS*-Panzer (-grenadier) Divisions. These two divisions were Panzer-Grenadier ones when the corps was formed, but were redesignated as Panzer after October 1943. The corps headquarters was formed in Italy in October–November 1943, before relocating to western Europe. First saw action in June 1944 in Normandy; suffered heavy casualties near Caen, in Falaise pocket, and along the Seine. After refitting, fought in the Ardennes from December 1944 to January 1945, then sent to Hungary; conducted successful SÜDWIND ("Southwind") offensive that destroyed the Soviet Gran Bridgehead in mid-February 1945. Next the corps had minor success during the FRÜHLINGSERWACHEN offensive in early March 1945, before retreating west into Austria. The corps surrendered to American forces near Steyr at the end of the war.

---

*Symbols used are confirmed wartime vehicle and sign identification symbols. Many shown in other publications are unconfirmed, fabrications, or postwar creations for veterans' associations.

II SS-Panzer Corps

SS-Panzer Corps (retitled II SS-Panzer Corps, 1943–45)

SS-Panzer Corps at Kursk, assigned, may not have been used

SS-Obergruppenführer und General der Waffen-SS Paul Hausser (May 1942–28 June 1944)

SS-Gruppenführer und Generalleutnant der Waffen-SS, later *SS-Obergruppenführer und General der Waffen-SS* Wilhelm "Willi" Bittrich (29 June 1944–8 May 1945)

SS-Corps-Signal Battalion 502
SS-Rocket Launcher Battalion 502
Heavy SS-Artillery Battalion 502
Heavy SS-Panzer Battalion 502 (served with XI SS-Panzer Corps 1945)

Organized 14 September 1942 as the *SS-General Kommando* (SS Corps Command) to control the original three *Waffen-SS* divisions. First saw action early February 1943 in the Kharkov region, retreated southwest before playing a leading role in the counteroffensive that recaptured Kharkov and Belgorod by mid-March 1943. The corps again had a major role on the southern wing of the Zitadelle ("Citadel") offensive in early July 1943, before moving south to the Mius bridgehead later that month. The corps headquarters and the 1st SS-Panzer-Grenadier Division relocated to Italy early in August 1943, and later helped to disarm the Italian Army. Corps assumed command of the 9th and 10th SS-Panzer Divisions and returned to action at the beginning of April 1944 in Galicia, helping to free the surrounded 1st Panzer Army. With the same divisions, the corps moved west during June 1944, entering combat in Normandy 28 June, and suffering heavy casualties during the next two months. Survivors regrouped near Arnhem, and helped to defeat the Allied airborne landings at Arnhem and Nijmegen. The 2d SS-Panzer Division then replaced the 10th SS-Panzer Division for the remainder of the war. After refitting, the corps fought in the Ardennes, December 1944–January 1945, then relocated to Hungary for the early March Frühlingserwachen offensive. The corps retreated west into Austria, through the Vienna area, and surrendered to US forces at Steyr on 8 May 1945.

III (Germanic) SS-Panzer Corps

SS-Gruppenführer und Generalleutnant der Waffen-SS, later *SS-Obergruppenführer und General der Waffen-SS* Felix Steiner (1 May 1943–25 February 1944)

SS-Gruppenführer und Generalleutnant der Waffen-SS Matthias Kleinheisterkamp (25 February–16 April 1944)

SS-Obergruppenführer und General der Waffen-SS Felix Steiner (16 April–30 October 1944)

SS-Obergruppenführer und General der Waffen-SS Georg Keppler (30 October 1944–4 February 1945)

Generalleutnant Martin Unrein (4 February–early April 1945)

SS-Obergruppenführer und General der Waffen-SS Felix Steiner (early April–8 May 1945)

    SS-Corps-Signal Battalion 503
    SS-Rocket Launcher 503 (not formed)
    Heavy *SS*-Panzer Battalion 503 (joined corps February 1945)
    SS-Nebelwerfer Battery 521
    Waffen-Grenadier Regiment of the *SS* 103 (Romanian volunteers, from March 1945)

Ordered to form on 15 April 1943 to control the Germanic volunteer units, to be based around the 5th *SS*-Panzer (-grenadier) and 11th *SS*-Volunteer-Panzer-Grenadier Divisions. The 5th *SS*-Panzer Division was never able to join the corps, and was replaced by the 4th *SS*-Volunteer Panzer-Grenadier Brigade (later retitled the 23d *SS*-Volunteer-Panzer-Grenadier Division). The corps trained and saw combat against partisans in Croatia from September to early December 1943, before relocating to the Oranienbaum front west of Leningrad. The corps was hit hard by the Soviet offensive of January 1944, and forced to retreat west to the Narva River line in Estonia, where it assumed positions in and around Narva and held them from early February until late July 1944. The corps then took over the Tannenberg Line defenses 20 kilometers to the west, and held them in very heavy fighting until the retreat from Estonia in mid-September 1944. After defensive fighting near Riga, the corps took over a portion of the Kurland defense line, and held it successfully through the First, Second, and Fourth Battles of Kurland, until relocating to Pomerania in early February 1945. After small success that month in the S*onnenwende* offensive, the corps retreated to the Altdamm bridgehead, which was held until late March 1945. After holding positions along the Oder River east of Berlin, the corps split because of the Soviet offensive of 16 April 1945, and elements retreated to the north, to the south, and through Berlin. Survivors surrendered to Allied forces along the Elbe River during early May 1945.

IV *SS*-Panzer Corps

SS-Gruppenführer und Generalleutnant der Waffen-SS und Polizei, later *SS-Obergruppenführer und General der Waffen-SS und Polizei* Alfred Wünnenberg (1 June–late August 1943)

SS-Gruppenführer und Generalleutnant der Waffen-SS Matthias Kleinheisterkamp (June–20 July 1944)

Gruppenführer und Generalleutnant der Waffen-SS Herbert Otto Gille (20 July 1944–8 May 1945)

SS-Corps-Signal Battalion 504
SS-Rocket Launcher Battalion 504 (not formed)
Heavy SS-Panzer Battalion 504 (not formed)
Heavy Panzer Battalion 509 (*Heer*, served as the corps Tiger battalion during 1945 in place of the never-formed Heavy Panzer Battalion 504)

Ordered to form on 1 June 1944, however formation not seriously begun. During June 1944, the forming staff of the VII SS-Panzer Corps was retitled as the IV SS-Panzer Corps, and it took control of the 3d and 5th SS-Panzer Divisions in central Poland the next month. After delaying actions east of Warsaw, the corps fought near Warsaw, suffering heavy casualties, until late December 1944. At that time, it was moved to Hungary. There it entered combat in early January 1945, fought in unsuccessful offensives KONRAD 1–3, and suffered further heavy losses. The corps then fought defensively for the remainder of the war, retreating with the rest of the German forces from Hungary from mid-March 1945, passing into Austria and surrendering to American forces west of Graz on 8 May 1945.

V SS-Mountain Corps

SS-Obergruppenführer und General der Waffen-SS Artur Phleps (8 July 1943–18 September 1944)

SS-Obergruppenführer und General der Waffen-SS und Polizei Friedrich-Wilhelm Krüger (late September 1944–15 March 1945)

SS-Obergruppenführer und General der Waffen-SS und Polizei Friedrich Jeckeln (15 March–8 May 1945)

SS-Corps Reconnaissance Battalion 505
SS-Corps Signal Battalion 505
SS-Artillery Battalion 505
SS-Flak Battalion 505
SS-Flak Battalion 550 (formed 1945 and subordinated to the 32d SS Volunteer-Infantry Division)
SS-Panzer Battalion 505 (captured tanks)
SS-Anti-Tank Battalion 560 (assigned 1945)
SS-Anti-Tank Battalion 561 (assigned 1945)
SS-Assault Gun Battalion 505 (never formed, was to be based on the assault gun battery within SS-Anti-Tank Battalion 7)
SS-Rocket Launcher Battalion 505
SS-Rocket Launcher Battalion 506 (intended for the VI *Waffen*-Army Corps, but fought on Oder River front under V SS-Mountain Corps)

Created on 1 July 1943 to control the 7th *SS*-Volunteer-Mountain Division and related units in occupied Yugoslavia. At first known as the V *SS*-Volunteer-Mountain Corps, but the "Volunteer" designation was dropped early 1945 when the corps headquarters and some support elements relocated to the Oder River front in eastern Germany. Until then, the corps directed anti-partisan operations, mainly in Bosnia. During 1945, the corps consisted largely of non-*SS* elements.

VI *Waffen*-Army Corps of the *SS* (Latvian)

SS-Gruppenführer und Generalleutnant der Waffen-SS und Polizei Karl Pffeffer-Wildenbruch (27 September 1943–11 June 1944)

SS-Gruppenführer und Generalleutnant der Waffen-SS Karl von Treuenfeld (11 June–25 July 1944)

SS-Obergruppenführer und General der Waffen-SS Walter Krüger (25 July 1944–8 May 1945)

>   *SS*-Corps Signal Battalion 506
>   *SS*-Flak Battalion 506
>   *Waffen*-Grenadier Regiment of the *SS* 106 (combined with the 19th *Waffen*-Grenadier Division late 1944)

Formed beginning 8 October 1943 (ordered into existence 27 September 1943) as the VI *SS*-Volunteer-Army Corps to control the Latvian *Waffen-SS* formations. Later renamed to final corps title. Arrived at the front along the Velikaya River early spring 1944 after the two Latvian divisions had retreated from the Volkhov River line. The corps retreated into Latvia; from October 1944 until the end of the war, it occupied the central portion of the Kurland defense line.

VII *SS*-Panzer Corps

Absorbed by IV *SS*-Panzer Corps early summer 1944.

SS-Gruppenführer und Generalleutnant der Waffen-SS Matthias Kleinheisterkamp (May–June 1944)

Ordered to form on 25 June 1943, but the corps staff only began to organize during May 1944, and was then renamed to become the staff for the IV *SS*-Panzer Corps.

VIII *SS*-Cavalry Corps

Never formed, would have controlled the 8th *SS*-Cavalry Divison and the 22d *SS*-Volunteer Cavalry Division.

IX *Waffen*-Mountain Corps of the *SS* (Croatian)

SS-Brigadeführer und Generalmajor der Waffen-SS, later *SS-Gruppenführer und Generalleutnant der Waffen-SS* Karl-Gustav Sauberzweig (1 June–mid-November 1944)

SS-Obergruppenführer und General der Waffen-SS und Polizei Karl Pffeffer-Wildenbruch (mid-November 1944–12 February 1945)

> *SS*-Mountain-Artillery Regiment 509
> *SS*-Reconnaissance Battalion 509 (former *Waffen*-Reconnaissance Battalion 23)
> *SS*-Flak Battalion 509

Ordered to form June 1944 to control the two Bosnian Muslim divisions, reassigned to Hungary in November 1944 to control the 8th *SS*-Cavalry and 22d *SS*-Volunteer-Cavalry Divisions. Corps destroyed in Budapest between late December 1944 and early February 1945.

X *SS*-Army Corps

SS-Obergruppenführer und General der Waffen-SS und Polizei Erich von dem Bach (4–10 February 1945)

Generalleutnant Günther Kappe (10 February–7 March 1945)

Formerly the XIV *SS*-Army Corps, retitled when reassigned early 1945 from the Upper Rhine to the Pomeranian front. Controlled miscellaneous, largely non-*SS* units. During 1944, this was considered as the possible title for an Estonian corps, if a second Estonian division had been formed.

XI *SS*-Panzer Corps

SS-Obergruppenführer und General der Waffen-SS Matthias Kleinheisterkamp (1 August 1944–2 May 1945)

> *SS*-Corps Signal Battalion 111
> Heavy *SS*-Panzer Battalion 502 (served as the corps Tiger battalion during 1945)

Organized 1 August 1944 as XI *SS*-Army Corps, the corps was retitled 1 February 1945 as XI *SS*-Panzer Corps. During 1944 and early 1945, the corps controlled *Heer* units in western Poland and Slovakia as a conventional infantry corps; during February 1945, took over armored elements on the Oder front. After Soviet offensive of April 1945, caught in the Halbe pocket south of Berlin with 9th Army, and spearheaded the costly breakout.

XII SS-Army Corps

SS-Obergruppenführer und General der Waffen-SS und Polizei Curt von Gottberg (7 August–18 October 1944)

General der Infanterie Günther Blumentritt (18 October 1944–28 January 1945)

Generalleutnant Eduard Crasemann (28 January–16 April 1945)

    SS-Corps Signal Battalion 112

Formed from the staff of Combat Group von Gottberg (a corps-sized collection of anti-partisan formations in Belorussia) to control *Heer* and *Polizei* units plugging the gap in German defenses in Poland, after the destruction of Army Group Center, summer 1944. During September 1944, corps staff relocated to the Netherlands, and remained on the northern part of the Western Front, as a *Heer* infantry corps, until destroyed in the Ruhr pocket April 1945.

XIII SS-Army Corps

SS-Gruppenführer und Generalleutnant der Waffen-SS Hermann Priess (7 August–24 October 1944)

SS-Gruppenführer und Generalleutnant der Waffen-SS Max Simon (16 November 1944–8 May 1945)

    SS-Corps Signal Battalion 113
    SS-Artillery Battalion 113

Ordered to form 1 August 1944. The next month, it took over a section of the Western front in Lorraine. Served mainly as a *Heer* infantry corps during the following fighting, participated in NORDWIND offensive in Lorraine in January 1945 before retreating east into the Danube valley by the end of the war.

XIV SS-Army Corps

SS-Obergruppenführer und General der Waffen-SS und Polizei Erich von dem Bach (November 1944–25 January 1945)

General der Panzertruppen Karl Decker (25 January–late March 1945)

SS-Gruppenführer und Generalmajor der Waffen-SS und Polizei Heinz Reinefarth (late March–early April 1945)

Formed November 1944 by converting the superfluous staff of the "Head of Anti-Partisan Warfare" into a military headquarters. Controlled miscellaneous *Heer* elements on the upper Rhine front until reassigned to Pomerania in January 1945 and retitled as "X *SS*-Army Corps." A shadow headquarters seems to have remained in existence, perhaps as a deception measure.

XV *SS*-(Cossack) Cavalry Corps

Generalleutnant Helmuth von Pannwitz (25 February–8 May 1945)

>Corps-Combat Engineer Regiment
>Corps Reconnaissance Battalion

During February 1945, the *Heer* Cossack Cavalry Corps passed into the *Waffen-SS* for administrative matters, while the officers and men did not assume *SS* membership or rank.

XVI *SS*-Army Corps

SS-Obergruppenführer und General der Waffen-SS Karl-Maria Demelhuber (15 January–April 1945)

Organized in January 1945 by converting the "Leadership Staff—East Baltic Coast" to a combat headquarters to control formations in Pomerania. Dissolved after retreat from Pomerania.

XVII *Waffen*-Army Corps of the *SS* (Hungarian)

Waffen-General der Waffen-SS Franz Zeidner (early January–18 March 1945)

Waffen-General der Waffen-SS Eugen Ranzenberger (18 March–8 May 1945)

This was to be the headquarters to control the 25th and 26th *SS-Waffen*-Grenadier Divisions, but since those were never ready for combat, the corps only underwent the initial stages of formation.

XVIII *SS*-Army Corps

SS-Gruppenführer und Generalmajor der Waffen-SS und Polizei Heinz Reinefarth (December 1944–12 February 1945)

SS-Obergruppenführer und General der Waffen-SS Georg Keppler (12 February–8 May 1945)

Organized December 1944, it served as a *Heer* infantry corps on the Upper Rhine front until the end of the war.

Divisions

1st SS-Panzer Division "Leibstandarte SS Adolf Hitler," 1939–40

SS-LAH, 1940

1st SS-Panzer Division "Leibstandarte Schützstaffel Adolf Hitler"

SS-Obergruppenführer und General der Waffen-SS Josef "Sepp" Dietrich (17 March 1933–4 June 1943)

SS-Standartenführer, later *SS-Oberführer* and *SS-Brigadeführer und Generalmajor der Waffen-SS* Theodor "Teddy" Wisch (4 June 1943–20 August 1944)

SS-Obersturmbannführer Franz Steineck (temporary, 20–31 August 1944)

SS-Standartenführer, later *SS-Oberführer* and *SS-Brigadeführer und Generalmajor der Waffen-SS* Wilhelm Mohnke (31 August 1944–6 February 1945)

SS-Brigadeführer und Generalmajor der Waffen-SS Otto Kumm (6 February–8 May 1945)

> *SS*-Panzer-Grenadier Regiment 1 *"LSSAH"*
> *SS*-Panzer-Grenadier Regiment 2 *"LSSAH"*
> *SS*-Panzer Regiment 1 *"LSSAH"*
> *SS*-Armored Artillery Regiment 1 *"LSSAH"*
> *SS*-Flak Battalion 1 *"LSSAH"*
> *SS*-Armored Reconnaissance Battalion *"LSSAH"*
> *SS*-Anti-Tank Battalion *"LSSAH"*
> *SS*-Armored Signal 1 *"LSSAH"*

The "Asphalt Soldiers." An early view of men of the *SS-LAH*, circa 1935. They still wear the original black uniforms and First World War helmets, but have the second version of helmet insignia. The *SS-LAH* and *SS-V* changed the next year to field grey uniforms and M-1935 helmets.

SS-LAH, 1941

SS-LAH, 1942

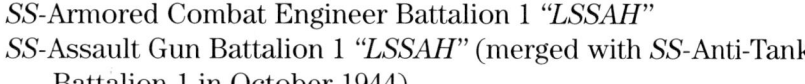

SS-LAH, 1943–45

SS-Armored Combat Engineer Battalion 1 *"LSSAH"*
SS-Assault Gun Battalion 1 *"LSSAH"* (merged with SS-Anti-Tank Battalion 1 in October 1944)
SS-Rocket Launcher Battalion 1 *"LSSAH"* (added May 1944, renumbered as 501 in March 1945)
SS-Field Replacement Battalion 1 *"LSSAH"*

Formed in 1933 as *Stabwache Adolf Hitler* with 120 men. Retitled as *Leibstandarte Adolf Hitler* on 9 November 1933. Expanded to a full regiment, then to brigade size before becoming a full division during 1942. Became an armored division at this time, and received its final full designation on 22 October 1943.

The *Leibstandarte* saw heavy combat in Poland in September 1939 and advanced into the Netherlands during the initial stage of the Western Campaign, before shifting to the Dunkirk perimeter, and then advancing south into France. During the invasion of the Soviet Union, Operation BARBAROSSA, it advanced with Army Group South, capturing Rostov during November 1941, and then settling into winter positions along the Ssambek River. Remaining in the east until early July 1942, the *Leibstandarte* moved to Normandy to reform as a panzer-grenadier division, and returned to combat in Ukraine in late January 1943. After heavy defensive fighting near Kharkov, the division retreated to the southwest, before participating in the counteroffensive that recaptured Kharkov and Belgorod by mid-March 1943. Partial success on the southern wing of the Kursk salient during early July 1943 was followed by a move to Italy late that month, where the division disarmed Italian Army units and fought partisans until late October. The *Leibstandarte* then returned to Ukraine, fighting west of Kiev and suffering very heavy

Men of *SS-LAH* pose at the Olympic monument in Greece during the invasion in April 1941.

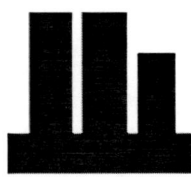

SS-LAH at Kursk, 1943, assigned but not used

casualties during the retreat into Galicia. Elements were gradually withdrawn for reconstitution in Belgium, with the last departing the east during in April 1944. After replenishment and inadequate retraining, the division began to enter combat in Normandy piecemeal from late June 1944, and sustained very heavy casualties again in the fighting near Caen, at Mortain, and in the Falaise pocket. The *Leibstandarte* was reformed in Germany during that autumn, and again entered combat in mid-December 1944 during the Ardennes offensive. After heavy losses around Stavelot and Bastogne, the division was withdrawn during January 1945 and took in replacements while *en route* to Hungary, where it participated in the successful SÜDWIND offensive of late February that destroyed the Gran Bridgehead. After partial success during the FRÜHLINGSERWACHEN offensive of early March 1945, the *Leibstandarte* gradually withdrew into Austria, surrendering to American forces near Steyr on 8 May 1945.

2d SS-Panzer Division "Das Reich"

2d SS-Panzer Division "Das Reich" 1941–45

Das Reich at Kursk, used into autumn 1943

SS-Gruppenführer und Generalleutnant der Waffen-SS, later *SS-Obergruppenführer und General der Waffen-SS* Paul Hausser (19 October 1939–14 October 1941)

SS-Oberführer, later *SS-Brigadeführer und Generalmajor der Waffen-SS* Wilhelm Bittrich (14 October–31 December 1941)

SS-Brigadeführer und Generalmajor der Waffen-SS Matthias Kleinheisterkamp (1 January–1 April 1942)

SS-Gruppenführer und Generalleutnant der Waffen-SS Georg Keppler (1 April 1942–10 February 1943)

SS-Oberführer Herbert-Ernst Vahl (10 February–18 March 1943)

SS-Gruppenführer und Generalleutnant der Waffen-SS Walter Krüger (3 April–late December 1943)

SS-Oberführer, later *SS-Brigadeführer und Generalmajor der Waffen-SS* Heinz Lammerding (late December 1943–26 July 1944)

SS-Obersturmbannführer Christian Tychsen (temporary, 26–28 July 1944)

SS-Standartenführer, later *SS-Oberführer* Otto Baum (28 July 1944–24 October 1944)

SS-Brigadeführer und Generalmajor der Waffen-SS Heinz Lammerding (1 November 1944–20 January 1945)

SS-Standartenführer Karl Kreutz (20 January–10 February 1945)

SS-Gruppenführer und Generalleutnant der Waffen-SS Werner Ostendorff (10 February–9 March 1945)

A radio command armored car of the *SS-Reich* (later *Das Reich*) Reconaissance Battalion in Russia during the summer of 1941. It carries the tactical sign for the 1st Company of its battalion, and a "G" for Guderian, indicating that it was part of Panzer Group (later Panzer Army) 2, commanded by *Generaloberst* Heinz Guderian.

SS-Standartenführer Rudolf Lehmann (9 March–13 April 1945)

SS-Standartenführer Karl Kreutz (13 April–8 May 1945)

- *SS*-Panzer-Grenadier Regiment 3 "*Deutschland*"
- *SS*-Panzer-Grenadier Regiment 4 "*Der Führer*"
- *SS*-Regiment (mot.) "*Germania*" (late 1939–late 1940)
- *SS*-Infantry Regiment 11 (late 1940–October 1941)
- *SS*-Motorcycle Regiment "*Langemarck*" (June 1942–May 1943, former *SS*-Infantry Regiment 4)
- *SS*-Panzer Regiment 2
- *SS*-Armored Artillery Regiment 2
- *SS*-Flak Battalion 2
- *SS*-Armored Reconnaissance Battalion 2
- *SS*-Anti-Tank Battalion 2
- *SS*-Armored Signal Battalion 2
- *SS*-Armored Combat Engineer Battalion 2
- *SS*-Assault Gun Battalion 2 (merged with *SS*-Anti-Tank Battalion 2 October 1944)
- *SS*-Rocket Launcher Battalion 2 (added 1944)
- *SS*-Field Replacement Battalion 2

Formed in late 1939 as the *SS-Verfügungstruppe* (*SS-V*) Division, which was based on the *SS-V* regiments *Deutschland*, *Germania*, and *Der Führer*. Full divisional supporting elements were gradually added, so that the division was fully operational for the 1940 Western Campaign, after *Deutschland* and *Germania* had fought in Poland. The division was renamed *Deutschland* on 3 December 1940, but this was soon changed to *Reich* ("Empire") on 28 January 1941. Finally, the title became *Das Reich* in May 1942.

The division fought well in the invasion of western Europe in the Netherlands and France, and then was with Army Group Center during BARBAROSSA for the drive on Moscow. It suffered heavy losses defending the Yelna position as the Kiev Pocket was formed and closed, and then sustained further severe casualties defending against the Moscow counteroffensive. Gradually withdrawn from the front, *Das Reich* was reconstituted in France, and returned to combat in January 1943, defending Kharkov as part of the *SS*-Panzer Corps. After withdrawing from the city, it played a leading role in the "miracle on the Donets" counteroffensive during February–March 1943. Early in July, it fought in the southern pincer of Operation ZITADELLE, and then moved south, to help destroy the Soviet Mius bridgehead, before returning to the Kharkov sector for the Fourth Battle of Kharkov. Next, it participated in the withdrawal towards the Dnieper, and by December, was badly depleted.

A combined arms combat group (*Kampfgruppe Das Reich*) remained in Ukraine, while the mass of the division returned to France to again rebuild. The last elements of the combat group rejoined the main body in France by April 1944, but rebuilding was not complete when the Allies invaded France on 6 June. Parts of the division fought the Maquis in the Dordogne, before moving north to Normandy, where the remainder joined them by early July. After weeks of heavy fighting, most of the surviving elements escaped the Roncey pocket in late July, and the division was outside the Falaise pocket when that formed in mid-August. *Das Reich* distinguished itself in assaulting the Allied ring around the Falaise pocket, enabling many encircled units to escape.

After withdrawing to Germany by September 1944, *Das Reich* rebuilt quickly, and then participated in the Ardennes Offensive between December 1944 and January 1945. After a final reconstitution, the division moved to Hungary with the 6th *SS*-Panzer Army for the FRÜHLINGSERWACHEN Offensive near Lake Balaton during March 1945. It then withdrew into Austria, where it briefly defended Vienna in early April 1945. Again badly depleted, the remnants surrendered to American forces near St. Pölten up to 8 May, with the detached *"Der Führer"* Regiment first passing through Prague before surrendering near Pilsen.

3d *SS*-Panzer Division *"Totenkopf"*

SS-Gruppenführer Theodor Eicke (14 November 1939–11 July 1941)

SS-Brigadeführer und Generalmajor der Waffen-SS Georg Keppler (15 July–21 September 1941)

SS-Gruppenführer und Generalleutnant der Waffen-SS, later *SS-Obergruppenführer und General der Waffen-SS* Theodor Eicke (21 September 1941–26 February 1943)

Formations of the *Waffen-SS*

3d *SS*-Panzer Division "*Totenkopf,*" 1939–45

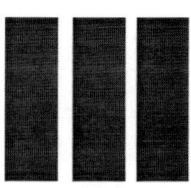

Totenkopf at Kursk, 1943

SS-Brigadeführer und Generalmajor der Waffen-SS Max Simon (26 February–early April 1943)

SS-Oberführer, later *SS-Brigadeführer und Generalmajor der Waffen-SS* and *SS-Gruppenführer und Generalleutnant der Waffen-SS* Hermann Priess (early April 1943–20 June 1944)

SS-Obersturmbannführer Karl Ullrich (20 June–13 July 1944)

SS-Oberführer, later *SS-Brigadeführer und Generalmajor der Waffen-SS* Hellmuth Becker (13 July 1944–8 May 1945)

- *SS*-Panzer-Grenadier Regiment 5 "*Totenkopf*" (former *SS-Totenkopf* Infantry Regiment 1)
- *SS*-Panzer-Grenadier Regiment 6 "Theodor Eicke" (former *SS-Totenkopf* Infantry Regiment 3)
- *SS-Totenkopf* Infantry Regiment 2 (October 1939–summer 1941)
- *SS*-Motorcycle Regiment "Thule" (June 1942–May 1943, former *SS-*Infantry Regiment 9)
- *SS*-Panzer Regiment 3
- *SS*-Armored Artillery Regiment 3
- *SS*-Flak Battalion 3
- *SS*-Armored Reconnaissance Battalion 3
- *SS*-Anti-Tank Battalion 3
- *SS*-Armored Signal Battalion 3
- *SS*-Armored Combat Engineer Battalion 3
- *SS*-Assault Gun Battalion 3 (later merged with *SS*-Anti-Tank Battalion 3)
- *SS*-Field Replacement Battalion 3

The "*Totenkopfverbände*" consisted of the guard detachments at concentration camps during the 1930s. These forces were brought to a strength above what was needed, so that Heinrich Himmler would have another armed force at his disposal during wartime. After war was declared in September 1939, the 6,500 fittest men of the *SS-TV* were combined with older-age *Allgemeine-SS* reservists to form a division, which became known as the *SS-Totenkopf* Division. While motorized, it lacked the lengthy peacetime training of the *SS-V* units, and so did not fight as well as those did in the 1940 Western Campaign. Still, *Totenkopf* fought respectably, and during the following year, the older men were replaced with young wartime volunteers, and the division was thoroughly trained. It then fought during BARBAROSSA with Army Group North in the advance on Leningrad, before shifting south to the Lake Ilmen area. Already depleted, *Totenkopf* was caught in the Demyansk pocket, and was a mainstay in its defense between February and October 1942. From May, elements were withdrawn to rebuild in France, and new subunits were formed, so that a new *Totenkopf* Division organized even as the last of the old version bled to death in the Valdai Hills.

One of the *SS-Totenkopf* Infantry Regiments on the march, circa 1941. The NCO at center, with sword drawn, is a combat veteran, as indicated by his decorations.

The new *SS*-Panzer-Grenadier Division *Totenkopf* returned to combat during February 1943, joining the *SS-Panzer Corps* southwest of Kharkov, and participating in the successful counteroffensive. It next fought with the corps during Operation ZITADELLE, and during the destruction of the Mius Bridgehead, and then in the withdrawal across the Dnieper and to the west. During 1944, *Totenkopf*, in greatly weakened form, retreated through Ukraine to Romania, joining *Heer* Panzer-Grenadier Division *Grossdeutschland* in the successful defense of the Targul Frumos sector during the spring. During June and early July 1944, the division rested and rebuilt, and then joined the 5th *SS*-Panzer Division *Wiking* in the IV *SS*-Panzer Corps for action east and north of Warsaw. *Totenkopf* again suffered heavy losses defending the "Wet Triangle" between Warsaw and Modlin in the autumn of 1944, before entraining to Hungary at the end of the year. Still with IV *SS*-Panzer Corps, *Totenkopf* went into combat on 4 January 1945 during Operation KONRAD 1, in an attempt to relieve the Budapest garrison. The division played little part in KONRAD 2 during the next week, but was fully involved in KONRAD 3 beginning on 18 January. This attempt to restore a German frontline on the Danube failed, and the division was exhausted and almost out of armored vehicles by the end of the month. *Totenkopf* played a defensive role during Operation *FRÜHLINGSERWACHEN*, and then served as a rear guard for the retreat of 6th Army and 6th *SS*-Panzer Army during the retreat from Hungary. The division briefly defended Vienna in early April, before surrendering to American units northwest of the city in early May 1945. The division was then forcibly turned over the Soviets, where its members faced lengthy captivity.

4th *SS-Polizei*-Panzer-Grenadier Division

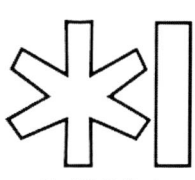

SS-Brigadeführer und Generalmajor der Polizei, later *SS-Gruppenführer und Generalleutnant der Polizei* Karl Pfeffer-Wildenbruch (1 October 1939–10 November 1940)

SS-Gruppenführer und Generalleutnant der Schutzpolizei Artur Mülverstedt (10 November 1940–10 August 1941)

SS-Brigadeführer und Generalmajor der Waffen-SS Walter Krüger (10 August–15 December 1941)

SS-Brigadeführer und Generalmajor der Polizei, later *SS-Gruppenführer und Generalleutnant der Polizei* Alfred Wünnenberg (15 December 1941–10 June 1943)

SS-Oberführer und Oberst der Schutzpolizei, later *SS-Brigadeführer und Generalmajor der Waffen-SS und Polizei* Fritz Schmedes (10 June 1943–18 June 1944)

SS-Standartenführer und Oberstleutnant der Schutzpolizei Karl Schümers (temporary, 18 June–13 July 1944)

SS-Brigadeführer Herbert-Ernst Vahl (13–22 July 1944)

SS-Standartenführer und Oberstleutnant der Schutzpolizei Karl Schümers (23 July–18 August 1944)

SS-Standartenführer und Oberstleutnant der Schutzpolizei Helmut Dörner (temporary, 18–24 August 1944)

SS-Brigadeführer und Generalmajor der Waffen-SS und Polizei Fritz Schmedes (24 August–27 November 1944)

SS-Standartenführer Walter Harzer (28 November 1944–8 May 1945)

- *SS-Polizei*-Panzer-Grenadier Regiment 7 (former *SS-Polizei*-Infantry Regiment 1)
- *SS-Polizei*-Panzer-Grenadier Regiment 8 (former *SS-Polizei*-Infantry Regiment 2)
- *SS-Polizei*-Infantry Regiment 3 (late 1939–early 1943)
- *SS-Polizei*-Artillery Regiment 4
- *SS-Polizei*-Flak Battalion 4
- *SS-Polizei*-Armored Signal Battalion 4
- *SS-Polizei*-Panzer Battalion 4 (formed from *SS-Polizei*-Assault Gun Battalion 4 July 1944)
- *SS-Polizei*-Armored Reconnaissance Battalion 4
- *SS-Polizei*-Anti-Tank Battalion 4
- *SS-Polizei*-Armored Combat Engineer Battalion 4
- *SS-Polizei*-Assault Gun Battalion 4 (retitled *SS-Polizei*-Panzer Battalion 4 July 1944)
- *SS*-Field Replacement Battalion 4

4th *SS-Polizei*-Panzer-Grenadier Division, 1941–44

4th *SS-Polizei*-Panzer-Grenadier Division, 1944–45

Organized from militarily-capable members of the *Ordnungspolizei* (the "Order Police," or ordinary policemen) in October 1939. Assigned to the *Waffen-SS*, though most of division did not hold *SS* membership. Fought along the Maginot Line in June 1940. Next fought with Army Group North in the advance on Leningrad, seeing heavy combat in the first half of 1942 in the Volkhov River sector. Heavy combat in September 1942 outside Leningrad in the First Battle of Lake Ladoga, then in the Second Battle of Lake Ladoga early 1943. Most of division withdrawn to Greece to rebuild while a combat group remained behind in the north, rejoining the division in late spring 1944. Particiapted in antipartisan operations in Greece through 1944, until the unit was committed against the Red Army in the Banat (a then-predominantly ethnic German portion of Yugoslavia) in October 1944. Withdrew into Slovakia in late January 1945 and transported north to Stettin and on to the Danzig area. Heavy combat, evacuated by sea in April, reemployed on the Oder front north of Berlin, retreated to the Elbe River, and surrendered to American forces in early May 1945.

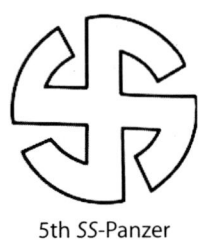

5th *SS*-Panzer Division *"Wiking"*

SS-Brigadeführer und Generalmajor der Waffen-SS, later *SS-Gruppenführer und Generalleutnant der Waffen-SS* Felix Steiner (1 December 1940–1 May 1943)

SS-Brigadeführer und Generalmajor der Waffen-SS, later *SS-Gruppenführer und Generalleutnant der Waffen-SS* Herbert Otto Gille (1 May 1943–20 July 1944)

SS-Standartenführer Johannes-Rudolf Mühlenkamp (20 July–9 October 1944)

SS-Standartenführer, later *SS-Oberführer* Karl Ullrich (9 October 1944–8 May 1945)

    SS-Panzer-Grenadier Regiment 9 *"Germania"*
    SS-Panzer-Grenadier Regiment 10 *"Westland"*
    SS-Panzer-Grenadier Regiment *"Nordland"* (December 1940–May 1943)
    SS-Panzer Regiment 5
    SS-Armored Artillery Regiment 5
    SS-Flak Battalion 5
    SS-Armored Reconnaissance Battalion 5
    SS-Anti-Tank Battalion 5
    SS-Armored Signal Battalion 5
    SS-Armored Combat Engineer Battalion 5
    SS-Assault Gun Battalion 5 (never fully formed, elements reassigned to *SS*-Anti-Tank Battalion 54 early 1944)

SS-Field Replacement Battalion 5
Finnish Volunteer Battalion of the *SS* (January 1942–May 1943)
SS-Volunteer-Panzer-Grenadier Battalion "*Narwa*" (July 1943–February 1944)*

Formed in late 1940 as the *Germania* Division, with detached *Germania* Regiment from *SS-V* joined by new regiments *Nordland* (Danish and Norwegian volunteers) and *Westland* (Dutch and Flemish volunteers) and supporting units. Always primarily German in composition, but also included Swedes, Swiss, Walloons (anti-Rexists from the AGRA movement), and Finns (who formed a separate battalion from January 1942). *Wiking* first saw action in June 1941 in Operation BARBAROSSA, invading Ukraine, fought across Dnieper River, spent winter 1941–42 on the Mius River line. From early July 1942, advanced through Rostov, fought in the western Caucasus, then eastern Caucasus, seeing heavy combat and sustaining severe losses. In December 1942, retreated west through Rostov, then saw defensive combat on the lower Donets before participating in the counteroffensive to the north. The Finns left in March 1943, and were replaced with the Estonian "*Narwa*" Battalion. The *Nordland* Regiment was detached in April 1943. The division returned to action in July 1943 west of Kharkov, retreated to the Dnieper; saw heavy combat and sustained heavy losses in October 1943 south of Kiev. Received final divisional designation in the same month. Encircled in January 1944 in the Cherkassy-Korsun Pocket, then led the breakout on 15 February 1944. Rebuilt in Poland, most of division was back into combat in late March 1944 in the Kovel zone, successful by

*"Narwa" is the German spelling for the Estonian "Narva."

The first difficult battle for *SS-Wiking* came during the establishment of a bridgehead across the Dnieper River from Dniepropetrovsk, at Kamenka during early September 1941. Dug in near Kamenka are Danish volunteer Sibbern Rasmussen, left, and an unknown ethnic-German (one of the first in the *Waffen-SS*), both from the 2nd Company of *SS-Nordland*. (Natedal)

Two experienced tankers of *SS*-Panzer Regiment 5 relax outside an isba in this undated photo.

late April 1944, north to Poland, fighting east of Warsaw, then 12 August 1944 heavy losses north of Warsaw in the "Wet Triangle" near Modlin. End of December 1944, transported to Hungary, and participated in the Konrad 1 operation in early January 1945 against Budapest, followed by Konrad 2 on 9 January, then Konrad 3 to the south from 18 January. After failure of these operations, retreated west, held defensive line during Operation Frühlingserwachen, sustaining heavy losses near Stuhlweissenburg. An escape route was opened for *Wiking* by the 9th *SS*-Panzer Division "Hohenstaufen," then the division withdrew into Austria and surrendered to US forces in May 1945.

6th *SS*-Mountain Division *"Nord"*

SS-Brigadeführer und Generalmajor der Waffen-SS Richard Herrmann (28 February–25 May 1941)

SS-Brigadeführer und Generalmajor der Waffen-SS Karl-Maria Demelhuber (17 June 1941–21 April 1942)

SS-Oberführer Hans Scheider (21 April–15 June 1942)

SS-Brigadeführer und Generalmajor der Waffen-SS, later *SS-Gruppenführer und Generalleutnant der Waffen-SS* Matthias Kleinheisterkamp (15 June 1942–15 December 1943)

6th SS-Mountain Division "Nord," 1941–45

SS-Brigadeführer und Generalmajor der Waffen-SS, later *SS-Gruppenführer und Generalleutnant der Waffen-SS* Lothar Debes (15 December 1943–20 May 1944)

SS-Obergruppenführer und General der Waffen-SS Friedrich-Wilhelm Krüger (20 May–late August 1944)

SS-Gruppenführer und Generalleutnant der Waffen-SS und Polizei Karl-Heinrich Brenner (1 September 1944–2 April 1945)

SS-Standartenführer Franz Schreiber (2 April–8 May 1945)

    SS-Mountain Infantry Regiment 11 "Reinhard Heydrich"
    SS-Mountain Infantry Regiment 12 "Michael Gaissmair"
    SS-Mountain Artillery Regiment 6
    SS-Reconnaissance Battalion 6
    SS-Flak Battalion 6
    SS-Mountain Combat Engineer Battalion 6
    SS-Signal Battalion 6
    SS-Panzer-Grenadier Battalion 506
    SS-Anti-Tank Battalion 6
    SS-Mountain Field Replacement Battalion 6

SS-Totenkopf Regiments 6 and 7 were sent to Norway as occupation troops during 1940. Not collectively trained for combat as a formation before committed in Finland as Motorized *SS-Kampfgruppe Nord*, 1 July 1941, it suffered heavy losses at the Soviet fortress at Salla. Withdrawn for retraining and reconstitution, the division was trained by and with experienced Finnish units for several months. Reorganized and redesignated as an *SS* mountain division in June 1942. Defensive operations in Kiestinki-Louhi sector of north Karelia throughout 1942, 1943, first nine months of 1944. Especially heavy combat in June 1944, with the attached Norwegian *SS*-Ski Battalion *Norge* almost destroyed. After the Finnish/Soviet armistice in September 1944, withdrew north in October and November, conducting a 1,600-kilometer foot march through Finland and Norway including a withdrawal through Rovaniemi, Finland, which was burned when Finnish commandos attacked an ammunition train on a siding there. The division reached Norway in November 1944, and Denmark in December. The division then began arriving in the Palatinate at the end of December 1944, and was committed to *NORDWIND* Offensive in Low Vosges Mountains in early January 1945, where it saw heavy combat and sustained serious losses. Static defensive patrolling near Bitche in February 1945. Transferred to the Saar-Moselle sector in March and destroyed as a division, although survivors fought on with elements of the 38th *SS*-Panzer Grenadier Division *Nibelungen*.

7th SS-Volunteer-Mountain Division *"Prinz Eugen"*

SS-Brigadeführer und Generalmajor der Waffen-SS, later *SS-Gruppenführer und Generalleutnant der Waffen-SS* and *SS-Obergruppenführer und General der SS* Artur Phleps (1 March 1942–3 July 1943)

SS-Brigadeführer und Generalmajor der Waffen-SS Carl *Reichsritter* (Imperial Knight) von Oberkamp (3 July–28 November 1943)

SS-Standartenführer August Schmidhuber (temporary, 28 November–late December 1943)

SS-Brigadeführer und Generalmajor der Waffen-SS Carl *Reichsritter* von Oberkamp (late December 1943–11 January 1944)

SS-Standartenführer August Schmidhuber (temporary, 11 January–early February 1944)

SS-Oberführer, later *SS-Brigadeführer und Generalmajor der Waffen-SS* Otto Kumm (early February 1944–20 January 1945)

SS-Oberführer, later *SS-Brigadeführer und Generalmajor der Waffen-SS* August Schmidhuber (20 January–8 May 1945)

- *SS*-Volunteer Mountain Infantry Regiment 13 "Artur Phleps"
- *SS*-Volunteer Mountain Infantry Regiment 14 (possibly unofficially titled "Skanderbeg" after taking on German cadre from that disbanded division)
- *SS*-Volunteer Mountain Artillery Regiment 7
- *SS*-Flak Battalion 7
- *SS*-Signal Battalion 7
- *SS*-Panzer Battalion 7 (captured French tanks)
- *SS*-Anti-Tank Battalion 7
- *SS*-Combat Engineer Battalion 7
- *SS*-Field Replacement Battalion 7

Organized in March 1942 from ethnic Germans in Yugoslavia, later supplemented by Siebenburgen *Volksdeutschen*. Fought in Bosnia in late 1942–early 1943, then Croatian coastline, then Montenegro in late 1943. Final full designation attained on 22 October 1943. By mid-1944, was back in Bosnia, and by late 1944 was fighting outside Belgrade, followed by retreat into Croatia. Early in 1945, participated in the offensive into Hungary, then retreated into Carinthia. Surrendered to British forces in May 1945; its personnel were turned over to Yugoslavian Communists.

8th SS-Cavalry Division "Florian Geyer"

SS-Brigadeführer und Generalmajor der Waffen-SS Wilhelm "Willi" Bittrich (1 June–29 November 1942)

SS-Obersturmbannführer der Reserve Gustav Lombard (29 November 1942–13 January 1943)

8th SS-Cavalry Division "Florian Geyer," 1942–45

SS-Standartenführer und Oberstleutnant der Schutzpolizei Fritz Freitag (13 January–late March 1943)

SS-Obersturmbannführer, later *SS-Standartenführer* August Zehender (late March–early May 1943)

SS-Brigadeführer und Generalmajor der Waffen-SS Hermann Fegelein (early May–13 September 1943)

SS-Gruppenführer und Generalleutnant der Polizei (*Waffen-SS Standartenführer der Reserve*, later *Oberführer der Reserve*) Bruno Streckenbach (13 September 1943–1 April 1944)

SS-Obersturmbannführer, later *SS-Standartenführer* and *SS-Oberführer* and *SS-Brigadeführer und Generalmajor der Waffen-SS* Joachim Rumohr (1 April 1944–11 February 1945)

    SS-Cavalry Regiment 15
    SS-Cavalry Regiment 16
    SS-Cavalry Regiment 17 (assigned as cadre for the 22d *SS*-Volunteer-Cavalry Division April 1944 and not reformed)
    SS-Cavalry Regiment 18 (from August 1943)
    SS-Artillery Regiment 8
    SS-Flak Battalion 8
    SS-Signal Battalion 8
    SS-Armored Reconnaissance Battalion 8
    SS-Anti-Tank Battalion 8 (absorbed planned *SS*-Assault Gun Battalion 8)
    SS-Combat Engineer Battalion 8 (not surrounded in Budapest, reassigned 1945 to 37th *SS*-Volunteer Cavalry Division)
    SS-Assault Gun Battalion 8 (not fully formed, merged with *SS*-Anti-Tank Battalion 8 late 1944)

First established on 15 September 1939, as the *SS-Totenkopf* Mounted Regiment at battalion strength to perform rear area security duties in Poland. After several reorganizations, it became *SS*-Cavalry Regiments 1 and 2 under control of the *Waffen-SS* on 25 February 1941. Expanded into the *SS*-Cavalry Brigade on 21 July 1941 and used for mopping-up and rear-area operations in the Pripet Marshes region; committed numerous atrocities against civilians and Red Army stragglers. Most of the brigade saw front line action with Army Group Center from December 1941 to May 1942, with units gradually withdrawn for reconstitution. Reorganization into the *SS*-Cavalry Division ordered on 1 June 1942, with the unit now having a military rather than police character. The division—the cavalry regiments of which were actually infantry mounted on horses—was engaged in anti-partisan operations during the last quarter of 1942, with elements again sent to the front lines from December 1942 to January 1943. Anti-partisan operations resumed until August 1943, when the division was sent to stabilize the front west of

Kharkov, followed by fighting along the Dnieper River. Elements fought near Kirovograd while the main body was withdrawn to Hungary to rebuild. Retitled the 8th *SS*-Cavalry Division Florian Geyer on 12 March 1943. *SS*-Cavalry Regiment 17 fought separately in the Pripet sector into April 1944 before becoming the cadre for the 22d *SS*-Volunteer Cavalry Division. The main body returned to action in September 1944 in Transylvania, where survivors of the battalion-sized *SS*-Regiment "Siebenbürgen" were incorporated. The division gradually retreated to the Budapest area, where it was under siege from 24 December 1944 until the breakout attempt on 11 February 1945. Only 170 men of the 8th and 22d *SS*-Cavalry Divisions escaped the city.

9th *SS*-Panzer Division "Hohenstaufen"

SS-Brigadeführer und Generalmajor der Waffen-SS, later *SS-Gruppenführer und Generalleutnant der Waffen-SS* Wilhelm "Willi" Bittrich (15 February 43–29 June 1944)

SS-Standartenführer Thomas Müller (temporary, 29 June 1944 –10 July 1944)

SS-Standartenfüher, later *SS-Oberführer* and *SS-Brigadeführer und Generalmajor der Waffen-SS* Sylvester "Vestl" Stadler (10 July 1944–29 July 1944)

SS-Standartenführer, later *SS-Oberführer* Friedrich-Wilhelm Bock (temporary, 29 July 1944–10 October 1944)

SS-Oberführer, later *SS-Brigadeführer und Generalmajor der Waffen-SS* Sylvester "Vestl" Stadler (10 October 1944–8 May 1945)

    SS-Panzer-Grenadier Regiment 19
    SS-Panzer-Grenadier Regiment 20
    SS-Motorcycle Regiment "Hohenstaufen" (planned, never fully formed)
    SS-Panzer Regiment 9
    SS-Armored Artillery Regiment 9
    SS-Flak Battalion 9
    SS-Armored Reconnaissance Battalion 9
    SS-Anti-Tank Battalion 9
    SS-Armored Signal Battalion 9
    SS-Armored Combat Engineer Battalion 9
    SS-Assault Gun Battalion 9 (merged with *SS*-Panzer Regiment 9 during formation)
    SS-Field Replacement Battalion 9

Formation ordered in December 1942; organized in spring 1943 in France. *Reichs Arbeit Dienst* (*RAD*, the German Labor Service) volunteers combined with conscripts; changed from panzer-grenadier

9th *SS*-Panzer Division "Hohenstaufen," 1943

division to full panzer division on 22 October 1943. Committed to action in March 1944 in Galicia with the Panther Battalion not yet ready for action. Heavy combat into April 1944, then in reserve. Sent back west in June 1944, into action in Normandy on 29 June, joined by Panthers. Heavy combat in the Odon Valley, reduced to one infantry regiment, on outside of Falaise pocket, retreated through Belgium, rested in Arnhem area of Netherlands, *en route* to Germany when British airborne assault aspect of Operation MARKET-GARDEN occurred. After successful battle, withdrawn to Germany to rebuild. Participated in Ardennes Offensive from 25 December, with heavy combat at St. Vith, then Bastogne; withdrawn January 1945. Hastily rebuilt, in action in Operation *FRÜHLINGSERWACHEN* in Hungary 18 March 1945; subsequently covered withdrawal, rescued the almost-surrounded *Wiking* at Stuhlweissenberg, then went west into Austria. Surrendered to American forces in May 1945.

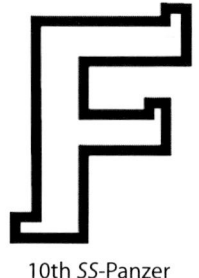

10th *SS*-Panzer Division "Frundsberg"

SS-Brigadeführer und Generalmajor der Waffen-SS Lothar Debes (15 February–12 November 1943)

SS-Brigadeführer und Generalmajor der Waffen-SS, later *SS-Gruppenführer und Generalleutnant der Waffen-SS* Karl von Treuenfeld (12 November 1943–22 April 1944)

SS-Standartenführer, later *SS-Oberführer* and *SS-Brigadeführer und Generalmajor der Waffen-SS* Heinz Harmel (27 April 1944–27 April 1945)

SS-Obersturmbannführer der Reserve Franz Roestel (27 April–8 May 1945)

    SS-Panzer-Grenadier Regiment 21
    SS-Panzer-Grenadier Regiment 22
    SS-Motorcycle Regiment "Karl der Grosse" (planned, never fully formed)
    SS-Panzer Regiment 10
    SS-Armored Artillery Regiment 10
    SS-Flak Battalion 10
    SS-Armored Reconnaissance Battalion 10
    SS-Anti-Tank Battalion 10
    SS-Armored Signal Battalion 10
    SS-Armored Combat Engineer Battalion 10
    SS-Field Replacement Battalion 10

Formation order in January 1943, organized during the spring of that year from *RAD* volunteers and conscripts. Initially received the honor title "Karl der Grosse" ("Charlemagne" in English and French) and organized as a Panzer-Grenadier Division. On 22 October 1943, renamed and retitled as 10th *SS*-Panzer Division "Frundsberg." Committed to action in concert with the 9th *SS*-Panzer Division in Galicia in March 1944, saw heavy combat into the next month before going into reserve. Moved west during June 1944, entering combat in Normandy on 29 June. Heavy losses in the Odon valley, but the division was not caught in the Falaise pocket, and was able to retreat to the Arnhem area. After successful defensive fighting at Nijmegen in September 1944, and near Aachen from November to early December 1944, the division was rebuilt in Germany and returned to action on the Rhine Plain in Alsace (joined finally by its Panther Battalion) during the latter part of the NORDWIND offensive in January 1945. It was then shipped east to participate in the SONNENWENDE offensive in Pomerania the next month, before retreating into the Altdamm bridgehead. Sent south to Saxony in April 1945, fought in the Dresden area, and largely destroyed by the end of the war.

11th *SS*-Volunteer-Panzer-Grenadier Division *"Nordland"*

SS-Brigadeführer und Generalmajor der Waffen-SS, later *SS-Gruppenführer und Generalleutnant der Waffen-SS* Friedrich "Fritz" von Scholz (1 May 1943–27 July 1944)

Oberst i.G., later *SS-Brigadeführer und Generalmajor der Waffen-SS* Joachim Ziegler (28 July 1944–25 April 1945)

SS-Brigadeführer und Generalmajor der Waffen-SS Dr. Gustav Krukenberg (25 April–8 May 1945)

- *SS*-Volunteer-Panzer-Grenadier Regiment 23 "*Norge*" (Norwegian no. 1)
- *SS*-Volunteer-Panzer-Grenadier Regiment 24 "*Danmark*" (Danish no. 1)
- *SS*-Artillery Regiment 11
- *SS*-Flak Battalion 11
- *SS*-Signal Battalion 11
- *SS*-Panzer Battalion 11 "Hermann von Salza" (was to be expanded into *SS*-Panzer Regiment 11 on several occasions, but this never occurred)
- *SS*-Armored Reconnaissance Battalion 11
- *SS*-Anti-Tank Battalion 11 (absorbed by with *SS*-Assault Gun Battalion 11)
- *SS*-Combat Engineer Battalion 11
- *SS*-Assault Gun Battalion 11 (absorbed *SS*-Anti-Tank Battalion 11)
- *SS*-Field Replacement Battalion 11

Created on 22 March 1943, to combine all the Dutch and Scandinavian volunteers in the *Waffen-SS* with the Dutch, Danish, and Norwegian Legions. At first, the divison was to be named *"Wäräger"* ("Varangian" in English, as a counterpart to the *"Viking"* Division), but its cadre was the

11th *SS*-Volunteer Panzer-Grenadier Division *"Nordland,"* 1943–45

Nordland Regiment from the 5th *SS*-Panzer (-Grenadier) Division, so on 22 October 1943, the final designation of 11th *SS*-Volunteer Panzer-Grenadier Division *Nordland* was assigned. The Dutch had meanwhile been assigned to their own brigade, so the division consisted of a majority of ethnic Germans supplemented by Scandinavians and German nationals. It deployed to Croatia in September 1943 and trained while fighting partisans until gradually sent piecemeal to the Oranienbaum front, west of Leningrad from November to December 1943. The division suffered heavily in the Soviet offensive that began on 14 January 1944, and was forced to retreat to the Luga River, and then to the Narva River in Estonia by early February 1944. After intense fighting in the Narva area into May 1944, the division retreated west to the Tannenberg Line in late July 1944, and successfully held positions there until ordered to retreat into Latvia in mid-September 1944. The division formed a defensive screen near Riga, and then assumed responsibility for a sector on the western end of the Kurland defenses, seeing heavy fighting in the first, second, and fourth Battles of Kurland. Redeployed to Pomerania during early February 1945, the division participated in the *Sonnenwende* offensive, freeing Arneswalde, before retreating to the Altdamm bridgehead. This was evacuated by 19 March 1945 and the division assumed positions along the Oder River northeast of Berlin. Most of the division was caught in Berlin after the Soviet offensive of 16 April 1945, and a few survivors broke out of the city on 2 May 1945. They and scattered elements that avoided encirclement surrendered to Allied forces along the Elbe River in the following days.

12th *SS*-Panzer Division *"Hitlerjugend"*

SS-Oberführer, later *SS-Brigadeführer und Generalmajor der Waffen-SS* Fritz Witt (31 July 1943–14 June 1944)

SS-Standartenführer, later *SS-Oberführer* and *SS-Brigadeführer und Generalmajor der Waffen-SS* Kurt Meyer (14 June–6 September 1944)

SS-Sturmbannführer Hubert Meyer (6 September–24 October 1944)

SS-Brigadeführer und Generalmajor der Waffen-SS und Oberst i.G. Fritz Kraemer (24 October–13 November 1944)

SS-Standartenführer, later *SS-Oberführer* and *SS-Brigadeführer und Generalmajor der Waffen-SS* Hugo Kraas (19 November 1944–8 May 1945)

> *SS*-Panzer-Grenadier Regiment 25
> *SS*-Panzer-Grenadier Regiment 26
> *SS*-Panzer Regiment 12
> *SS*-Armored Artillery Regiment 12

SS-Flak Battalion 12
SS-Armored Reconnaissance Battalion 12
SS-Anti-Tank Battalion 12
SS-Armored Signal Battalion 12
SS-Armored Combat Engineer Battalion 12
SS-Rocket Launcher Battalion 12 (renumbered as 512, March 1945)
SS-Field Replacement Battalion 12

The division was ordered into existence 24 June 1943 to use members of the Hitler Youth in forming a sister division for the 1st SS-Panzer Division in the I SS-Panzer Corps. At first organized as a Panzer-Grenadier Division, on 22 October 1943, it received its final full designation. The division trained in Belgium, and first saw action in Normandy on 7 June 1944. It fought near Caen for the remainder of the campaign, and by mid-August 1944 only combat groups remained in the front sector. Reforming elements fought on the Seine River later that month. After reconstitution, the division participated in the Ardennes offensive from 17 December 1944, and suffered heavy losses near Elsenborn and at Bastogne. Again reformed, the division transferred to Hungary and helped destroy the Soviet Gran bridgehead in late February 1945. The division next had small successes in the *FRÜHLINGSERWACHASEN* offensive in early March 1945, before retreating west into Austria. Survivors surrendered to American forces in the Steyr area on 8 May 1945.

13th *Waffen*-Mountain Division of the SS "Handschar" (Croatian no. 1)

SS-Brigadeführer und Generalmajor der Waffen-SS und Oberst i.G. Karl-Gustav Sauberzweig (1 August 1943–1 June 1944)

SS-Standartenführer, later *SS-Oberführer* and *SS-Brigadeführer und Generalmajor der Waffen-SS* Desiderius Hampel (19 June 1944–8 May 1945)

Waffen-Mountain Infantry Regiment of the SS 27 (Croatian no. 1)
Waffen-Mountain Infantry Regiment of the SS 28 (Croatian no. 2)
Waffen-Mountain Artillery Regiment of the SS 13 (Croatian no. 1)
Waffen-Reconnaissance Battalion of the SS 13 (later reassigned to *Waffen*-Mountain Division 23)
Waffen-Flak Battalion of the SS 13
Waffen-Signal Battalion of the SS 13
Waffen-Anti-Tank Battalion of the SS 13
Waffen-Combat Engineer Battalion of the SS 13

Began formation on 1 March 1943 as "Croatian SS-Volunteer Division." The intention was to use Bosnian Muslims in defense of their home region against attacks by partisan bands. To remove outside influences, the division was trained in France. Partisan infiltrators instigated a small mutiny in mid-September 1943, but training progressed satisfactorily, and the division returned to its home region during February 1944 to defend the Muslim community from partisan and Chetnik attacks. The division was never deployed in areas populated by Bosnian Serbs, so the allegations about mass atrocities committed by this division are unlikely. When the Germans withdrew from the Bosnian Muslim heartland during September 1944, many of the division's soldiers remained behind to protect their families. German personnel from various small units in the Balkans were incorporated, and *Handschar* fought on as a small brigade-sized combat group (with divisional status) until the end of the war, seeing heavy combat in Croatia and Hungary, and surrendering to British forces near Klagenfurt during early May 1945.

14th *Waffen*-Grenadier Division of the *SS* (Ukrainian no. 1)

SS-Brigadeführer und Generalmajor der Waffen-SS und Polizei Walter Schimana (15 July–20 October 1943)

SS-Oberführer und Oberst der Schutzpolizei, later *SS-Brigadeführer und Generalmajor der Waffen-SS und Polizei* Fritz Freitag (20 October 1943–27 April 1945)

> *Waffen*-Grenadier Regiment of the *SS* 29 (Ukrainian no. 1)
> *Waffen*-Grenadier Regiment of the *SS* 30 (Ukrainian no. 2)
> *Waffen*-Grenadier Regiment of the *SS* 31 (Ukrainian no. 3)
> *Waffen*-Artillery Regiment of the *SS* 14
> *Waffen*-Reconnaissance Battalion of the *SS* 14 (replaced by *Waffen*-Füsilier Battalion 14 during 1944 rebuild)
> *Waffen*-Flak Battalion of the *SS* 14
> *Waffen*-Füsilier Battalion of the *SS* 14 (from former *Waffen*-Reconnaissance Battalion of the *SS* 14)
> *Waffen*-Signal Battalion of the *SS* 14
> *Waffen*-Combat Engineer Battalion of the *SS* 14
> *Waffen*-Field Replacement Battalion of the *SS* 14

A "Galician *SS*-Volunteer Division" began to assemble during July 1943 as the predecessor to further planned formations. Numerous volunteers stepped forward, and the best were formed into a standard German infantry division, which was thoroughly trained through June 1944. A 2,000-man combat group was detached for anti-partisan duties from February to March 1944, but the main body of the division only entered combat in early July 1944 in Galicia, west of Brody. The Galician Division was caught later that month in the Brody-Tarnov pocket, and suffered enormous losses after fighting well. The unit was reformed at Neuhammer in Silesia with survivors, formerly excess personnel, and new volunteers from the Ukrainian refugee community during August and September 1944, before moving to Slovakia where elements battled the military revolt and performed security duties into early February 1945, while the division trained. Moved to Slovenia, the division, now known as "Ukrainian," fought partisans until the end of March 1945. It then returned to frontline combat, serving against the Red Army on the Austro-Slovenian border. On 27 April 1945, the division became the 1st Division of the Ukrainian National Army, leaving the *Waffen-SS*.

15th *Waffen*-Grenadier Division of the *SS* (Latvian no. 1)

SS-Brigadeführer und Generalmajor der Waffen-SS Peter Hansen (25 February–1 May 1943)

SS-Brigadeführer und Generalmajor der Waffen-SS Carl *Graf* (Count) von Pückler-Burghauss (1 May 1943–16 February 1944)

SS-Oberführer Nikolaus Heilmann (17 February–21 July 1944)

SS-Oberführer Herbert von Obwurzer (21 July 1944–26 January 1945)

SS-Oberführer Adolf Ax (26 January–15 February 1945)

SS-Oberführer, later *SS-Brigadeführer und Generalmajor der Waffen-SS* Karl Burk (15 February–8 May 1945)

> *Waffen*-Grenadier Regiment of the *SS* 32 (Latvian no. 3)
> *Waffen*-Grenadier Regiment of the *SS* 33 (Latvian no. 4)
> *Waffen*-Grenadier Regiment of the *SS* 34 (Latvian no. 5)
> *Waffen*-Artillery Regiment of the *SS* 15 (Latvian no. 1) (merged into *Waffen*-Artillery Regiment 19 in August 1944, thereafter only at battalion strength)
> *Waffen*-Flak Battalion of the *SS* 15 (merged with *Waffen*-Flak Battalion 19 in July 1944 to form *SS*-Flak Battalion 506)
> *Waffen-Füsilier* Battalion of the *SS* 15
> *Waffen*-Signal Battalion of the *SS* 15
> *Waffen*-Anti-Tank Battalion of the *SS* 15
> *Waffen*-Combat Engineer Battalion of the *SS* 15
> *Waffen*-Field Replacement Battalion of the *SS* 15

After the January 1943 establishment of the Latvian Legion, the first full division began forming 23 May 1943. Trained men were sent to replenish the 2d *SS*-Infantry Brigade (later the 19th *Waffen*-Grenadier Division) which delayed the combat readiness of what became the 15th *Waffen*-Grenadier Division. The division was gradually committed west of Velikiye Luki between November 1943 and January 1944 and served in pieces attached to various German formations. During February 1944, the division relocated to positions south of Staraya Russa, which were soon evacuated, as the unit retreated west to the Velikaya River by the end of the month. Here it was joined by the 2d *SS*-Infantry Brigade, which was enlarging into the 19th *Waffen*-Grenadier Division, and both units suffered heavy losses in fierce combat that lasted until late April 1944. The divisions then assumed quieter positions to the southeast, but were forced to abandon them during July 1944. The 15th Division suffered enormous losses during the withdrawal to Latvia, and was evacuated to Germany beginning in late July 1944. After incomplete reconstitution, the 15th Division returned to combat in West Prussia during late January 1945, immediately incurring heavy losses. The division gradually retreated west through Pomerania, with the detached Füsilier Battalion being destroyed in the Berlin fighting. The survivors of the 15th Division surrendered to the Allies near Schwerin in early May 1945.

16th SS-Panzer-Grenadier Division *"Reichsführer-SS"*

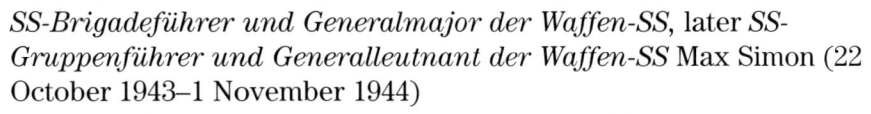

SS-Brigadeführer und Generalmajor der Waffen-SS, later *SS-Gruppenführer und Generalleutnant der Waffen-SS* Max Simon (22 October 1943–1 November 1944)

SS-Oberführer Otto Baum (1 November 1944–8 May 1945)

    SS-Panzer-Grenadier Regiment 35
    SS-Panzer-Grenadier Regiment 36
    SS-Artillery Regiment 16
    SS-Flak Battalion 16
    SS-Signal Battalion 16
    SS-Panzer Battalion 16
    SS-Armored Reconnaissance Battalion 16
    SS-Combat Engineer Battalion 16
    SS-Assault Gun Battalion 16 (became *SS*-Anti-Tank Battalion 32 in February 1945)
    SS-Field Replacement Battalion 16

16th *SS*-Panzer-Grenadier Division *"Reichsführer-SS"*

First organized during 1941 as the Escort Battalion *Reichsführer-SS* (a bodyguard for Heinrich Himmler, abbreviated as *RFSS*), it expanded during 1943 into the partially-armored Assault Brigade *RFSS*. The expansion took place on Corsica, and the brigade saw action there against the French during September 1943, evacuating the island at the beginning of the next month. The expansion into the 16th Division was ordered on 23 October 1943, and commenced the following month in Slovenia. A combat group of two reinforced battalions fought against the Anzio beachhead between late January to early April 1944, while the main body of the division helped occupy Hungary beginning on 19 March 1944 in Operation Margarethe. From May 1944, the united division fought on the Italian Ligurian coast, and then south of Bologna. During February 1945, the division moved to Hungary, and fought in the retreat from south of Lake Balaton into Austria, surrendering to British forces near Klagenfurt during early May 1945.

17th SS-Panzer-Grenadier Division "Götz von Berlichingen"

SS-Oberführer, later *SS-Brigadeführer und Generalmajor der Waffen-SS* Werner Ostendorff (January–15 June 1944)

SS-Standartenführer Otto Baum (18 June–30 July 1944)

SS-Standartenführer Otto Binge (30 July–29 August 1944)

SS-Standartenführer Dr. Eduard Deisenhofer (30 August–30 September 1944)

SS-Standartenführer Thomas Müller (30 September–October 1944)

SS-Brigadeführer und Generalmajor der Waffen-SS Werner Ostendorff (21 October–late November 1944)

SS-Standartenführer Hans Lingner (November 1944–8 January 1945)

SS-Standartenführer Fritz Klingenberg (22 January–22 March 1945)

SS-Standartenführer Georg Bochmann (30 March–8 May 1945)

> *SS*-Panzer-Grenadier Regiment 37
> *SS*-Panzer-Grenadier Regiment 38
> *SS*-Artillery Regiment 17
> *SS*-Flak Battalion 17
> *SS*-Signal Battalion 17
> *SS*-Panzer Battalion 17
> *SS*-Armored Reconnaissance Battalion 17
> *SS*-Anti-Tank Battalion 17
> *SS*-Combat Engineer Battalion 17
> *SS*-Field Replacement Battalion 17

Ordered into existence 3 October 1943; received its full designation 19 days later. Created from replacement units and ethnic German conscripts; not fully motorized; it trained in France. Committed to American sector of the Normandy front from 10 June 1944, it suffered heavy losses in the Carenten area. Elements fought in Mortain offensive early August 1944, but most of the depleted division avoided the Falaise encirclement. The survivors regrouped in the Saar in September, incoporating *SS*-Panzer-Grenadier Brigades 49 and 51, and assorted *Heer* stragglers. It again suffered heavy losses around Metz in October and November, then retreated into the Saar. There it saw further heavy fighting and sustained heavy casualties in December, with stragglers used as replacements. In late December 1944, the *SS*-Panzer-Grenadier *Lehr* (Training) Regiment from the *SS*-Panzer-Grenadier School "Kleinschlag" at Prosetschnitz, near Prague, assigned and retitled as the new *SS*-Panzer-Grenadier Regiment 38. Heavy fighting in Lorraine, January 1945, in the NORDWIND offensive, followed by defensive operations until March. From mid-March, a gradual retreat to the Nuremburg area. Most of the division was destroyed by late March 1945, although survivors fought on until the end of the war, surrendering to US forces in Bavaria.

18th SS-Volunteer-Panzer-Grenadier Division "Horst Wessel"

SS-Standartenführer, later *SS-Oberführer* August-Wilhelm Trabandt (25 January 1944–3 January 1945)

SS-Standartenführer Georg Bochmann (3 January–27 March 1945)

SS-Standartenführer Heinrich Petersen (27 March–8 May 1945)

> *SS*-Volunteer-Panzer-Grenadier Regiment 39
> *SS*-Volunteer-Panzer-Grenadier Regiment 40
> *SS*-Volunteer-Artillery Regiment 18
> *SS*-Flak Battalion 18
> *SS*-Signal Battalion 18
> *SS*-Panzer Battalion 18
> *SS*-Armored Reconnaissance Battalion 18
> *SS*-Anti-Tank Battalion 18
> *SS*-Combat Engineer Battalion 18
> *SS*-Field Replacement Battalion 18

Created from the 1st *SS*-Infantry Brigade on 25 January 1944; originally planned to include *SA* volunteers. Instead, conscripted Banat ethnic Germans filled out the ranks. During training, part of the division fought partisans near Zagreb through June 1944, while the rest participated in Operation MARGARETHE, the occupation of Hungary, March 1944. *SS*-Volunteer Panzer-Grenadier Regiment 40 fought in Galicia during the summer 1944 alongside a battalion from the French *SS*-Assault Brigade, while the division completed its formation. Elements were committed in Slovakia in September and October 1944, while the division as a whole first saw combat south of Budapest in November 1944. Transferred to Moravia, the division fought in Silesia from February 1945, seeing heavy combat and breaking out of encirclement against orders. After further heavy combat in Bohemia, survivors surrendered to Czech and Soviet forces during the last days of the war; many were executed.

19th *Waffen*-Grenadier Division of the *SS* (Latvian no. 2)

SS-Oberführer Hinrich Schuldt (February–15 March 1944)

SS-Standartenführer Friedrich-Wilhelm Bock (15 March–13 April 1944)

SS-Oberführer, later *SS-Brigadeführer und Generalmajor der Waffen-SS* and *SS-Gruppenführer und Generalleutnant der Waffen-SS und Polizei* Bruno Streckenbach (13 April 1944–8 May 1945)

> *Waffen*-Grenadier Regiment of the *SS* 42 "Voldemars Veiss" (Latvian no. 1)
> *Waffen*-Grenadier Regiment of the *SS* 43 "Hinrich Schuldt" (Latvian no. 2)
> *Waffen*-Grenadier Regiment of the *SS* 44 (Latvian no. 6)

> *Waffen*-Artillery Regiment of the *SS* 19 (Latvian no. 2)
> *Waffen*-Flak Battalion of the *SS* 19 (merged with *Waffen*-Flak Battalion 15 in July 1944 to form *SS*-Flak Battalion 506)
> *Waffen-Füsilier* Battalion of the *SS* 19 (formed 1944 from *Waffen* Field Replacement Battalion 19)
> *Waffen*-Signal Battalion of the *SS* 19
> *Waffen*-Anti-Tank Battalion of the *SS* 19
> *Waffen*-Combat Engineer Battalion of the *SS* 19
> *Waffen*-Field Replacement Battalion of the *SS* 19 (converted 1944 into the *Waffen-Füsilier* Battalion 19)

Originally formed during 1941 with two former *SS-Totenkopf* Infantry Regiments as the 2d *SS*-Infantry Brigade, emplyed for rear area security. During 1942, the staff of the brigade took over several foreign legions, controlling them in front line combat along the Leningrad siege lines. Latvian *Schuma* battalions ("*Schuma*" is short for "*Schutzmannschaft*," and indicated as an auxilliary battalion raised by the German *Heer* or Police from the native population in the Baltic states and Soviet Union) were added. During January 1943, it was decided to convert the brigade into a purely Latvian unit, the first element of the Latvian *Waffen-SS* Legion. This took effect by May 1943, when the unit took up positions along the Volkhov River. These were held until the retreat of late January 1944, which finally ended a month later when the brigade took over positions along the Velikaya River. Here it was enlarged into the 19th *Waffen*-Grenadier Division during the following months. Its first two infantry regiments were considered senior to those of the 15th Division, which were formed at a later date. The 19th Division took heavy casualties along the Velikaya, and moved with the 15th Division to a quieter zone to the southeast, but both were forced to retreat during July 1944, and the 19th Division suffered very heavy casualties during the withdrawal and following defense of eastern Latvia. By early October 1944, the division assumed a position in the central portion of the Kurland defense line, and held its zone successfully until the end of the war, seeing especially heavy fighting during the first, third, fifth, and sixth Battles of Kurland. Survivors either went into Soviet captivity at the end of the war, or became partisans.

20th *Waffen*-Grenadier Division of the *SS* (Estonian no. 1)

SS-Oberführer, later *SS-Brigadeführer und Generalmajor der Waffen-SS* Franz Augsburger (January 1944–19 March 1945)

SS-Oberführer, later *SS-Brigadeführer und Generalmajor der Waffen-SS* Berthold Maack (March–8 May 1945)

> *Waffen*-Grenadier Regiment of the *SS* 45 (Estonian no. 1)

Waffen-Grenadier Regiment of the *SS* 46 (Estonian no. 2)
Waffen-Grenadier Regiment of the *SS* 47 (Estonian no. 3)
Waffen-Artillery Regiment of the *SS* 20
Waffen-Flak Battalion of the *SS* 20 (destroyed September 1944 and not rebuilt)
Waffen-Füsilier Battalion of the *SS* 20 (former *SS*-Volunteer-Panzer-Grenadier Battalion "Narwa")
Waffen-Signal Battalion of the *SS* 20
Waffen-Anti-Tank Battalion of the *SS* 20
Waffen-Combat Engineer Battalion of the *SS* 20
Waffen-Field Replacement Battalion of the *SS* 20 (expanded to a regiment during December 1944)

Creation of an Estonian *Waffen-SS* Legion was announced 28 August 1942; serious formation began early the next year using a mixture of volunteers and conscripts. The best men were concentrated in the first battalion which, as the Volunteer Panzer-Grenadier Battalion "Narwa," was sent to the 5th *SS*-Panzer Division *Wiking* in July 1943. It remained with the division until late February 1944, when it joined the Estonian division as *Waffen-Füsilier* Battalion 20. Meanwhile, the Estonian Legion evolved into a two regiment (plus supporting elements) brigade, which entered combat near Nevel as the 3d Estonian *SS*-Volunteer Brigade during October 1943. After battling partisans for two months, the brigade relocated to the vicinity of Staraya Russa during January 1944, was redesignated as a division on the 24th of the month, and was quickly caught up in the retreat to the "Panther" line. During February 1944, the division was moved to the Narva sector, taking up positions along the Narva River, immediately north of the town of Narva. These were held in heavy combat until the late July 1944 retreat to the Tannenberg Line, where the division suffered heavy casualties while successfully defending the central portion of the defenses around Grenadier Hill. During August 1944, the 20th Division fought in southeastern Estonia near Tartu. When the Germans withdrew from Estonia during late September 1944, the division was evacuated to Germany, where it began reconstitution at Neuhammer, Silesia, the next month. Here it incorporated any available Estonians, including former naval and air force members, recovered wounded, and survivors of the six Frontier Guard Regiments destroyed the previous month while defending Estonia. Before the process was complete, the 20th Division was rushed back into combat in Silesia during late January 1945 near Breslau. In the ensuing retrograde operations it was caught in the Oppeln pocket, making an organized but costly escape in late March 1945. The survivors fought on until the end of the war, when many were killed by Czech partisans near Prague in early May 1945. Most of the division went into Soviet captivity, while some individuals went into American captivity near Pilsen.

21st *Waffen*-Mountain Division of the *SS* "Skanderbeg" (Albanian no. 1)

SS-Standartenführer, later *SS-Oberführer* August Schmidhuber (17 April–11 December 1944)

> *Waffen*-Mountain Infantry Regiment of the *SS* 50 (Albanian no. 1)
> *Waffen*-Mountain Infantry Regiment of the *SS* 51 (Albanian no. 2)
> *Waffen*-Mountain Artillery Regiment of the *SS* 21 (one battalion)
> *Waffen*-Reconnaissance Battalion of the *SS* 21
> *Waffen*-Mountain Combat Engineer Battalion of the *SS* 21
> *Waffen*-Signal Battalion of the *SS* 21
> *Waffen*-Anti-Tank Battalion of the *SS* 21

Ordered into existence in 17 April 1944, the *Waffen-SS* believed a small division could be formed from Albanians to fight Communist partisans. Though 6,500 Albanians were accepted for service, they proved highly unreliable. The division fought without success in anti-partisan operations during August and September 1944. Desertion became endemic during the summer of 1944, and only 5,000 men (3,500 of them Albanians) were on hand by 1 October 1944. German naval personnel evacuated from the Adriatic were added, and with the German cadre filled out *Waffen*-Mountain Infantry Regiment 51 and the anti-tank battalion, which fought alongside the 7th *SS*-Volunteer Mountain Division until the end of the year. The last Albanians were then released from service, the divisional staff elements were reassigned to the planned 32d *SS*-Volunteer Grenadier Division, and the German/ethnic German cadre became replacements for *SS*-Volunteer Mountain Infantry Regiment 14.

22d *SS*-Volunteer-Cavalry Division "Maria Theresia"

SS-Standartenführer, later *SS-Oberführer* and *SS-Brigadeführer und Generalmajor der Waffen-SS* August Zehender (1 May 1944–12 February 1945)

> *SS*-Cavalry Regiment 17 (to be renamed *SS*-Cavalry Regiment 54)
> *SS*-Volunteer-Cavalry Regiment 52
> *SS*-Volunteer-Cavalry Regiment 53 (partially formed)
> *SS*-Volunteer-Cavalry Regiment 55 (never formed)
> *SS*-Volunteer-Artillery Regiment 22
> *SS*-Flak Battalion 22
> *SS*-Signal Battalion 22
> *SS*-Armored Reconnaissance Battalion 22
> *SS*-Anti-Tank Battalion 22
> *SS*-Combat Engineer Battalion 22

Sister division of the 8th *SS*-Cavalry Division; ordered into existence 1 May 1944. Based around the already-detached *SS*-Cavalry Regiment 17, to which three new regiments and supporting elements were to be added. The personnel came from ethnic Germans released from Hungarian Army service and newly conscripted ethnic Germans and ethnic Magyars. The formation took place west of Budapest, and was far from completed when Regiments 17 and 52—which were actually infantry mounted on horses—were declared combat ready in late August 1944. Because of the disaster in Romania, these units were needed to man the defenses in Transylvania. They saw heavy combat during September and October 1944. The rest of the division participated in the occupation of Budapest, Operation PANZERFAUST, 16 October 1944. Then it fought east of Budapest, but was forced back to Pest by early December 1944. Encircled by the end of the year, it was destroyed in the ensuing fighting, with only a handful of men (170 combined from the 8th and 22d SS-Cavalry Divisions) escaping from Buda on 11–12 February 1945.

23d *Waffen*-Mountain Division of the *SS* "*Kama*" (Croatian no. 2)

SS-Standartenführer Hellmuth Raithel (6 June–late October 1944)

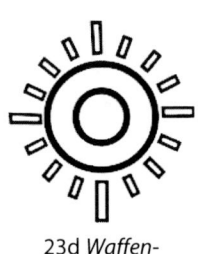

> *Waffen*-Mountain Infantry Regiment of the *SS* 55 (Croatian no. 3)
> *Waffen*-Mountain Infantry Regiment of the *SS* 56 (Croatian no. 4)
> *Waffen*-Mountain Artillery Regiment of the *SS* 23 (Croatian no. 2)
> *Waffen*-Reconnaissance Battalion of the *SS* 23 (former *Waffen*-Reconnaissance Battalion 13; reassigned, corps-level command)
> *Waffen*-Flak Battalion of the *SS* 23
> *Waffen*-Anti-Tank Battalion of the *SS* 23
> *Waffen*-Combat Engineer Battalion of the *SS* 23

23d *Waffen*-Mountain Division of the *SS* "*Kama*"

Ordered in to existence 17 June 1944 as the sister division to the Bosnian 13th *Waffen*-Mountain Division, although formation actually commenced a week earlier. Organized in the Batschka region (today known as the "Vojvodina") around a cadre from *Handschar*, the formation was never completed. By 10 September 1944, the division only numbered 3,793 officers and men, and two weeks later, the Bosnians were ordered to Bosnia to join *Handschar*. The German cadre of *Kama* remained in the Batschka to become the cadre of the new 31st *SS*-Volunteer Grenadier Division. A combat group of Bosnians commanded by Germans (*Kampfgruppe* Syr) did briefly fight on the Tisza River in late September 1944, but the division was dissolved on 31 October 1944.

23d *SS*-Volunteer-Panzer-Grenadier Division "*Nederland*" (Dutch no. 1)

SS-Brigadeführer und Generalmajor der Waffen-SS Jürgen Wagner (10 February–8 May 1945)

> *SS*-Volunteer-Panzer-Grenadier Regiment 48 "General Seyffardt" (Dutch no. 1)

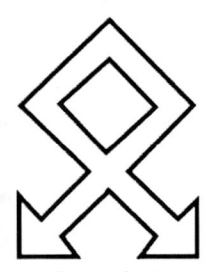

23d SS-Volunteer Panzer-Grenadier Division "Nederland"

    SS-Volunteer-Panzer-Grenadier Regiment 49 "De Ruyter" (Dutch no. 2)
    SS-Volunteer-Artillery Regiment 23 (Dutch no. 1)
    SS-Reconnaissance Company 23
    SS-Flak Battery 23
    SS-Signal Battalion 23
    SS-Anti-Tank Battalion 23
    SS-Combat Engineer Battalion 23
    SS-Field Replacement Battalion 23

Upgraded former 4th *SS*-Volunteer-Panzer-Grenadier Brigade *Nederland* (based on the Volunteer Legion *Nederland)* and was actually a miniature division in structure. First organized summer 1943, the brigade expanded to include additional assault guns and a full regiment of artillery. It conducted anti-partisan operations in Croatia, autumn 1943; then committed to the Oraniembaum front, west of Leningrad during January 1944. Retreated west in late January 1944; assumed positions in the Narva bridgehead in early February 1944. Remained in the bridgehead through heavy fighting until late July 1944. The "General Seyffardt" regiment nearly destroyed during its retreat to the Tannenberg Line circa 26–28 July 1944 (20 percent of already-depleted regiment escaped). Retreated into Latvia, September 1944; elements returned to Germany for rebuilding, main body fought in Kurland from October 1944 through January 1945, including the first, second, and fourth battles of Kurland. Evacuated to Pomerania, rejoined by detached elements and fought in the SONNENWENDE Offensive at Arneswalde, then withdrew to the Altdam bridgehead in March 1945. Withdrew toward Oder River line, late March 1945; joined by rebuilt "General Seyffardt" Regiment (in action since January 1945 in West Prussia and Pomerania). After Soviet Berlin offensive on 16 April 1945, withdrew south of Berlin, caught in Halbe pocket. Survivors surrendered to American forces along the Elbe (mostly at Tangermünde) May 1945. The divisional units with the number "23" formerly carried the number "54" in the brigade.

24th *Waffen*-Mountain Division of the *SS* "Karstjäger"

SS-Obersturmbannführer Karl Marks (designated commander circa July–5 December 1944)

    Waffen-Mountain Infantry Regiment of the *SS* 59
    Waffen-Mountain Infantry Regiment of the *SS* 60 (never formed)
    Waffen-Mountain Artillery Regiment of the *SS* 24 (one battalion)
    Waffen-Signal Battalion of the *SS* 24 (one company)

Karstwehr Battalion was formed in 1942 from South Tyrolian ethnic Germans to patrol the *Karst* (especially difficult terrain dominated by unusual limestone and dolomite rock formations) the border area where Austria, Italy, and Slovenia meet. Expanded into a regiment; then full division status by incorporating ethnic Germans, Italians, and Slovenians. Second regiment never formed; unit was a reinforced regiment, officially downgraded to the *Karstjäger* Brigade in January 1945. Engaged in anti-partisan operations; committed to front-line action against the British in April 1945, fought well as part of Combat Group Harmel.

25th *Waffen*-Grenadier Division of the *SS* "*Hunyadi*" (Hungarian no. 1)

Waffen-Gruppenführer der SS Josef Grassy (10 October 1944–8 May 1945)

> *Waffen*-Grenadier Regiment of the *SS* 61 (Hungarian no. 1)
> *Waffen*-Grenadier Regiment of the *SS* 62 (Hungarian no. 2)
> *Waffen*-Grenadier Regiment of the *SS* 63 (Hungarian no. 3)
> *Waffen*-Artillery Regiment of the *SS* 25 (Hungarian no. 1)
> *Waffen-Füsilier* Battalion of the *SS* 25
> *Waffen*-Signal Battalion of the *SS* 25
> *Waffen*-Anti-Tank Battalion of the *SS* 25
> *Waffen*-Combat Engineer Battalion of the *SS* 25
> *Waffen*-Ski Battalion of the *SS* 25 (fought independently)
> *Waffen*-Field Replacement Battalion of the *SS* 25

First planned in late October 1944 after the Szalasi regiment took power in Hungary, the details for the creation of a Hungarian *Waffen-SS* were finalized by 24 November 1944. The *Waffen-SS* was to train and equip four infantry divisions of ethnic Magyars as a solid base for the reestablishment of the Royal Hungarian Army (*Honved*). The formation of the first had already begun on 2 November, and it took the patriotic name, "*Hunyadi*." It was formed around *Honved* veterans, civilian volunteers, and the latest group of conscripts. First collected in Hungary, the division relocated to Neuhammer, Silesia, in late November 1944. On 27 November 1944, 800 men were killed and another 650 wounded in an American air attack on the train in which they were being transported. The division, still in training and awaiting most of its authorized equipment, evacuated Neuhammer on 8–9 February 1945, leaving behind two combat-ready battalions. These saw heavy combat up to 14 February before rejoining the division, which relocated to Bavaria, and then to Austria by the end of the war. The division surrendered to American forces after sporadic combat with American advance units.

26th *SS*-Panzer Division

No commander assigned.

Planned to be formed in the summer of 1944 by expanding *SS*-Panzer-Grenadier Brigade 49, but cancelled because of the need to replenish

26th *Waffen*-Grenadier Division of the *SS* "*Hungaria*" (Hungarian no. 2)

Waffen-Oberführer der SS Zoltan von Pisky (23 December 1944–21 January 1945)

SS-Brigadeführer und Generalmajor der Waffen-SS Berthold Maack (22 January–20 March 1945)

Waffen-Gruppenführer der SS Josef Grassy (21 March–8 May 1945)

    Waffen-Grenadier Regiment of the *SS* 64 (Hungarian no. 4)
    Waffen-Grenadier Regiment of the *SS* 65 (Hungarian no. 5)
    Waffen-Grenadier Regiment of the *SS* 85 (Hungarian no. 6)
    Waffen-Artillery Regiment of the *SS* 25 (Hungarian no. 2)
    Waffen-Füsilier Battalion of the *SS* 26
    Waffen-Signal Battalion of the *SS* 26
    Waffen-Anti-Tank Battalion of the *SS* 26
    Waffen-Combat Engineer Battalion of the *SS* 26
    Waffen-Ski Battalion of the *SS* 26 (fought independently)

The second Hungarian *Waffen-SS* division was ordered into existence during November 1944, and was to have only two infantry regiments. As it became clear that the third and fourth Hungarian *Waffen-SS* divisions could not be formed, excess men were assigned to the first two. As a result, *Waffen*-Grenadier Regiment 85 was added to the division on 24 December 1944. Again, *Honved* veterans were combined with civilian volunteers and recent conscripts. The division relocated from Hungary to Neuhammer during December 1944, but because of overcrowding there, moved again to Sieradtz, Poland, in early January 1945. It began to retreat to the west on 19 January 1945, losing 2,570 men in combat by the time it again reached Neuhammer in early February 1945. The division evacuated Neuhammer on 8–9 February 1945, also leaving behind two combat-ready battalions. It relocated to Austria, and surrendered there to American forces during early May 1945 after sporadic combat with American advance forces.

27th *SS*-Panzer Division

No commander assigned.

Planned to be formed summer 1944 by expanding *SS*-Panzer-Grenadier Brigade 51, but cancelled because of the need to replenish other divisions. *SS*-Panzer-Grenadier Brigade 51 incorporated into the 17th *SS*-Panzer-Grenadier Division.

27th SS-Volunteer-Grenadier Division *"Langemarck"* (Flemish no. 1)

27th SS-Volunteer Grenadier Division "Langemarck"

SS-Standartenführer Thomas Müller (27 November 1944–8 May 1945)

- *SS*-Volunteer-Grenadier Regiment 66 (Flemish no. 1) (two battalions)
- *SS*-Volunteer-Grenadier Regiment 67 (Flemish no. 2) (two battalions)
- *SS*-Volunteer-Grenadier Regiment 68 (Flemish no. 3) (only partially formed)
- *SS*-Volunteer-Artillery Regiment 27
- *SS*-Signal Battalion 27
- *SS*-Anti-Tank Battalion 27
- *SS*-Combat Engineer Battalion 27

Ordered into existence on 18 September 1944 to take advantage of the Flemish refugees arriving in Germany in the wake of the Allied liberation of Belgium. A full infantry division was to be organized around the *SS*-Volunteer Assault Brigade "Langemarck." The new personnel came from Flemish members of the *Nationalsozialistisches Kraftfahrkorps* (*NSKK*, the Nazi Party "Motor Vehicle Organization" used to furnish auxilliary transportation) and the *Organisation Todt* (*OT*, the German heavy construction agency), refugees from collaborationist groups such as the Flemish Guard, Germanic-*SS* and Hitler Youth, and from Flemish workers from German industry. Around 15,000 Flemish men of military

Officers and men of *SS*-Motorcycle Regiment "Langemarck" try out the first of the newly assigned *Schwimmwagen* amphibious jeeps. These vehicles greatly enhanced the capabilities of reconnaissance troops in the *Heer* and *Waffen-SS,* and relegated motorcycles to use by dispatch riders.

Officers and soldiers of *SS*-Langemarck in a *Schwimmerwagen* amphibious jeep.

age were available, so the division could have attained full strength, had time and equipment allowed. A combat group of two infantry battalions and an anti-tank battalion were readied for service in Flanders in December 1944 had the Ardennes offensive succeeded; this group was then sent to Pomerania in late January 1945. After heavy combat during February and March 1945, the combat group reassembled west of the Oder River in April 1945. The mass of the division organized on the Lüneburg Heath, and trained elements were sent to the Oder front, so that up to 6,000 men were ready for combat when the Berlin offensive began on 16 April 1945. Heavy combat in late April 1945 as the combat portion of the division retreated west, before surrendering to Allied forces along the Elbe River in early May 1945.

28th *SS*-Panzer Division

No commander assigned.

Planned for formation during the summer of 1944, but cancelled because of the need to replenish other divisions.

28th *SS*-Volunteer-Grenadier Division *"Wallonien"* (Walloon no. 1)

SS-Oberführer Karl Burk (18 September–12 December 1944)

SS-Oberführer Nikolaus Heilmann (12 December 1944–early January 1945)

SS-Obersturmbannführer, later *SS-Standartenführer* Leon Degrelle (30 January–8 May 1945)

> *SS*-Volunteer-Grenadier Regiment 69 (Walloon no. 1) (two battalions)

28th SS-Volunteer Grenadier Division "Wallonien"

SS-Volunteer-Grenadier Regiment 70 (Walloon no. 2) (one battalion)
SS-Volunteer-Grenadier Regiment 71 (Walloon no. 3) (not formed)
SS-Volunteer-Artillery Regiment 28 (one battalion)
SS-Signal Battalion 28 (one company)
SS-Anti-Tank Battalion 28 (two companies)
SS-Combat Engineer Battalion 28 (not formed)
SS-Panzer-Grenadier Replacement Battalion 36

Ordered into existence on 18 September 1944 to take advantage of the Walloon refugees arriving in Germany in the wake of the Allied liberation of Belgium. A full infantry division was to be organized around the SS-Volunteer Assault Brigade *"Wallonien,"* though far fewer Walloons were on hand than was the case for the Flemings. By combining *NSKK* and *OT* veterans with political and para-military men and workers from German industry, 8,000 Walloons could be found, although many wanted no part of *Waffen-SS* service. Only about 4,000 men could be readied for combat, even with several hundred French and Spanish volunteers added. A regimental-sized combat group was prepared for service in Wallonia in December 1944, had the Ardennes offensive succeeded. It was sent to Pomerania late January 1945, and saw heavy combat during February and March 1945. Newly trained men joined the combat element during a reconstitution west of the Oder River in early April 1945, so that perhaps 2,000 men were available when the Berlin offensive struck on 16 April 1945. Heavy combat in late April 1945 as the unit retreated west, before it surrendered to Allied forces in northern Germany in early May 1945.

Waffen-Grenadier Division of the *SS* (Russian no. 1)

SS-Brigadeführer Bronislav Kaminski (1–19 August 1944)

SS-Oberführer Christoph Diehm (19 August–December 1944)

Waffen-Grenadier Regiment of the *SS* 72 (Russian no. 1) (not formed)
Waffen-Grenadier Regiment of the *SS* 73 (Russian no. 2) (not formed)
Waffen-Grenadier Regiment of the *SS* 74 (Russian no. 3) (not formed)

This was the former "Kaminski Brigade" of Soviet citizens that fought partisans in the rear of Army Group Center. Demoralized after the German retreat from Belorussia during June and July 1944, this unit was to pass into the *Waffen-SS*. The one regiment committed in Warsaw in August 1944 committed so many atrocities that Kaminiski was executed and the survivors of the brigade were sent to Vlasov's Russian Liberation Army.

29th *Waffen*-Grenadier Division of the *SS* (Italian no. 1)

SS-Oberführer der Reserve Otto Jungkunz (10–15 February 1945)

SS-Standartenführer der Reserve Constantin Heldmann (15 February–8 May 1945, he had deputized for Jungkunz since 20 August 1944)

>   *Waffen*-Grenadier Regiment of the *SS* 81 (Italian no. 1)
>   *Waffen*-Grenadier Regiment of the *SS* 82 (Italian no. 2)
>   *Waffen*-Artillery Regiment of the *SS* 29 (two battalions)
>   *Waffen*-Füsilier Battalion of the *SS* 29 (known as "Battalion Debica")
>   *Waffen*-Anti-Tank Battalion of the *SS* 29
>   *Waffen*-Signal Company of the *SS* 29
>   *Waffen*-Combat Engineer Company of the *SS* 29

Formation of new, pro-Fascist Italian military units began after Mussolini's rescue from captivity on 12 September 1943. This included an Italian *SS*-Legion, which organized battalion by battalion in the autumn of 1943. The 1st Assault Brigade of the Italian Volunteer Legion was established on 1 March 1944 to control the initial battalions, and was redesignated as the *Waffen*-Grenadier Brigade of the *SS* (Italian no. 1) on 7 September 1944. Two reinforced battalions fought Allied troops in front-line action at Anzio between 18 March 1944 and early June 1944. The other battalions operated against Italian partisans throughout 1944. The divisional designation took effect on 10 February 1945, and anti-partisan operations continued through the end of April 1945, when the separated battalions surrendered to Allied and partisan units in northern Italy.

30th *Waffen*-Grenadier Division of the *SS* (Russian no. 2)

SS-Obersturmbannführer und Oberstleutnant der Schutzpolizei Hans Siegling (1 August 1944-8 May1945)

>   *Waffen*-Grenadier Regiment of the *SS* 75 (Russian no. 4)
>   *Waffen*-Grenadier Regiment of the *SS* 76 (Russian no. 5)
>   *Waffen*-Grenadier Regiment of the *SS* 77 (Russian no. 6)
>   *Waffen*-Artillery Battalion of the *SS* 30
>   *Waffen*-Reconnaissance Battalion of the *SS* 30 (formerly known as the "Cavalry Battalion")
>   *Waffen-Füsilier* Company of the *SS* 30
>   *Waffen*-Signal Company of the *SS* 30
>   *Waffen*-Armored Car Company of the *SS* 30
>   *Waffen*-Field Replacement Battalion of the *SS* 30

Organized during the summer of 1944 by collecting *Schuma* battalions no longer needed in Belorussia after the destruction of Army Group

Center. The members were a German police cadre supplemented by Russians, Belorussians, Ukrainians, and others. In Poland, four infantry regiments were formed, and on 20 July 1944 titled *Schuma* Brigade "Siegling." The divisional designation followed on 3 August 1944, and the fourth regiment was disbanded the next month. The forming division was transported to eastern France during the second half of August 1944, and faced constant desertion before and after its arrival. The division fought partisans with mixed results as it trained during September and October 1944. Relocated to the Colmar region, it fought Free French units in frontline combat in mid-November 1944 and suffered heavy losses. Withdrawn east of the Rhine, the unit was redesignated as *Waffen*-Grenadier Brigade of the *SS "Weissruthenian"* ("Belorussian") during January 1945. Most manpower was sent to the Vlasov Army, with only the *Waffen* Grenadier Regiment 75 and limited support elements maintained on the active rolls. Much of the German cadre went into the forming 25th *Waffen*-Grenadier and 38th *SS*-Panzer-Grenadier Divisions. On 9 March 1945, the brigade received a paper redesignation to again become the 30th *Waffen*-Grenadier Division (Belorussian no. 1), but the strength remained that of a reinforced regiment. The remaining men surrendered to American forces in Bavaria at the end of the war.

31st SS-Volunteer-Grenadier Division

SS-Oberführer, later *SS-Brigadeführer und Generalmajor der Waffen-SS* Gustav Lombard

31st *SS*-Volunteer Grenadier Division

SS-Volunteer-Grenadier Regiment 78
SS-Volunteer-Grenadier Regiment 79
SS-Volunteer-Grenadier Regiment 80
SS-Volunteer-Artillery Regiment 31
SS-*Füsilier* Battalion 31
SS-Signal Battalion 31
SS-Anti-Tank Battalion 31
SS-Combat Engineer Battalion 31

A full-strength division formed from the draconian conscript of the military age manpower of the ethnic German Batschka region, based around the German cadre of the disbanded 23d *Waffen*-Mountain Division. First ordered into existence on 24 September 1944. The division never received an honor title, but was informally known as "Batschka." It was rushed into combat in Hungary in November 1944, before being fully trained, and suffered heavy losses. After rest and replenishment, it returned to combat in Silesia in January 1945 until the end of the war, when it passed into Soviet captivity.

32d SS-Volunteer-Grenadier Division "January 30th"

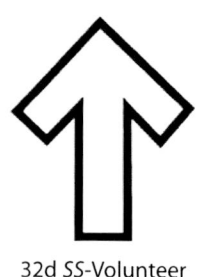

SS-Standartenführer Johannes-Rudolf Mühlenkamp (organized the division mid-January–5 February 1945)

SS-Standartenführer Joachim Richter (5–17 February 1945)

SS-Oberführer Adolf Ax (17 February–mid-March 1945)

SS-Obersturmbannführer Hans Kempin (mid-March–8 May 1945)

- SS-Volunteer-Grenadier Regiment 86 "Schill"
- SS-Volunteer-Grenadier Regiment 87 "Kurmark"
- SS-Volunteer-Grenadier Regiment 88 (partially formed)
- SS-Panzer-Grenadier Regiment "Falke" (subordinated to the division)
- SS-Volunteer-Artillery Regiment 32
- SS-Flak Battalion 550 (corps troops from V SS-Mountain Corps)
- SS-*Füsilier* Battalion 32 (former SS-Music School Braunschweig)
- SS-Signal Battalion 32
- SS-Anti-Tank Battalion 32 (former SS-Assault Gun Battalion 16)
- SS-Combat Engineer Battalion 32
- SS-Rocket Launcher Battalion 506 (intended to be corps troops for the VI *Waffen*-Army Corps)
- SS-Field Replacement Battalion 32

SS-Regiment "Schill" was created 20 July 1944 for possible use against an insurrection, and consisted of officer cadets and elements from training units. Fought well against the Slovak revolt during September and October 1944 and retitled as SS-Panzer-Grenadier Regiment 86. With the success of the Soviet Vistula offensive after 12 January 1945, any available German units were rushed to the Oder River line, including SS-Regiments "Falke" and "Kurmark," formed from the cadre and recruits at training grounds. Joined by SS-Panzer-Grenadier Regiment 86 and additional training and miscellaneous units and superfluous administrative staffs, the division came together during February 1945 near Frankfurt. After defensive fighting that month, the division finished its organization, and then was heavily engaged in the Berlin offensive beginning on 16 April 1945. Forced west, most of the division was destroyed in the Halbe pocket south of Berlin in late April. Survivors surrendered to Allied forces along the Elbe River early the next month.

33d SS-Volunteer-Grenadier Division

No commander assigned

This was to be an infantry division organized from the Hungarian *Heimatwacht* (HW), the militia of the German community in western Hungary that protected the population from partisan attacks. As most men of military age had already volunteered or been conscripted, the *HW* consisted mainly of older men. At first intended to be the local version of the *Volkssturm*, it was then planned to form them into a division. But the *HW* was badly armed and had little in the way of equipment or uniforms (which led to it being referred to as the "Slouch Hat Division" because of the wearing of civilian caps) and most of its men were scattered while defending their home regions during the autumn of 1944. The survivors were evacuated to Austria and merged with the Austrian *Volkssturm*. This was the unit that is often described as the "33d *SS*-Cavalry Division."

33d *Waffen*-Grenadier Division of the *SS* "Charlemagne" (French no. 1)

Waffen-Oberführer Edgar Puaud (10 February–5 March 1945)

SS-Brigadeführer und Generalmajor der Waffen-SS Dr. Gustav Krukenberg (5 March–25 April 1945)

SS-Standartenführer Walter Zimmermann (25 April–8 May 1945)

> *Waffen*-Grenadier Regiment of the *SS* 57 (French no. 1)
> *Waffen*-Grenadier Regiment of the *SS* 58 (French no. 2)
> *Waffen*-Artillery Battalion of the *SS* 33
> *Waffen*-Anti-Tank Battalion of the *SS* 33
> *Waffen*-Signal Battalion of the *SS* 33
> *Waffen*-Combat Engineer Company of the *SS* 33
> *Waffen*-Field Replacement Company of the *SS* 33
> Divisional Honor Company/Close Combat School

The French *SS*-Volunteer Regiment was created on 18 August 1943, and became the French *SS*-Assault Brigade spring 1944. One battalion saw heavy combat in Galicia in summerm 1944. On 10 August 1944, the French *Waffen*-Grenadier Brigade of the *SS* was ordered into existence, to combine the *Heer* French Volunteer Legion (*LVF,* 1941–1944) with the French *SS*-Assault Brigade and former Milicien, *NSKK,* and *OT* volunteers. The Assault Brigade veterans formed the cadre of *Waffen* Grenadier Regiment 57, and the *LVF* formed that of Regiment 58, with ex-Miliciens and others spread throughout the unit. Committed to action in West Prussia in January 1945, and redesignated as a division on 10 February 1945 with no expansion. After heavy combat in Pomerania into March 1945, survivors regrouped in Mecklenburg. Redesignated as *Waffen*-Grenadier Regiment Charlemagne on 25 March 1945. A volunteer battalion from this regiment fought in Berlin late April through early May 1945 and was destroyed. The detached training regiment of the division surrendered to Allied forces in southwest Germany at the end of the war, the main body near Salzburg, and part with *Nibelungen*.

34th *SS*-Volunteer Grenadier Division *"Landstorm Nederland"* (Dutch no. 2)

SS-Oberführer Martin Kohlroser (10 February–8 May 1945)

>   *SS*-Volunteer-Grenadier Regiment 83 (Dutch no. 3)
>   *SS*-Volunteer-Grenadier Regiment 84 (Dutch no. 4)
>   *SS*-Volunteer-Artillery Regiment 34 (Dutch no. 2) (partially formed)
>   *SS*-Anti-Tank Battalion 60 (former *SS*-Anti-Tank Battalion "*Nordwest*")
>   *SS*-Flak Battery 60 (former *SS*-Flak Battery "Clingendaal")
>   *SS*-Signal Company 60
>   *SS*-Combat Engineer Company 60
>   *SS*-Field Replacement Battalion 60

First formed 1943 to combat the Resistance and ensure order in the event of an Allied invasion. Changed from police to military status on 16 October 1943, becoming the *SS*-Grenadier Regiment "*Landstorm Nederland*." The cadre consisted of Dutch *Waffen-SS* veterans and Dutch and German police officers and NCOs. Elements firat saw action September 1944 along the Albert Canal, one battalion fought later that month near Arnhem. Expanded on 1 November 1944 into the *SS*-Volunteer Brigade *"LN,"* with miscellaneous units and Dutch fascist National Socialist Movement (*NSB*) party members added. Redesignated as a division on 10 February 1945, fought in the Arnhem area and broke up in heavy fighting during April 1945, gradually surrendered during April and May 1945.

35th *SS-Polizei*-Grenadier Division

SS-Oberführer und Oberst der Schutzpolizei Johannes Wirth (late February–mid-March 1945)

SS-Standartenführer und Oberst i.G. Rüdiger Pipkorn (mid-March–24 April 1945)

>   *SS-Polizei*-Grenadier Regiment 89 (former *SS-Polizei* Regiment 29)
>   *SS-Polizei*-Grenadier Regiment 90 (former *SS-Polizei* Regiment 30)
>   *SS-Polizei*-Grenadier Regiment 91 (former *SS-Polizei* Regiment 14 with 1st and 3d Battalions, 2d Battalion remained a police unit on detached service)
>   *SS-Polizei*-Artillery Regiment 35 (partially formed)
>   *SS-Polizei*-Signal Battalion 35

35th *SS-Polizei*-Grenadier Division

> *SS-Polizei*-Tank Destruction Battalion 35 ("Tank Destruction" indicated that the unit lacked the normal heavy weapons of an "anti-tank" unit)
> *SS-Polizei*-Combat Engineer Battalion 35
> *SS*-Field Replacement Battalion 35

Organized in February 1945 as Police Brigade Wirth, *SS*-Police Regiments 29 and 30, which were formed by police personnel evacuated from France. With added units, soon retitled as the 35th *SS*-Police Grenadier Division and committed in the Guben area along the Oder River. The division was caught in the Halbe pocket south of Berlin after the Soviet offensive of 16 April 1945, and disintegrated by the end of the month. Survivors fought on with other units, and only a handful made their way west to surrender to American forces.

36th *Waffen*-Grenadier Division "Dirlewanger"

SS-Brigadeführer und Generalmajor der Waffen-SS und Polizei Fritz Schmedes (20 February–8 May 1945)

> *Waffen*-Grenadier Regiment 72
> *Waffen*-Grenadier Regiment 73
> *Waffen*-Grenadier Regiment 74 (number assigned, but regiment never formed)
> *Waffen*-Artillery Battalion 36 (two batteries)
> *Waffen-Füsilier* Company 36
> *Waffen*-Signal Company 36
> *Waffen*-Field Replacement Company 36

First created spring 1940 as *SS-Sonderkommando* (Special Unit) Dirlewanger to make use of convicted poachers as a rear area security force. After service in Poland, the unit was sent to Belorussia early 1942, and used for anti-partisan operations into 1944. The unit was expanded by adding additional criminals, military convicts, and local auxilliaries. The unit engaged in many pitched battles, but also gained a reputation for looting and atrocity. After the German withdrawal from Belorussia during June and July 1944, the Dirlewanger unit was expanded with additional military convicts and sent to Warsaw to battle the Polish Home Army from early August to early October 1944. It suffered heavy losses and was believed to have committed many crimes. Reformed as a brigade, the unit fought in Slovakia against the uprising during October 1944, and now included many political prisoners in its ranks. The brigade fought badly on the Slovakian/Hungarian border during late 1944 and early 1945, before being sent to the Guben sector of the Oder Front in early February 1945. Here, during heavy fighting, it was reformed as the 36th *Waffen*-Grenadier Division of the *SS*, with that title taking effect on 10 February. The division organized during the lull in

37th *SS*-Volunteer Cavalry Division "Lützow"

SS-Standartenführer Waldemar Fegelein (organized division late February 1945)

SS-Obersturmbannführer Karl Gesele (circa 3 March–8 May 1945)

    SS-Volunteer Cavalry Regiment 92
    SS-Volunteer Cavalry Regiment 93 (partially formed)
    SS-Volunteer Cavalry Regiment 94 (one battalion)
    SS-Artillery Battalion 37
    SS-Reconnaissance Battalion 37
    SS-Anti-Tank Battalion 37 (two batteries)
    SS-Combat Engineer Battalion 37 (renamed *SS*-Combat Engineer Battalion 8, which avoided Budapest encirclement)
    SS-Signal Company 37

Began to organize on 26 February 1945 from elements of the 8th and 22d *SS*-Cavalry Divisions that escaped from Budapest, or avoided encirclement, along with recovered wounded and the cadre and recruits of cavalry training schools. From early March 1945, fought in two combat groups near Gran and Bratislava. After heavy combat, one group surrendered with the 6th *SS*-Panzer Army along the Enns River, the other surrendered to Allied forces south of Prague.

38th *SS*-Panzer-Grenadier Division "Nibelungen"

SS-Obersturmbannführer Richard Schulze (early April 1945)

SS-Gruppenführer und Generalleutnant der Waffen-SS Heinz Lammerding (potential commander April 1945)

SS-Obergruppenführer und General der Waffen-SS Carl *Reichsritter* von Oberkamp (potential commander April 1945)

SS-Oberstumbannführer Martin Friedrich Stange (22 April–8 May 1945)

    SS-Panzer-Grenadier Regiment 95
    SS-Panzer-Grenadier Regiment 96
    SS-Panzer-Grenadier Regiment 97 (not formed, intended men used to create a 4th Battalion for Regiments 95 and 96, respectively)
    SS-Artillery Battalion 38
    SS-Anti-Tank Battalion 38

SS-Combat Engineer Battalion 38 (understrength)
SS-Field Replacement Battalion 38 (not fully formed)

Began to organize late March 1945 with a cadre from the staff and last classes at the *SS* officer candidate school at Bad Tölz, and 8,000 Hitler Youths and *RAD* inductees. Survivors from other units were added, and the unit was committed in the Danube valley on 24 April 1945. Heavy fighting against American forces followed through 5 May 1945, and the division surrendered three days later.

A small number of additional formations are below listed by name only, as a point of reference.

Brigades

SS-Panzer-Grenadier Brigade 49
SS-Panzer-Grenadier Brigade 51
Waffen-Mountain Brigade (Tartar no. 1)
SS-Panzerbrigade "Gross"
Indian Volunteer Legion of the *SS*
Eastern-Turkic Volunteer Legion of the *SS*
Caucasian *Waffen-Verbände* (Groups) of the *SS*

Regiments

SS-Regiment Siebenbürgen
Waffen-Grenadier Regiment 103 (Romanian no. 1)
Waffen-Grenadier Regiment 106 (Latvian no. 7)
SS-Fortress Regiment 1 ("Besslein")
1st Hungarian *SS-Sturmjäger* (Assault Light Infantry) Regiment
SS-Volunteer Regiment "*Nordwest*"
SS-Panzer-Grenadier *Lehr* (Instructional) Regiment
SS-Regiment "Ney"
SS-Command-Signal Regiment 500 (formerly numbered 501)
SS-Command-Signal Regiment 503
SS-Regiment "Kurt Eggers" (staff controlling war reporters)
1st Bulgarian Regiment of the *SS*
2d Romanian Regiment of the *SS*

Battalions

SS-Military Geology Battalion 500
SS-Röntgen Battalion (X-Ray technicians)

Heavy *SS*-Panzer Battalion 501
Heavy *SS*-Panzer Battalion 502
Heavy *SS*-Panzer Battalion 503
SS-Anti-Tank Battalion 560
SS-Anti-Tank Battalion 561
Waffen-Ski Battalion 25
Waffen-Ski Battalion 26
1st Hungarian-*SS*-Ski Battalion (actually three battalions strong)
SS-Jäger Battalion 500
SS-Jäger Battalion 501
SS-Jäger Battalion 502
SS-Raiding Detachment "Middle" (former *SS*-Jäger Battalion 502)
SS-Raiding Detachment "Northwest"
SS-Raiding Detachment "East"
SS-Raiding Detachment "South"
SS-Raiding Detachment "Southeast"
SS-Raiding Detachment "Southwest"
SS-Parachute Battalion 500 (retitled as 600)

Never Formed

SS-Motorcycle (or "*Schnell*") Regiment Kalevala (Finnish no. 1)
26th *SS*-Panzer Division
27th *SS*-Panzer Division
28th *SS*-Panzer Division
33d *SS*-Volunteer-Grenadier Division
3d Romanian Regiment of the *SS*

Structure of *Waffen-SS* Divisions

The *Waffen-SS*, as with the *Heer*, possessed a great variety of divisional structures. The complexities of this variety were further complicated by a more or less continuous evolution of authorized division structures throughout the war. For example, the first *Waffen-SS* divisions were organized as motorized infantry ones, with little armor. Four of the earliest divisions (*SS-LAH*, *SS-Das Reich*, *SS-Totenkopf*, and *SS-Wiking*) were then re-formed as *Panzer* (armored) divisions, and three new armored divisions joined them (*SS*-Hohenstaufen, *SS*-Frundsberg, and *SS-Hitlerjugend*). Four additional divisions were raised as Panzer-Grenadier (armored infantry) (*SS-Nordland*, *SS-Reichsführer-SS*, *SS*-Götz von Berlichingen, and *SS*-Horst Wessel).

The motorized *SS*-Combat Group *Nord* evolved into *SS-Nord*, which set the standard for the establishment of an *SS* mountain division. This was used as the intended structure for *SS-Prinz Eugen*, *SS-Handschar*, *SS*-Skanderbeg, and *SS-Kama*, though the last two didn't complete formation. Similarly, the *SS*-Cavalry Brigade developed into *SS*-Florian Geyer, which had a structure copied for *SS*-Maria Theresia (though not for *SS*-Lützow, which had a structure similar to an infantry division).

The *SS* infantry divisions, in particular the 14th, 15th, 19th, and 20th *Waffen*-Grenadier Divisions and the 31st *SS*-Volunteer Grenadier Division, used a standard *Heer* infantry division structure, first found in the 1940 version of *SS-Polizei* (which by the spring of 1944 had reformed into a Panzer-Grenadier division of the same structure as *SS-Nordland*). This was also the intended model for the 25th and 26th *Waffen*-Grenadier Divisions, the 27th, 28th, and 32d *SS*-Volunteer Grenadier Divisions, and the 35th *SS-Polizei*-Grenadier Division, none of which completed their formation, though they did take the field in a semblance of what was intended.

The remaining divisions of the *Waffen-SS* were essentially enlarged brigades or combat groups, and had unique structures, especially as they often fought in several separate parts. This sounds like, and is, a complex subject. The following represents the idealized structure of *Waffen-SS* early war motorized, Panzer, Panzer-Grenadier, mountain, cavalry, and infantry divisions. Each division usually differed slightly in one way or another, and the divisional list in this book is the best way to trace each individual *Waffen-SS* division. Only the major combat elements are included; the supply regiment, for example, is not listed in detail. Units that are not described as "motorized" or "armored" can be assumed to be horse-drawn or dismounted, as appropriate.

Early War

In 1940–41, the few *Waffen-SS* divisions that existed were organized as motorized infantry divisions. These divisions consisted of the following subunits.

Three motorized infantry regiments, each of three infantry battalions. These regiments also had separate companies of combat engineers, anti-tank guns, heavy infantry guns (short-range howitzers), and motorcycle reconnaissance.

One motorized artillery regiment of four battalions, with two light howitzer battalions, one heavy howitzer battalion, and one mixed howitzer and field gun battalion.

One motorized reconnaissance battalion, including one company of armored cars, three of motorized infantry, and one of heavy weapons.

One motorcycle infantry battalion.

One motorized anti-tank battalion with three batteries of towed anti-tank guns.

One motorized anti-aircraft battalion, with three batteries of 88mm pieces, two batteries of 37mm, and one battery of 20mm.

One motorized combat engineer battalion.

One motorized signal battalion.

One battery of assault guns.

Panzer Divisions

Panzer divisions had two infantry regiments, one motorized and one armored. Each regiment had three battalions, and one of the three battalions in the armored infantry regiment was mounted aboard armored halftracks. All five remaining infantry battalions were motorized. Each

Early War Waffen-SS Motorized Infantry Division

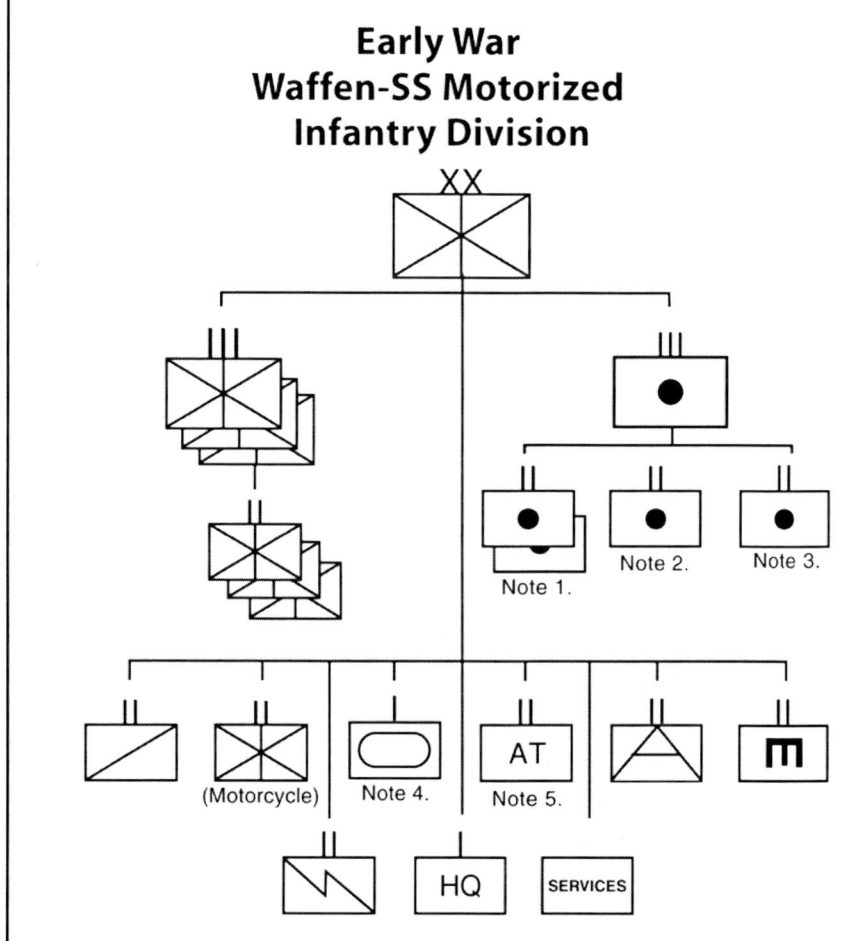

Notes:
1. Each battalion consisted of three 4-gun batteries of towed 105mm howitzers.
2. Consisted of three 4-gun batteries of towed 150mm howitzers.
3. Consisted of two 4-gun batteries of 150mm howitzers and one 4-gun battery of 105mm field guns.
4. The assault gun battery was equipped with twelve assault guns.
5. The anti-tank battalion consisted of three 6-gun batteries of 75mm anti-tank guns.

regiment had separate companies of combat engineers, heavy infantry guns, light anti-aircraft guns, and motorcycle reconnaissance. The heavy infantry guns in the armored regiment were self-propelled.

One regiment of tanks, with one battalion of Panzer IVs and one battalion of Panzer V "Panthers." Each battalion had four companies of tanks, each with four platoons (although later in the war, the tank companies of *SS-LAH* and *SS-Hitlerjugend* were authorized five platoons). The regiment included separate companies of motorized combat engineers and armored anti-aircraft guns.

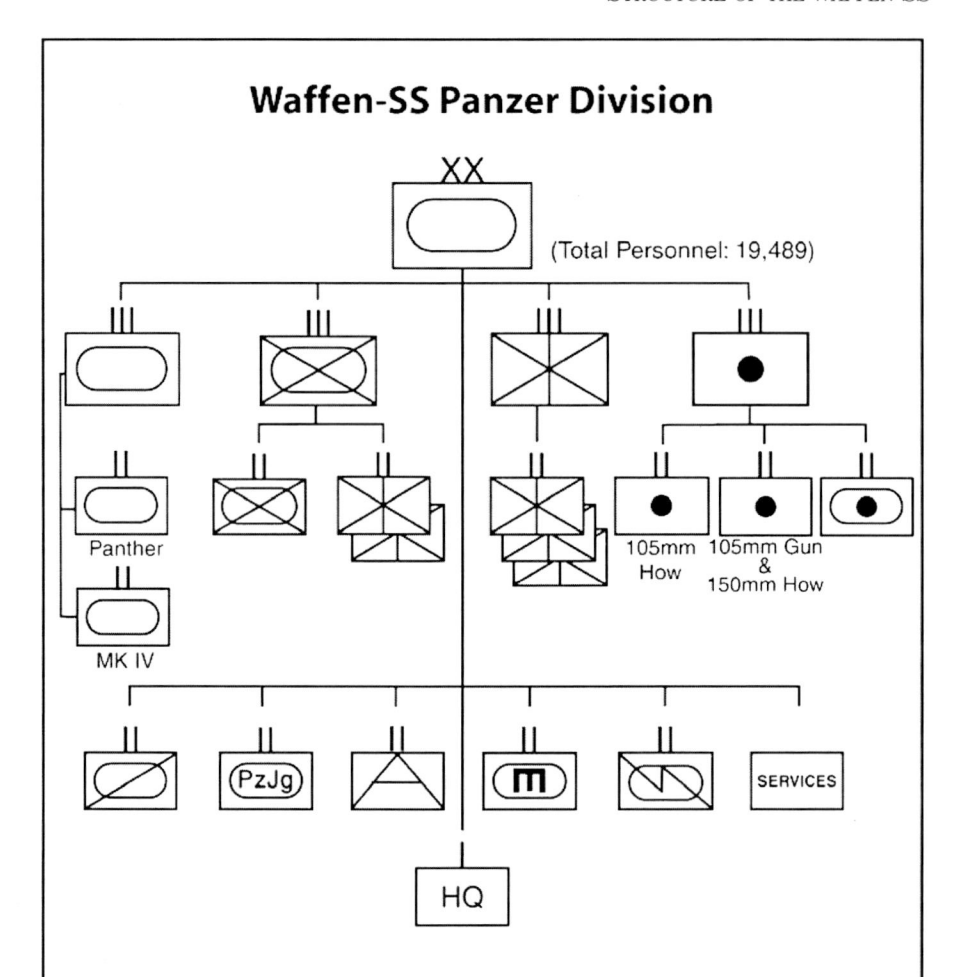

Waffen-SS Panzer Division

(Total Personnel: 19,489)

Panther

MK IV

105mm How

105mm Gun & 150mm How

PzJg

SERVICES

HQ

Notes:
1. The quantity of tanks authorized in an *SS* Panzer regiment varied according to changing tables of organization and equipment during the war. In the last year of the war, a battalion was authorized four companies, each of 17 tanks, with an additional 8 tanks in each battalion headquarters company for a total of 76 tanks per battalion. Another 8 in the regimental headquarters company brought the total to 160 tanks authorized for the regiment.
2. At the same time, the tank companies of the *SS-LAH* and *SS-Hitlerjugend* were authorized an additional platoon of five tanks each, bringing their totals to 96 tanks per battalion, and 200 tanks in the regiment.
3. The artillery regiment was authorized a battalion of 12 *Wespe* and 6 *Hummel* self-propelled howitzers, a battalion of 18 towed 105mm howitzers, and a battalion with two batteries of towed 150mm howitzers and one of towed 105mm field guns. Late in the war, *SS-LAH* and *SS-Hitlerjugend* were each authorized a battalion of *Nebelwerfers* as well.
4. The *Panzerjäger* (antitank) battalion consisted of two companies with 14 *Jagdpanzer* IVs each and battery of towed antitank guns.
5. The anti-aircraft battalion consisted of 20mm, 37mm, and 88mm guns.
6. Total armored personnel carriers for the division was 230.

One regiment of artillery, with one light howitzer battalion, one heavy howitzer battalion, one mixed battalion with light cannon and multi-barrel rocket launchers, and one armored battalion with two batteries of *Wespe* (self-propelled 105mm howitzers) and one battery of *Hummel* (self-propelled 150mm howitzers).

One armored reconnaissance battalion, with one company of armored cars, three infantry companies mounted on armored halftracks, and one heavy weapons company mounted on armored halftracks.

One armored anti-tank battalion, with two batteries of *Jagdpanzer* IV tank destroyers and one motorized battery of anti-tank guns.

One motorized anti-aircraft battalion, with three batteries of 88mm guns, two batteries of 37mm automatic cannon, and one battery of 20mm automatic cannon.

One armored combat engineer battalion, with two motorized companies, one motorized heavy weapons company, and one company mounted on armored halftracks.

One armored signal battalion, with one field telephone company and one radio company, both with a mix of armored halftracks and unarmored vehicles.

Panzer-Grenadier Divisions

Two motorized infantry regiments, each of three infantry battalions, with separate companies of combat engineers, heavy infantry guns, light anti-aircraft guns, and motorcycle reconnaissance.

One motorized artillery regiment, with two battalions of light howitzers and one battalion of heavy howitzers.

One battalion of tanks, equipped with assault guns, but organized in a tank manner with four companies, each with four platoons.

One battalion of anti-tank guns, equipped with assault guns in all three batteries.

One armored reconnaissance battalion, with two motorized infantry companies, two infantry companies mounted on armored halftracks, and one heavy weapons company mounted on armored halftracks.

One motorized anti-aircraft battalion with three batteries of 88mm pieces and one battery of 37mm pieces.

One motorized combat engineer battalion with companies.

One motorized signal battalion with one field telephone and one radio company.

Waffen-SS Panzer-Grenadier Division

(Total Personnel: 18,000)

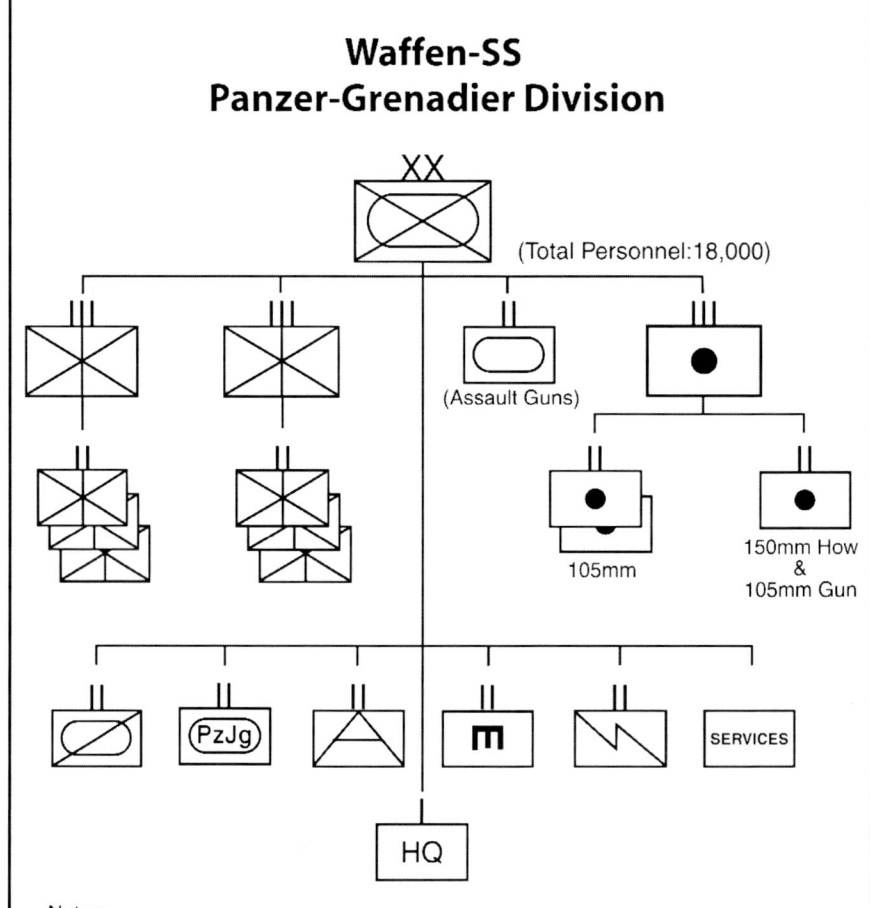

(Assault Guns)

105mm

150mm How & 105mm Gun

HQ

SERVICES

Notes:
1. The panzer battalion was authorized 70–76 armored fighting vehicles, and was usually assigned assault guns.
2. The artillery regiment consisted of two battalions with 18 towed 105mm howitzers in each and a battalion with two batteries of towed 150mm howitzers and one battery of 105mm field guns.
3. The *Panzerjäger* (anti-tank) battalion consisted of 45 assault guns or tank destroyers.
4. The anti-aircraft battalion consisted of 20mm, 37mm, and 88mm guns.
5. The infantry regiments used wheeled vehicles for transport.
6. The armored reconnaissance battalion was authorized 141 armored personnel carriers.

Mountain Divisions

No two *Waffen-SS* mountain divisions were organized alike. The following shows an idealized structure, but only *SS-Nord* was so organized. (The notes on the wire diagram explain the fundamental differences between the structures of the six *Waffen-SS* mountain divisions.)

Two mountain infantry regiments, each with three mountain infantry battalions and separate companies of anti-tank guns, heavy infantry guns, and combat engineers.

Waffen-SS Mountain Division

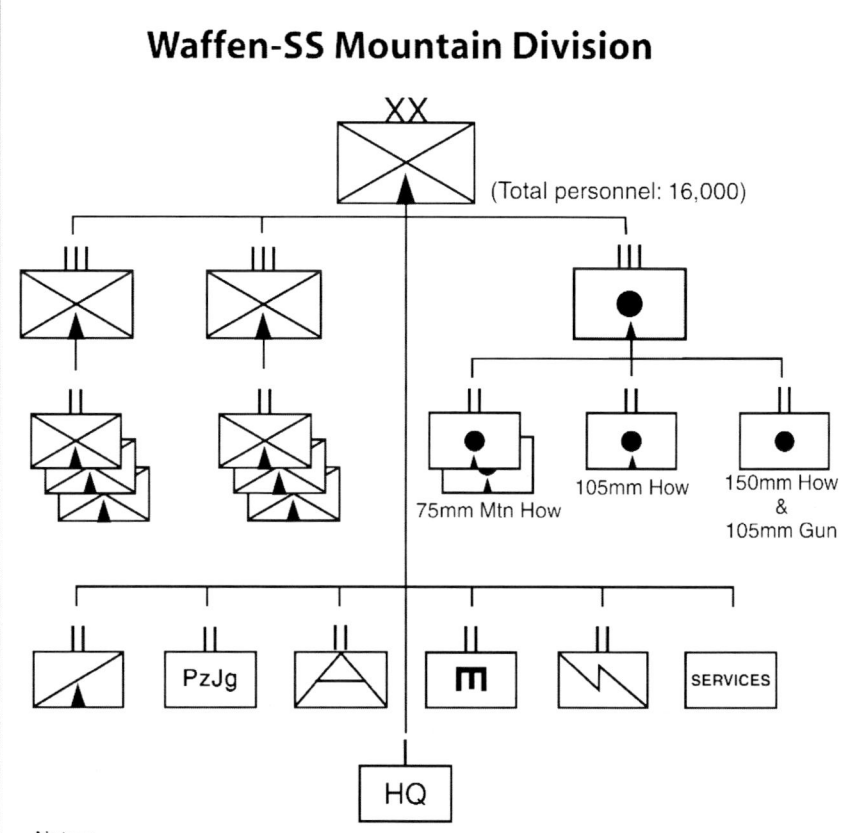

(Total personnel: 16,000)

75mm Mtn How

105mm How

150mm How
&
105mm Gun

PzJg

SERVICES

HQ

Notes:
1. The reconnaissance battalion consisted of three infantry companies and one heavy weapons company.
2. The artillery regiment consisted of two battalions of mule-packed 75mm mountain howitzers, (12 howitzers per battalion), one battalion of 12 towed 105mm howitzers, and one battalion with two batteries of towed 150mm howitzers (four howitzers each) and one battery of four towed 105mm field guns.
3. *SS-Nord* also possessed *SS*-Motorized Infantry Battalion 6 (later *SS*-Panzer-Grenadier Battalion 506), a battalion of motorized infantry, left over from *SS-Nord's* days as a motorized division) and, from September 1943–September 1944. *SS*-Ski Battalion *"Norge"* was attached.
4. *SS-Prinz Eugen* differed in the following especially significant ways:
    a. Two mountain infantry regiments of four battalions each.
    b. The 75mm and 105mm battalions possessed only two batteries each.
    c. The division possessed two companies of horse cavalry.
5. *SS-Handschar* differed in the following especially significant ways:
    a. Two mountain infantry regiments of four battalions each.
    b. The 75mm and 105mm battalions possessed only two batteries each.
6. *SS-Skanderbeg* differed in the following especially significant ways:
    a. Three 75mm battalions, each of three four-gun batteries, and one towed battalion of 150mm howitzers.
    b. No anti-aircraft battalion.
7. *SS-Kama* never achieved full divisional status, and possessed two mountain infantry regiments of two battalions each, with some division support troops.
8. *SS-Karstjäger* differed in the following especially significant ways:
    a. The 105mm battalion of the artillery regiment was equipped with mule-packed 105mm mountain howitzers.
    b. No anti-aircraft battalion.

One mountain artillery regiment with four battalions, including two with 75mm mountain guns, one with towed 105mm howitzers, and one with towed 150mm howitzers and 105mm guns.

One reconnaissance battalion with three mountain infantry companies and one heavy weapons company.

One motorized anti-tank battalion with three batteries of anti-tank guns.

One anti-aircraft battalion with two batteries of 37mm automatic cannon and two batteries of 20mm automatic cannon.

One combat engineer battalion with three companies.

One signal battalion with one field telephone and one radio company.

Cavalry Divisions

Three cavalry regiments, each of battalion size, each with six cavalry squadrons (companies).

One artillery regiment with two light howitzer battalions and one heavy howitzer battalion.

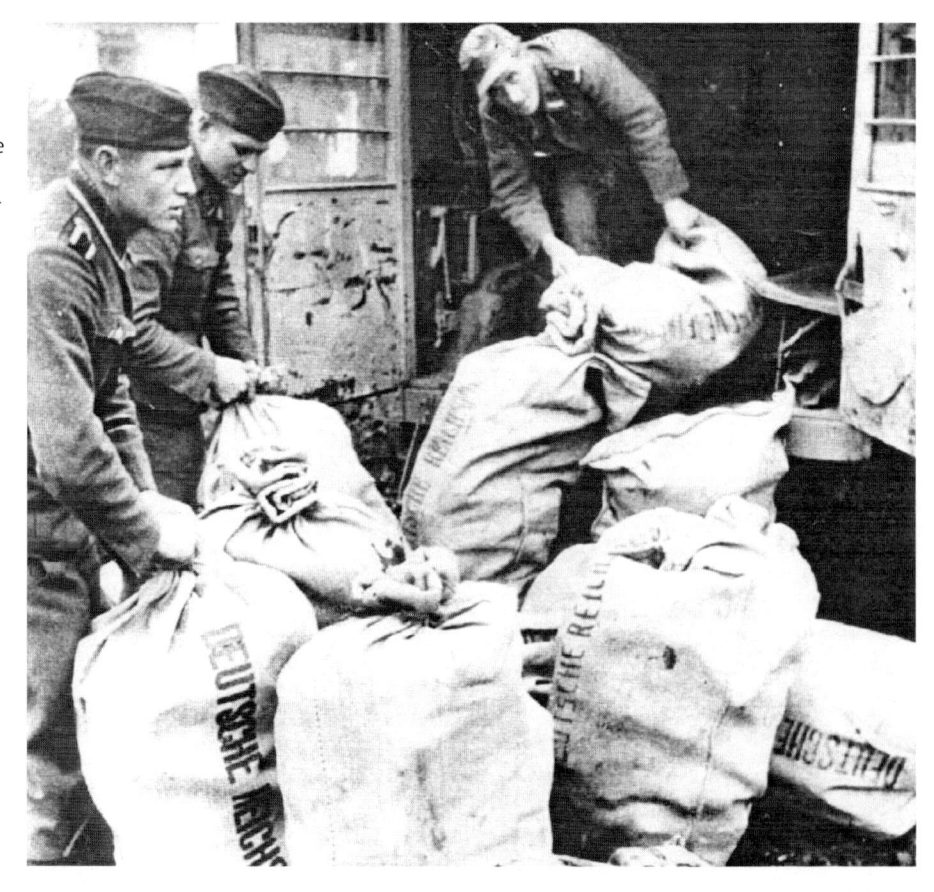

"German National Postal System" proclaims the stencilled letters on the bags, and these were some of the happiest words a frontline soldier could read. Bags of mail are delivered to a Waffen-SS unit, along with another important item, jerrycans of fuel.

Structure of the Waffen SS

One armored reconnaissance battalion with four motorized infantry companies and one motorized heavy weapons company.

One anti-tank battalion with two motorized batteries and one battery of assault guns.

One anti-aircraft battalion with a battery each of 88mm guns, 37mm automatic cannon, and 20mm automatic cannon.

One motorized combat engineer battalion with three companies.

One motorized signal battalion with one field telephone company and one radio company.

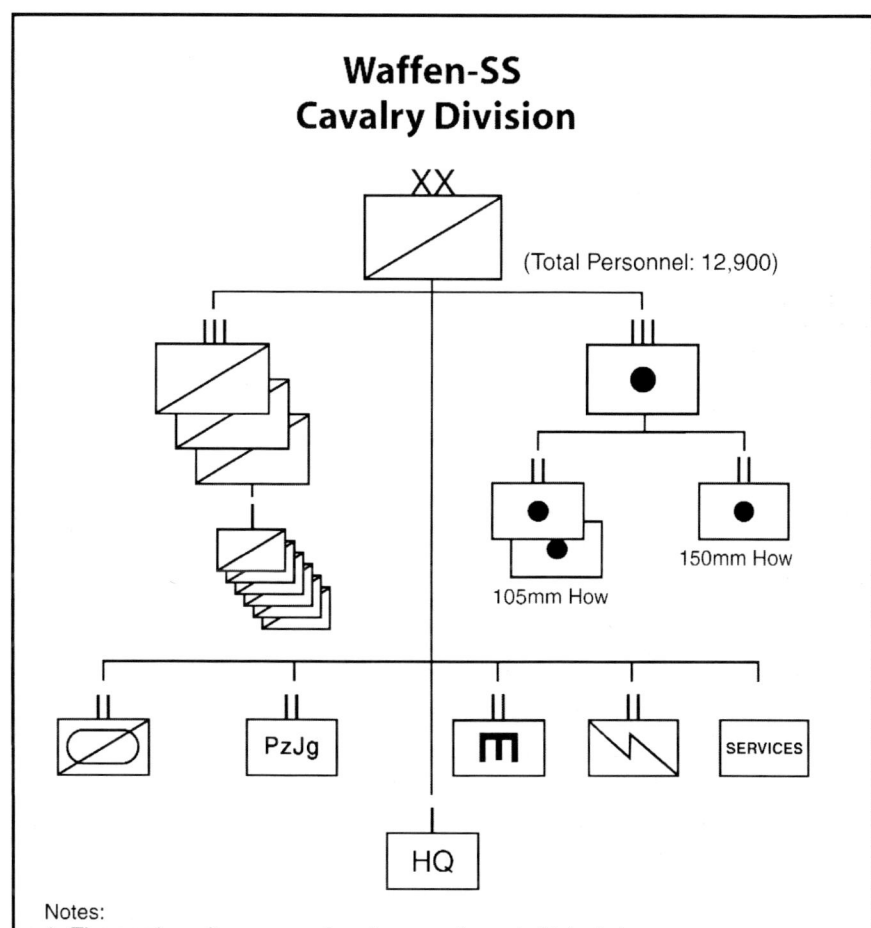

Waffen-SS Cavalry Division

(Total Personnel: 12,900)

[Organizational chart showing division structure with cavalry regiments, artillery regiment with 105mm Howitzers and 150mm Howitzers, PzJg (anti-tank), and other support units including HQ and Services]

Notes:
1. The cavalry units were used as dragoons (mounted infantry).
2. The artillery regiment consisted of two battalions of horse-drawn 105mm howitzers (12 howitzers per battalion) and one battalion with two batteries of horse-drawn 150mm howitzers (four per battery) with a four-gun battery of horse-drawn 105mm field guns.
3. Later in the war, the armored reconnaissance battalion was redesignated as a *Füsilier* battalion, and became a dismounted organization.

Grenadier (Infantry) Divisions

Three infantry regiments, each with three infantry battalions and separate companies of anti-tank guns and heavy infantry guns.

One artillery regiment with three battalions of light howitzers and one battalion of heavy howitzers.

One *Füsilier* battalion with three infantry companies and one heavy weapons company.

One anti-tank battalion with two motorized batteries and one battery of assault guns.

One anti-aircraft battalion with a battery each of 88mm, 37mm automatic cannon, and 20mm automatic cannon.

One combat engineer battalion with three companies.

One signal battalion with one field telephone and one radio company.

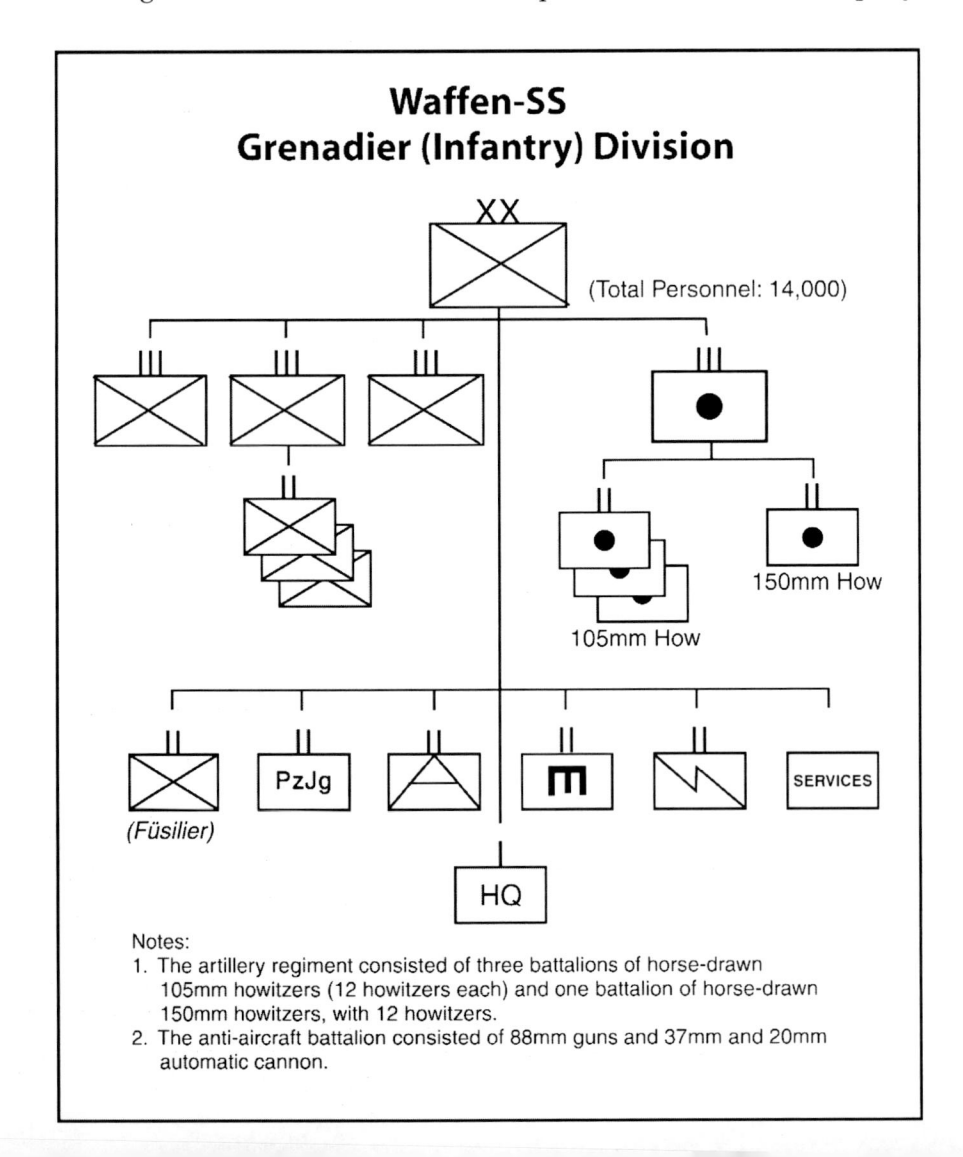

Waffen-SS Grenadier (Infantry) Division

(Total Personnel: 14,000)

105mm How

150mm How

PzJg

(Füsilier)

SERVICES

HQ

Notes:
1. The artillery regiment consisted of three battalions of horse-drawn 105mm howitzers (12 howitzers each) and one battalion of horse-drawn 150mm howitzers, with 12 howitzers.
2. The anti-aircraft battalion consisted of 88mm guns and 37mm and 20mm automatic cannon.

Germans in the *Waffen-SS*

The First World War was the decisive event in the lives of millions of Germans, not least for those who would influence and shape the *Waffen-SS*. By early 1919, Adolf Hitler was convinced that Germany had been betrayed from within. He was determined that if he had a say during a future war, Germany would obtain the resources it needed from eastern Europe, negating any British blockade. An armed force loyal to the government would preserve order at home.

Heinrich Himmler, born in 1900, missed seeing combat by a few months, but retained dreams of military glory. He would seek to live those out vicariously for the rest of his life.

Paul Hausser had attained a coveted posting to the General Staff before the war, and as a trained staff officer served in elite units with royal connections. He would later seek the reestablishment of a military elite after the homogeneity of the *Reichswehr* years.

Felix Steiner was a participant in the 1917 fighting against the Russians, during which *Stosstrupp* ("shock troop") tactics were mastered. The next spring, he helped put those methods to use against the Allies in the *"Kaiserschlacht"* offensives. Steiner was convinced that the future of warfare lay with small groups of highly-trained, elite soldiers.

Hausser and Steiner both fought in the east during 1919, defending German territory against the Poles and Bolsheviks. Steiner, in particular, was able to get a feel for the political climate in the eastern Baltic, which featured Russians and Baltic Germans attempting to maintain political power in the face of Communism and local nationalist aspirations. As highly competent professional officers, Hausser and Steiner were both able to find a place in the 100,000-man *Reichswehr*, the limited army allowed to Germany under the Treaty of Versailles.

Hundreds of thousands of other soldiers were unable to continue their military careers. While most drifted into various civilian occupations, several thousand of the more promising soldiers were taken into the police forces, and these semi-militarized groups (collected in 1934 as the *Ordnungspolizei*, or "Order Police") became a means for Germany to circumvent the Versailles limitations.

Paramilitary organizations called *Freikorps* allowed some men to continue military activity for a few years after the war. Tens of thousands of former soldiers, and other men too young to fight by 1918, saw action in these unofficial units during the early 1920s. Some *Freikorps* men enlisted in the *Reichswehr* or the *Ordnungspolizei* in the following years, but the best most could manage was to maintain their old contacts with each other by joining the *Sturmabteilungen* (Storm Units, or *SA*) of the Nazi Party. The *SA* leadership came to hope that their men, numbering over 100,000 by 1931, could form the new army of Germany.

It was little noticed during 1929 that Himmler was appointed as *Reichsführer* of the *Schutzstaffeln* ("Protection Detachments," or *SS*), those carefully-selected Nazi adherents who served as bodyguards for Nazi speakers at political rallies. The *SS* was still only a small force at this time, but Himmler had big plans, and retained his hopes to be involved in a military endeavor.

Hausser and Steiner were able to advance in the *Reichswehr*, but neither was happy with their experience. They considered the *Reichswehr* leadership too old fashioned, and found little audience for their ideas on creating a new guard corps or special attack force.

Hitler came to power in Germany on 30 January 1933. This provided an opportunity for the longtime head of his protection detail, a former *Reichswehr* senior noncommissioned officer (NCO), Josef "Sepp" Dietrich, to resume a military career. Dietrich was a veteran of tank combat during the Great War, and had then drifted from the *Freikorps* to the police and into the *SS*. On 17 March 1933, Dietrich was instructed to collect 117 reliable young *SS* men into a militarized *SS* bodyguard for Hitler. It was the origin of what became the *Leibstandarte* ("Body Guard Regiment") Adolf Hitler (*SS-LAH*). Eight of these 117 men went on to become regimental commanders in the *Waffen-SS*, and three (Wilhelm Mohnke, Theodor Wisch, and Fritz Witt) attained division command.

The *SS* now began to grow rapidly. *Politisches Bereitschaften* ("Political Readiness Detachments") were set up in major cities to act in the event of a Communist strike. These consisted of both dedicated party members and men who could not find semi-military service elsewhere. German Army and discharged *Reichswehr* veterans provided the leadership.

On 1 October 1934, the term *SS-Verfügungstruppen* ("Special Use Troops," or *SS-V*) replaced the former "Political Readiness" label.

Service in the *SS-V* was recognized by law as a fulfillment of a man's military obligation, because the *SS-V* received military—rather than exclusively political—training. Organized by battalions during 1935, the next year the loose regimental structures became formalized into the *SS-V* Regiments *Deutschland* and *Germania*. The *SS-LAH* was considered "related" to the *SS-V*, but retained separate status.

Hausser had reached the rank of *Generalmajor* during 1931, and retired a year later with the pension status of a *Generalleutnant*. He met Himmler, and was persuaded to join the *SS* in late 1934, to help reinforce the soldierly nature of the *SS-V*.

The *SA* had grown remarkably since early 1933. By the following spring, it numbered approximately three million men, and its leaders sought to exercise some sort of power. Hitler perceived a threat, as did the leaders of the *Reichswehr*. The latter turned a blind eye when Hitler used *SS* men to murderously purge the *SA* leadership on 20 June 1934 in the "Night of the Long Knives." Hitler had made a gesture to the *Reichswehr*, demonstrating that it was the armed force for Germany's future instead of the *SA*. In return, the *Reichswehr*, soon to become the openly-conscripted *Wehrmacht* in violation of the Versailles provisions, agreed to not interfere with the small, highly-select *SS-V* units. It was even provided that the *SS-V* units could come together into a division in the event of war.

The *SA* declined, and in the following years, most of its manpower joined the German Army (*Heer*) and the *Luftwaffe*. A number of *SA* military instructors, including Felix Steiner, instead joined the *SS-V*.

Most of the junior enlisted men of the *SS-V* continued to be drawn from young volunteers, but as *SS-Deutschland*, *SS-Germania*, and the *SS-LAH* grew to full regimental size, they met their need for officers and

SS-LAH on parade, circa 1935, still with early uniform elements.

NCOs by taking on veterans from the police, from the *SA*, and from the political *SS* (known as the *Allgemeine-SS*). The *SS-V* addressed the creation of an organic officer corps by creating two officer candidate schools, with Hausser founding one and setting the curriculum. The *SS* system differed from that of the *Heer* in not requiring an *Abitur* (certificate generally gained upon matriculation from a *Gymnasium*, or academic high school, around age 19), and also in insisting that any man lacking military experience had to first serve time in the ranks. In the *Heer*, a well-educated man could join immediately as an officer candidate.

These *SS* stipulations turned away some potential recruits, who wished to become officers quickly. It also brought in hundreds of young men with lower-class backgrounds, however, who lacked education but desired professional military careers. Hausser's school system was designed to provide the necessary education to men who demonstrated potential.

An element of the *SS-V* parades circa 1935. The early style of uniform is worn, though the black was initially kept for use in official functions.

The regimental flag of *SS-Germania* at a pre-war parade. This flag had been "consecrated" through being touched by the "Blood Flag" carried in the 1923 "Beer Hall" Putsch in Munich.

By 1936, the *SS-V* was highly selective. For recruits, it only accepted young men who were healthy, in good physical shape, and who had clean police records. Additionally, recruits had to show proof of pure "Aryan" ancestry back to 1800, while those who became officers had to further demonstrate this to 1750. Politics was not specifically an issue—though obviously few sought to join who were in outright opposition to the Nazi party—and party membership was not required for joining the *SS-V.* Surveys revealed that many potential enlistees were attracted by the chance to serve in a new sort of guard force, and by the opportunity to become an officer.

Only the best applicants were accepted into the *SS-V* (others were claimed by the *Wehrmacht* and not allowed to join). Of those, only the most promising were selected for officer training, and only 60 percent of these passed their courses. Afterwards, especially during peacetime, it was the best officers who received promotion. Those men who became battalion and higher-level commanders in the *SS-V* and *Waffen-SS* after beginning their careers as simple enlisted men were in many ways the "best of the best," and in that light, it is not surprising that so many were highly considered.

Hausser's curriculum emphasized tactical training and leadership principles, with political education forming only a small portion of the whole. The same was true in the *SS-V* units where, thanks to Steiner, a new initiative had taken hold. Steiner had assumed command of the 3d Battalion of *SS-Deutschland* during 1935, and implemented his ideas on creating modern "shock troops." He replaced most parade drill with strenuous exercise to create an athlete-soldier, and emphasized initiative over blind obedience, and infiltration over direct attack. Officers and men exercised and trained together, breaking down social barriers and creating comrades, with each man prepared to take the place of his superior, should the latter become a casualty.

Steiner took command of *SS-Deutschland* the next year, and spread his methods to the entire regiment. Due to their obvious validity, Hausser, as Inspector of the *SS-V* from the autumn of 1936, instigated Steiner's reforms throughout the *SS-V*. Hausser imparted to the *SS-V* the notion that its men were soldiers, and not political activists, and sought to combine the traditional Prussian notion of professionalism with the modern training reforms of Steiner.

Heer observers and training advisors were impressed by the *SS-V* and the *Wehrmacht* actively included the *SS* units (which were expanding through the creation of those supporting elements necessary for a division) in its plans. The *Heer* allowed the *SS-V* to be equipped with scarce motor vehicles, in place of the initial horse-drawn ones. Motorized units were perceived as vital to offensive operations, and thus *SS-V* units participated in the occupation of that part of Czechoslovakia known to the Germans as the Sudetenland, the annexation of Austria, and the seizure of the rump of the Czech lands.

If the *SS-V* had earned the respect of the *Heer*, that wasn't the case for *LAH*, which possessed superb human material but hadn't undergone the same high level of training. Dietrich was a proud man, and it was well into 1938 before he agreed to an exchange of officers between *LAH* and the *SS-V*. He also acknowledged that Hausser's authority as inspector extended to the *LAH*, which previously acted as a law unto itself. During 1939, the military character of *LAH* gradually improved, though discipline problems such as looting and poor fire control still arose during the Polish and Western campaigns.

Himmler continued to seek ways to have armed men under his control, and another means developed with the cooperation of Theodor Eicke, who had become Inspector of the concentration camp system (run by the *SS*) during 1936. Eicke possessed tremendous energy, and he devoted much of his attention to recruiting men to be camp guards. The pre-war camps required only a few thousand guards, but Eicke enlisted 3,500, and then many thousands more into the *SS-Totenkopfverbände* ("Death's Head Organizations," a name based on their insignia, and abbreviated *SS-TV*). The standards were somewhat lower than those for the *SS-V* and *SS-LAH*, with men not needing to meet the same stringent height and health requirements.

The excess men were recruited with an eye toward commitment in a military role. Eicke had emerged from the First World War with a hatred of aristocratic professional officers, and he rejected the traditional German notion of "Prussian discipline." He instead sought to instill political fanaticism, teaching his men that it was their duty to destroy Germany's enemies. While the *SS-TV* gained some measure of military proficiency, it lagged behind the standard necessary for service during wartime.

Austrian Nazis had first come to Germany during 1933, when the *SS* and *SA* were banned in their country. Those desiring military service were collected into a battalion, which became the 2d Battalion of *SS-Deutschland*. After the *Anschluss*, this unit was detached to serve as the cadre of a new regiment of the *SS-V*, raised in Austria. This unit kept the same high recruiting standards as *Deutschland* and *Germania*, and received the honor title *"Der Führer"* to symbolize Austrian loyalty to the new regime.

When the Second World War began on 1 September 1939, the future *Waffen-SS* consisted of the regiments *SS-LAH*, *SS-Deutschland*, *SS-Germania*, and *SS-Der Führer*, along with an artillery regiment and supporting battalions (anti-tank, combat engineer, signal, and so on). *SS-LAH* was intended to operate as a reinforced motorized infantry regiment, while the rest of the *SS-V* would be collected into a motorized infantry division, the *SS-V* Division. Himmler, as head of the *SS* and Chief of German Police, had a say in the formation of two additional divisions.

The *Wehrmacht* had no control over the growth of the *SS-TV* during peacetime, but wanted its excess trained men to serve in the *Heer* during the war. The *Ordnungspolizei* had also grown considerably during the preceding years, and possessed many men capable of military service. Both of these branches were committed to providing the manpower for a division each, respectively, and Himmler asserted his authority to have those divisions belong to the *SS*. During October 1939, Hitler decided that the *SS-TV* men could form the core of an *SS-Totenkopf* Division, while the police would become the *SS-Polizei* Division.

Tens of thousands of *Allegemeine-SS* men were *Wehrmacht* reservists, and they served during the war in the same manner as non-*SS* men. Thousands of others belonged to an older category (over the age of 25) and these men were added to a base of 6,500 *SS-TV* men and cadres from the *SS-V* to form the *SS-Totenkopf* Division. This had a strength of 18,000 men, a minority of whom were former concentration camp guards. The *SS-V* officers, in particular, helped oversee a tough training program to bring the division's training up to military standards.

The *SS-Polizei* Division was able to fill its command positions with military veterans, and it soon attained a level of efficiency comparable to *Heer* infantry divisions. In common with the latter, only individual officers and men were *SS* or Nazi party members, and its association with the *SS* was largely on paper. During the war, hundreds of men from the *SS-Polizei* Division would go on to serve with other *Waffen-SS* units, though the division itself only became fully a part of the *Waffen-SS* during early 1942. After that, its members held *Waffen-SS* rank instead of their police rank, or as an additional commission, in the case of officers.

The term *Waffen-SS* became official during the spring of 1940, and it indicated those units concerned with frontline military duty. The *SS-TV* organizations remained extant, and aside from camp guards, included units used for rear area security and occupation duties. Himmler and Hitler still foresaw the *SS-LAH* and *SS-V* forming a force for maintaining postwar state security, but considered their wartime duty as doubly advantageous. It would provide necessary practical experience in fighting, and would lend legitimacy to postwar duty.

The men of the *SS-LAH* and *SS-V* had considered themselves as elite soldiers since well before the war. This was because of the teachings of their officers, inspired by Hausser and Steiner, and as a logical consequence of their rigorous military training. The *SS-Totenkopf* Division maintained a higher degree of political awareness because of its many *SS-TV* and *Allegemeine-SS* members. In the *SS-Polizei* Division, the officers and men saw themselves as simply fulfilling the military role which had always been their intention, no matter that they had served with the police out of clandestine necessity.

Himmler had the *Wehrmacht*'s approval to raise 100,000 "Police Reinforcements" in the event of war. In fact, the men he enlisted were young wartime volunteers for the *Waffen-SS*, who were collected into over a dozen new *Totenkopf* regiments. These reorganized gradually, many dissolving and amalgamating before fully forming, with the surviving units becoming *SS-Totenkopf* infantry regiments, an indication of their intended use as military formations. Initially, many were used for occupation and pacification duties, but by the time the Soviet Union was invaded on 22 June 1941, the final title of "*SS*-Infantry Regiment" was in place, and most of the regiments were used as military, rather than police units. The *Totenkopf* infantry units were at times used in anti-partisan operations, which often involved the killing of innocent civilians.

The officer corps for these new *Waffen-SS* infantry regiments came from *SS-V* transfers, from the *Ordnungspolizei,* and from *Allegemeine-*

SS reservists. The overall quality of leadership was far below that of the *SS-V*, and there wasn't sufficient time to train the newly inducted men well, much less to prewar standards. For these reasons, the regiments usually did not fight well, and suffered heavy casualties in their initial battles. Some regiments were broken up to reinforce more established units, while others became more dependable as they gained experience. In the latter category was a unit organized out of the pre-war *SS* equestrian branch. The *SS*-Cavalry Brigade grew out of a Death's Head Riding Regiment to become a police force, and finally a military one by early 1942. Its officers and men were of a much lower standard than the prewar *SS*-V, but from early 1942, as it became a full *Waffen-SS* division, it received the same replacements as other *Waffen-SS* units.

During 1940 and 1941, Himmler remained officially limited in the number of men he could recruit for his armed forces. Foreigners were not subject to *Wehrmacht* service, however, so Himmler turned to non-Germans as a reservoir of manpower. Initially, this involved recruiting "Germanic" Western Europeans, primarily from the countries occupied during 1940. Some Swiss had already joined before the war, as had Baltic Germans, and individual men of German or Germanic ancestry from around the world (694 non-Germans were counted in the *Waffen-SS* as of 1 May 1940). As the following section demonstrates, tens of thousands of Europeans would follow the initial volunteers. The first Danes, Dutch, Flemings, and Norwegians were concentrated, along with Finns, into the new *SS-Wiking* ("Viking") Division, which, unlike the *Totenkopf* Infantry Regiments, did receive first-class officers and training before it went into action during late June 1941. The base of the division was *SS-Germania*, which gradually came to include many foreigners in its ranks.

Himmler, and his recruiting chief Gottlob Berger, cultivated ties before the war with leaders in the *Volksdeutsche*, or ethnic German communities of Eastern Europe. Individual ethnic Germans moved to Germany and joined the *Waffen-SS* through 1940, and the "1,000-man action" (in which the ethnic Germans were to be trained as instructors for the Romanian Army, but instead remained in Germany) brought hundreds of Romanian ethnic Germans into the *Waffen-SS*. It was the conquests of the next year that opened the gates to recruiting these men *en masse*. Several thousand came to Germany with the support units of the *SS-V* Division (renamed *"Reich"* and then *"Das Reich,"* or "The Empire"), which had passed through the Banat region during the Yugoslavian campaign.

The Banat was the area around the city of Temesvar (Timisoara in Romanian) settled by Germans at the behest of the Holy Roman Emperor of the German Nation during the eighteenth century. These German settlers were to form a wall of Christians between the Empire and the Muslim Ottoman Turks, who had only recently been driven back from what is today Austria. After April 1941, this region came to be split between the German occupation government in Serbia, Romania, and, in the largest part, Hungary. Aside from the men who came to Germany with *SS-Das Reich*, the *Waffen-SS* initially only had access to those ethnic Germans in the Serbian zone. The others were liable for Hungarian or Romanian Army service. The same was true for ethnic Germans in Hungarian-controlled Batschka-Vojvodina, and Romanian-controlled Siebenbürgen (Transylvania) and Bessarabia, while Croatian ethnic Germans were left to the new Croatian Army.

A partisan war developed in the former Yugoslavia by the end of 1941, so Himmler decided to raise a mountain division of ethnic Germans from the Serbian Banat. When only a few thousand volunteered, conscription was introduced. For the first time, the *Waffen-SS* included draftees. These men were usually not up to the pre-war *SS-V* standard, and the leaders were primarily demobilized ethnic German officers and NCOs from the former Yugoslavian Army. Together, they formed the Volunteer Mountain Division *Prinz Eugen*, the first element of the *Waffen-SS* to carry the designation "Volunteer," despite few of its men actually fitting that description. The title was designed to indicate that the division was not formed from German citizens (the vast majority of men in *Wiking* were German nationals), and recalled the pivotal role played by Prince Eugene of Savoy during the defense of Vienna and expulsion of the Turks from Croatia, Hungary, Transylvania, and Slovenia in the early eighteenth century. The *Prinz Eugen* Division was at first ridiculed by the rest of the *Waffen-SS*, but it eventually developed into an effective unit.

During 1943, the *SS* High Command worked out arrangements with the Croatian and Romanian governments for ethnic Germans in their military establishments to be allowed to transfer into the *Waffen-SS*. These men, veteran soldiers, brought with them an altogether higher level of competency than those who were conscripted before or after. The Croatians primarily served with *Prinz Eugen*, or its sister division *Handschar* ("Scimitar"), organized from Bosnian Muslims and ethnic Croatian Catholics. The Romanians were used to flesh out III (Germanic) *SS*-Panzer Corps, which collected the majority of Western European volunteers in the Volunteer Panzer-Grenadier Division *Nordland* and Volunteer Panzer Grenadier Brigade *Nederland*. *SS-Prinz Eugen*, *SS-Handschar*, *SS-Nordland*, and *SS-Nederland* all contained sizable cadres of German nationals from the pre-war *SS-V* or early-war formations such as *SS-Wiking*.

The next year, new agreements required ethnic Germans in Hungary and Romania to perform German military service, and most of these men went into the *Waffen-SS*. While individuals volunteered, conscription was widely applied in the Banat and Siebenbürgen, with these men assigned to every element of the *Waffen-SS*. The Batschka/Vojvodina area became the last ethnic German region to experience extensive conscription, with its men suffering often brutal press-ganging during the summer of 1944. These draftees were primarily used to form the Volunteer Cavalry Division Maria Theresia and the 31st *SS-Volunteer Grenadier Division* (which never received an honor title). They also filled out the Volunteer Panzer-Grenadier Division Horst Wessel, which had its origins in a brigade formed from two *SS-Totenkopf* Infantry Regiments.

The so-called "classic" *SS* Divisions—*SS-LAH* (raised to a division 1941), *SS-Das Reich*, *SS-Totenkopf*, and *SS-Wiking*—began receiving small quantities of ethnic German replacements by the spring of 1942, and as a rule, considered them inferior, since they were not the fine physical specimens of the pre-war era. The majority of their replacements consisted of young wartime volunteers from Germany. While these men lacked the extensive training seen before the war, almost all were veterans of the Hitler Youth, and had received training in such military skills as marksmanship, route marching, map reading, and military courtesy and drill. This eased their transition to military life, and made them far more prepared for its rigors than were their comrades from other countries.

A *Waffen-SS* soldier from the summer of 1942. He typifies the young men who joined the *Waffen-SS* during the early war as volunteers, and helped rebuild *SS-LAH, Das Reich,* and *Totenkopf* prior to the Kharkov campaign. They were some of the last men to receive thorough training, close to the pre-war standard, before being committed to combat.

The supply of volunteers was largely exhausted during 1942, and the *Waffen-SS*, including its elite German divisions (which received armored vehicles from the summer of 1942), then had to rely heavily on conscripts from ordinary German draft pools, just as did the *Heer*. It also became common for excess *Luftwaffe* and Navy personnel to be assigned to the *Waffen-SS*, without any say in the matter. The Hohenstaufen and Frundsberg Panzer Divisions, raised during 1943, were supposed to attain the same elite level as the "classic" divisions, yet included a majority of young German conscripts. The *Hitlerjugend* ("Hitler Youth") Panzer Division was forming at the same time, using volunteers from the Hitler Youth who were otherwise considered a year too young for military service, being 16 to 17 years old at the time of induction.

It should be noted that *SS-Totenkopf* suffered heavy losses during 1941, and was almost completely destroyed the next year at Demyansk. As the original complement of camp guards and *Allegemeine-SS* reservists bled to death in the Valdai Hills, a new *SS-Totenkopf* Division gradually formed around small cadres from the original during the summer and autumn of 1942. The new men were primarily young wartime volunteers, and afterwards, the division received replacements in the same manner as the other "classic" divisions. Eicke was killed in action on 26 February 1943, and even before his death, the command of the division came to be primarily in the hands of officers from the pre-war *SS-V*. The *TV* influence declined for the remainder of the war. (It should be noted here that exchanges of personnel between concentration camps and field units were not limited to *SS-Totenkopf*, but included most *Waffen-SS* units, as well as *Wehrmacht* and *Polizei* veterans who were assigned as camp guards when no longer fit for frontline service due to wounds and illness.)

The "classic" divisions were able to maintain a degree of quality, and the three new armored divisions reached a comparable level, because their experienced cadre carried on the traditions established in the pre-war *SS-V*. The young Germans, whether volunteers or draftees, and the *Luftwaffe* and Navy levies, were taught that they were an elite, and part of a new type guard force. As much as time allowed, instruction focused on the training methods developed by Steiner, with modifications based on wartime experience.

This was also true in the other units raised by the *Waffen-SS*, though the later "German" divisions usually contained large numbers of ethnic German conscripts and men transferred from other branches of service, with smaller cadres possessing *SS-V* experience. The training times were often short, and the men themselves were not always as enthusiastic as young German draftees, who tended to become caught up in the *SS-V* spirit in the "classic" divisions. The Germanic *Waffen-SS* also caught this spirit, and by 1944 its men were interchangeable with experienced German *Waffen-SS* soldiers.

The divisions raised from Ukrainians and Balts (14th, 15th, 19th & 20th Waffen-Grenadier Divisions) fought as well as veteran German infantry divisions, but were in the Waffen-SS only by organizational association, and had no relation to the pre-war elite. The other foreign units were usually, at best, comparable to Heer divisions hastily thrown together from German conscripts and stragglers. At worst, units such as the Free India Legion were Nazi Party propaganda fronts that wasted valuable weapons and German cadre.

By 1945, the pre-war *SS-V* members who weren't dead or disabled had been spread remarkably thinly by Himmler's desire to create new military units under his nominal control. The *Waffen-SS* listed 38

An *SS-LAH* soldier displays a knocked out Soviet T-34 for Max Büschel, *Waffen-SS* war reporter, in this photo released to the press on 1 March 1944. The moment would have taken place during the heavy fighting in western Ukraine in the preceding months. (Bando)

divisions in its order of battle, though several never got beyond the organizational stage, and numerous separate regiments and battalions. The roster included divisions of Italians, Hungarians, Albanians, and even Russians. It was a far cry from both Himmler's conception of a state security police force and the Hausser/Steiner plan for the new elite guards.

For more information about the non-combat units added by Himmler to the *Waffen-SS*, see page 259.

Germanics in the *Waffen-SS*

Heinrich Himmler envisioned the *SS* as more than an organization for Germans. He intended that the "best Nordic blood" would be represented, whether in the form of German nationals, ethnic Germans from outside Germany, or "Germanics" from the related countries. For this reason, the *SS* cultivated contacts with influential persons in many foreign countries, in preparation for the time when these nations would unite with Germany into a Nordic union. As a first step, non-German nationals of German or Germanic extraction were welcomed into the ranks of the *SS-V* before the war. By 1 May 1940, 694 such men served in the *Waffen-SS*, and the number grew considerably in the following months and years.

Germanic volunteers were particularly prized for two reasons. First, in many cases, joining the German military meant aiding an occupying power. Both sides hoped that the act of volunteering would lessen tensions between the aggressor and the victim. Second, those without German citizenry or ancestry were outside the bounds of *Wehrmacht* recruiting, offering the *Waffen-SS* a unique source of manpower. But which nations qualified as Germanic?

To the *SS*, the related "brother" nations were: Denmark, Flemish Belgium (Flanders), Great Britain, Iceland, Liechtenstein, Luxembourg, the Netherlands, Norway, Sweden, and Switzerland. During the war, Walloon Belgium was given Germanic status and Luxembourg was annexed to Germany, so that its men were considered German nationals. Finland became an "honorary Germanic" nation due to its unique ethnic origin. Non-Jewish citizens of these countries were eligible to become full members of the *SS* and could, in theory, qualify for all the same rights and benefits due to German nationals. Men (and often women nurses) from all of these countries served with the *Waffen-SS* during World War II, and their story is complex and interesting, not least because it is often told simplistically and inaccurately.

Germanic volunteers served in the *Waffen-SS* in both closed formations and in multinational ones, and before examining each Germanic nation individually, it is best to examine the history of the major multinational units.

The *"Wiking"* Division

The unit which eventually became the 5th *SS*-Panzer Division *"Wiking"* was created to use Germanic manpower from the countries occupied during 1940. On 20 April of that year (Hitler's birthday), the *Nordland* Regiment was authorized, incorporating Danes and Norwegians. The *Westland* Regiment followed two months later, on 15 June, to take in Dutch and Flemish volunteers.

Recruiting went slowly, partly because Germany and the Soviet Union were officially on friendly terms, by virtue of the conclusion of the Non-Aggression Pact of August, 1939. Consequently, many did not perceive the *Waffen-SS* as an outlet for anti-Communist feelings. The Norwegian political scene was still sorting itself out, so few men stepped forward until early the next year, when Quisling solidified his power and called for volunteers for *Nordland*. In Denmark, only the members of the small, minority DNSAP felt favorably towards Germany, and although some of these men quickly volunteered, few others joined them. Meanwhile, the Flemish *VNV* party adopted a wait-and-see attitude and avoided committing its members to the German military. Only in the Netherlands was a collaborationist party, the *NSB*, firmly in place and the subject of popular support. Nearly 1,000 men enlisted in the *Westland* Regiment, though 120 later dropped out when they realized that they would receive difficult military training in place of political police instruction.

During October 1940, *SS-Germania*, one of the original units of the *SS-V*, was detached from the *SS-V* Division to form the core of a new division. This was ordered into existence on 1 December of that year as the *SS*-Division *Germania*, incorporating the regiments *SS-Germania*, *SS-Nordland*, and *SS-Westland*, along with newly-created supporting elements. The fully-motorized division was retitled as the *SS*-Division *Wiking* soon after, on 21 December 1940.

During the spring of 1941, 400 Finns were added to *Wiking*. These were men with previous military experience who were to gain familiarity with German methods, while another 800 men of the new Finnish Volunteer Battalion of the *Waffen-SS* received full military training. The initial 400 were spread around the division, which now also began to receive Norwegian volunteers and small numbers of Flemings and Swedes.

When the invasion of the USSR began on 22 June 1941, *SS-Wiking* included roughly 1,143 Germanic volunteers comprised of 631 Dutch, 294 Norwegians, 216 Danes, 1 Swede, and 1 Swiss (the Finns were not counted). Other Germanics were still in training, while a few were assigned to other *Waffen-SS* units outside *SS-Wiking*. Despite casualties, replacements which arrived during the summer of 1941 allowed *SS-Wiking* to carry on its rolls by 19 September approximately 821 Dutch, 291 Norwegians, 251 Danes, 45 Flemings, and eight Swedes. These numbers would fluctuate during the following months as the division suffered heavy casualties, but then took in replacements.

SS-Wiking was given priority over the national legions in receiving recovered wounded who were returning to active duty, and so the number of Germanics in it rose beyond the level represented solely by new recruits. The Flemings were most represented in this, with so many men being sent to *Wiking* that the strength of the Flemish Legion suffered. Meanwhile, their fellow countrymen, the Walloons, began to turn up in the division. These were primarily members of the AGRA party who were opposed to Leon Degrelle and the Rexists, and thus avoided the Walloon Legion.

The Walloons were not the only ones to begin volunteering once the war with the Soviet Union began. Additional Swedes, Swiss, and now Liechtensteiners joined the *Waffen-SS*, and were primarily assigned to *Wiking*. Individual Icelanders, largely students at German universities, also made their way to the division, while Luxembourgers found themselves German citizens subject to conscription if they didn't volunteer for military duty. Luxembourgers, therefore, were not singled out in nationality head counts, while the Icelanders were few enough to escape notice.

Detached elements of *SS-Wiking* saw limited combat during the last days of June 1941, but the division as a whole finally went into action at the beginning of the following month. *SS-Westland* commander, Hilmar Wäckerle, was one of the first to die, shot by a crewman as he investigated a knocked-out Soviet tank. He was soon succeeded by Artur Phleps, an experienced staff officer who had previously held General rank in the Romanian Army. Phlep's military career had begun well before the First World War in the Austro-Hungarian Army, and having this highly experienced professional in charge no doubt hastened *SS-Westland*'s development into a dependable unit.

SS-Nordland was commanded by another Austro-Hungarian Army veteran of long experience, Fritz von Scholz, who soon gained the respect and soldierly affection of his men. Von Scholz was nicknamed "*der Alte Fritz*" (Old Fritz), which had been the appellation fondly afforded Frederick the Great by his men almost two centuries previously. Both *SS-Nordland* and *SS-Westland* at this time contained many German officers, including von Scholz, who would go on to have a long association with the Germanic volunteers.

SS-Wiking crossed the Dnieper Reiver at Dniepropetrovsk during late August 1941, after fighting past the Korsun-Schanderovka area, where it would again see combat two and a half years later. The bridgehead at Kamenka was expanded in heavy fighting during September, after which *SS-Wiking* participated in the advance to the east, across the Mius River. The German drive was halted, and *SS-Wiking* settled into winter positions along the Mius, which were held into the following summer.

The division gradually replaced its serious losses from the summer and autumn campaign. The Finnish Volunteer Battalion finished its training in early December 1941, and joined *SS-Wiking* the following month. The surviving Finns already in the division were merged into the new battalion, which became the 4th Battalion of *SS-Nordland*. The former 3d Battalion of the regiment was broken up to replenish the first two battalions, so the Finns were renumbered as the 3d Battalion, a designation they retained until leaving *SS-Wiking*.

Another change for *SS-Wiking* was that staff officer Christian Fredrik von Schalburg was reassigned to command the *Frikorps Danmark* during February 1942. The Russian-born Danish aristocrat had become a legend for his daring reconnaissance missions, and had served as the spokesman for the European volunteers in the division. Another Danish professional officer with *SS-Wiking* was Poul Rantzau-Engelhardt, who became von Scholz's trusted advisor on the *SS-Nordland* staff.

Several more Danish officers, including Tage Petersen and Johannes Brenneke, were also found in *SS-Wiking*, but otherwise, non-German officers were few. This would change beginning late during 1942, as young volunteers began to graduate from officer training schools and small numbers of older professional soldiers in each nation joined the *Waffen-SS*. Command within *SS-Wiking* at battalion level and above, however, remained almost exclusively among German nationals.

SS-Wiking assisted in the capture of Rostov in mid-July 1942, then advanced across the Kuban river into the Western Caucasus. After heavy fighting near Maikop, the division shifted east, fighting south of the Terek River near Malgobek until Christmas. The Finnish Battalion

Christian Fredrik von Schalburg, left, the Finland veteran and first combat commander of the *Frikorps Danmark*, greets his former student from the NSU, Sören Kam, during the spring of 1942. Von Schalburg was readying his men for combat, while Kam was on home leave prior to attending the *Waffen-SS* officer training school at Bad Tölz. Soon after, von Schalburg was killed in action in the Demyansk pocket. Kam later earned the Knight's Cross, on 7 February 1945. (H.T. Nielsen)

had its single hardest day of combat when it captured Hill 701 on 16 October, suffering very heavy casualties. During late December, *SS-Wiking* was hastily withdrawn to be recommitted northeast of Rostov in the anticipated relief of Stalingrad. This instead became a fighting withdrawal, with *SS-Wiking* and other units from the Caucasus barely succeeding in escaping to the west through Rostov.

SS-Wiking passed through Rostov on 5 February 1943, and was immediately committed to defensive fighting to the north, containing the Soviet drive towards Dniepropetrovsk. It then particpated in the successful counteroffensive to the north that resulted in the recapture of Kharkov and the "miracle on the Donets." The division had incurred significant losses during the eight months of continuous fighting, and now reorganized.

Von Scholz had left *SS-Wiking* during November 1942, but soon resumed his affiliation with the Germanic volunteers by taking command of the 2d *SS*-Infantry Brigade during January 1943. His place as *SS-Nordland* commander was assumed by Wolfgang Joerchel. Phleps had departed to form *SS-Prinz Eugen* during the spring of 1942, and his successors had proved ineffectual. Veteran *SS-Nordland* battalion commander Harry Polewacz took over *SS-Westland* during September 1942, and led the regiment ably until he was killed by a sniper in January 1943. He was replaced by the division's 1st General Staff Officer, Erwin Reichel, who himself was mortally wounded in late February. His successor was August Dieckmann, who had developed an outstanding reputation as a battalion commander in *SS-Germania*.

On 16 February 1943, a breakdown of *SS-Wiking*'s personnel indicated that the division included roughly 1,972 Germanic volunteers. These were comprised of 1,061 Dutch, 418 Danes, 252 Norwegians, and 241 Flemings. Not counted were roughly 900 Finns, 20 or so Swedes, and perhaps 100 or more Swiss and Liechtensteiners. Hundreds of additional volunteers were either in hospitals or recovering with reserve (training) units.

SS-Wiking now underwent a substantial transformation. It was to become the foundation of a Germanic corps, which ultimately became known as III (Germanic) *SS*-Panzer Corps. The idea was to combine the Germanic legions into a sister division to *SS-Wiking*, and as a cadre *SS-Nordland* was detached. It formed the core of the eventual 11th *SS*-Volunteer Panzer-Grenadier Division *"Nordland,"* and in fact, most of the Scandinavians and Dutch in *SS-Wiking* were reassigned to this new division (which became the separate *SS-Nordland* Division and *SS-Nederland* Brigade).

Meanwhile, the two Belgian legions became full-fledged *Waffen-SS* formations, and so the Flemings and Walloons in *SS-Wiking* were sent to join them. The two-year contract for service by the Finnish Battalion had ended, and the Finnish government did not wish to renew it. Consequently, almost all of the Finns in the *Waffen-SS* returned to Finland. To replace the Finns, the first combat-ready battalion of the Estonian *SS*-Legion was assigned to *SS-Wiking* as the *SS*-Volunteer Panzer-Grenadier Battalion "Narwa" (pronounced "Narva," and named after the town of Narva in Estonia). The Estonian people were ethnically related to the Finns, and were being considered for Germanic status, but by 1944, were considered non-Germanic (aside from members of the small Estonian ethnic Swedish community). *SS*-Battalion Narwa joined *Wiking* during July 1943, and returned to Estonia in late winter 1944.

Aside from the Estonians, from the summer of 1943 on, *SS-Wiking* primarily consisted of German nationals, supplemented by ethnic Germans. Germanic volunteers were found mainly holding NCO or officer rank, and were spread throughout the division, without regard to nationality. A survey from 14 July 1943 returned a total of 11,254 men in the division, broken down into 8,892 German nationals, 715 ethnic

Germans, 664 Estonians, 619 Dutch (many likely soon left to join the *Nederland* Brigade), 177 Danes, 130 Flemings, 47 Norwegians, 5 Swedes, 1 Finn, and 4 "others" (probably Swiss/Liechtensteiners).

SS-Wiking never was able to join up with the III (Germanic) *SS*-Panzer Corps and for the remainder of the war, it was essentially a German division, little different from the 1944 version of *SS-Totenkopf*, which became its sister division in IV *SS*-Panzer Corps. Both divisions suffered heavy losses during the retreat from Ukraine between summer 1943 and spring 1944, and after rebuilding, suffered further heavy losses during the second half of 1944 in the greater Warsaw area. Their infantry strength was quite low by the time they reached Hungary at the beginning of 1945 for the attempted relief of Budapest. Without attached units of non-Germans, *SS-Wiking* and *SS-Totenkopf* would have been unable to achieve any success during the three Konrad offensives.

These supplemental infantry units consisted of the 1st Battalion each of the *SS-Norge* and *SS-Danmark* Regiments (actually composed mainly of young German conscripts), the Hungarian *SS*-Regiment "Ney," and the three-battalion strong 1st Hungarian *SS*-Ski Battalion (the name was a deliberate mislabelling for intelligence reasons). The Hungarian units consisted of highly motivated Hungarian Army veterans who were happy to be under *Waffen-SS* administration. They were issued with the best available weapons and performed ably under German operational control. They were not, however, Germanic in the least, and so fall outside the scope of this study.

SS-Wiking was the first *Waffen-SS* unit to incorporate non-German volunteers on more than an individual basis. Its service allowed various trouble spots, such as differences in national character, to be identified, and demonstrated that foreigners could be turned into effective "German" soldiers. Had *SS-Wiking* not proved to be a solid, elite division, the later Germanic formations might have been relegated to serving as second-class infantry.

SS-Volunteer Regiment *"Nordwest"*

SS-Westland had been established as a purely military unit, intended to match the quality of the pre-war *SS-V* elements. Many young men in Western Europe were willing to join the Germans for military service, but preferred not to serve in such an overtly German unit, which could conceivably be used in combat against the British. To attract men of this sort, a new regiment, named *"Nordwest,"* was created on 3 April 1941. It was intended that the regiment would serve in a police role, rather than in frontline combat, and that it would see duty in Western Europe rather than on the far frontiers of the German *Reich*. Enlistment was open to Dutch, Flemings, and Danes.

The recruiting drive for *SS-Nordwest* met an immediate response in the Netherlands and Flanders, but lagged in Denmark, where most men willing to aid the Germans had already joined *SS-Nordland*. By August 1941, *SS-Nordwest* reported a strength of 1,400 Dutch, 805 Flemings, and 108 Danes, but that month marked the effective end of the regiment. The war against the Soviet Union had erupted weeks earlier, on 22 June, and national legions were forming to join the struggle in the Netherlands, Flanders, and Denmark. *SS-Nordwest* had been segregated by nationality into companies, and these were used as the cadre for the respective legions. *SS-Nordwest* had recruiting standards well below what the *Waffen-SS* required, and so it included some men who were physically disqualified even from service in the new legions, whose requirements were almost as high as for *Waffen-SS* formations such as *SS-Westland* and *SS-Nordland*. So after the creation of the legions, *Nordwest* continued to exist on paper, but it consisted of a small cadre of le*SS*-physically-able men, who were supplemented by new recruits who moved on to other units after finishing training.

The *SS-Nordland* and *SS-Nederland* Divisions

These were originally to be one unit, an *SS*-Volunteer Panzer-Grenadier Division. All available Germanic volunteers were to be concentrated in this division, which would join with *SS-Wiking* to form the III (Germanic) *SS*-Panzer Corps. *SS-Wiking* supplied the *SS-Nordland* Regiment as a cadre for the the new division, which at first was to be named *"Wärager"* in reference to the Varangians, who were medieval rovers and raiders related to the Vikings. Adolf Hitler considered the reference too obscure, and changed the name to *"Nordland"* to reflect the source regiment.

The *SS-Nordland* Division (ultimately titled the 11th *SS*-Volunteer Panzer-Grenadier Division *"Nordland"*) was to include three infantry regiments, one Danish (based on the *Frikorps Danmark*), one Norwegian (based on the *SS-Nordland* Regiment combined with the Norwegian *SS*-Legion), and one Dutch (based on the Dutch *SS*-Legion), along with supporting units (which would include Germanic volunteers). All available Swedes in the *Waffen-SS* (perhaps 50 at this time) were also concentrated in *SS-Nordland*, where they formed the 4th Platoon of the 3d Company of *SS*-Armored Reconnaissance Battalion 11.

The assembled Dutch volunteers considerably outnumbered the other nationalities, with far more than enough manpower to constitute a regiment. This would have led to many Dutchmen being used to fill out the rest of *SS-Nordland*, where they would serve outside of a specifically-Dutch unit. Anton Mussert and the *NSB* leadership protested this, and the *SS*-High Command finally honored their wish by establishing the separate 4th *SS*-Volunteer Panzer-Grenadier Brigade *"Nederland,"* which, in effect, was a scaled-down division.

The total of available Danes, Norwegians, Dutch, and other Germanics remained insufficient to completely fill out one division, let alone a division and a large brigade, so the rosters of *SS-Nordland* and *SS-Nederland* were completed with ethnic Germans, primarily the most recently recruited men from the Banat. These were primarily experienced soldiers of the Romanian Army who transferred voluntarily. Most officers and NCOs in both units were German nationals, though Germanics were well represented among the ranks of the junior officers and junior NCOs, and this improved as more young men graduated from officer and NCO training courses. The senior leadership remained almost entirely German, however, as relatively few professional officers joined the *Waffen-SS*, and many of those who had been present during 1941–1942 left German service as the tide of war changed.

German nationals always constituted at least 25 percent of *SS-Nordland*'s strength, and ethnic Germans usually made up another 35 percent, leaving a maximum of 40 percent Germanics. This number

A grenadier of the Norwegian *SS*-Legion manning a First World War vintage Hotchkiss machine-gun in a defensive position outside Leningrad, probably during the summer of 1942. The Germans captured versions of this gun in various countries, including Norway, and reused them extensively as they remained reliable, despite their heaviness and a relatively low rate of fire.

decreased as casualties depleted the division and—with German defeat in sight—fewer Germanic volunteers stepped forward. During December 1943, a study showed that German nationals in *SS-Nordland* numbered 232 officers, 1,496 NCOs, and 2,403 men (the latter primarily in the various supporting elements). Danes amounted to 41 officers, 193 NCOs, and 1,123 men (1,357 total); and Norwegians to 29 officers, 62 NCOs, and 705 men (796 total). It should be noted that the number of Danes in *SS-Nordland* always exceeded that of Norwegians because of the existence of the separate Norwegian *SS*-Ski Battalion (assigned to *SS-Nord* until late 1944), in which many Norwegians preferred to serve. In December 1943, *SS-Nordland* also included roughly 100 assorted Germanic volunteers of other nationalities, including Swiss, Swedes, Dutch, and Flemings. The entire division counted 11,393 men on its rolls at this point.

SS-Nederland was in a similar state, with around 2,500 Dutch volunteers forming the core of its two infantry regiments, and ethnic Germans filling out the enlisted men. One thousand ethnic Germans were added to each infantry regiment during formation, when the original single Dutch regiment was removed from *SS-Nordland*. German nationals again made up most of the officer and NCO corps, with the brigade's strength at approximately 6,000 men. This would increase as the brigade gradually became a division in all but name, and was finally reclassified as such in early 1945.

SS-Wiking could not be removed from combat, and eventually it joined with the 3d *SS*-Panzer Division *Totenkopf* to form IV *SS*-Panzer Corps from the summer of 1944 until the end of the war. The III (Germanic) *SS*-Panzer Corps thus consisted of the *SS-Nordland* Division, the *SS-Nederland* Brigade, and supporting elements. While the specialist supporting elements of the brigade, division, and corps finished their formation at various schools and training grounds, the main combat portions of *SS-Nordland* and *SS-Nederland* relocated to Croatia, beginning at the end of August 1943.

In Croatia, *SS-Nederland* took over an area north of Zagreb, while *SS-Nordland* deployed to an area southeast of the capital. Both formations carried out sub-unit exercises while also acquiring some seasoning for the minority of inexperienced men through anti-partisan actions. During September 1943, after the Allied invasion of the Italian mainland and subsequent official Italian surrender, the corps helped disarm various Italian units in its vicinity, and Italian weapons were sometimes incorporated into the training.

Eventually, between late November and late December 1943, the elements of III (Germanic) *SS*-Panzer Corps were gradually united in a combat zone, along the perimeter of the Oranienbaum pocket to the west of Leningrad. This theater of war was familiar to many of the volunteers, since the Dutch and Norwegian *SS*-Legions had spent most of their service on the Leningrad siege lines. It was certain that the next attempt to raise the siege of Leningrad would involve an attack out of the large beachhead around Oranienbaum, and so the corps was spread out along the frontline to support the weak formations already dug in (primarily from two *Luftwaffe* Field Divisions). Small bits and pieces from the corps, along with odds and ends from *Wehrmacht* units in the corps' zone, were deployed to the west under the command of the corps artillery commander, Danish *SS-Brigadeführer* Christian Peder Kryssing, as *SS*-Combat Group "*Küste*" ("Coast"). It defended against any attempted landings to the rear of the Oranienbaum defenders.

The anticipated attack began on 14 January 1944, and after a week of delaying actions, III (Germanic) *SS*-Panzer Corps was caught up in the general German retreat from the Leningrad area. An attempt was made to stabilize the front along the Luga River, but the Soviet pressure was too strong, and the river was crossed at the end of the month (with *SS-Nederland* and Combat Group Coast crossing at Keikino, and *SS-Nordland* crossing to the south at Jamburg). The retreat continued west to the line of the Narva River in northeastern Estonia, which was reached during the first days of February. Here the front at last stabilized during the course of heavy fighting.

The Estonian 20th *Waffen*-Grenadier Division of the *SS* was rushed north from the Nevel sector, and assumed positions north of the town of Narva. Combat Group Coast held the line north of them, to the Baltic coast. *SS-Nordland* and *SS-Nederland* set up their command posts in Narva, while the *SS-Danmark*, *SS*-General Seyffardt, and *SS*-De Ruyter Regiments remained on the east bank directly across from the town, carving out fortifications to hold a bridgehead. *SS-Norge* occupied a long line in the swamps on the west side of the river, south of the town. The Narva position extended like a finger into the Soviet lines, and while some Soviet forces attempted to smash the fingertip at the Narva bridgehead, others tried to take the region from the rear, by breaking through *SS-Norge* and *Heer* infantry units to cut off the supply line into Narva.

The bridgehead and swamp areas were successfully defended in exceptionally heavy fighting during February and March 1944, until both sides paused to regroup and wait out the muddy season. *SS-Norge* commander, Arnold Stoffers, an experienced *SS-Wiking* veteran, was killed in action personally leading a critical attack on 25 February, and casualties were high in every combat unit of the corps. Enough replacements and recovered wounded were added that *SS-Nordland* numbered 11,018 men on 30 June 1944. A month earlier, in late May, the Norwegians were at a low ebb of 21 officers, 48 NCOs, and 269 men. The Danes were better off, including 37 officers, 220 NCOs, and 832 men.

Even with modest replenishment, the Narva front was too weak to successfully resist the Soviet attacks expected during the summer. Due to the Soviet success in Belorussia during June and July 1944, no substantial reinforcements could be sent to Estonia. The German forces in the Narva sector, therefore, constructed a new defensive position on a much shorter front 20 kilometers to the rear. It was known as the Tannenberg Line, and the defenses were hinged on three small hills, known as Orphanage Hill, Grenadier Hill, and Hill 69.9 (sometimes referred to as Love's Hill). A small battalion from the reforming Flemish *SS*-Assault Brigade Langemarck had been sent to the Narva sector, and its men dug in on Orphanage Hill on 25–26 July 1944, as the Narva bridgehead was evacuated. A large Soviet attack tried to catch the German and Germanic forces during their withdrawal, and the *SS*-General Seyffardt Regiment was surrounded and destroyed. The regiment was already depleted, and only 20 percent (perhaps 200 men) escaped to the west.

The other units withdrawing from the bridgehead and the Narva River line successfully made their way to the new line, but the Soviet attack prevented proper cohesion. Units became intermingled, but they had brought along their weapons and manpower, and thus a defense coalesced on the core formed by the Flemings. The full weight of a Soviet offensive was repulsed over the next four days in the heaviest fighting yet seen in that theater. Flemings fought side by side with Dutch, Danes, Norwegians, Swedes, ethnic Germans, and Estonians, along with German naval infantry and a German cadre from the *Waffen-SS* formations. The opening days of the Tannenberg Line defense witnessed perhaps the most international grouping of the *Waffen-SS* seen during the war. The motto coined in the Narva bridgehead was continued, "All Europe at Narva."

The Tannenberg fighting again caused heavy casualties to the Germanics. Most of the Flemish officers from the *SS*-Langemarck battalion were killed. *SS*-General Seyffard regimental commander Richard Benner died with his regiment. *SS*-De Ruyter regimental commander Hans Collani (formerly commander of the Finnish *SS*-Volunteer Battalion) was killed in action a few days later, as was *SS*-*Nordland* commander "*Alte Fritz*" von Scholz. Scholz was succeeded by the Chief of Staff of III (Germanic) *SS*-Panzer Corps, the *Heer* General Staff officer Joachim Ziegler. He quickly proved himself as able a troop commander as he had been a staff officer.

The Tannenberg front then settled down to sporadic fighting that lasted into September. The Soviets switched their focus south, to the Tartu (Dorpat, in German) sector, where the defenses were weaker. The III (Germanic) *SS*-Panzer Corps was forced to divert elements under *SS*-*Nederland* commander Jürgen Wagner to delay the enemy advance. Part of this force was a weak battalion from the reforming *SS*-Assault

Brigade *"Wallonien."* It had been sent to the Narva zone in parallel fashion to the Langemarck battalion, but had not yet seen combat.

The Soviets were sufficiently delayed during the following fighting, and the Walloons distinguished themselves at the cost of overwhelming casualties. Another unit that performed very well was *SS-Nordland*'s *SS*-Armored Reconnaissance Battalion 11, which included volunteers from every Germanic nation in Europe (except Great Britain, though some Britons would serve with it during 1945). This unit repeatedly launched key counterattacks which disrupted the Soviet advance.

The Tartu sector stabilized by the beginning of September 1944, but the region was abandoned a couple of weeks later, when the deteriorating situation in central Latvia forced the Germans to evacuate Estonia. The forces defending the Tannenberg Line withdrew to the west and southwest, with some embarking at Tallinn and Pärnu for evacuation by sea. The main portions of *SS-Nordland* and *SS-Nederland* moved by land to the Riga area, where they set up blocking positions to the east of the city, allowing many other units to make an orderly withdrawal west to Kurland. The two units then screened to the south of Riga, providing cover as the Kurland front took shape. This was accomplished by the second week of October.

The III (Germanic) *SS*-Panzer Corps then assumed responsibility for a sector on the western part of the Kurland defenses, protecting the main route toward the key port of Liepaja (Libau, in German). This area was successfully defended in heavy fighting during the First and Second Battles of Kurland, both during the second half of October. The main Soviet effort during the Third Battle of Kurland struck the lines of VI (Latvian) *Waffen*-Army Corps of the *SS* farther east, but the Germanics were again the center of action for the Fourth Battle of Kurland, fought during late January and early February 1945.

The III (Germanic) *SS*-Panzer Corps was pulled out of Kurland at this time, gradually embarking from Liepaja, to be shipped by sea to Stettin to go on the offensive in Pomerania. The Soviet advance across Poland had reached the Oder River at Frankfurt and Küstrin, leaving long, exposed northern and southern flanks. The Germans planned to attack into both flanks, with a southern group advancing north from Küstrin, while another force, including the III (Germanic) *SS*-Panzer Corps, attacked south in Pomerania.

It was at this time, on 10 February 1945, that the *SS-Nederland* Brigade was retitled as the 23d *SS*-Volunteer Panzer-Grenadier Division. *SS*-General Seyffardt, rebuilt with Dutch volunteers and German conscripts, had been in combat independently in West Prussia since the previous month, fighting alongside the Latvian 15th *Waffen*-Grenadier Division of the *Waffen-SS* and the French 33d *Waffen*-Grenadier Division of the *SS* Charlemagne under the headquarters of the XVI *SS*-Army

Corps. These forces were gradually forced west through Pomerania, where *SS*-General Seyffardt rejoined *SS-Nederland* during March 1945.

SS-Nordland and the main body of *SS-Nederland* attacked as part of the SONNENWENDE offensive on 15 February 1945. Fighting nearby were the 4th *SS-Polizei*-Panzer-Grenadier Division and the 10th *SS*-Panzer Division Frundsberg, along with combat groups from the Flemish 27th *SS*-Volunteer Grenadier Division and the Walloon 28th *SS*-Volunteer Grenadier Division.

The *SS-Nordland* assault was able to reach the town of Arneswalde, where a 3,000-man garrison and many civilians were rescued. The other attacking units had less success, and the overall operation was a failure by 18 February, after which the units withdrew to their start lines. Under heavy pressure, the III (Germanic) *SS*-Panzer Corps withdrew west, forming a bridgehead around Altdamm, immediately east of Stettin across the Oder River. This was held through the middle of March at the cost of seeing the formations involved (*SS-Nordland*, *SS-Nederland*, *SS*-Langemarck, *SS-Wallonien*, and *SS*-Frundsberg) lose almost all of their fighting strength. *SS-Danmark* commander Albrecht Krügel, who had been awarded the Oakleaves to his Knight's Cross after the Second Battle of Kurland, was killed in action leading an emergency counterattack on 16 March. He had earned the German Cross in Gold in early 1943 as the commander of the 6th Company of the *SS-Nordland* Regiment.

The III (Germanic) *SS*-Panzer Corps, along with the combat groups of *SS*-Langemarck and *SS-Wallonien*, then withdrew across the Oder, and at last had a chance to refit. Recovered wounded, German naval infantry, and superfluous personnel (for example, mechanics for vehicles which could not be replaced) were integrated into the combat elements. This allowed them to reach an acceptable fighting strength, though time for personal and unit training did not exist. While the two Belgian combat groups remained largely Flemish and Walloon in composition, *SS-Nordland* and *SS-Nederland* contained fewer Scandinavians and Dutch than ever before. Aside from the few Swiss and Swedes, they had little to look forward to if they returned to their liberated homelands, and many had seen for themselves the atrocities the Soviets committed against German civilians. Those Germanics still in German service thus considered themselves dead men, and they were determined to go down fighting. Most of the Germanic volunteers wanted to remain in service, to protect German civilians and perhaps eventually to join the Western Allies in an anti-Soviet war. During this last refit of the Germanic corps, roughly 30 members of the British Free Corps arrived, and were assigned to *SS*-Armored Reconnaissance Battalion 11. Most were later withdrawn at the order of corps commander Felix Steiner, but a few saw action in the following fighting.

The Soviet Berlin offensive opened on 16 April 1945, and *SS-Nordland* and *SS-Nederland* immediately rushed south to counter the Soviet forces that had crossed the Oder. The two Germanic divisions were quickly forced to retreat, with *SS-Nordland* withdrawing west into Berlin, and *SS-Nederland* moving to the south of the city. *SS*-DeRuyter remained to the north of Berlin, and retreated to the west with the Belgians of *SS*-Langemarck and *SS-Wallonien*.

The final struggle began for *SS-Nordland* and the mass of *SS-Nederland*. *SS-Nordland* and the multi-national Tiger tank battalion of the III (Germanic) *SS*-Panzer Corps (Heavy *SS*-Panzer Battalion 503) were wiped out defending Berlin. Fighting alongside them was a battalion formed from the hardcore remnants of the French *SS*-Charlemagne. Most survivors were taken into Soviet captivity, while some individuals escaped the city and surrendered to the Western Allies. *SS-Nordland* commander Joachim Ziegler, who had earned the Knight's Cross for his leadership on the Tannenberg Line, was removed from command on April 24. He was despondent after failing to keep his men out of the doomed capital. Ziegler had intended to lead his European volunteers west, to join Steiner's III (Germanic) *SS*-Panzer Corps headquarters (which remained northwest of Berlin) and then offer the proven anti-Communist forces for service with the Western Allies. Now, he saw his hopes dashed and felt that he and his men were doomed. Ziegler was replaced with *SS*-Charlemagne commander Dr. Gustav Krukenberg, but his abilities were still recognized through his award on 25 April of the Oakleaves to his Knight's Cross, for his leadership of *SS-Nordland* during Operation SONNENWENDE and then in the Altdamm bridgehead.

Danes and ethnic-Germans of *SS*-Panzergrenadier Regiment *"Danmar*k" at the funeral for men who were killed in action fighting partisans in Croatia during the autumn of 1943. The flag at center is that of the former *Frikorps Danmark*. (H.T. Nielsen)

Ziegler was killed along with *SS*-Armored Reconnaissance Battalion 11 commander and Knight's Cross holder Rudolf Saalbach during a failed attempt to break out of Berlin during the early hours of 2 May 1945.

SS-Nederland joined with the mass of the 9th Army that was falling back from the Oder front south of Berlin. This force included the survivors of the 32d *SS*-Volunteer Panzer-Grenadier Division *30. Januar*, the 35th *SS-Polizei*-Grenadier Division, and the 36th *Waffen*-Grenadier Division of the *SS* (the former Dirlewanger Brigade). The 9th Army found itself caught in a pocket around Halbe during the last days of April, and only barely succeeded in punching an escape hole to the west, following the last King Tiger tanks of Heavy *SS*-Panzer Battalion 502 (which served as the Tiger battalion for XI *SS*-Panzer Corps). *SS-Nederland* commander Jürgen Wagner had only 300 men of his division with him when he surrendered to American forces along the Elbe River at Tangeründe on 6 May 1945. Wagner was later turned over to the Yugoslav government, which executed him on 27 June 1947 for crimes allegedly committed while commanding *SS-Deutschland* during the April 1941 invasion of Yugoslavia.

The 11th *SS*-Volunteer Panzer-Grenadier Division *Nordland* and the 23d *SS*-Volunteer Panzer-Grenadier Division *Nederland* only served in combat for approximately 16 months, but during that time, they established reputations second to none within the *Waffen-SS*. In these divisions, Germanic volunteers and ethnic Germans proved their mettle to be fully equal to that of the German nationals in the ranks of the *Waffen-SS* and the *Wehrmacht*.

The Germanic Nations

With the history of the multinational formations laid out, the next step is to examine the Germanic nations and their contribution to the *Waffen-SS* individually.

Denmark

Denmark had prevailed against Prussia in the First Schleswig War (1848–50), but then lost the Second to Prussia and Austria in 1864, and was forced to surrender the southernmost part of Jutland to these powers, i.e. Schleswig to Prussia and Holstein to Austria. After the Seven Weeks War of 1866, Holstein came under Prussian control as well, and both duchies were incorporated into the German Empire (the Second

Reich) in 1871. Schleswig and Holstein were to be returned to Denmark after World War I, but a plebiscite was held in 1920 to allow the population to speak. Ethnic Danes still outnumbered ethnic Germans in the north part of the region, and North Schleswig again became Danish South Jutland, but German influence remained.

As much of Europe became divided into Fascist and Communist camps, Nazism gained limited support in Denmark and two political parties arose in South Jutland. Dr. Frits Clausen formed the Danish National Socialist Workers Party (DNSAP), while Dr. Jens Möller organized what became the National Socialist German Workers Party-Nordschleswig (NSDAP-N). The former party was for ethnic Danes, and included members from throughout the country, while the latter consisted of ethnic Germans, and advocated the reunion of South Jutland with Germany. Both parties sought a close association between Denmark and Germany, and while the National Socialists were popular among ethnic Germans, the Danish version found much less success, and the DNSAP had little influence on Danish politics.

During 1939, the province of Volhynia passed from Romania to the Soviet Union, and hundreds of ethnic German families fled that area. Many settled in South Jutland, with others emigrating to Germany proper. Some of the young men from these Volhynian exile families in South Jutland decided to cross into Germany and offer their services to the German military, and they brought along friends from the existing ethnic German community. One hundred and ten men offered their service to the *SS-V*, which welcomed men of German and Germanic descent who were not liable for *Wehrmacht* conscription. Soon after, by early September 1939, however, Germany was at war with France and Britain, and in the uncertainty of the time, most of the volunteers decided to return to their homes.

Only a dozen ethnic German Danish citizens remained in the *SS-V* during the campaigns of 1940. No *Waffen-SS* unit was involved in the invasion of Denmark and Norway on 9 April 1940, but the ethnic Germans, including Fritz Weber and the Volhynian Johann Velde, were fully involved in the fighting in the Low Countries and France. Their comrade Julius Übel was killed in action on 28 May, becoming the first Danish citizen to die in *Waffen-SS* service.

Meanwhile, Finland had been invaded by the Soviet Union on 30 November 1939, and volunteers from all around the Baltic hurried to Finland to offer assistance. The Danish contingent amounted to 1,200 men, who formed a battalion under the command of Danish Army officers. At the head was V. Tretow-Loof, assisted by staff officer Poul Rantzau-Engelhardt, who had fought in Finland in 1919 during that country's war of independence. The second company was commanded Christian Fredrik von Schalburg, who had been removed from the Royal

SS-Wiking officers confer during the summer of 1941. At right is the ethnic-German Johann "Panje" Velde, who earned the German Cross in Gold and the Honor Roll Clasp. He gained his nickname due to his large head and un-Germanic features. (H.T. Nielsen)

Guard in Copenhagen after becoming Youth Leader for the DNSAP. An outspoken National Socialist, von Schalburg's anti-Communist convictions had formed during his childhood, when his aristocratic Danish and Ukrainian family had fled Russia to escape the civil war.

Among the Danes who went to Finland were Robert L. Hansen, Heinrich Husen, Alfred Jonstrup, and the young officer Johannes Just Nielsen. The Danes completed training during January 1940, but had seen only brief combat when Finland made peace with the Soviets in March. The Danes were awaiting transport home when word arrived of the German invasion, and von Schalburg was heard to comment, "So now we will have to go and kick the Germans out."

The volunteers from Finland finally made it home in late May 1940, and found that the German occupation was very lenient. Danish resistance to the German invasion had been light, and only 13 Danish soldiers had died during the brief hostilities on 9 April, before the Danish government had ordered a ceasefire. The government and King Christian X were allowed to remain in place, and the 6,500-man Danish Army remained mobilized. Many army officers, however, felt disgraced by the ceasefire. They recognized that Denmark could not have successfully resisted the German invasion, but they felt that a longer resistance would have demonstrated Danish resolve to the rest of the world. Then Denmark could have surrendered with honor, as happened with the Netherlands a month later.

The *Waffen-SS* established the *Nordland* Regiment on 20 April 1940 to attract Danish and Norwegian volunteers, and word of this new unit quickly spread in Danish Army and National Socialist circles. The first 40 Danish volunteers from Copenhagen left for Germany on 20 June, and 72 more from the rest of Denmark followed a week later. Finland veterans such as Rantzau-Engelhardt, von Schalburg, Husen and Just Nielsen volunteered from September, believing that a showdown between Germany and the Soviets was inevitable. They were joined by army officers such as Erik Brorup and Kristen Madsen Brodersen, who were eager to show the Germans and the world that Danes could fight. South Jutland was again officially called "North Schleswig," and man ethnic Germans from this area also volunteered for the *Waffen-SS*, some for the second time.

The DNSAP maintained a youth section known as the NSU, and some of these young men, including Sören Kam, were among the first volunteers to join the *Waffen-SS*, along with veterans of the Danish *SA*. Other Danes, including Hansen and Jonstrup, went to Germany as civilian workers, and only joined the *Waffen-SS* during 1941.

As mentioned previously, when *SS-Wiking* entered combat in June 1941, it already included 216 Danes, and the number rose to 251 a few months later by 19 October, despite 65 Danes becoming casualties. Heinrich Husen was the second ethnic Dane to die in the *Waffen-SS*; he was killed in action leading a patrol on 2 August 1941, 13 days after the first ethnic Dane, Gunnar Christiansen, lost his life.

New Danish recruits were constantly in training, and these men gradually joined *Wiking*. The number of Danes in German military service greatly expanded, however, only after the German invasion of the USSR. Now large numbers of men stepped forward, volunteering expressly to fight the Soviets. In common with Flanders, Wallonia, the Netherlands, and Norway, a national legion was created, which obstensibly was to be a Danish force under Danish leadership, and not a part of the German military, although it would fight alongside German forces.

The legions were intended to appeal to those who wanted to serve their country by joining a nationalist force, where they would be soldiering alongside their countrymen, instead of joining the army of their occupier. The legions would receive training and administration from the *Waffen-SS*, but the men would not hold *SS* membership, and did not have to meet physical standards as high as those required by the *Waffen-SS*. To show that the legion members were not *SS* men, their ranks were prefixed differently, for example a private was known as a *"Legion-Mann"* instead of as an *"SS-Mann."*

The forces raised in other countries were titled as "Volunteer Legions," but Denmark was treated differently since it nominally remained independent (its legal government eventually signing the Anti-Comintern Pact). The Danish legion was known as the *"Frikorps Danmark"* (Free Corps Denmark), which denoted the special status of

Denmark and recalled the Danish force that had fought Communism in the Baltic states after World War I.

The Danish government sought to ensure that the *Frikorps* was apolitical, and tried to limit DNSAP influence. King Christian X asked an aristocratic artillery officer, Lieutenant Colonel Christian Peder Kryssing, to take command. The anti-Nazi Kryssing accepted, and since the *Frikorps* was to be an infantry battalion, like-minded Captain Thor Jörgensen agreed to serve as chief of staff, to oversee training. Several other anti-Nazi officers joined, but many junior officers and up to 40 percent of the enlisted men were DNSAP members or sympathizers. This included Just Nielsen, who transferred from *SS-Wiking*.

Many of those who were not initially pro-DNSAP soon joined the DNSAP men in oppostion to Kryssing. Even with the help of Jörgensen, he had proved inadequate as an infantry instructor, and was too conservative to smooth over the difficulties with the DNSAPers in the *Frikorps* who wished to politicize the unit. Training stagnated, and talk of mutiny spread. Gradually, the anti-DNSAP officers were reassigned to regular *Waffen-SS* units (principally *Wiking*), since they were unable to improve the situation. This was no criticism of their military ability; well-regarded officers such as Tage Petersen and Johannes Hellmers (who had seen action against the Germans on 9 April 1940) were involved. This eroded what remained of Kryssing's support. The other legions were already in action on the Eastern Front, while the *Frikorps* still required extensive training. This was enough for the German authorities, and on 23 February 1942, Kryssing and Jörgensen were removed from command and replaced by Christian Fredrik von Schalburg, who had made established his reputation as a staff officer in *SS-Wiking*, before taking command of the 1st Battalion of *SS-Nordland*.

Von Schalburg was well known as a professional solider, and had earned both classes of the Iron Cross for his daring intelligence gathering missions with *SS-Wiking*. He had the respect of every member of the *Frikorps*, and this allowed an atmosphere to prevail in which pro- and anti-DNSAPers could set aside their differences and get on with training. The *Frikorps* was at last ready for frontline duty by early May 1942, when it was flown into the Demyansk pocket to support *SS-Totenkopf*.

In the swamps at Demyansk, the *Frikorps* quickly proved its worth as a combat unit. It fought well against several attacks, and made an attack of its own on the night of 27–28 May 1942. Von Schalburg selected Johannes Just Nielsen and his platoon to eliminate a small, but dangerous, Soviet bridgehead across the Robja River at Ssutoki. The attack was a complete success, but as the Danes prepared to withdraw at dawn, they came under heavy shelling, and Just Nielsen was hit instantly. His body rolled into the river, from where it could not be recovered. The death of the idealistic young officer was a blow to the entire

Frikorps, and his accomplishment was recognized by the German high command, which awarded him the *Führer* Commendation Certificate (A decoration that later evolved into the Honor Roll of the German Army. Those listed on the Honor Roll received a clasp to wear on their uniform, and the award was considered almost as prestigious as the Knight's Cross of the Iron Cross. While the Knight's Cross recognized outstanding bravery that was of decisive importance to military success, the Honor Roll Clasp represented outstanding heroism that was of a more personal nature.)

A worse loss came soon after, as the Danes attacked the reestablished Ssutoki bridgehead in the early hours of 2 June. Von Schalburg went to the frontlines to rally his men, whose assault had bogged down under heavy fire. He stepped on a mine, which wounded his leg, exposing him in an open area. His messenger, Alfred Jonstrup, and two others tried to carry him to safety, but before they could get him away, a barrage of Soviet mortar shells killed von Schalburg and two of his handlers. The untouched Jonstrup brought von Schalburg's remains from the scene, and the attack was broken off.

Knud Borge Martinsen took command of the *Frikorps*, as the senior Danish officer present. He was an experienced Danish Army staff officer and a dedicated National Socialist, who had developed a good relationship with von Schalburg. On 10 June 1942, however, a new "permanent" commander for the *Frikorps* arrived in the person of Hans Albert von Lettow-Vorbeck, an *SS-Wiking* veteran and a nephew of the

Knud Borge Martinsen, von Schalburg's friend and successor as commander of the *Frikorps Danmark*. He went on to form the Danish branch of the Germanic-SS, which he named the "Schalburg Corps" to honor his comrade. (H.T. Nielsen)

famous World War I general Paul von Lettow-Vorbeck. He had briefly commanded the Flemish *SS*-Legion, and was sympathetic toward non-Germans, which could have helped him become a good commander for the Danes. Before he could properly establish himself, von Lettow-Vorbeck was killed in action the day after he arrived, and Martinsen again took command, this time for the remainder of the history of the unit. The Danes had resented having a German as commander, and if Martinsen lacked the inspiring personality of von Schalburg, he was tactically competent and almost as importantly, he was Danish.

Martinsen led the *Frikorps* through continued combat at Demyansk until early August 1942, when the unit was withdrawn to Latvia for refitting. The men then received three weeks of home leave, after arriving back in Denmark and parading through Copenhagen during early September. Almost a month later, the reassembled *Frikorps* returned to Latvia, training and organizing at Mitau, before arriving at the front near Velikiye Luki during the first days of December. With a strength of 1,000 men, the *Frikorps Danmark* was subordinated to the 1st *SS*-Infantry Brigade.

The Danes manned frontline defensive positions, which were initially quiet. They successfully resisted heavy attacks on Christmas Day, and sporadic fighting continued during the first part of 1943. Martinsen temporarily gave up command to return to Denmark during February, to establish a Danish branch of the Germanic-*SS* (a political, not military force, intended to mirror the *Allegemeine-SS* in the Germanic nations), which he named the "Schalburg Corps" in honor of the fallen *Frikorps* commander. Martinsen was succeeded by another Danish professional officer, Per Neergard-Jacobsen, and it was under his command that the *Frikorps* left the front and arrived at the training area at Grafenwöhr, Bavaria at the end of March 1943.

With the establishment of the *SS-Nordland* Division, the *SS* High Command had decided to use the *Frikorps* as the basis for the new *SS*-Panzer-Grenadier Regiment *"Danmark."* This was to be fully a part of the *Waffen-SS*, and was not considered to be, even on paper, an extension of the Danish Army. The *Frikorps* was to be combined with the Danes from the *SS-Nordland* Regiment and the rest of the *Waffen-SS* to compose the regiment. Including recovered wounded and its replacement company, the *Frikorps* consisted of 1,150 men. Martinsen resumed command to oversee a dissolution parade, after which the history of the *Frikorps Danmark* ended.

Most *Frikorps* veterans wanted to continue serving against the Soviets, but they had doubts about doing so in a regiment that was considered a German, not Danish unit. The Danish government shared their objections, in part because a German officer, Hermenegild *Graf* (Count) von Westphalen, had been named regimental commander. Ultimately, only a few Danes refused to join the regiment, and the government renewed its approval—granted the year after the German occupation and just after the commencement of Operation BARBAROSSA—for Danish citizens to serve in the German or Finnish military establishments (some Danes again chose to go to Finland to fight in the Continuation War).

As the new regiment, ultimately titled *SS*-Panzer-Grenadier Regiment 24 *"Danmark,"* trained during the summer of 1943, several more Danes left specifically to serve with the Schalburg Corps or pro-German paramilitary organizations. After the dissolution of the *Frikorps*, *SS-Danmark* included 1,280 Danes, which was far less than regimental strength. Filling out the unit were 1,120 ethnic Germans and 800 German nationals. Officer positions were evenly split between 16 Danes and 16 Germans. Knud Borge Martinsen commanded the 1st Battalion, while Per Neergard-Jacobsen was in charge of the 3d Battalion. Danish Army officer Per Sörensen had distinguished himself as a company commander with *Frikorps*, and initially remained at that level in the new regiment. He was more apolitical than many other DNSAP members, but he had earned the respect of all of the Danish volunteers. Sörensen took command of 1st Battalion during the course of 1943, when Martinsen left the *Waffen-SS*. He had been annoyed at not receiving command of the regiment, and decided to instead devote his energy to the Schalburg Corps.

Most of the history of *SS-Danmark* has been related previously, in the context of *SS-Nordland*. The regiment saw more extensive combat than the other corps elements while in Croatia, and much of the 5th Company was destroyed. Four hundred new recruits from Denmark bolstered the regiment and the entire division, which numbered 1,357 Danes when it redeployed to Oranienbaum. *SS-Danmark* suffered heavy casualties in the retreat to Narva, with Neergard-Jacobsen wounded badly enough that he never returned to service. The Luxembourg volunteer Fritz Sidon took command of 9th Company during the withdrawal from Oranienbaum, and for his bravery was awarded the Honor Roll Clasp. The casualties continued in the Narva bridgehead, and von Westphalen was mortally wounded on 9 April 1944 while crossing the Kreenholm bridge into the bridgehead. He was awarded the German Cross in Gold on 23 April for his mens' efforts, and died on 28 May. Albrecht Krügel, who had earned the Knight's Cross as a battalion commander in *SS-Norge*, succeeded von Westphalen.

The colors and cadre of the 1st Battalion of *SS-Danmark* (and also that of *SS-Norge*) were sent back to Germany during March 1944 for reconstitution of the battalion. Its remaining equipment and most of its enlisted soldiers were distributed among the rest of the regiment. For the remainder of the war, *SS-Danmark* would consist of two infantry battalions instead of the previous three. The rebuilt 1st Battalion of *SS-Danmark* would return to combat in the autumn of 1944 with mainly Germans in its ranks. It fought with *SS-Wiking* and *SS-Totenkopf* in IV *SS*-Panzer Corps in the Wet Triangle north of Warsaw, and then was destroyed during combat in Hungary in January and February 1945.

Aside from patrol activities, the Narva bridgehead was quiet during June 1944, until the Soviets tried to capture Outpost Sunshine at the extreme southeast corner of the German defenses. This was a strongpoint the Danes had set up beyond their lines, in No-Man's Land, as a jumping-off site for patrols and as a listening post for enemy activity. It was being manned by the 7th Company on 12 June when a surprise attack overwhelmed it. As the survivors fell back, Danish NCO and *SS-Wiking* veteran Egon Christophersen rallied a handful of men and launched a counterattack that recaptured Outpost Sunshine. Christophersen had been awarded the Iron Cross 1st Class two weeks earlier, and was immediately recommended for the Knight's Cross, which was approved on 11 July 1944.

The confusion around Outpost Sunshine allowed other Soviet forces to strike the main defenses of *SS-Danmark*'s 2d Battalion that same day. In an action similar to Christophersen's, the battalion's German commander, Heinz Hämel, rallied his headquarters staff and led them in an attack that restored the frontline positions. Hämel also received the Knight's Cross, which was approved soon after the events, on 16 June, 1944. He had been the second NCO in *SS-Wiking* to receive the German Cross in Gold, as a platoon commander in *SS-Germania* on 13 June 1942, and in two years had risen to the post of battalion commander.

Hämel was wounded during the intense Tannenberg Line fighting, and was with *SS-Nordland* commander Fritz von Scholz when the latter died in an ambulance. *SS-Danmark* was again heavily engaged in the Kurland fighting. Per Sörensen's distinguished service was recognized at this time through the award of the German Cross in Gold on 14 October 1944, which rewarded his service through the summer. He again distinguished himself during the Second Battle of Kurland, by commanding an emergency combat group that plugged a hole in the regiment's front. The message to correctly place this reserve force had been carried by Alfred Jonstrup, who persisted in his vital mission even after a shell fragment tore off part of his jaw. Sörensen and Jonstrup were both awarded the Honor Roll Clasp on 25 December 1944. The German commander of *SS-Danmark*'s 3d Battalion, Rudolf Ternedde, also received this decoration that day, for the same battle.

Small numbers of Danes were still serving in other elements of *SS-Nordland* all during this time. The adjutant of *SS*-Armored Reconnaissance Battalion 11 was the North Schleswiger Georg Erichsen, who had graduated as the top student of the 9th Shortened Wartime Course

Danish volunteer Egon Christophersen on a propaganda trip to Germany after his 11 July 1944 award of the Knight's Cross. His bravery helped retake Outpost Sunshine on the edge of the Narva bridgehead, and his Knight's Cross was the first awarded to a Dane. (H.T. Nielsen)

for officer candidates at Bad Tölz. This brought him a direct promotion to *Untersturmführer* upon completion of the course. Erichsen was killed in action in late January 1945, during the Fourth Battle of Kurland, and recommended for the Honor Roll Clasp. The war ended before the decision to award it could be made.

SS-Danmark was fully involved in the battles of the III (Germanic) *SS*-Panzer Corps during the Fourth Battle of Kurland, and then the Sonnenwende offensive in Pomerania. It had already been severely depleted before the costly defensive fighting in the Altdamm Bridgehead, during which Albrecht Krügel was killed in action, leading some of his headquarters staff in a desperate, futile counterattack. He had been awarded the Oakleaves to his Knight's Cross for his regiment's performance during the Second Battle of Kurland.

Another German, Rudolf Klotz, replaced Krügel, as *SS-Danmark* finally got a rest on the west side of the Oder River. The regiment was partially rebuilt by incorporating any military men available, and these were almost entirely German, further diluting the Danish nature of the unit. Sörensen held command of 2d Battalion when the regiment went into combat east of Berlin, and he took command of *SS-Danmark* when

The North-Schleswig ethnic German Georg Erichsen, who was the adjutant for SS-Armored Reconaissance Battalion 11 commander Rudolf Saalbach, and was killed in action in late January 1945. (H.T. Nielsen)

Klotz suffered a mortal wound on 20 April. He held command for only four days, as *SS-Nordland* retreated into Berlin. On 24 April 1945, Per Sörensen was killed by a sniper while trying to observe Soviet troop movements. Danish veterans felt they had lost their best officer. Ternedde commanded the last remnants of *SS-Danmark* and *SS-Norge* for the final days of the war, until the fighting in Berlin ended on 2 May.

Danes had also seen combat during the last year of the war with other units. Kryssing had remained with the *Waffen-SS* after losing his post as commander of the *Frikorps*, and because of his abilities as an artillery officer, had risen in rank to *SS-Brigadeführer*. This made him the highest-ranking Germanic volunteer. This was little comfort, however, because he lost two sons killed in action with the *Waffen-SS*, and his wife was crippled during an air raid while serving as a Red Cross nurse. Kryssing was the Artillery Commander for the III (Germanic) *SS-*Panzer Corps when it deployed to Oranienbaum, and he had then commanded *SS-*Combat Group Coast into the summer, protecting the Baltic flank of the corps. Rantzau-Engelhardt served as his chief of staff, and many other Danes were in his headquarters, including some who were his opponents from late 1941! After the war, Kryssing received a jail sentence, but he was most upset that King Christian X abandoned him, refusing any assistance to the man he had helped to select.

During the summer of 1944, Rantzau-Engelhardt served as a brigade commander, taking charge of two of the Estonian *SS*-Frontier Guard Regiments with a loose brigade staff. He escaped abroad after the war, and had his memoirs published in Argentina.

Dozens of Danes remained in *SS-Wiking* after the spring of 1943, primarily as officers and NCOs. Sören Kam commanded a platoon in the 1st Company of the *SS-Germania*, and he took emergency command of his company during the incredibly heavy fighting in the Wet Triangle. He briefly led his entire battalion when all officers were out of action during October 1944, and for this he was awarded the Knight's Cross on 7 February 1945.

Johannes Hellmers had remained in *Waffen-SS* service afer leaving the *Frikorps*. He fought with *SS*-Thule (the former *SS*-Infantry Regiment 9), and then with *SS-Totenkopf*, before being assigned to command a company in the Dutch *SS*-De Ruyter. His distinguished leadership of 6th Company during the summer of 1944 was recognized with the award of the German Cross in Gold on 18 December 1944. Soon after, on 25 January 1945, at the height of the Fourth Battle of Kurland, Hellmers led a counterattack with a handful of men that succeeded in preventing an incursion in the *SS*-De Ruyter lines from becoming a full breakthrough. For this, he was awarded the Knight's Cross on 5 March 1945, the third and final Dane to receive this decoration.

Robert Hansen, a classmate of Erichsen at Bad Tölz, survived the war, having risen to command a company in *SS*-Armored Reconnaissance Battalion 5. For men such as he, it had been a long odyssey from volunteering to serve in Finland in late 1939 until the German defeat in May 1945. Over 10,000 ethnic Danes and 1,200 North Schleswiger ethnic Germans had volunteered for the *Waffen-SS*, and more than 3,500 of them were killed in action. The survivors faced prison sentences and losses of rights, and those involved in anti-resistance activities with the Schalburg Corps were sometimes executed. This was the fate of Knud Borge Martinsen, though his execution was literally repudiated decades later by the Danish parliament. Also executed was the anti-Nazi Tage Petersen, who had served against his will in an anti-resistance police force during the final months of the war. Other Danes died in Soviet prison camps, including Danish Army engineer officer Ernst Christian Hartvig Viffert, who had become Combat Engineer Commander of VI (Latvian) *Waffen*-Army Corps of the *SS*. A handful had "happy" endings, including Johann Velde, who had earned the German Cross in Gold on 21 November 1943 as the commander of the 3d Company of *SS-Germania*. He then became the adjutant to that regiment's decorated commander, Hans Dorr, and earned the Honor Roll Clasp on 17 December 1944. "Panje" Velde was able to forge a

On the left is *SS-Sturmbannführer* Ernst Christian Hartvig Viffert, the Royal Danish army officer who became the combat engineer Commander ("Stopi") for the Latvian VI *Waffen*-Army Corps. He died in Soviet captivity during 1950. (H. T. Nielsen)

successful career in the West German *Bundeswehr* and retired as an *Oberst*, one of the few former members of the *Waffen-SS* to rise above the rank of *Oberstleutnant*.

To the end, a minority of the Danish volunteers belonged to the DNSAP or the NSDAP-N. The majority had come forward not out of love for Germany, but rather out of fear of a Soviet-dominated Baltic. They hoped that through fighting in Finland and with the *Waffen-SS*, no other country would have to face the the sort of occupation that engulfed Latvia and Estonia, and severely hurt Finland. For their troubles, the Danish volunteers were branded as criminals and traitors by the post-war Danish government, despite having had permission to serve granted by the Danish government and king during the war.

Finland

In 1914, Finland was part of the Russian Empire, but the Finns and ethnic Swedes in the lands north of St. Petersburg desired autonomy. During World War I, enough Finns made their way to German-held areas to constitute a unit of the German Army, the 27th *Jäger* (light infantry) Battalion. This unit helped form the core of the eventual Finnish Army, and many Germans (and various Scandinavians) fought in Finland as the country gained independence during the Russian Civil War. These events laid the background for future German-Finnish cooperation.

Under the terms of the German-Soviet Non-Aggression Pact of 1939, Finland and the Baltic states were designated a Soviet sphere of influence. Germany took no action when the Soviet Union first demanded territorial concessions from Finland, and then invaded on 30 November 1939. The Finns fought back fiercely, and Soviet troops—under the command of the survivors of the recent purges of the Soviet officer corps—also struggled with the vast size and undeveloped nature of Karelia. The Soviet Army suffered hundreds of thousands of casualties, and while it could have mobilized millions of men to occupy all of Finland, Stalin instead agreed to a negotiated peace. The Finns had suffered proportionally heavy losses, and were willing to cede some territory to end the conflict.

The Finns had earned the respect of the world, and Germany now considered Finland a worthy ally for their planned invasion of the Soviet Union. The Finnish government was informed of the plans for BARBAROSSA during January 1941, and agreed to cooperate with Germany to recover its lost territory. The Germans wanted a Finnish volunteer unit within their armed forces as a propaganda coup, and as a reminder of the service of the old 27th *Jäger* Battalion. Volunteers were gathered during the first months of the year.

The Baltic coast in 1941 included many Swedish communities, and in Finland these constituted up to 15 percent of the population, with the remainder being ethnic Finns. The precise distribution was and remains hard to determine, because of the gradual assimilation of the ethnic Swedes. This meant that many Finnish citizens with Swedish names spoke Finnish as their first language. Ethnic Swedes dominated the 27th *Jäger* Battalion, and the Finnish government sought to ensure that this did not happen again with the new volunteer unit. So ethnic Finns were given preference among the volunteers for service in Germany.

A new factor for the Finnish government was the rise of right-wing political groups sympathetic to Germany, such as the *Samfundet Folkgemenskap* which, as its name indicates, was primarily an ethnic Swedish organization. The Germans expected that most of the volunteers would be ethnic Swedes with National Socialist sympathies, but the Finnish government was determined to limit the participation of right-wing activists. It had no wish to see these men become heroes with increased political influence, nor did it want them having excessive influence on the future Finnish Army, since it was anticipated that service in the modern German military would groom the volunteers for important duties once back in Finland.

The *Waffen-SS* took over the administration of the Finnish volunteers, since it was anticipated that they would be pro-Nazi ethnic

Swedes. In fact, only 3 to 4 percent of the volunteers were full ethnic Swedes, though others were assimilated Finnish-speakers with Swedish names. About 20 percent of the men were political activists, and the unit retained an apolitical nature throughout its existence. The Germans requested that half the volunteers be experienced soldiers, but in reality, two-thirds were untried young men. The Germans accepted the Finnish demand that the 1,200 volunteers only be committed against the Soviet Union.

The 400 experienced volunteers were distributed throughout *SS-Wiking* in the weeks before BARBAROSSA began on 22 June 1941. Most of them, 7 officers and 200 men, went into *SS-Nordland*. Another 5 officers and 76 men fought with *SS-Westland*, while 9 officers were with *SS-Germania*. The other Finns were in the artillery, reconnaissance, and anti-tank elements of *SS-Wiking*.

The 800 remaining inexperienced men began training in Vienna, and later at several military camps, as *SS*-Volunteer Battalion *"Nordost"* (northeast). Hans Collani, a long-serving German *SS* officer who had been an original member of *SS-LAH* in 1933, was appointed as commander. Years earlier, Collani had failed his *Abitur* examinations, and then made a career as a merchant seaman. He sailed widely, including through the Baltic, and this gave him a familiarity with other peoples and cultures which made him a good choice as leader of the Finnish battalion. Assisting Collani was a cadre of German officers and NCOs, and these men initially held most command positions within *SS-Nordost*, even though qualified Finns were available. In fact, too many Finnish officers and NCOs were present, since the Germans toyed with the idea of organizing a full regiment of Finns. This did not develop because of resistance from the Finnish government. The Finnish volunteers resented their lack of representation in leadership positions, and this was particularly strong among excess NCOs, who were forced to serve as junior enlisted men.

Most of the excess officers and NCOs were returned to Finland before the end of 1941 and during early 1942. Once the battalion, known from late 1941 as the Finnish Volunteer Battalion of the *Waffen-SS*, went into action, Finnish candidates were increasingly used to fill leadership vacancies caused by casualties. This mollified the volunteers, and the Germans that remained were largely sympathetic men, respected for their competency.

The 400 men with *SS-Wiking* fought well, despite language difficulties, while the battalion finished its training. It departed for the front during December 1941, but weather and fuel problems kept it from arriving at *SS-Wiking*'s positions on the Mius River until early January. It left 60 percent of its vehicles along the route, as the French trucks with which they had been equipped were not designed with the

Finnish volunteer Tauno Manni as an officer cadet at Bad Tölz during the 9th Shortened Wartime Course. He graduated successfully, and survived the war. (Natedal)

conditions of the Ukrainian winter in mind. Many Finns had to walk for hundreds of kilometers to reach *SS-Wiking*.

During the first months of 1942, the Finnish *SS*-Volunteer Battalion incorporated half of the survivors of the initial 400 Finns serving in *SS-Wiking* (81 had been killed in action, and others returned to Finland). Replacement German vehicles were received, and the unit finally was assigned to serve as the 3d Battalion of *SS-Nordland* (the previous 3d Battalion was disbanded and its former members distributed to strengthen the other two battalions of the regiment).

SS-Wiking advanced into the Caucasus during the late summer of 1942, with the Finns arriving in the West Caucasus on 13 August after a 700-kilometer drive. The battalion saw light combat as the German attempt to capture the West Caucasus oilfields failed. *SS-Wiking* gradually shifted 500 kilometers east to participate in the attack on the East

Caucasus oil fields. The Finns went into action on 26 September near Malgobek, and heavy fighting lasted for the next several weeks. The crescendo was on 16 October when the Finns captured Hill 701 (known as "Killing Hill") in desperate combat that caused many casualties. All German units suffered during this campaign, and the Finnish portion amounted to 88 killed and 346 wounded, along with 80 men evacuated due to illness (Malaria was a particular problem for the German forces in this region). The Finns lost 60 percent of their fighting strength, and this was typical of all of *SS-Wiking*'s infantry elements.

About this time, a handful of Finns were detached from the battalion after volunteering to assist the *Heer* Brandenburg Commandos with an operation against the Soviet rail line south of Murmansk. They were ideal helpers due to their familiarity with both Finnish weather and terrain conditions and German military methods. Later, during 1944–1945, another group of Finns, of roughly platoon size, would serve with the *SS-Jagdverbände*, the successor to the Brandenburgers.

Prior to the East Caucasus fighting, reinforcements had been dispatched from Finland. The 200 men were all combat veteran volunteers, who were integrated into the companies of the Finnish *SS*-Volunteer Battalion after arriving at *SS-Wiking* on 23 November. Two of the new arrivals almost immediately distinguished themselves: Kalevi Könönen and Yrjö Pyytiä defended their machinegun position for eight hours against continuous heavy attacks on 4 December, and were awarded the Iron Cross 1st Class. They were nominated for the Honor Roll of the German Army, and had their names published on 27 August 1943.

The Finns had fought well, and were accepted as full comrades within *SS-Wiking*. Heinrich Himmler decided that the ethnic Swedish community had positively influenced all of Finland, and that all Finns, therefore, could be considered Germanic and given full *SS* membership. The *Waffen-SS* leadership again wanted to increase the Finnish presence to a regiment, which was intended to become the *SS*-Motorcycle Regiment *"Kalevala"* within the III (Germanic) *SS*-Panzer Corps. The Finnish government had no faith in a German victory after the end of 1942, and they preferred to have the Finnish involvement in the *Waffen-SS* end when the contract for the Finnish Volunteer Battalion expired during the spring of 1943.

Up to that time, the Finnish battalion was involved in all of *SS-Wiking*'s battles, fighting in the Kalmuck Steppe, in the retreat through Rostov, and finally, along the Donets during the campaign which saw the recapture of Kharkov. The battalion was returned to Finland for a month of home leave at the beginning of June 1943, as negotiations continued between the *SS* and the Finnish government. Hitler finally stepped in, and on 4 July, accepted the Finnish request that the men of the battalion be incorporated into the Finnish Army. A week later, the

Finnish *SS*-Volunteer Battalion of the *Waffen-SS* held a final parade at Hanko. Commander Collani shook hands with every man of the unit as he expressed the thanks of his nation for their service. The Finns then changed into Finnish Army uniform and accepted into the Finnish Army.

Individual Finns remained with the *Waffen-SS*. A few, such as Lars Olsson, were attending specialist schools, and were allowed to continue their courses up to September 1943, before returning to Finland. Others continued in the *Waffen-SS*, including Finnish Army officer Ulf-Ola Olin and his cousin, Lars Erik Ekroth. Olin served in *SS*-Panzer Regiment 5, where he commanded a Panther tank platoon in 7th Company, under Knight's Cross recipient Otto Schneider. Olin's successful leadership in the fighting near Warsaw during the summer of 1944 was rewarded with the German Cross in Gold on 28 February 1945. He later succeeded Schneider as company commander, and remained in Germany after the war.

Another Finnish Army officer, Jouko Itälä, left the Finnish *SS*-Volunteer Battalion to become a winter conditions specialist for the *Waffen-SS*. He is best known for his role as the instructor for the Norwegian *SS*-Ski Company. Itälä also remained in German service until 1945, returning to Finland after the war.

Many members of the disbanded Finnish Volunteer Battalion wanted to continue serving in the *Waffen-SS*, but were unable to do so because of their assignment to various Finnish Army units, which were often in heavy combat. Finnish sources list 113 veterans of the battalion who were killed in action with the Finnish Amy during the continuation war, mostly during the summer 1944 fighting. This included Kalevi Könönen, who lost his life on 23 June. A few individual Finns were able to reach German-held territory and join the *Waffen-SS* during 1943 and 1944, such as Kenneth Henriksson and Olavi Koistinen, who served with *SS*-Nord in Finland and then on the Western Front.

After Finland concluded an armistice with the Soviets during September 1944, the Soviets pressured the Finnish Army into sporadic against the German forces withdrawing to Norway. Sadly, at least six Finnish *SS*-Volunteer Battalion veterans were killed in action against the Germans, including Teuvo Hatara, Kauko Kauppi, Jaako Kohola, Keijo Koskelin, Raine Ritari, and Niilo Sääskilahti. The Germans captured hundreds of Finnish prisoners as they left Finnish territory. In Norway, several of the prisoners volunteered for the *Waffen-SS*, and they were joined by other men who left Finland for the same purpose. Together with those already serving, between 100 and 200 Finns fought with the *Waffen-SS* from late 1944 until the end of the war.

Roughly 1,400 Finnish citizens, mostly ethnic Finns, served with the Finnish Volunteer Battalion of the *Waffen-SS*, and 256 were killed in action. Most of the others were wounded at least once. Combined with the later volunteers, the Finnish contribution to the *Waffen-SS* reached perhaps 1,500 men. The Finnish volunteers received sound, advanced training, which is what the Finnish military had hoped for them. It sent many of the veterans to officer schools, and 282 former NCOs and junior enlisted men later became Finnish Army officers. Another 21 Finns graduated from the *Waffen-SS* officer school at Bad Tölz, and one of these men, Sulo Suorttanen, eventually rose to become Defense Minister in the Finnish government.

The German cadre of the Finnish Volunteer Battalion was used as the cadre for the Dutch and ethnic German *SS*-Panzer-Grenadier Regiment 49 "De Ruyter." Hans Collani commanded the regiment, and with him came Karl-Heinz Ertel, Helmut Scholz, and Eugen Deck. Collani, Ertel, and Scholz won the Knight's Cross with *SS*-De Ruyter, and Deck the German Cross in Gold, but all these men had honed their military craft while serving with the Finns.

Flanders

Belgium is a union of two peoples: Dutch-speaking Flemings and French-speaking Walloons. The Flemings live in the more northern and western parts of Belgium, but Flemish and Walloon cells overlap in many regions, most of all around Brussels. Thus, it is not unusual to find Dutch speakers with French names, and vice versa.

Flemings of the Black Brigade (the militia of the VNV) assemble after volunteering for the Flemish *SS*-Legion during the summer of 1941. (De Vos)

The name was not important to a Belgian of the World War II era; rather, it was political outlooks that separated people. Flemings made up over half of the Belgian population, but society and the government were dominated by Walloons. Many Flemings felt themselves second-class citizens, while most Walloons were content with the *status quo*, even if the Belgian government was corrupt.

The debate among discontented Flemings concerned what future form Flanders should take. Autonomists had been active during the World War I German occupation, but they had been severely punished after the war. The dominating idea became that all Dutch speakers should unite to form a "Greater Netherlands" based around the Netherlands, Flanders, and French Flanders (the coastal region just across the border, which was culturally Flemish, but belonged to France). At first, the principal party to espouse this was the Union of *Dietsch* National Solidarity (*"Dietsch"* referring to all Dutch speakers, not merely those in the Netherlands), a movement founded by decorated First World War veteran Joris van Severen in 1931 and commonly abbreviated as *"Verdinaso."* The party maintained a militia known as the *DMO*, headed by Jef Francois.

Verdinaso did not try to join the Belgian establishment, and so another party soon took the dominant role in Flemish right-wing politics. Several smaller groups came together during 1933 under Staf de Clercq to form the Flemish National Union, abbreviated *VNV*. This movement was strongly Catholic, unlike *Verdinaso*, and it received wide support in Flanders. This included getting several members elected to parliament. The *VNV* received monetary aid from Germany, and Nazi influence was found in the establishment of a paramilitary arm which roughly emulated the *SA*. It was known as the *Dietsch Militia*, and the largest branch was the Black Brigade (because of its black uniforms). This was headed by Dr. Reimond Tollenaere, and numbered 12,000 men by 1942, out of a total *VNV* membership of 100,000 men and women.

The above numbers include most *Verdinaso* members, since all right-wing political movements were obliged to merge with the *VNV* after the German occupation of Belgium. Although *Verdinaso* was an anti-religious movement, its members were welcomed into the *VNV* and its traditions were maintained. Joris van Severen had been shot in captivity by Belgian authorities during May 1940, but his name was given to a memorial badge worn by former *Verdinaso* members. During the war, it was often seen on the uniforms of Flemish *Waffen-SS* volunteers.

Two additional factions became prominent during the war. Jef van de Wiele founded a German-Flemish cultural exchange group in 1935, which was really a closeted National Socialist movement. The party's name was abbreviated as *DeVlag*, which conveniently was Flemish for "the flag," and it advocated the incorporation of Flanders into Germany as a district of the *Reich*. After the occupation, *DeVlag* attracted many with pro-German feelings, so that by late 1943, it counted 51,000 members.

A smaller force was established in September 1940 as the Flemish branch of the *Allegemeine-SS*. Eventually known as the Germanic-*SS* in Flanders, this also drew those with strongly pro-German feelings. Perhaps 4,000 men ultimately joined the Germanic-*SS*, and many of them already belonged to *DeVlag*, while a few were *VNV* and former *Verdinaso* members. While *DeVlag* had a limited focus of Flemish-German relations, the Germanic-*SS* (in all its nations) concerned itself with the future of all the Germanic peoples. Its members in Flanders and abroad hoped to eventually see all the Germanic nations united into one body.

All of these organizations contributed volunteers to the *Waffen-SS*, and as indicated, many individuals belonged to two or more of them (Willy Carpels was photographed wearing the Joris van Severen memorial badge on his Germanic-*SS* uniform, for example). Recruiting for the *Waffen-SS* in Flanders initially went slowly, however, since the *VNV* hesitated to encourage its young men to volunteer for German military service. Flemings were also uncertain about joining an overtly German unit such as *SS-Westland*, so that by early 1941, only a handful of adventure seekers and Germanophiles had volunteered.

This changed when *SS-Nordwest* was established on 3 April 1941. The *VNV* had decided to support limited recruitment for this unit, which was intended for service in Western Europe. Six hundred Flemings quickly volunteered, and were formed into three companies. The day after the German invasion of the Soviet Union, on 22 June 1941, a Flemish Legion was created which was intended to be a nationalist unit under Flemish command and German (*Waffen-SS*) administration, rather than a part of the German military. The Flemish companies from *SS-Nordwest* became the cadre of the *SS*-Volunteer Legion Flanders.

Many collaborationist leaders volunteered for the *Waffen-SS* soon after the war in the east began. This included Dr. Tollenaere and Francois, and they were followed by hundreds of their supporters. DeClercq and the *VNV* leadership, however, refrained from endorsing the efforts to recruit Flemings for combat duty until the Germans had made various concessions, which theoretically ensured that the Flemish Legion would be under Flemish leadership and *VNV* influence. Once the matter had been resolved, the *VNV* officially endorsed the Flemish *SS*-Legion on 6 August 1941.

The German promises proved impossible to keep. A major problem was the condition of the former Belgian Army, which had been Walloon-dominated. French was the language of command until immediately before the war, and officer candidates needed to speak that language to

Volunteers of the Flemish Legion during the spring of 1942. Second, third, and fourth from the left are Bert Mathys, Meulders, and Richard Geldhof. The latter was killed in action soon after during the fighting in the Volkhov swamps. (De Vos)

be trained and commissioned. As a result, the Belgian Army officer corps of 1940 had been over 90 percent Walloon. There simply was no more than a handful of available Flemish officers, and only a few of these volunteered for the legion, which had to rely on Germans to fill out most of the officer and even NCO ranks.

In common with the other legions from Germanic countries, the Flemish Legion was organized and trained by the *Waffen-SS*. The Flemings in the legion were not considered *SS* men, although the Flemings who went into *SS-Westland* did hold this status. This hazy difference would evaporate as Flemings were reassigned to various other *Waffen-SS* formations. The German commander of the Flemish *SS-Legion* was Michael Lippert, a harsh man who formerly had been Theodor Eicke's assistant in the *SS-TV* (he had personally participated in the execution of *SA* members during the "Night of the Long Knives" in 1934). Lippert seems to have resented his assignment to command the Flemings, and he created an atmosphere in which the German cadre showed them little sympathy. The situation worsened because most

Flemings lacked a military background and could not communicate in German, and further lacked officers and NCOs of their own to intercede for them with the Germans. So the confused and intimidated Flemings were seen by some of the German cadre as a sorry bunch who would make poor soldiers.

Word of the conditions reached the *VNV*, and DeClerq strongly protested to Himmler, who had the charges investigated. Himmler instigated a program resembling cultural sensitivity training, and chastised Lippert for the mistreatment of the Flemings. Conditions improved, and the Flemings became fond of certain German officers who treated them fairly, above all the 2d Company commander, Helmut Breymann. "Germans" came from a variety of provinces and regions, and among them, the Austrians had been raised with the heritage of their former multinational empire, and tended to be quite understanding towards non-Germans. The Flemings came to consider Austrians such as Breymann a separate class from other German nationals. The understanding Austrian attitude first displayed with the Flemish *SS*-Legion led to Austrians forming the cadre of non-German units whenever possible throughout the *Waffen-SS*.

The Flemings proved to be hard workers, and most were dedicated Catholics who looked forward to seeing combat against "Godless Bolshevism" in the east. With most of the former problems solved, or at least reduced, the Flemish *SS*-Legion quickly finished its training, and formed into an overstrength infantry battalion of 1,114 men. It was shipped to a staging area in Latvia, where it arrived on 23 November 1941. During the following weeks, company-sized groups were sent to frontline German positions on the Leningrad siege lines for short periods of seasoning. Casualties were light as no major battles took place.

By early 1942, the *Heer* 250th Infantry Division, the "Blue" Division of Spanish volunteers, was fighting close by the Flemish *SS*-Legion. Tragedy struck on 21 January when short rounds fired by the Spanish artillery fell onto a forward outpost of the Flemings. Dr. Tollenaere was visiting this post, and died in the bombardment. He was the first of many Flemish officers to be killed on the Eastern Front. In his memory, the *VNV* later that year began issuing the Tollenaere Memorial Badge to proven combat veterans. Tollenaere's younger brother, Leo, enlisted in the legion to replace him. Leo Tollenaere became a driver and survived the war, although he served in several of the most intense campaigns. Despite the accidental death of Dr. Tollenaere, relations were very good between the Flemings and the Spaniards since both were (for the most part) devout Catholics who found themselves far from home serving with a foreign army.

During February 1942, the Flemish *SS*-Legion successfully defended against heavy Soviet attacks, and at the beginning of the following month, the Flemings went on the offensive to retake positions lost by *Heer* units. This was accomplished with such flair that the Flemish *SS-Legion* was mentioned in the 4 March *Wehrmacht* Press report. The victories of the previous weeks, however, had been paid for in blood; death, wounds, and frostbite had reduced the legion to only 100 men ready for action by 9 March.

The Flemish *SS*-Legion was withdrawn to briefly rest and reorganize, but it returned to action on 17 March, and Lippert was wounded and evacuated the next day. Few were sorry to see him leave. Hans-Albert von Lettow-Vorbeck was named as Lippert's replacement, but after he had toured Flanders and met with the *VNV* leadership, he was instead placed in the *Waffen-SS* officer reserve, and later sent to the *Frikorps Danmark*. In his place, on 20 April 1942, the Austrian Jozef Fitzthum became the commander of the Flemings. He was an *Allegemeine-SS* officer who served in the *Waffen-SS* at a lower rank. Fitzthum had little military command experience, but soon demonstrated his tactical abilities.

During early 1942, the Soviets had attempted to relieve the siege of Leningrad from the east by launching a massive offensive across the frozen swamps of the Volkhov River region (an area known to the Axis soldiers as "The End of the World"). This had been contained in desperate fighting, and as the snow and ice melted, the Soviet forces became stuck in nearly impassable bogs. The Germans managed to seal the rear of the penetration, trapping the Soviet attack force in the so-called Volkhov pocket. This was gradually reduced during the spring, with the final push beginning in June 1942. The Flemish and Dutch *SS*-Legions were sent east to take part in this battle, and the Flemings had to defend their lines against a determined breakout attempt on 25 June. The next day, they joined their neighboring units in an offensive that had largely destroyed the Soviet forces in the Volkhov pocket by the end of the month.

Fitzthum was recalled on 26 June to straighten out a training course for Germanic volunteers that had stalled due to poor leadership. Soon after, he assumed command of the regiment-sized Dutch *SS*-Legion, while a battalion commander from that formation became the new commander of the Flemish *SS*-Legion on 14 July. This was Conrad Schellong, who would remain with the Flemings until the end of the war. He was considered an ardent Nazi and a hard man by those who only knew him from a distance. The Flemings who served close to him, however, soon came to realize that he was merely a "no-nonsense" type, and was tolerant of dissenting political views . . . as long as they came from good soldiers.

Under Schellong, the Flemings completed mopping up along the Volkhov before returning to the Leningrad siege lines towards the end of July. By this stage, many young Flemings were proven veterans, and some were sent to NCO training classes. Due to this, the NCO corps of the Flemish Legion gradually became mostly Flemish, with men such as Georg D'Haese and Bert DeGruyter becoming well known to their comrades.

The sporadic fighting in the last part of 1942 allowed the Flemings to rebuild their strength, which had sunk below 300 on the Volkhov. As new volunteers and recovered wounded arrived, on 31 December 1942, the Flemish *SS*-Legion numbered almost 700 men. One of the new arrivals was Richard "Remy" Schrijnen, who had been trained as an anti-tank gunner, but initially served as a foot messenger.

Even as the Flemish *SS*-Legion licked its wounds, hundreds of additional Flemings were fighting with *SS-Wiking* during the advance to the Caucasus and then in the defensive and offensive struggles that followed. Most of these Flemings had been assigned to *SS-Wiking* (usually to *SS-Westland*) after volunteering for the legion, or after being wounded with it. Their first choice was to serve in a Flemish unit, and this was later granted.

Meanwhile, a few Flemings were concentrated in yet another formation, the *SS*-Motorcycle Regiment "Langemarck." This unit had first been the *SS*-Infantry Regiment 4, and it had been nearly destroyed in successful defensive fighting during early 1942. It received the honor title "Langemarck" to relect its record. The Flemish town of Langemarck was the scene of a suicidal attack by young German student volunteers during the First World War, and its name had come to represent sacrifice to those familiar with German military history. The remnants of *SS*-Langemarck were combined with the Motorcycle Battalion of *SS-Das Reich* to form a new, two-battalion regiment. Flemish volunteers were among the assigned replacements, probably as a nod towards history. Soon after the regiment was established, it was broken up, with the 2d Battalion converted to an armored unit, becoming the 2d Battalion of *SS*-Panzer Regiment 2. In this manner, a handful of Flemings became tankers, and fought with the regiment at Kharkov, at Kursk, on the Mius, and then again near Kharkov. On 27 August 1943, Georg Colemonts distinguished himself as the driver of a Panzer IV in Knight's Cross recipient Dieter Kesten's 6th Company. With his tank burning from a direct hit, and under heavy enemy fire, he carried his wounded commander to safety, and made the vehicle operational again. Colemonts was entered in the German Army Honor Roll on 25 May 1944, becoming one of only two Flemings to win the Honor Roll Clasp.

Back near Leningrad, the Flemish *SS*-Legion remained in the line during the first weeks of 1943. It was then moved south to support its old comrades in the Spanish Blue Division. That unit had suffered severely in the recent fighting, and one of its regiments had been nearly destroyed while evacuating the town of Krasny-Bor. The Flemish Legion attacked on 22 March and retook the town. The Flemish unit, organized as a battalion, had to spread itself thin to occupy positions designed to hold a regiment.

The Soviets counterattacked the next day, with a tank brigade leading the assault on Krasny Bor. The Flemings defended themselves furiously in close combat, and eventually received limited support from several 88mm anti-aircraft pieces and two Tiger tanks. This enabled the Flemings to hold the town, though at one point, Schellong had to lead his staff into action to halt a potential breakthrough. Until this point, 23 March 1943 was the single heaviest day of combat the Flemings had seen, and although 450 men had gone into combat the day before, only 50 men were ready for action 48 hours later.

The greatly reduced Flemish *SS*-Legion remained at Krasny-Bor until the end of March, when it was withdrawn to rest. During May 1943, it was removed from the Leningrad area and sent to the *SS* Training Center at Debica to reform. During 15 months of nearly uninterrupted combat, the Flemish *SS*-Legion had developed a reputation as a reliable unit, so the *SS*-High Command decided to increase its combat capability.

The fiction that the Flemish Legion was not a part of the *Waffen-SS* was removed. The veterans of the legion were combined with most of the Flemings in *SS-Wiking* and *SS-Das Reich*, and with new volunteers, to form a brigade. The legion had been an infantry battalion, but the Flemish unit was upgraded into the partially-armored, fully-motorized *SS*-Assault Brigade Langemarck. The title was seen by the *Waffen-SS* as a symbol of honor, and of finding a common tie between Germans and Flemings, but did not have the intended effect, since at this same time, the late spring of 1943, the Walloon volunteer battalion of the *Heer* became the *SS*-Assault Brigade *Wallonien*. The Flemings were jealous that the Walloons could fight under their regional name, and also that they had been accepted into the elite *Waffen-SS*, since for two years the Flemish had received preferential treatment.

The *SS*-Langemarck Brigade was roughly twice the size of the former Flemish *SS*-Legion. It was based around the old legion infantry battalion, but with nearly another battalion's worth of heavy weapons, including a battery of *Sturmgeschütz III* assault guns. During the summer and autumn of 1943, dozens of qualified Flemings attended *Waffen-SS* officer and NCO schools, so that as *SS*-Langemarck came together, most command positions at company level and below were filled by Flemings, which was a marked departure from 1941. When the unit departed its Bohemian training area for Ukraine on 26 December 1943, it numbered 42 officers, 162 NCOs, and 1,864 enlisted men.

During the autumn of 1943, the Soviets had reoccupied Kiev and pushed west to the vicinity of Zhitomir, where a German counteroffensive had halted their advance. By the beginning of 1944, the Soviets were advancing again against the depleted German formations. *SS-Das Reich* had left a strong armored combat group in Ukraine when the main body of the division was withdrawn to France to rebuild during December 1943. *SS*-Langemarck soon found itself fighting alongside Combat Group *Das Reich* in costly delaying actions. New volunteers, and replacement officers and NCOs arrived to partially offset the casualties, and among them was the German officer Wilhelm Rehmann, who took over the leaderless 3d Company of *SS*-Langemarck. Remy Schrijnen began to build his reputation as a superb anti-tank gunner during these combats that lasted into early March.

SS-Langemarck was surrounded near the village of Jambol during the first days of March 1944, and went through several days of combat that rivalled Krasy-Bor for intensity and casualties. The sub-units of the brigade gradually broke out of Jambol on 3–5 March, with the anti-tank company covering the retreat and incurring the highest losses. The remnants of *SS*-Langemarck remained in combat for another two weeks, before being withdrawn from the front. In April 1944, the brigade was transported back to its training base in Bohemia to begin a new round of refitting. Only 400 were initially fit for duty, but the brigade's efforts were considered extremely successful under the tough conditions it had

An excerpt from a wartime publication, showing members of the Flemish Germanic-*SS* arriving for *Waffen-SS* training at the Germanic camp at Sennheim, Alsace. (Natedal)

faced. Conrad Schellong was awarded the German Cross in Gold on 29 March 1944 in recognition of his men's achievements.

Himmler was also impressed with the Flemish brigade. He ordered that it be expanded to include two infantry battalions along with the previous extensive supporting heavy weapons. Manpower was lacking, however, even as recovered wounded returned and a few new volunteers joined. German defeat began to look inevitable, and after the Allied landings in Normandy on 6 June 1944, the liberation of Belgium appeared to be within sight. By 30 June, *SS*-Langemarck numbered only 1,731 officers and men, though its new establishment called for roughly 3,000 personnel.

The next month, the Flemish and Walloon brigades, both rebuilding after heavy casualties, were each ordered to send a battalion to Estonia to support the III (Germanic) *SS*-Panzer Corps at Narva. Schellong dispatched his first infantry battalion, commanded by Wilhelm Rehmann. The unit was at less than full strength, but its 450 men were mostly veterans. Flemings made up most of the officer and NCO corps, with the recently-commissioned Georg D'Haese commanding the 3d Company. Instead of a full battery of anti-tank guns, Combat Group Rehmann had only three 75mm *Pak 40s (Panzerabwehrkanonen 40*, or Anti-Tank Gun Model 1940*)*, with Remy Schrijnen the gunner for one of them.

CG Rehmann departed Bohemia 19 July 1944, and arrived in the rear area of the III (Germanic) *SS*-Panzer Corps on 25 July. The corps was beginning its withdrawal to the Tannenberg Line, and there was much confusion as units lost their way and became entangled. The Flemings entrenched on 25 July in the key spot at the center of the defensive line, Orphanage Hill, to serve as an anchor as the defenses came together. The Dutch regiment *SS*-General Seyffardt should have also occupied that zone, but it was caught and destroyed in the woods to the east. This left the Flemings with much less support than intended.

Even as elements of the corps arrived at the Tannenberg positions on 26 July, and tried to sort themselves out, the first Soviet attacks hit Orphanage Hill, following tremendous artillery barrages. The Flemings considered themselves to have been assigned a suicide mission, and prepared to sell their lives as dearly as possible. Most of the officers of the combat group were soon killed or put out of action, and Rehmann went to the rear with what veterans describe as "a scratch." He was forever after considered a dishonorable coward by the survivors of the combat group. Corps commander Felix Steiner assigned D'Haese, who had only been commissioned 35 days previously, to take command of the battalion. The unit was then called Combat Group D'Haese, a name which brought great pride to the Flemings. They were commanded by one of their own, a man who had risen from the ranks after enlisting in *SS-Nordwest*.

The Flemings and stragglers from other units successfully defended Orphanage Hill on 26 July, despite having one of their three anti-tank guns put out of action. The next day, however, they were forced out of their postions, and fell back to Grenadier Hill immediately to the west. A second anti-tank gun was knocked out that morning, but Schrijnen with the last gun, remained in action in the flat ground to the north of Grenadier Hill. Schrijnen knocked out numerous Soviet tanks on 26 and 27 July.

On 28 July, Siegfried Scheibe, as commander of the 2d Battalion of *SS-Norge*, led some of his men and anyone else who could be rounded up in a last-ditch effort to retake Orphanage Hill. D'Haese and his adjutant, Walter van Leemputten, headed a group of 20 Flemings who joined this attack. They were particularly concerned with 50 or so Flemings who had not made it back from Orphanage Hill the day before. Scheibe's attack failed, and the 50 missing men were not seen again. Van Leemputten, who had been D'Haese's classmate at Bad Tölz, was fatally wounded and carried back to Grenadier Hill.

During that day, all of Schrijnen's crew was put out of action at one point. He manned the gun by himself, and continued to knock out Soviet tanks. Later, some men helped him shift his position slightly, and soon after, the old site received a direct hit. Schrijnen's soldier's luck continued in the late afternoon, as a Soviet tank brigade massed to overrun his gun. He and his new crew were ordered to retreat, abandoning the piece, but Schrijnen refused the order and remained in position. Loading and firing by himself, he broke up the Soviet attack, knocking out at least eight tanks, several of them Josef Stalin heavy models. Schrijnen was finally blown away from his anti-tank gun, but the Soviets broke off the attack for the night. The next day, as they prepared a larger force of armor, their concentration was broken up by elements of the 11th *SS*-Panzer Battalion "Hermann von Salza" under Paul-Albert Kausch. It was Kausch's crew that found Schrijnen's battered body and brought him to the rear for treatment. He was proposed for the award of the Honor Roll Clasp.

During 29 July, the Combat Group D'Haese survivors were withdrawn from the line for rest. D'Haese was presented to III (Germanic) *SS*-Panzer Corps commander, Felix Steiner, who offered profuse thanks for the sacrifices the Flemings had made. Steiner removed his German Cross in Gold and pinned it on D'Haese's tunic. Sadly, Georg D'Haese never officially received the German Cross in Gold, most likely because of his outspoken criticism of German policies and the Nazi leadership. As a loyal *VNV* member, he and many other Flemings in the *Waffen-SS* still sought an independent Flanders which would be more than a German province or colony. Schrijnen shared this view, but his single-handed courage was ideal for press reports, so his decoration was approved, and upgraded to the Knight's Cross, which was awarded on 21 September 1944.

By this date, the 130 men of Combat Group D'Haese still ready for duty had been evacuated from Estonia and were on their way to Germany by ship. Days before, the *SS*-Langemarck Brigade had been ordered to expand into a full division. The Allied liberation of Belgium during September 1944 had forced Belgian collaborators of every sort to go into exile in Germany. The *Waffen-SS* High Command decided to combine all available Flemish males into what became the 27th *SS*-Volunteer Grenadier Division "Langemarck." This meant that the hard core of Flemish *SS*-Legion and *SS*-Assault Brigade veterans would be joined by former members of the *NSKK*, the *Organization Todt*, the German Navy, and various paramilitary formations of the *VNV* and *DeVlag*.

Staf deClercq had died in late 1942, and his successor, Dr. Hendrik Elias, had steered the *VNV* away from its former active collaboration. The party was upset that Germany made no effort toward establishing Flemish independence. *DeVlag* had survived as independent movement because it had pretended to be a "cultural association" instead of a political one, but by 1944, it was operating openly as a pro-German party. It encouraged its members to enter German service, and supplied much of the manpower that went into the *SS*-Langemarck Division. Jef van de Wiele held an honorary commission as a *Sturmbannführer* in the Germanic-*SS*, and he became the political training officer for the new division.

Van de Wiele was also named head of the entire Flemish exile community in Germany. This gave him control of not only *DeVlag*'s youth movement, but also that of the *VNV*. From the autumn of 1944, German Hitler Youths had actively engaged in combat against advancing Soviet forces in the *Volksturm*. Van de Wiele decided that Flemish youth of the 15–17-year-old group would also do their part, though within the context of the *SS*-Langemarck Division. The Flemish youth formed a separate small battalion (and the nucleus of another) with experienced officers and NCOs as cadre. The Youth Battalions trained in northern Germany in common with thousands of other Flemings who lacked *Waffen-SS* training.

SS-Langemarck was intended to be a full division, with three infantry regiments of two battalions each, and full supporting elements. These included an artillery regiment, and anti-tank, combat engineer, and signal battalions. The Flemish males of military age in Germany, including workers for German industry, totalled 15,000 or more men, so the plan for Langemarck could have been met, had time for training and equipping existed. During the autumn of 1944, however, all German efforts went towards preparing the units intended for the Ardennes Offensive.

While many veteran Flemings formed the cadre of the forming units of *SS*-Langemarck, the majority were concentrated into a combat group based around the former brigade.

This Combat Group Schellong (named for the commander, who was to command a regiment in the foreseen division) consisted of two infantry battalions and a heavy weapons battalion (known as *SS*-Anti-Tank Battalion 27, but actually including one company/battery each of anti-tank guns, anti-aircraft guns, heavy infantry guns, and assault guns). CG Schellong was kept with the 6th Panzer Army during December 1944, so that it could be committed in Flanders for propaganda purposes when the region was reconquered. When this failed to become necessary, the unit was instead sent east, where it unloaded at Stettin at the end of January 1945.

East of Stettin, the Arneswalde area was the intended jumping-off zone for the III (Germanic) *SS*-Panzer Corps' offensive into the flank of the Soviet forces advancing to the Oder River. The main body of the corps was still in transit to Pomerania from Latvia, and only scratch forces defended around Arneswalde. CG Shellong joined the combat group of the *SS-Wallonien* Division and elements of the corps that had been reforming in Germany, and the front was finally secured in heavy fighting. When the SONNEWENDE offensive failed, the Flemings were caught up in the fighting retreat back to Altdamm and Stettin. The Flemings crossed the Oder River with other Axis forces in the early hours of 20 March. Combat Group Schellong numbered 200 men fit for duty, out of its original strength of 2,300.

A few Flemings remained with other *Waffen-SS* units, mainly in *SS-Wiking*. By this stage, *SS*-Panzer Artillery Regiment 5 was the most international element of the division. *SS-Nordwest* veteran Jan Vincx became the forward observer for the regiment's 4th Battery after his graduation from Bad Tölz. On 22 January 1945, during the KONRAD 3 offensive, he helped defend the division's flank as the emergency commander of his battery, and was proposed for the Honor Roll of the German Army. The war ended before his name could be published, and so he did not actually receive the Honor Roll Clasp, though he is considered an Honor Roll member because his name was accepted for publication.

During late March and April 1945, newly-trained Flemings were sent to the Oder River front and incorporated into the structures of two regiments, *SS*-Volunteer Grenadier Regiments 66 and 67. Regiment 68 was not fully formed, and most of its men were used to flesh out the other two regiments. The Flemish Youth battalion also arrived, and was designated as the 1st Battalion of Regiment 68. Additional youths were in the new 2d Battalion of the regiment, and these two units exchanged some personnel to reduce the chance that all of the Flemish youths would be wiped out at once. The reorganized *SS*-Volunteer Grenadier Regiment 68 did not function as a regiment, instead its two small battalions fought with other elements of the division as the situation dictated. On 1 April, the parts of the *SS*-Langemarck Division deployed along the Oder River numbered 167 officers, 408 NCOs, and 3,537 men. Aside from a few specialists of various nationalities, almost all of these 4,102 men were Flemings, including the officers and NCOs.

The infantry portions of *SS*-Langemarck were later joined by the incomplete *SS*-Combat Engineer Battalion 27, *SS*-Anti-Aircraft Battalion 27, and *SS*-Artillery Regiment 27, the latter commanded by the Dane Holger Arentoft (another Dane, Oluf von Krabbe, commanded the first youth battalion). These units brought the strength of the *SS*-Langemarck Division up to roughly 6,000 men, which was comparable to many neighboring German divisions. Perhaps 6,000 more Flemings were still in training, while others had refused to serve a Germany that was clearly almost finished. The men undergoing training did not see action before the end of the war. Those who were in the combat-ready elements and continued to fight did so for two main reasons: they were determined to protect German civilians from Soviet reprisals; and they had little to return to in Flanders. Some hoped to join with the British and Americans in an anti-Soviet war. The *SS*-Langemarck division was fortunate not to be sucked into the Berlin fighting or the Halbe pocket after the Soviet Berlin offensive began on 16 April 1945. Instead, it retreated to the west under heavy pressure and managed to surrender to Allied units along the Elbe River during the first days of May.

During the following months, the Flemish *Waffen-SS* soldiers were gradually returned to Belgium, where they were treated harshly by the Belgian government. The men were kept for months in primitive conditions, and many died from exposure. Individuals were arbitrarily selected and executed, simply for military collaboration (as opposed to those executed for specific crimes). Though most *Waffen-SS* veterans were released by 1950, they had lost their civil rights and citizenship—they literally became "resident aliens" under the law. Fortunately for them, Flemish nationalism remained a strong ideal among much of the population, so the veterans were able to form support groups and receive aid from the Flemish population at large. The veterans formed an organization they named the *Sint Maartensfonds* (*SMF*), and established the magazine, *Berkenkruis* ("Birch Crosses," in reference to embellishment found on thousands of Eastern Front graves) which remained in publication until the end of the 1990s. The power of the Flemish nationalist lobby made it possible for the *SMF* to meet frequently and openly, and to publish a series of books on the history of the Flemish collaboration. As the veterans reached their later years, they were considered heroes by much of the population in Flanders, even as Walloon *Waffen-SS* veterans remained pariahs in Wallonia.

The Flemish *Waffen-SS* volunteers, on the whole, had been the most idealistic of any in Western Europe. Collectively, they also met the happiest post-war fate, after the immediate reprisals were over. Remy Schrijnen was persecuted for his wartime celebrity, and for his demands that Flemish *Waffen-SS* veterans receive amnesty. Shrijnen finally received political asylum in Germany in 1962 and became a *Bundeswehr* reservist. Other Flemings had become Soviet prisoners during the war, and most died in the *gulag* system. Four survivors of the 50 Flemings captured on the Tannenberg Line were finally released during 1962, six years after the last German *Waffen-SS* prisoners!

Schrijnen, D'Haese, and Bert DeGruyter made particular contributions towards preserving the history of the Flemish *Waffen-SS*. Jan Vincx became the principal historian for the *SMF* until his death in 1996. Besides writing the seven-volume set, *Vlaanderen in Uniform*, about all aspects of the Flemish collaboration, he also co-authored the four-volume series, *Nederlandse vrijwilligers in Europese krijgsdiesnt 1940–1945* (Dutch Volunteers in European Wartime Service) specifically dealing with the Dutch *Waffen-SS* (published by the *SMF*).

The precise number of Flemings in the *Waffen-SS* is difficult to establish. Many of those incorporated after September 1944 never got beyond the training stage. Those that did see action were only in combat for a few months, and as many were conscripted, should be considered in a different light from those who volunteered between 1940 and mid-1943. A rough estimate is that over 8,000 Flemings had served in the *Waffen-SS* up to September 1944, and that the number grew to over 13,000 by the end of the war. The casualties of *SS*-Langemarck during the retreat from the Oder are undetermined, but it is likely that at least 5,000 Flemings were killed in action within the *Waffen-SS* during the war. The dead have been honored in recent years though memorials placed in Flanders and Eastern Europe. On these are carved the names: Volkhov, Krasny-Bor, Jambol, and Orphanage Hill. Young Flemish nationalists continue to study these battles, and dream of an independent Flanders in which the *Waffen-SS* volunteers will be considered founding fathers.

Great Britain

Oswald Mosley's British Union of Fascists (BUF) numbered perhaps 10,000 members before the war. From September 1939 forward, BUF men served in the British military in common with their countrymen, and without aiding Germany. The policies of the party stipulated not harming the interests of Britain.

Some British citizens, usually of mixed heritage, joined the *Waffen-SS* before the war. Eighteen were on duty with various units as of 1 May 1940. The most prominent such was Thomas Haller Cooper, whose mother was German. He became a junior NCO in *SS-LAH* after joining in 1938.

John Amery came from a distinguished family, but opted to join the Spanish Nationalists under Franco during the Spanish Civil War. He became a Spanish citizen and went to Germany during the Second World War, where he made anti-British propaganda speeches. Amery had the idea of recruiting PWs for propaganda duty, and German authorities expanded the concept into that of a unit for front line service against the Soviets, in the same manner as the Germanic *SS*-Legions. During the spring of 1943, the so-called Legion of St. George was authorized to accept up to 1,500 British volunteers.

The recruiting drives failed to generate much enthusiam in PW camps. Several hundred men did accept invitations to visit holiday camps and learn more about the legion, but most of these men were simply personally curious, or had been ordered by their superiors to collect information. Only a handful of men actually signed on for military service.

The Germans understood that British prisoners had no interest in serving against their homeland. The recruiting material, therefore, stressed that the British unit would only fight on the Eastern Front. Gradually, a few men volunteered. There was some hope that South African prisoners might hold anti-British feelings, but the Germans failed to realize that members of the South African Army had to specifically volunteer to fight outside their country, and these men were consequently anti-German, not anti-British.

A few South Africans did volunteer for the legion, which on 1 January 1944 became part of the *Waffen-SS* as the British Free Corps (BFC). Several each of Australians, New Zealanders, and Canadians also joined, so the unit was never entirely British, but should more aptly be considered "Commonwealth." The American George Hale also became a member of the BFC. He had been captured at Dieppe, and enlisted with several of his comrades from the Canadian Essex Scottish Regiment.

Cooper became an instructor for the BFC, which had a strength of roughly 40 men at any given moment. As new recruits trickled in, others would leave or desert because of the declining military situation for Germany. The most dedicated members of the BFC were detached singly or in small groups to serve as war reporters and observers on various fronts for weeks or months with assorted *Waffen-SS* divisions. The New Zealand volunteer, Ray Nicholas Courlander, was captured by British forces in Brussels in September 1944, while reporting on the German retreat from Belgium.

At least two other British soldiers served with the *Waffen-SS*, without joining the BFC. Serving in British units, James Conen and William Celliers were captured by Italian forces in North Africa, and sent to a PW camp in Italy. After the September 1943 Italian armistice, they were part of a group of PWs that attempted to march to Switzerland. They were intercepted by *SS*-Anti-Aircraft Battalion 1 from *SS-LAH*, and made it clear they had no wish to return to PW life. As the two were experienced drivers, they were accepted as "Hiwis" ("Volunteer helpers," a term which normally applied to Soviet citizens who served as auxilliaries in the German military), and went with the battalion to the Eastern Front during October 1943. They served dependably until the unit was withdrawn for refitting the following spring, at which point they were reassigned, since *SS-LAH* was expected to see combat against British forces in Western Europe. The two went on to serve with an *SS* staff headquarters, but their ultimate fate is unknown.

Several of the volunteers for the BFC were not PWs. Kenneth Edward Berry and Alfred Vivian Minchen were young merchant seamen whose ship was impounded by German authorities in 1940. Eric Pleasants and Dennis John Leister were pacifists assigned to perform farm labor on Jersey prior to the German occupation of the Channel Islands. Pleasants, who had been a member of Britain's boxing team at the 1936 Berlin Olympics, was actually sent to a PW camp after trying to escape from Jersey by boat. He enlisted in the BFC in the hopes of finding a means of getting away from the Germans while near the frontlines. While training with the BFC, he represented it successfully in several boxing matches against other German units.

In early 1945, a British Army officer known by the pseudonym "Webster" volunteered for the BFC. He joined after becoming angry witnessing several Allied bombing raids on German civilian targets, and received the rank of *Hauptsturmführer*. During March of that year, the BFC was declared fit for combat, and was assigned to the III (Germanic) *SS*-Panzer Corps, which was refitting west of the Oder River. The first squad to arrive was sent to a company of *SS*-Armored Reconnaissance Battalion 11, which was located by a village named Schöneberg. The company was attacked by a Soviet patrol on 22 March and the British volunteers saw their first combat that day. Kenneth Edward Berry became a Soviet prisoner during the fighting, and after the war claimed he had deliberately deserted.

Webster and the rest of the BFC arrived at the headquarters of the III (Germanic) *SS*-Panzer Corps on 6 April. Including those already on hand, the BFC totalled around 40 men. They were split among the companies of *SS*-Armored Reconnaissance Battalion 11, to prevent too many becoming casualties in a single firefight.

A week later, on 14 April, corps commander Felix Steiner decided to remove the BFC from the front. He did not want the British volunteers to suffer in what was certain to be the final campaign of a lost war, and he had doubts about the legality of their employment under any circumstances. Steiner sought to avoid having any of his subordinates face post-war punishment for commanding British PWs in battle. Many of the volunteers were upset at this decision, as they wanted to prove themselves in combat, and Webster was so annoyed that he resigned his commission and returned to PW status. Cooper took over the platoon-strength BFC, and led most of it west, where short of the Elbe River the men put on their old PW uniforms and attempted to pass themselves off as escapees.

Several British volunteers were in Berlin during the battle for the city, from the last remnants of the BFC coordination staff, as war reporters, or as volunteer medics with *SS-Nordland*. As one of the latter, Reginald Leslie Cornford knocked out a Soviet tank in close combat on 27 April, and was then killed by survivors of the tank's crew. Eric Pleasants was also in Berlin, and was able to escape from the city after killing two Soviet soldiers in hand-to-hand combat.

The British volunteers had varied fates after the war. Amery, who had never joined the *Waffen-SS*, was executed, and Cooper was also sentenced to this fate. His life was spared when the court took his German parentage into consideration, and he was released from prison in 1953. Webster escaped any punishment because he had highly-placed relatives in the British nobility. Men who had left BFC service, claimed to have deserted (such as Berry), or who had proven records of attempted escape from PW camps (and could be believed when they claimed to have volunteered solely to find an opportunity to escape) usually received light prison sentences, if any. The same was true for most of the non-British or Canadian volunteers. George Hale was imprisoned for ten years, and several of the more unrepentant members, who were considered "hardcore" cases received equal or longer sentences.

Eric Pleasants had married a German woman during the war, and remained in the American zone of occupation in Germany. He performed as a circus-type "strong man," even after the Soviets took control of the area in which he lived. They considered him a possible spy, so he was arrested during 1947 and sent to the infamous Vorkuta slave labor camp in northern Siberia. Pleasants survived his stay there, and was sent back to Britain in 1953. He was considered to have suffered enough, and avoided further punishment. He became something of a celebrity because of his experiences, which he recorded in the book, *I Killed to Live*, and was eventually the subject of a program on British television.

The British volunteers never made a significant contribution to the *Waffen-SS*. Their value was as a propaganda tool, though a few men were certainly anti-Communists who desired to actively fight on the Eastern Front. Only 50 or so men belonged to the BFC for any significant length of time, and such is the scandal that this small group created in Britain that the full story of the unit may never be known.

Iceland

Although released from Danish rule in 1918, Iceland still depended on Denmark for defense in 1940 when Denmark was invaded and occupied by Germany. Shortly thereafter, the British occupied Iceland to prevent it from falling into German hands, and the United States assumed responsibility for Iceland's defense in 1941, even before the attack on Pearl Harbor. The fully independent Republic of Iceland was declared on 17 June 1944. Some Icelanders attending universities or otherwise living in Europe at the outbreak of the Second World War are known to have joined the German military. The precise number is not recorded, but as many as 20 may have joined the *Waffen-SS*, either in Denmark or in Germany. The most prominent Icelandic volunteer was Björn Björnsen, who attended an officer training course at Bad Tölz, without graduating, before becoming an officer and war reporter. One of the only other identified Icelanders was Grettir "Egidir" Odiussen, who served with *SS-Wiking*, and never returned from Soviet captivity. Finally, it is known that Norwegian officer volunteer Odd Tordarson, who served in the 3d Battalion of *SS-Germania* and then was fatally wounded while commanding a platoon in the 4th Company of *SS-*Armored Reconnaissance Battalion 11, had an Icelandic father.

The Netherlands

National Socialism during the 1930s was more popular in the Netherlands than in any country outside of Germany. Various parties competed for the attention of the Dutch radical right, but by far the most successful was the National Socialist Movement (*NSB*), founded by Anton Adriaan Mussert on 14 December 1931. The *NSB* platform of Dutch patriotism held a greater appeal than the pro-German outlook of its competitors, yet even as the *NSB* gained parliamentary seats later in the decade, the seeds of its future impotence were being sewn. *NSB* parliamentary leader, Meinoud Marinus Rost van Tonningen, was forging a close friendship with Heinrich Himmler and the German *SS* leadership, and soon his loyalty was more to them than to Mussert. In the months before the German offensive of 10 May 1940, many of the NSB's 100,000 members were forced into exile in France to avoid the possibility that they might form a "fifth column" in the event of German invasion.

The Dutch Army of 1940 was unprepared for modern war, despite indications that a German invasion could be expected. Many Dutch units fought hard between 10 and 14 May, when conditions allowed, and the country surrendered with honor. While the tenacity of Dutch soldiers impressed the Germans, Dutch training and officer abilities were considered woefully inadequate.

The *NSB* came into the open after the occupation. Its suppressed militia, the *Weer Afdeeling* (WA, or Armed Detachment), reappeared under Arie "A. J." Zondervan. On 11 September 1940, J. Hendrik "Henk" Feldmeijer, the former commander of Mussert's bodyguard, created the Dutch-*SS*. This was intended to mirror the *Allegemeine-SS* in the same way that the *WA* mirrored the *SA*. While this was initially a branch of the *NSB*, by November 1942, it was made a component of the Germanic-*SS*, and retitled the Germanic-*SS* in the Netherlands (GSS). Thus it passed from Dutch to German control.

The creation of the *Westland* Regiment of the *Waffen-SS* on 15 June 1940 met a quicker response than had the previous creation of the *Nordland* Regiment. Hundreds of young Dutchmen volunteered during 1940, and after initial conflict with bullies in the training cadre, soon developed close bonds with their German comrades. Many of these early recruits were not overtly political; instead they had been impressed by the German victory in the west and by the initially lenient occupation. They desired to become professional soldiers in a first-class army. One of these early recruits was Gerrit-Jan Pulles, the son of the mayor of Eindhoven.

A hundred or so political activists from the *NSB* left *Westland* during December 1940, as they had sought political police work rather than tough military training. These men were able to pass along what they had learned to that point to the initial volunteers for the Dutch-*SS*, to give them some para-military instruction.

Over 600 Dutch were with the *Wiking* Division on 22 June 1941, making them by far the largest foreign body within the unit. As more volunteers finished training, the number of Dutch increased to over 800 a few months later, and that figure continued to increase.

With the German invasion of the Soviet Union, a Dutch Legion was created in common with the other Germanic nations. As with the other legions, it was intended to be a national unit, with Dutch officers and language of command. The retired chief of staff of the Dutch Army, General Hendrik Seyffardt, was an *NSB* member, and he used to his reputation to actively encourage volunteering for the Dutch Legion. Over 1,000 Dutch had already volunteered for the *Nordwest* Regiment, and they became the base of the regiment-sized Dutch Volunteer Legion, which was administrated by the *Waffen-SS*. Three of the early *Nordwest* volunteers who then went into the Dutch Legion were Gerardus Mooyman, Derk-Elsko Bruins, and Kaspar Sporck.

The Dutch Legion had a sizeable *NSB* representation, and Zondervan volunteered as an example to his men. The *WA* volunteers were then concentrated in the 3d Battalion of the unit. Dutch Army officers were encouraged to join, but few did as it became clear the Germans had a low regard for their abilities and would not generally grant rank matching what was held previously. So while the Dutch Legion had attained a strength of 2,933 men (including 26 Flemings) by 9 January 1942, only 26 of the 66 officers were Dutch.

Several hundred Dutch volunteers were removed from the legion prior to the completion of training, due to either concealed criminal pasts or "political unreliability," so that only 2,781 officers and men were with it when it deployed to the Volkhov River sector by early February 1942 under German officer, Otto Reich.

The Dutch Legion was quickly caught up in extremely heavy fighting in the inhospitable swamps of the Volkhov. It endured significant casualties by early April 1942, including the popular Dutch officer and *NSB* member, Olaf Westra, killed in action on 7 April. A few days later, the combat strength of the legion was down to only 200 men, and the unit was withdrawn to Poland to rebuild. The Dutch Legion had been honored a month earlier by receiving praise in the 4 March *Wehrmacht* Report.

New recruits who had just finished their training helped to rebuild the Dutch Legion. Mussert ordered members of the *WA* to volunteer to augment these men, and some recovered wounded also returned to duty. Unfortunately, as with the Flemish Legion, most of the Dutch recovered wounded were instead assigned to the *Wiking* Division, which had priority, as it was a full *Waffen-SS* unit, and not merely administered by the *Waffen-SS* (the Dutch Legion was still, in theory, a Dutch unit, and not a part of the German military). Despite this difficulty, the Dutch Legion numbered 1,418 officers and men by 1 June 1942.

Dutchmen continued to volunteer for full *Waffen-SS* service, and also usually ended up in *Wiking*, including Feldmeijer, who performed his military service with *SS*-Flak Battalion 5. *Wiking* and the Dutch Legion both absorbed heavy casualties during their 1942 combats (the Dutch Legion suffering just under 2,000 dead and wounded up to 30 November), so that the number of Dutchmen on duty with the legion or in the *Waffen-SS* was never nearly as high as the total of those who had joined. The *Waffen-SS* High Command released figures on 14 December 1942 which indicated that as of the previous 30 October, 5,228 Dutch had served with the *Waffen-SS* (with 219 dead and 1,289 released from service), and another 4,524 had served with the Dutch Legion (with 367 dead and 1,174 released from service). This figure of 9,752 volunteers was higher than the number of Norwegian volunteers during the entire war, and nearly matched the wartime total from Denmark.

As *Wiking* advanced to the Caucasus during the summer of 1942, the Dutch Legion returned to the Volkhov for the destruction of the Soviet forces cut off during their winter offensive. Some accounts credit the legion with capturing Soviet General Andre Vlasov, who later headed the German-sponsored Russian Liberation Army. This final phase of the Volkhov fighting was again costly, but ultimately successful. The Dutch Legion then assumed a place on the Leningrad siege lines by the end of July 1942, where new recruits were integrated. Despite further costly fighting into the autumn, by the end of 1942, the legion reported a strength of 1,755 officers and men.

Early in 1943, the heavy anti-tank guns of the 14th Company of the Dutch Legion were detached from their parent unit, and sent with the 14th Company of the Norwegian Legion to fight on the eastern portion of the German positions that blockaded Leningrad, near Schlüsselburg. While the 75mm *Pak 38/97* pieces (based on First World War French gun tubes) were less powerful than the modern 75mm *Pak 40*, they still exceeded the capabilities of the anti-tank weapons of most German infantry units in this sector, and provided much needed assistance during the Second Battle of Lake Ladoga. The terrain here was more open than usual in this region, and the Dutch and Norwegian gunners had frequent opportunity to defend against Soviet tank attacks, which were otherwise rare in the greater Leningrad area.

The soul of the anti-tank fighting was provided by Gerardus Mooyman, who was forced to switch from messenger to gunner because of casualties. The 19-year-old quickly demonstrated his abilities as a gunner during the February 1943 fighting. On 13 February alone, he knocked out 13 Soviet tanks, which brought him the award of the Knight's Cross a week later. Mooyman was the first Germanic volunteer to earn this decoration. While he was delighted with the recognition, the young man was in over his head when he was made a propaganda figure, and asked to pose for photos with many German and Dutch personalities. Mooyman later completed an officer training course at Bad Tölz, and became an officer in the anti-tank battalion of the *Nederland* Brigade/Division.

Back in the Netherlands, Hendrik Seyffardt was assassinated on 6 February 1943. (Dutch Communists claimed credit for the killing.) In his honor, the 1st Company of the Dutch Legion was titled "General Seyffardt."

The main portion of the Dutch Legion was also heavily engaged during February and March 1943, still as part of the ring around Leningrad. The next month, the unit received home leave in the Netherlands before reassembling during May 1943 at Grafenwöhr, in common with the Danes and Norwegians, for the creation of the *Nordland* Division. The Dutch Legion, which had usually been referred to internally as a regiment, was now to become one in name, as the Panzer-Grenadier Regiment *Nederland* of the *Nordland* Division.

This arrangement proved impractical for a couple of reasons. By the summer of 1943, *Waffen-SS* panzer-grenadier divisions were based around two, not three, infantry regiments, and *Frikorps Danmark* and the Norwegian Legion were already slated for expansion into panzer-grenadier regiments. Also, since the Dutch were to incorporate Dutch *Wiking* veterans, they formed the largest group in the concentration of Germanic volunteers at Grafenwöhr, with more than enough men to form a regiment. Mussert and *NSB* leadership requested that the Dutch be allowed to form their own division.

Josef Fitzthum had taken command of the Dutch Legion when it returned to the Volkhov during the summer of 1942. He became the first commander of the intended Panzer-Grenadier Regiment *Nederland*, and in recognition of his successful leadership of the legion was awarded the German Cross in Gold on 24 August 1943. By this time, the Dutch regiment had been removed from *Nordland,* and expanded into two smaller regiments (with two battalions each, instead of the three in

Dutch Army officer Gerard Peters, who served with the combat engineer battalion of *SS-Prinz Eugen*. He later served on the staff of the Higher *SS* and Police Leader for the Adriatic Coastline. (Mansson)

Danmark and *Norge*). The first regiment, which became *SS*-Volunteer Panzer-Grenadier Regiment 48, carried on the title "General Seyffardt," while the second, which became *SS*-Panzer-Grenadier Regiment 49, was titled "De Ruyter" for the seventeenth-century Dutch admiral of that name (the German spelling of "De Ruiter" was also extensively used).

The regiments General Seyffardt and De Ruyter were joined with the usual supporting services (but with no artillery initially) to form the *Nederland* Division, but insufficient men were on hand, even after a thousand ethnic Germans (from the same body used to fill out *Nordland*) were added to each regiment. On the Oranienbaum front, the 3d Battalion of the *SS-Polizei* Artillery Regiment 4, which was part of the combat group the 4th *SS-Polizei*-Panzer-Grenadier Division left behind when it moved to Greece to rebuild, joined the *Nederland* Brigade to give it an artillery component. With that, the initial structure of *Nederland* was complete, it now formed a sort of "mini-division," a scaled-down panzer-grenadier division, which could be expanded later. The unit continued to refer to itself as a division, but officially it was reclassified as the 4th *SS*-Volunteer Panzer-Grenadier Brigade *Nederland*.

Wiking had supplied 1,500 Dutch and, combined with those legion veterans who continued to serve, Dutch volunteers accounted for perhaps 3,500 of the 6,424 officers and men in the brigade on 31 December 1943. Thus, the Dutch character of the unit diminished in comparison to the old legion, and this would only increase as new, primarily German, units were added, including a second, and finally a third artillery battalion. Since the brigade was fully part of the *Waffen-SS*, and now officially part of the German military, it received more and better weaponry than the legion had enjoyed, including a battery of assault guns in its anti-tank battalion. But since *Brigade Nederland* was no longer considered an extension of the Dutch armed forces, the *NSB* had less influence than ever before. Also, Dutch officers and NCOs continued to be scarce, but this would improve from early 1944 as young Dutchmen joined the unit after completing courses at training schools.

This Dutch leadership rarely reached above the company level, so the brigade was fortunate that its predominently German officer corps was formed around highly experienced and competent *Wiking* veterans. Fitzthum was reassigned, and replaced as General Seyffardt commander by the last commander of the *Nordland* Regiment, Wolfgang Joerchel. Hans Collani and his German cadre from the former Finnish Volunteer Battalion formed the staff of De Ruyter, with Collani as commander. Command of the brigade was taken by Jürgen Wagner, who had recently won the Knight's Cross as *Germania* Regiment commander.

The General Seyffardt Regiment particularly distinguished itself during the retreat from Oranienbaum, with a decisive delaying action conducted by a combat group based around its 1st Battalion. The German battalion commander, Hans-Joachim Rühle von Lilienstern, was awarded the Knight's Cross on 12 February 1944. By this date, the General Seyffardt Regiment held the northernmost portion of the Narva bridgehead, around Popovka, with its neighbor, the De Ruyter Regiment, to the right around Lilienbach. The General Seyffardt Regiment held its positions in desperate fighting in early March 1944, but in the following days, De Ruyter was hard pressed. An extremely costly counterattack by the 9th Company of Regiment *Danmark* cleared up one crisis, and its commander, Luxembourg volunteer Fritz Sidon, was awarded the Honor Roll Clasp many months later on 5 November 1944. Another attack forced the De Ruyter Regiment out of Lilienbach, with several Soviet tanks making a clean breakthrough. Just before this force reached the vital Narva railroad bridge, Philipp Wild counterattacked with his Panther platoon from the 1st Company of *SS*-Panzer Battalion 11 "Hermann von Salza." The Soviet tanks were knocked out, and Collani's men restored the gap in their lines, though Lilienbach could not be retaken. Wild, a German, was awarded the Knight's Cross on 21 March 1944, and his Danish driver, Kurt Tebring, received the Iron Cross 1st Class.

The Soviets made two more attempts to capitalize on their success at Lilienbach and break through De Ruyter's new lines just to the west of the village. On 14 March, the 2d Battalion of the regiment was nearly overwhelmed but Helmut Scholz, a platoon commander in 7th Company took charge of the entire zone after the battalion commander was killed. At the head of a few men, the Finnish battalion veteran counterattacked and restored the situation. A day later, a new Soviet assault again almost broke through. The new 2d Battalion commander, Carl-Heinz Frühauf, gathered every rear services man he could find, and launched a counterattack. This nearly faltered under intense fire, but Frühauf repeatedly rallied his men, and finally stabilized the De Ruyter positions for good.

During the lull that followed during the spring of 1944, the *Nederland* Brigade was highly decorated for its defensive efforts. Joerchel was awarded the Knight's Cross on 21 April, and the same medal followed for Frühauf and Scholz on 4 June. Collani was awarded the German Cross in Gold on 24 April, as were two Dutchmen, platoon commander Frans Venema from the 3d Company of General Seyffardt and Herman Schoofs from the staff of *SS*-Combat Engineer Battalion 54.

The two infantry regiments of *Brigade Nederland* were rebuilt as well as possible, incorporating survivors of the 9th and 10th *Luftwaffe* Field Divisions (including Georg Schluifelder) and some new Dutch volunteers, but were still understrength as the late July 1944 withdrawal to the Tannenberg Line began. Days earlier, Joerchel had been reassigned and replaced by the former commander of the Norwegian *SS*-Ski

Battalion, Richard Benner. The General Seyffardt Regiment, with its roughly 1,200 men, was one of the last units of the III (Germanic) *SS*-Panzer Corps to evacuate Narva. As the regiment made its way west, it was beset by bad luck. During the night of 25/26 July, Benner had on several occasions to decide on the precise route of withdrawal for his men. His reasoning was sound, but the chosen route resulted in the General Seyffardt Regiment being surrounded. The regiment broke up into smaller groups to try to make their way to the west to the Tannenberg positions. Benner was quickly killed, but the survivors fought on into 28 July. Since the initial Soviet attacks on the Tannenberg Line were barely contained, the staff of the III (Germanic) *SS*-Panzer Corps believed that the efforts of General Seyffardt in tying down significant enemy forces made the successful defense possible.

Brigade Nederland's assault gun battery had attacked to the east from the Tannenberg positions to try to clear a way for the General Seyffardt Regiment. Dutch officer Cornelius Nieuwendijk-Hoek and perhaps 250 men of the regiment did succeed in reaching the Tannenberg Line, thanks to this effort. With them was the 2d Battalion commander, Helmut Breymann, who had previously been a favorite officer with the Flemish Legion. He was killed in action soon after, however, during the continued Tannenberg Line fighting. The assault guns included two Dutchmen among the gun commanders, Joop Cuypers and Derk-Elsko Bruins. The latter had pressed home his relief attack to the last possible moment, and knocked out numerous Soviet tanks in the process. For this, Bruins became the second Dutch recipient of the Knight's Cross on 23 August 1944.

The first stage of the Tannenberg fighting hit *Nordland* the hardest, but by 29 July, De Ruyter was fully involved. Frühauf was wounded, and advancing Soviet forces passed by the 2d Battalion command post north of Grenadier Hill. Scholz took emergency command of the battalion and led the defense of the command post as a strongpoint. Stefan Strapatin, the ethnic German leader of Scholz's messenger squad, contributed by knocking out several tanks using *Panzerfaust* anti-tank rocket launchers. The Soviet advance reached the De Ruyter regimental command bunker on Hill 69.9. Collani was badly wounded, and shot himself when the situation seemed lost. Karl-Heinz Ertel, the regimental adjutant who had served with Collani since the first days of the Finnish volunteer battalion, assumed temporary command of De Ruyter, and directed the defense which ultimately proved successful when Paul-Albert Kausch and the last armor of the Hermann von Salza Battalion counterattacked.

In the aftermath of the Tannenberg fighting, Collani received the Knight's Cross posthumously on 19 August 1944. Kausch and Ertel were awarded the same decoration on 23 August, and Scholz was awarded the Oakleaves to his Knight's Cross weeks later on 21 September.

By that date, Scholz had been injured in an accident and evacuated, with Otto Petersen replacing him. Petersen and Strapatin distinguished themselves during the retreat from Estonia, and both received the Knight's Cross after the Second Battle of Kurland. Strapatin, from the Banat, was one of the only ethnic Germans to earn this decoration.

After the Tannenberg front quieted in early August, but before the evacuation of Estonia, Soviet forces advanced around Lake Peipus and threatened the Estonian front from the south. *Nederland* Brigade commander Wagner led a combat group against this advance in the Tartu area. Among his sub-units was a small battalion from the Walloon Assault Brigade *Wallonien* and the *SS*-Armored Reconnaissance Battalion 11. In the 5th Company of the recon unit was a platoon equipped with "cannon-wagons," armored halftracks mounting low-velocity 75mm howitzers. These vehicles were too lightly armored and armed to engage enemy tanks in open combat, but sometimes were called upon in emergencies to deal with tanks. Kaspar Spork had commanded a cannon-wagon in 5th Company since before the retreat from Oranienbaum, during which he had earned both classes of the Iron Cross after developing a hit-and-run, strike-from-ambush technique which allowed him to destroy many Soviet armored vehicles. In the fighting near Tartu, Sporck brought his kill total to 15 tanks, as well as numerous anti-tank guns, and for this he was awarded the Knight's Cross on 23 October 1944 as the third and final Dutchman.

The General Seyffardt Regiment was reconstituted during the autumn of 1944, primarily with Germans, and then fought along the Baltic coast in West Prussia and Pomerania from January 1945 with training units of the III (Germanic) *SS*-Panzer Corps. As this went on, the main portion of the *Nederland* Brigade nearly bled to death in Kurland. The brigade was especially hard-pressed during the Second Battle of Kurland, but the key heights around Ozoli were held by the 1st Company of De Ruyter and the 5th Battery of *SS*-Artillery Regiment 54 in tremendously difficult fighting. Georg Schluifelder had already earned the German Cross in Gold since joining *Nederland*, and earned the Knight's Cross for this battle as the commander of 1st Company. Herbert-Albert Rieth also earned the Knight's Cross as 5th Battery commander, and his forward observer, Johann Täubl, received the Honor Roll Clasp. When the observation post was overrun, Täubl's radioman, Walter Jenschke, led a counterattack that recaptured the position, and for that action was awarded the Knight's Cross. It was a sign of the brigade's composition by this point that all of these men were German nationals.

By the time Johannes Hellmers earned his Knight's Cross during the Fourth Battle of Kurland, the combat strength of *Brigade Nederland* was down to a couple of hundred men. Fortunately, the command and administrative sections were preserved, so than new men could be continually added to the combat elements during the refit before action in Pomerania, and again west of the Oder River. Individual Dutchmen remained in the unit, which was retitled the 23d *SS*-Volunteer Panzer-Grenadier Division *Nederland* on 10 February 1945. One was Geert Pulles, who had distinguished himself in the Narva bridgehead as the commander of De Ruyter's 3d Company before being wounded. After recuperation service with the *Landstorm*, he rejoined *Nederland* in Kurland, was awarded the German Cross in Gold for his previous leadership on 18 December 1944. Pulles was killed in action after the *Sonnenwende* offensive.

West of the Oder, the General Seyffardt Regiment rejoined what was now a Dutch formation in name only. Schluifelder had died at Ozoli during the Fourth Battle of Kurland, and Rieth was killed in the Halbe pocket, but most of the other high award winners of the division survived the war, including Mooyman and Bruins. Sporck remained with *Nordland*'s recon battalion, and was fatally wounded in Pomerania, dying on 8 April 1945.

Back in the Netherlands, the German occupying authorities decided during 1942 to set up a Dutch defense force to combat resistance fighters and Allied agents, and to maintain order in the event of an Allied invasion. As this *"Landwacht Nederland"* came together during 1943, all able-bodied men of the *WA*, Germanic-*SS*, and *NSB* were asked to volunteer to undergo military training. The cadre was formed around Dutch *Waffen-SS* veterans (often invalided out of combat service) and Dutch and German police officers and NCOs. On 16 October 1943, the *Landwacht* was reorganized as the *SS*-Grenadier Regiment *Landstorm Nederland* in the strength of three battalions. Most men served part-time, but all members were mobilized for three-day regimental training sessions during November 1943 and the following April. By the end of 1943, the *Landstorm* numbered 1,938 officers and men.

On 15 May 1944, with the Allied invasion of Western Europe expected at any time, the *Landstorm* was fully mobilized. It had finished its organization, and consisted of a three-battalion regiment with full supporting services. It included 3,167 officers and men, all but a few Dutch, and commanded by *Leibstandarte* veteran Martin Kohlroser. As a *Waffen-SS* formation, it became part of the German military, and the Dutchmen in it were now under German command instead of that of the *NSB*.

Up to September 1944, the main activity of the *Landstorm* was to train, but early that month, as British forces approached Dutch territory, part of the *Landstorm* was committed to combat. The 1st Battalion fought with the 85th Infantry Division, while the 2d Battalion was under the 719th Infantry Division, both in the Albert Canal zone. The 3d Battalion and supporting elements remained in reserve in the vicinity of

Arnhem, and were committed there alongside the 9th *SS*-Panzer Division Hohenstaufen after Operation MARKET-GARDEN began on September 18.

The next month, following the successful conclusion of the Arnhem battle, the *Landstorm* was brought together to the east of the front, and enlarged on 1 November into the *SS*-Volunteer Grenadier Brigade *"Landstorm Nederland."* Several miscellaneous *Waffen-SS* and police formations were added and now all male Germanic-*SS*, *WA*, and other *NSB* members were conscripted for service. Rost van Tonningen, who had fallen out of favor with Mussert, became an officer in the embryonic artillery regiment. Former Dutch concentration camp guards were also added. Mussert now had hardly any of his followers under his control, as almost all of the men were either in German military service, had already ben killed, or were in Allied captivity.

As this force organized, it was retitled the 34th *SS*-Volunteer Infantry Division *Landstorm Nederland* on 10 February 1945. As with the original *SS*-Panzer-Grenadier *Brigade Nederland*, it had essentially a miniature division structure, with two infantry regiments, each of two battalions, and less than full divisional supporting elements. Morale was low for several reasons. The military enthusiasts and veterans of previous *Waffen-SS* service considered camp guards and conscripts as less than ideal comrades. The conscripts were often quite young or overage for military duty, and would have preferred not to be fighting. And they were the only *Waffen-SS* Germanic unit to see combat against the Western Allies, instead of against the Soviets.

This last fact is one of which *Waffen-SS* veterans of all nationalities are not proud. In various unit histories, it is always stressed that the Germanic volunteers joined to fight Communism, though hundreds actually joined before 22 June 1941. The 5,000 or so men of the *Landstorm Nederland* Division usually receive little attention from historians. Clearly, this is fertile ground for future scholarship.

How was this thrown-together division able to fight well? Its senior leadership was mostly German, and Germans held half of the company command positions, and these men naturally were dedicated to fighting their country's enemies. As to the Dutch rank and file, they considered their fate sealed. They were already dead men, with nothing to look forward to in the post-war world, after choosing to collaborate. The *Waffen-SS* veterans were able to instill a degree of discipline and camaraderie, which enhanced the fighting potential, and so the Dutch and Germans in the unit together prepared to sell their lives as dearly as possible.

The *Landstorm* returned to the frontlines during the winter of 1945, and quickly had an advantage over their opponents. As Dutch natives, they understood how to operate in the many rivers, canals, and flooded areas around Arnhem, terrain which confounded the British. While the

An unusual Dutch volunteer, who was killed in action in the Netherlands by Wilson Boback of Company G ot the US Army's 501st Parachute Infantry Regiment during Operation MARKET-GARDEN, or the follow-up fighting. This man is of Indonesian descent, and wears the collar patch, arm shield, and cuff-title of the Dutch *SS-Legion*. The latter two items are of Dutch manufacture, instead of the more common German-made versions. His helmet includes the flaming grenade decal of the *SS-Landstorm Nederland*. (Boback, via Bando)

front remained static, the *Landstormers* had the upper hand in the constant raiding and patrolling that extended into the spring. Dutch Germanic-*SS* commander Feldmeijer was killed during this stretch, when an Allied fighter bomber strafed his car on 22 February.

Despite early sucesses, the *Landstorm Nederland* Division was quickly defeated when the large British offensive to take Arnhem began on April 2. In common with other German formations, it was forced to disperse, and most of its men gradually surrendered in groups, up to the end of the war. Some perferred to go down fighting, including *Wiking* veteran and Germanic-*SS* officer Willem "Wim" Heubel, who had graduated from Bad Tölz and commanded the 5th Company of *SS*-Volunteer Infantry Regiment 83. He was killed on 28 April 1945 while leading an attack on a British anti-tank gun position.

Those members of the *Landstorm* that surrendered went into captivity with discipline that impressed British and Canadian observers. To their fellow Dutch, however, they were pariahs, and they were quickly given bad treatment in very harsh prison camps. Other Dutch gradually arrived who had surrendered with the remnants of the Panzer-Grenadier Division *Nederland* or with other *Waffen-SS* units. Rost van Tonningen was murdered in captivity, but *Waffen-SS* veterans were not executed merely for serving in the German military. Instead, they received prison sentences of several years and permanent loss of civil rights. Though these rights were often restored during the 1980s, many veterans moved to Germany after the war, where men like Bruins could build a career. After some time in Germany, Mooyman settled in the Netherlands, with house painting the best job he could find. Individual Dutch *Waffen-SS* veterans joined the French Foreign Legion after the war, and several hundred regained some measure of their rights by volunteering to fight with the Dutch Army in Korea.

It should be noted that as Dutch *Waffen-SS* veterans shared their experiences with each other after the war, many believed that two additional Dutch received the German Cross in Gold, though the documentation isn't known to exist. The first is *SS-Wiking* NCO Frans Goedhart, who attended the 18th Shortened Wartime Course at Bad Tölz from late 1944, where classmates observed him wearing the decoration. Next, Nieuwendijk-Hoek is supported by several veterans in his claim that he received the German Cross in Gold from *SS-Nederland* commander Wagner during the early 1945 sea-passage from Kurland to Pomerania. Nieuwendijk-Hoek is sometimes reported asbeing killed during the war, but he was a comrade of Joop Cuypers in post-war Dutch captivity.

Hundreds of other Dutch volunteers (including an *NSKK* group caught at Stalingrad) went into Soviet captivity, where many died. Some were released during 1950, but others were not sent home for another decade. Wagner, Ertel, and others from the German cadre were extradited to Yugoslavia, where they were tried on trumped up charges as revenge for their months of training in Croatia during 1943. Wagner was executed for unspecified warcrimes, but Ertel was fortunate to survive and return to Germany during October 1950. He became an important resource to historians because of his experience as a participant in several aspects of the Germanic *Waffen-SS* volunteer movement.

Dutch *Waffen-SS* veterans have never been able to form a strong association, as did their Flemish counterparts, and few wrote memoirs or accounts of their service as happened in Norway and Denmark. The detailed history of the Dutch *Waffen-SS*, published in Dutch, was actually prepared by the Flemish SMF under Jan Vincx's direction. This doesn't change the fact that up to 20,000 Dutch joined the *Waffen-SS*, mostly as volunteers, and tens of thousands of others served in organizations such as the *OT* and *NSKK*. While no Dutch veterans' association formed, Dutch were active participants in the veterans' groups for *Wiking* and for the III (Germanic) *SS*-Panzer Corps. The great preponderance of Dutch in the *Waffen-SS* made good soldiers, no matter with which unit they served, and their German comrades regarded them highly. Fortunately, German and Flemish veterans have preserved the history of the Dutch *Waffen-SS* for posterity.

Norway

Well-known Norwegian soldier Vidkun Quisling formed the National Unity (*NS*) party in May 1933, after his previous venture into politics with the Agrarian Party had failed. *NS* was obviously influenced by Hitler and the German National Socialists, and few Norwegians showed any interest in the new party. Quisling drew his limited support primarily from conservative military families, who embraced the aspects of his message embracing Norwegian patriotism. Among the original members of *NS* were Ragnar Berg, the Dane (married to a Norwegian) Gust Jonassen, and Björn Östring, who became the head of the Youth Movement (*NSUF*).

During the Winter War, the Norwegian government granted approval for Norwegian citizens to volunteer to fight in Finland. Around 750 did so, as did some Norwegians already living in Sweden and Finland. Fewer than 300 of the Norwegian volunteers actually went into military units, and almost all of these were integrated into the Swedish volunteer contingent. Among the Norwegians to make it to Finland was Per Imerslund, the controversial journalist. Imerslund was an outspoken anti-Communist who had fought with the Falangists during the Spanish Civil War. He seems to have been perpetually discontent, often feuding with the *NS* leadership, despite holding broadly similar views. Only a few of the Norwegian volunteers in Finland were *NS* members because that party was in turmoil at the time, just recovering from internal strife.

One of Quisling's rivals for radical right-wing political power was the police official Jonas Lie, who before the war befriended the Nazi party official Josef Terboven. After the German invasion during the spring of 1940, Terboven became the head German administrator for Norway, and Lie was appointed Chief of Norwegian Police. The two cooperated to plot against Quisling, who initially was without station.

Quisling had tried to seize power in the wake of the German occupation, but his authority was not recognized by the Germans. Most *NS* male members were active or reserve soldiers in the Norwegian military, and they loyally fought the German invaders until the Norwegian Army capitulated on 10 June 1940. Almost every Norwegian who became a *Waffen-SS* officer up to early 1944 had seen combat against the Germans during 1940 (By mid-1944, many Norwegians born in 1924 and 1925 began to attend officer training schools. They, of course, had been too young for military duty in 1940).

The Germans gradually realized that *NS* was the only segment of the Norwegian populace to show them much good will. During September 1940, *NS* became the sole recognized political party allowed in Norway, and many right-wing sympathizers joined. This included Immerslund, who hoped the party had changed for the better. The old *NS* party was not the political outlet that he and certain other, mostly young, Norwegians sought.

With its expansion, *NS* was able to set up seven regiments of its uniformed militia, known as the *Hird*. As with the party militias in other Germanic nations, much of the *Hird* membership eventually joined the *Waffen-SS*. The *NS* grew to 55,000 members, and adult males up to age 45 were to serve in the general *Hird*, or one of its specialized branches. The most prominent sub-group was Quisling's personal Leader Guard, commanded by Östring in addition to his position as head of the *NSUF*.

During May 1941, Lie and Justice Minister Sverre Riisnaes established a Norwegian branch of the *Allegemeine-SS*, which eventually became known as the Germanic-*SS* in Norway (*GSSN*). This attracted the more radical, often younger, members of *NS*, who wanted to be part of a new Europe. While NS was a Norwegian nationalist party, the *GSSN* advocated a pan-Germanic policy which would have seen Norway become Germany's partner in a union of Nordic states. Although *GSSN* members were simultaneously *NS* members, the *GSSN* was often in conflict with the *NS* leadership, which was seen as too old fashioned. Men such as Imerslund found themselves at home in the *GSSN*, though ultimately fewer than 2,000 Norwegians ever joined.

Meanwhile, the *Nordland* Regiment of the *Waffen-SS* had already been established on 20 April 1940 (Hitler's birthday), well before the end of hostilities in Norway. Norwegian volunteers were initially few, since the *NS* was busy consolidating its power. On 12 January 1941, however, a Quisling speech was broadcast in which he called for volunteers. Several hundred men answered, though most would not complete training and did not join *Wiking* in Ukraine until the summer and autumn of 1941. As mentioned elsewhere, only 294 Norwegians were with *Wiking* at the start of the Eastern campaign on 22 June 1941.

The invasion of the USSR changed the recruiting situation. On 29 June, Terboven gave a speech announcing the creation of a Norwegian Legion to fight against the Soviets in Finland. Enthusiasm for this formation was high, with thousands of Norwegians quickly volunteering. The Norwegian Legion was planned to take the form of an infantry regiment, and several hundred professional officers who did not support *NS* offered their services. The enthusiasm dampened as it became clear that the legion would fight in German uniform, instead of in Norwegian or Finnish attire. It was to be administered by the *Waffen-SS*, in common with the other Germanic legions, and many Norwegians wanted nothing to do with the *SS*.

Since the German advance into the USSR was progessing well, the Norwegian volunteers for the legion were allowed to initially sign on for a three-month trial term of duty. It was anticipated that the war in the east would soon be over, so this was considered sufficient. After the disappointments concerning the uniforms and *SS* association, two further events caused many volunteers to not renew their contracts. It became clear that the Germans intended to use the Norwegian Legion near Leningrad alongside the Dutch and Flemish Legions, and after 7 December 1941, the United States joined the war.

After the departure or non-enlistment of thousands of volunteers, the Norwegian Legion could only form a reinforced infantry battalion. This received the honor title *"Viken,"* which was to have been the title of the first of the three intended infantry battalions. The others would have been *"Gula"* and *"Frosta."* The composition was almost entirely Norwegian, aside from a few German liaison officers. Most of the volunteers were *NS* members, and since *NS* drew support primarily from military families, the legion had sufficient Norwegian officers. Ragnar Berg had helped form the *GSSN*, and most of the early members of that organization found their way into the 4th Company of the legion, which he commanded. Charles Westberg who was, like Berg, a Norwegian Army officer and *NS* member, commanded the company's first platoon.

Norwegian Army Colonel Finn Hannibal Kjelstrup was at first to command the regiment-sized Norwegian Legion, but he resigned at the end of November 1941. His son, Sverre, remained in service, and eventually became an officer. *Viken* Battalion commander *Major* Jörgen Bakke replaced Kjelstrup, but he could not get along with the Germans or his fellow Norwegians, and he soon resigned as well. At the end of 1941, the command of the Norwegian Legion, at battalion size, finally resided with Norwegian Army Captain of Cavalry Arthur Qvist. He was a firm member of *NS*, but refused to actively politicize the unit, despite the wishes of some of his officers. Not withstanding this, Qvist was a popular commander, and held the respect of Norwegians and Germans.

The Norwegian Legion was ready for combat by the beginning of 1942, but a shortage of transportation meant that its 1,218 men had to wait another month before being assigned to positions along the seige lines outside of Leningrad. The German strength in this area had decreased, as many units were sent east to deal with the crisis on the Volkhov River. The Norwegians had to defend against attacks coming out of the city during March. Westberg became the first officer fatality on 19 March, when his command bunker took a direct hit during an artillery barrage.

The Norwegian Legion shifted positions during April 1942 and needed intelligence about the enemy situation in its new sector. Berg led a trench raid for this purpose in the predawn hours of 16 April. Despite careful preparation, the assault was caught in a minefield, then shot up by Soviet artillery. Berg and seven of his men were killed, and most of the rest were wounded. This was a black day for the Norwegian Legion, and Berg became a martyr for the combat veterans and the *GSSN*.

The Norwegian Legion reorganized during May 1942 after suffering many wounded and sick losses. It was soon back in action on the

Leningrad siege lines, which at this stage were "quiet." Combat amounted primarily to artillery duels and trench raids. New recruits arrived, and most were from the *NS*-run Labor Service. Since many were fairly young, they were concentrated in the 1st Company, in which Östring commanded a platoon. The company commander was the *GSSN* officer Olaf Lindvig.

Since the Norwegian sector remained quiet, the anti-tank guns of the 14th Company were sent wherever they were needed in the Leningrad sector. On 20 July 1942, a heavy attack penetrated the positions of a Latvian *Schuma* (auxilliary police) unit, and the platoon of Arnfinn Vik was sent there. In heavy fighting, Vik and his gunners successfully delayed the Soviet advance until counterattacks restored the front.

On 3 September 3, Lie arrived in the legion sector with the 1st Norwegian Police Company, which he had raised from volunteers within the forces under his command. These men proved a welcome addition, and fought alongside the legion into the following spring. By early 1943, Lie had taken temporary command of the legion from Quist, who was back in Norway.

A Norwegian survivor of the disastrous trench raid led by Ragnar Berg on 16 April 1942. A nurse shows off his Iron Cross 2d class, and a portrait of Vidkun Quisling is visible behind her right hand. (Jervas)

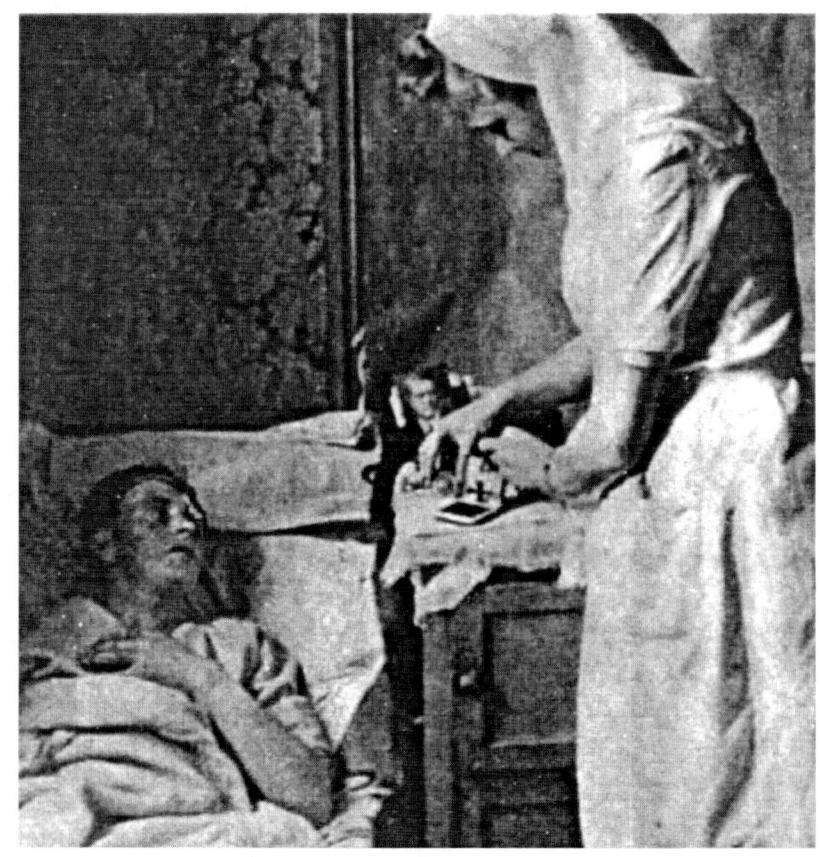

The Norwegian Legion was withdrawn from the front lines for a few days at the end of November 1942, but quickly had to return to combat on 3 December to eliminate a breakthrough in the zone of the Dutch Legion. After heavy fighting, the front settled down again, but attrition had reduced the strength of the Norwegian Legion to only 700 officers and men by the end of 1942.

While the main Norwegian positions remained free of major enemy attacks, the 14th Company did see heavy fighting. During the Second Battle of Lake Ladoga in February 1943, it supported the Spanish Blue Division near Krasny Bor, to the east of Leningrad. This was the area in which the Flemish Legion would be nearly destroyed a month later. The Norwegian anti-tank gunners were officially commended by Himmler for their achievements.

The Norwegian Legion and 1st Police Company were relieved from the front and prepared for transport back to Norway at the beginning of March 1943. The Norwegians received another commendation, this time from Fritz von Scholz, who had commanded the legion as part of the 2d *SS*-Infantry Brigade. Von Scholz was well acquainted with Norwegian volunteers after previously commanding the *Nordland* Regiment in the *Wiking* Division, and he would serve with them again a few months later as commander of the new *Nordland* Division.

The Norwegian Legion had suffered only 158 men killed during just over a year of frontline service. This was a remarkably small percentage in comparison with the other volunteer legions and the Norwegians in *Wiking*, but future Norwegian formations would not be so lucky. The Legion survivors received two weeks of home leave in Norway during May 1943, though those who signed on for the new Regiment *Norge* received their leave sooner. The legion was then dissolved in a ceremony in Oslo. The volunteers for *Norge* had already been shipped to Bavaria, where the *Nordland* Division was organizing. The new Norwegian *SS*-Panzer-Grenadier Regiment *Norge* ("Norway") organized at Grafenwöhr.

Already during the history of the Norwegian Legion, many volunteers had decided not to renew their enlistments when they expired. Of the 700 men who served to the end, only about 300 made their way into Regiment *Norge*. The others left German military service or transferred into the newly-raised Norwegian *SS*-Ski Battalion. Through the spring of 1943, around 800 Norwegians had served with *Wiking* (and a handful in other units), but because of casualties and expired enlistments, only 250 Norwegians from *Wiking* joined *Regiment Norge*. The *GSSN* contributed 160 new volunteers, and most of these men went into the new regiment's 1st Company, commanded by Lindvig. New recruits trickled in during the summer and autumn, but by late 1943, the *Nordland* Division counted only 810 Norwegians (300 ex-legionnaires, 250 *Wiking* veterans, 160 *GSSN* volunteers, and 100 new recruits). Quisling had hoped that 3,000 Norwegians would volunteer for *Norge*.

While the Norwegian Legion included only individual German liaison officers, *Regiment Norge* required the addition of a great many Germans and ethnic Germans to reach full strength. Fortunately, the officers and NCOs of the old *Nordland* Regiment were highly competent. The first commander of *Norge* was Wolfgang Joerchel, but he soon left to take command of a Dutch regiment. Arnold Stoffers, who had been with *Wiking* from its formation, replaced him. Fritz Vogt, who had been one of the first men in the *Waffen-SS* to win the Knight's Cross back in 1940, commanded the 1st Battalion, while *Nordland* Regiment veterans Albrecht Krügel and Hanns-Heinrich Lohmann commanded the 2d and 3d Battalions. All of these men held the German Cross in Gold. Norwegian officers were well represented at the company and platoon level, with other Norwegians serving in other parts of the *Nordland* Division. Additional Norwegians would join *Regiment Norge* in the spring of 1944, after completing officer training courses.

Regiment Norge suffered heavy losses during the retreat from Oranienbaum to the Luga River, then to Narva during January 1944. Lohmann was wounded during the last stage of the withdrawal, and did not return to combat until early November, when he assumed command of a *SS*-De Ruyter in Kurland. He was awarded the Knight's Cross on 12 March 1944 for his men's distinguished conduct during their first combat. Krügel received the same award on the same day for his role in a successful attack on a Soviet bridgehead across the Narva River north of the town of Narva during mid-February. He later succeeded the mortally-wounded *Graf* von Westphalen as commander of *Regiment Danmark*.

Regiment Norge fought in separated combat groups during the February and March struggle around Narva. While Krügel led part of the regiment as described, Stoffers led other elements to the southwest of Narva, where two Soviet positions threatened the Narva supply lines. He was killed in action on 25 February personally leading an attack on one of these, known as the "West Sack." This failed, but the West and East sacks were both eventually reduced to the point they no longer presented threats. Stoffers was posthumously awarded the Knight's Cross on the same day as Lohmann and Krügel. Fritz Knöchlein, whose name was associated with the Le Paradis incident in 1940, replaced him.

After the Narva zone settled down, *Regiment Norge* reorganized. The cadre of the 1st Battalion left for Germany to reorganize, with most survivors reassigned to 3d Battalion. Vogt briefly took command of 3d Battalion, but the typhus he had first contracted outside Moscow recurred, and he was evacuated for recovery. Josef Bachmeier took over the 2d Battalion and Martin Gürz replaced Vogt. Most of *Norge*'s replacements were former members of the *Luftwaffe* Field Divisions destroyed at Oranienbaum, and the Norwegian character of the unit, not strong to begin with, was diluted. After recovering briefly during the late spring through the addition of recovered wounded, it would only diminish as the war continued.

Regiment Norge suffered heavy losses again on the Tannenberg Line, outside Riga, and in Kurland. Bachmeier was awarded the Knight's Cross after being wounded at Grenadier Hill. He was succeeded by *Nordland* Regiment veteran and German Cross in Gold holder, Richard Spörle. Gürz was mortally wounded near Riga, and posthumously awarded the Knight's Cross. Killed at about the same time was 11th Company commander, Peter Thomas Sandborg, an original *GSSN* member, and a respected judge. *Norge* successfully held its positions during the Second Battle of Kurland, and Knöchlein and Spörle both earned the Knight's Cross for this, as did German NCO Siegfried Lüngen. Another German, 7th Company commander Willy Hund, received the Honor Roll Clasp.

Knöchlein was not well liked by his men, and he was replaced by *Wiking* veteran Wilhelm Körbel when *Regiment Norge* arrived in Pomerania in early February 1945. The regiment was now mostly German in composition. Hund distinguished himself again at Altdamm, and was awarded the Knight's Cross at the end of the war, as was the regimental adjutant Walter Körner, who had died of wounds in Pomerania.

Only a handful of Norwegians remained in *Regiment Norge* by the end of the war. Lage Sögaard and Kasper Sivesind were in 12th Company until the end, and they succeeded in escaping from Berlin on 2 May 1945. In the confusion of the Berlin fighting, it wasn't noted until decades later that Körner had been wounded and gone missing in action (dying in a field hospital away from his men). He had earned the German Cross in Gold as commander of *Norge*'s 8th Company during the spring of 1944. Spörle was killed in action east of Berlin, and Körbel badly wounded. The last remnants of *Norge* were led by Rudolf Ternedde in a combat group with the remnants of *Danmark*.

A few Norwegians remained in *Wiking* after the spring of 1943, mostly as officers and NCOs. Three Norwegian NCOs were awarded the Iron Cross 1st Class after the breakout from Cherkassy: Alf Fjeld and Helge Tollefsen from *Germania*, and Inge Martin Bakken from *Westland*. Haakon Sundberg was wounded outside Warsaw as an officer with the 3d Company of *Germania*. Arne Gunnar Smith had been one of the first volunteers for Regiment *Nordland* in early 1941. After completing officer training in the spring of 1944, he was sent to *Wiking* and assigned to command a platoon in the 7th Company of *Germania*. The decision was deliberate, as 7th Company was commanded by another early Norwegian volunteer, *GSSN* officer Fredrik Jensen. When Jensen was wounded outside Warsaw on 10 August, Smith succeeded him, but was killed in action only five days later. Jensen never returned to combat, but

Fredrik Jensen, the most highly decorated Norwegian volunteer in the *Waffen-SS*. He won the German Cross in Gold on 7 December 1944 as the commander of 7th Company of *SS-Germania*. This photo shows him in *Waffen-SS* uniform, though he also was an officer in the *GSSN* (Norwegian version of the *Allgemeine-SS*). (Brenden)

while he was recovering from his wounds at home in Norway, he became the most highly-decorated Norwegian veteran in the *Waffen-SS*. His award of the German Cross in Gold on 8 December 1944 reflected his more than three years of distinguished service.

By this time, additional Norwegians had come to *Wiking* in the ranks of the reformed 1st Battalion of *Regiment Norge*. Fritz Vogt had created the battalion in Germany during the summer of 1944 from young German conscripts, ethnic Germans, and German Navy men who had been assigned to the *Waffen-SS*. The unit was almost entirely German, but gradually some Norwegian officers and NCOs were added from recovered wounded men from other units. When the reformed 1st Battalions of *Norge* and *Danmark* joined *Wiking* north of Warsaw in early November, the *Norge* Battalion (as it was known) included 40 Norwegians among its 600 men.

Vogt got along very well with his Norwegian soldiers in the old and the new 1st Battalion of *Norge*. For the reformed unit, he had several of his former men assigned to him. This included his personal radio man Alf Guttorm Johnsen, and *Nordland* Regiment veteran Sverre Larsen. "*Nahkampf*" Larsen, nicknamed for his close combat proficiency, had served as Vogt's driver until losing an arm in combat during the retreat from Oranienbaum.

Norge was heavily engaged in repelling a Soviet attack on Christmas Day 1944, during which 19-year-old Norwegian officer Karl Aagard Östvig was killed. His Norwegian father and Hungarian mother were famous opera singers.

The *Norge* Battalion travelled with *Wiking* to Hungary at the end of 1944, and operated with *SS*-Panzer Regiment 5 during Operation KONRAD I in early January 1945. This drive towards Budapest stalled around Bieske, and the two units were surrounded at the Hegeyks estate for a week before breaking out. The reduced *Norge* Battalion next participated in KONRAD III, the attempt to relieve Budapest from the south. As IV *SS*-Panzer Corps advanced towards the Vali River, the *Norge* Battalion captured Pettend on 24 January, and had to defend the village the next day. If Pettend fell, the entire left flank of the corps would be torn open, so Vogt led his men in desperate combat against 180 Soviet tanks. He personally knocked out six with *Panzerfaust* rockets. Most of the battalion had become casualties by the time Pettend was abandoned on 28 January. The unit's Norwegian surgeon, Dr. Tor Storm, remained behind with the wounded, who could not be evacuated. During a 1988 visit to Pettend, veterans learned from Hungarian civilians that Storm and the wounded were burned alive in a wine cellar by the Soviets after their capture. *GSSN* officer and Norwegian Legion veteran Fritjof Rössnaes was also killed at Pettend. His family had helped found *NS* back in 1933, and when he was fighting at Pettend, his older brother, Knut, was serving nearby as an officer in *SS*-Panzer Artillery Regiment 5.

The *Norge* Battalion joined the IV *SS*-Panzer Corps retreat after the breakout from Pettend. On 3 February 1945, the German officer Heinz Fechner was killed in action. He had earned the German Cross in Gold with *Regiment Norge* at Narva. The battalion was down to a strength of only 100 men when it defended alongside the *Danmark* Battalion on 15 February. *Danmark* was destroyed in this fighting, and not reconstituted. By the 19 February, the *Norge* Battalion was down to 36 officers and men.

Recovered wounded were added to ex-*Luftwaffe* and German Navy replacements, so that the *Norge* Battalion numbered 250 men by the beginning of March. Vogt left to take over *SS*-Armored Reconnaissance Battalion 5, and one of the last Norwegian officers in the unit, Oskar Stömsnes, was killed in action on 19 March. He had fought the Germans in 1940 and then been an early *Waffen-SS* volunteer. Vogt was awarded the Oakleaves to his Knight's Cross on 30 March 1945 for his bravery at Pettend. Two days later, he was fatally wounded by a strafing airplane. *Wiking* commander Karl Ullrich placed his own Oakleaves around

Vogt's neck, so that he could die wearing them. The remnants of the *Norge* Battalion surrendered to American forces with the rest of *Wiking* at the end of the war.

A rift developed within the NS movement during the war. Quisling and the higher leadership of the party drew away from their previous policy of collaboration as it became clear that the German foreign ministry intended to treat Norway as a conquered colony. Quisling also was upset over the lack of acceptance of his proposal, first made in 1940, that the Norwegian volunteers in the German military form the base of a new Norwegian Army.

Meanwhile, the GSSN developed ties with the German SS leadership, a group that often pursued a different policy than that of the foreign ministry. The SS was planning for an eventual alliance of Germanic states, and the GSSN saw a future for themselves in such a situation. Many in the GSSN, including Imerslund, were openly critical of both the NS leadership and the non-SS German authorities. To them, the NS represented the same old-fashioned political right of the past, a group that was too Norwegian-centric, placing the good of Norway ahead of that of Europe as a whole. This pan-Germanic vision was especially attractive to young, idealistic members of the NS, who often joined the GSSN.

Gust Jonassen did not join the GSSN. As Sports Leader of the NSUF, however, he had considerable influence over young men who were home in Norway while their friends and brothers were in the Norwegian Legion or *Wiking*. Jonassen was an expert skier, and during the summer of 1942, he received permission to raise a "youth company" for ski patrol duty alongside the *Nord* Division in Finland. The German authorities allowed this second unit to form in order to mollify the NS elements that were upset that the Norwegian Legion was not sent to Finland. The unit quickly received enough volunteers, and went to Germany to train at the Germanic Camp at Sennheim, Alsace, where Finnish volunteer Jouka Itälä was the principal instructor. Classified as a Police unit, it next moved to the German Police Instructional School at Hallerau, where ski techniques were practiced, despite a lack of snow. The Norwegian Police Ski Company arrived in Karelia during March 1943, and soon proved a valuable addition.

Jonassen was killed on 26 May 1943 when he stepped on a mine. During July of that year, the unit received home leave, and the service contracts of many of the young volunteers expired. Most would reenlist, and with new volunteers, the Norwegian skiers later reassembled in Finland. Many Norwegians were eager to join this unit, which was almost entirely Norwegian and fought in Finland. Enough volunteers were available to form a small battalion, and additional Norwegians transferred in from *Regiment Norge*. The expanded company became known as the SS-Ski Battalion *"Norge"* and most of its 450 or so men were young members of the NSUF and GSSN. As mentioned previously,

Danish-born Gust Jonassen as commander of the Norwegian Ski Company in Karelia during the spring of 1943. He was killed soon after this, on 26 May, when he stepped on a mine. (Natedal)

existence of this second Norwegian unit is main reason the *Nordland* Division always included fewer Norwegians than Danes.

The Ski Battalion *Norge* trained in Finland, and joined the *Nord* Division for combat duty during January 1944. It consisted of a headquarters company and three infantry companies. As a patrol unit, it lacked a heavy weapons company. Command at first was given to German officer and German Cross in Gold holder Richard Benner, but it soon passed to Norwegian Army veteran Frode Halle.

At the front, the Norwegian battalion was misused to hold static positions. The *SS-Nord* Division had been assigned to defend a sector far too large to be able to cover it continuously, so much of the front was covered by patrols ranging between strongpoints; in any case, every available man was needed for the defense. The Norwegians dug in on Hasselmann and Kaprolat hills, which dominated the largely-flat countryside. The German commander of the 3d Company, Fritz Grond, was wounded early in the year, and Arnfinn Vik, now an officer, took over. When Vik was wounded in early April, Norwegian Army officer and *GSSN* member Axel Steen transferred in from the *Nord* Division. With Vik and then Steen heading 3d Company, all of the command positions in the battalion were held by Norwegians.

The 1st Company, under Norwegian Legion veteran Sophus Kahrs, had been in reserve, but during April 1944, it had to take over defensive positions of its own. These were vacated by the Norwegian 2d Police Company, which had served in Finland for six months. As with Lie's 1st Police Company, it consisted of members of the Norwegian police who volunteered for front service. The 2d Police Company was formed by Norwegian Army officer Egil Hoel, but as he was an engineering specialist, he was soon reassigned to the staff of the III (Germanic) *SS-Panzer Corps*.

By mid-June 1944, all signs pointed toward an imminent Soviet offensive against the sector being defended by *SS-Nord*, namely the "Road Postion" along the Kiestinki-Louhi Corridor. Despite this, many members of the Norwegian battalion had been sent home to Norway on leave, so the battalion was considerably understrength (with only perhaps 200 men present) by late June 1944. Part of the expected attack struck the *SS*-Ski Battalion *Norge* on 25 June, when the 3d Company was overrun on Kaprolat Hill. Steen was wounded, and shot himself in the command bunker, as did *SS-Standarten-Oberjunker* Birger Ernst Jonsson. Officers Rolf Walström and Tor Torjussen were killed in action, the latter just days after his twentieth birthday. Torjussen had served with *Wiking* during 1941 at the age of 17, and had only recently graduated from Bad Tölz. His classmate, Kaare Börsting, led the survivors of 3d Company south to 2d Company's positions on Hasselmann Hill. Only 57 men had defended Kaprolat Hill, but Soviet reports indicate that a Soviet Army battalion was reduced from 400 fit for duty to only 36 during the fighting.

Hasselmann Hill was struck the next day, and Börsting died when his stick grenade detonated before he released it. Hasselmann Hill was also overrun, and the President of the Norwegian Sporting Association, Sverre Andersen Österdal, was killed in action as a platoon commander in 2d Company. Most of the survivors of 2d and 3d Companies were captured, with only a few men men escaping through the woods to report the disaster suffered by their units. Norwegian researchers believe that 135 men from the battalion died at Kaprolat and Hasselmann Hills, with another 40 captured. Only 15 of these men ever returned to Norway.

The *Nord* Division was hard pressed by this Soviet offensive, and could send no help to the Norwegians. The 1st Company distinguished itself during the June and July fighting, and commander Sophus Kahrs earned the Iron Cross 1st Class. By 18 July, the Soviet offensive wound down, and the Norwegian battalion was able to reorganize. Since the autumn of 1943, approximately 200 Norwegians had been killed in action, most of which were killed at the end of June 1944, with many more wounded. The battalion's strength finally rose as recovered wounded and the 150 on leave returned. Fifty new volunteers arrived, along with the 3d *SS* and Police Company. (The title had "*SS*" added to attract members of the *GSSN* in addition to active police officers. Despite this, the company had only three *GSSN* members.)

The situation for the reformed *SS*-Ski Battalion *Norge* changed drastically when Finland concluded a separate armistice with the Soviet Union and withdrew from the war in late September 1944. Now the Norwegians had lost their reason for service and, tragically, they even fought isolated skirmishes with Finnish troops as the German forces marched 1,000 kilometers across Lapland to Norwegian territory. Back in Norway during December 1944, several Norwegian officers left for Germany to join *Regiment Norge*. Egil Hoel took command of the battalion after Halle refused to agree to lead his men against the Norwegian resistance. The ski battalion transformed into a motorized police force which would act in the event of an attempted Communist coup in Norway. At the same time, the 3d *SS* and Police Company served in northern Norway with German forces that guarded against a Soviet invasion.

During the spring of 1945, the contract of the 3d *SS* and Police Company expired. Lie and the leadership of the *GSSN* and *NS* did not realize just how close the war was to ending, and Lie solicited volunteers for a 4th *SS* and Police Company, to replace the 3d in northern Norway. The war ended before it could fully form. Only a few members of the former ski battalion were caught up in anti-resistance operations during the last weeks of the war, with most successfully avoiding such service.

After the war, the restored Norwegian government dealt harshly with collaborators, including the 6,000 who served in the German military. No one was executed solely for military service. Jonas Lie shot himself, while Sverre Riisnaes was committed to a mental institution. Per Immerslund had died of wounds suffered while serving with the *Nord* Division as a *Waffen-SS* war reporter, otherwise he would have been prosecuted. Hoel and Halle and other high-ranking soldiers received long prison sentences, though few Norwegian veterans actually spent more than three to five years behind bars. Some Norwegians in Soviet hands were not released until 1955, but most Norwegians in Allied captivity were returned to Norway by 1947.

The Norwegian Axis veterans were outcasts in Norway, but eventually could rebuild their lives, providing they kept quiet about the past. Olaf Lindvig, in fact, was something of a celebrity 50 years after the war, often in demand by various media outlets for his politically incorrect viewpoint. Frode Halle and other veterans wrote memoirs and accounts of service and Björn Östring helped to found the Institute for the History of the Norwegian Occupation (INO). Through the efforts of the INO, much material has been preserved so that future generations of Norwegians will be able to study the military and political collaboration in Norway during the World War II era.

Sweden

Many Swedes were alarmed by the Soviet invasion of Finland during November 1939. They considered Finland, with its substantial Swedish minority, a brother country. "For the honor of Sweden and the freedom of the North" became the recruiting cry to attract volunteers to fight alongside the Finnish Army. Up to 30,000 men attempted to volunteer, but the strength of the *SFK* (the Swedish Volunteer Force) was limited by the Swedish government to 10,000 men. Ultimately, 12,705 volunteers were taken in, and those accepted for service amounted to 8,260 Swedes and 727 Norwegians. Another 500 Swedes enlisted directly in the Finnish Army. These numbers demonstrated that anti-Communist feelings ran strongly in some of the Swedish population, even though the government maintained a strict policy of neutrality.

After the Winter War ended during March 1940, the Swedes gradually returned home. Many of the Norwegians with them were still in Sweden when word arrived of the German invasion of Norway and Denmark. Several hundred Norwegians and Swedes from the *SFK* immediately rushed to Norway, where they battled this new threat to Scandinavia in the Narvik area. Several were killed, but many of the survivors considered the Soviets the greater danger, and some of these men enlisted in the *Waffen-SS* the next year.

National Socialism and similar movements were not popular in Sweden, but small political movements did arise during the troubled economic times of the 1930s. Gösta Borg was a leader in Sven-Olov Lindholm's Swedish National Socialists Party (*NSAP*), which was very pro-German. The Swedish National Federation (SNF) was more successful. To create a more patriotic image, the *NSAP* changed its name to the Swedish Socialist Union (*SSS*) in 1938, after which its membership eventually rose to 5,000. These parties both made substantial contributions to the manpower of the volunteer forces in Finland, with 650 coming from the *SSS*.

A dozen or more of the most pro-German Swedes made their way to Germany during late 1940 and early the next year to join the *Waffen-SS*. This included Borg, who fought with the *Westland* Regiment from late 1941. Several other Swedes were assigned to the *Der Führer* Regiment, before the logical decision was made to concentrate the Swedes in *Wiking*, where they could serve alongside Danes and Norwegians.

With the German invasion of the USSR on 22 June 1941, additional Swedes began to enlist in the *Waffen-SS*, usually by crossing into Norway and volunteering at Oslo. Others, from the south of the country, enlisted in Copenhagen. Several actually joined the *Frikorps Danmark*, including Hans-Gösta Perhsson. He had lived in Denmark before the war, and was a member of the DNSAP as well as the *SSS*.

Swedish volunteer Bo Wikström displays his Iron Cross 2d class, Infantry Assault Badge, and *SS-Germania* cuff-title. (Rundkvist)

Back in Sweden, a volunteer battalion was established to continue the tradition of the *SFK* from the Winter War. It included many men who had volunteered to help Finland for a second time, and who came from a variety of political backgrounds. This unit fought beside the Finnish forces laying siege to the port of Hanko, which had been ceded to the Soviets after the Winter War. When the siege concluded successfully, much of the battalion enlisted in the Finnish Army, but most of the *SSS* and *SNF* members opted to join the *Waffen-SS*.

These men served primarily in *Wiking*, bolstering the number of Swedes so that at least 50 had passed through the division by the spring of 1943. Roughly 75 percent of the Swedes who joined the *Waffen-SS* during the war were veterans of service in Finland, with the rest primarily consisting of men too young to have fought during 1939–1941. Thousands of Swedes continued to serve in the Finnish Army throughout the war, and individuals left or deserted to join the *Waffen-SS*. These included Johann Westrin, who became engaged to a German woman, and Arvid S. Harry Gauffin, who had been a Finnish Army lieutenant, but who was killed in action as a private in the Norwegian *SS*-Ski Battalion.

During 1941, the Swedish government was secretly interested in having Swedish professional soldiers serve with the German military as guest officers to observe and learn new military techniques. This idea never bore fruit, but many Swedish officers were initially interested in fighting with the Germans as a means of professional advancement. As with the many Danish soldiers who joined the *Waffen-SS*, these Swedes would also have been professing their anti-Communist beliefs. Their enthusiasm quickly dampened, however, as they realized that the Germans were not granting Swedes rank equivalent to that they held in Sweden or Finland.

The Swedish Army was highly outmoded and weakened by defense cuts during the 1920s and 1930s. Swedish officers were considered by the Germans to require considerable retraining before being commissioned. This caused most Swedish professionals with pro-German feelings to fight instead in Finland, where they could acquire command positions with greater ease.

Still, a number of Swedes were granted officer ranks by the *Waffen-SS*, usually after taking familiarization courses (the so-called "Courses for Germanic Officers," which were for men with command experience, and were distinct from "Officer-Cadet Courses" which instructed men who had not previously held leadership positions). Another 15 to 20 became *Waffen-SS* officers after attending the *SS*-Officer Training School at Bad Tölz. Wolfgang Eld-Albitz graduated first in his class for the 11th Shortened Wartime Course, and was promoted directly to *SS-Untersturmführer*.

Swedes in the *Waffen-SS* also had more than their share of war correspondents, probably because the Germans hoped to positively influence Swedish public opinion towards Germany. Thorolf Hillblad had covered the *SS-LAH* as early as 1941, and Hans-Caspar Krüger was with *SS*-Panzer Battalion 5 during 1943. Swedish anti-aircraft gunnery specialist Carl Svensson became a reporter after his graduation from Bad Tölz, as did Gösta Borg.

With the creation of the III (Germanic) *SS*-Panzer Corps, the *Waffen-SS* High Command decided to concentrate the Swedes into one unit. All available Swedes, including some new recruits, were sent to the *SS*-Armored Reconnaissance Battalion 11, which became the most international unit of the *Waffen-SS*. This battalion, based on a cadre from *Wiking*, was formed around ethnic German enlisted men and German officers. They were supplemented by enlisted men from every Germanic country, and many Germanic officers. Approximately 40 Swedes formed the 4th (heavy) Platoon of the 3d (armored) Company. They crewed heavy machine guns and mortars mounted on armored personnel carriers. Additional Swedes, including Estonian ethnic Swedes, were found throughout the company, and, to a lesser extent, throughout the battalion. Further, Swedes trickled into *Nordland* and its armored reconnaissance battalion, but casualties and desertions gradually reduced the number present. At least 75 Swedes are believed to have served in *Nordland* at one point or another.

The Estonian ethnic Swedes mentioned above came from the 6,000-strong ethnic Swedish community found among Estonia's coastal islands. This tiny minority had long received special treatment, first from the Czarist Russians, and then from the Estonian government. During 1942, the Swedish *Waffen-SS* officer Sven Ryden had visited the ethnic Swedes, and convinced 50 to 60 to join the *Waffen-SS*. They were treated in the same manner as Swedish citizens, and considered Germanics, though a handful of ethnic Swedes who served in the Estonian 20th *Waffen*-Grenadier Division of the *SS* were considered Estonians. The first 30 ethnic Swedish volunteers were placed in a training group commanded by the Finnish *SS* officer Jouka Itälä, who spoke Swedish fluently and eased their transition to German military life.

Almost all of the Estonian ethnic Swedes in the *Waffen-SS* served in *SS*-Armored Reconnaissance Battalion 11, and they suffered heavy casualties along with every other nationality present. The ethnic Swedes could at least take some small satisfaction in not needing to worry about their families, as the German and Swedish governments cooperated to evacuate the ethnic Swedish community of Estonia to Sweden during 1944, before the Soviets could overrun the area. The ethnic Swedish volunteers who survived the war and avoided Soviet captivity usually settled in Sweden after the war.

SS-Armored Reconnaissance Battalion 11 was one of the most mobile, yet also most heavily-armed units in the III (Germanic) *SS*-Panzer Corps. As such, it was often used to provide rear guard screens during withdrawals, or to plug sudden gaps in defensive positions. The battalion covered the retreat of the corps from the Oranienbaum front during January 1944, and the first commander of the Swedish 4th Platoon, Walter Nilsson, was killed in action on 25 January. The Swedish *SS-Wiking* veteran had been very popular with his comrades, but his successor, Hans-Gösta Pehrsson, soon proved his worth.

Later in the year, the German commander of the 3d Company, Kaiser, was killed in action. Pehrsson took command of the company, which had become known as the "Swedish Company," despite being far from completely Swedish (and ethnic Swedish) in composition. Other Swedish officers commanded platoons in this unit, including Gunnar-Erik Eklöf, Heino Meyer, and Rune Ahlgren. The latter had left the Swedish Military Academy at Karlberg before completing his studies. He was killed in action with the battalion's 2d Company during the

Second Battle of Kurland, while carrying one his wounded men to safety. One source states that Ahlgren's name was added to a memorial plaque for Karlberg cadets killed in action, but only after serious debate about the merits of including an *SS* man.

Meyer and Eklöf commanded the 3d Company for brief periods when Pehrsson was absent due to wounds. The heavy casualties incurred during the retreat to Narva and the ensuing defensive operations there disheartened many Swedish volunteers. Unlike the Danes, Norwegians, Dutch, and Flemings serving alongside them, they did not have to fear any sort of retribution once they got home, and this convinced many to desert. Pehrsson was sympathetic toward those who wanted out of the *Waffen-SS*, and he aided the efforts of some to cross the Baltic to Sweden.

When the Germans evacuated Estonia during September 1944, the armored personnel carrier of *Wiking* veterans Sven Alm, Ingemar Johansson, and Markus Ledin broke down on the retreat route (though it is also claimed that they deliberately were deserting). They fixed the vehicle under cover, and then drove at night behind Soviet lines to the Baltic coast. Here they found a fishing boat to take them across the Baltic. They landed in Finland, and were apprehended by Finnish authorities. The Finns had just concluded their armistice with the USSR, and were turning over stray German soldiers to the Soviets. This almost happened to the three Swedes, but Ledin showed his medals from the Winter War, and convinced the Finns to let them "escape" to Sweden. Other Swedish volunteers may have had similar adventures.

Pehrsson remained the commander of the 3d Company. During the Second Battle of Kurland, he was sent with a small group of his men to plug a gap in the *Nordland* Division lines at Trekni, south of Preekuln. The position was held in heavy fighting for a week at the end of October 1944, and when it was almost overrun, Pehrsson counterattacked with twelve men and restored the situation. For his determination, Pehrsson was awarded the Honor Roll Clasp on 25 December 1944, becoming the most-highly-decorated Swede in the *Waffen-SS*.

Few Swedes and ethnic Swedes remained in *SS*-Armored Reconnaissance Battalion 11 after the bloody Kurland fighting. The unit suffered further heavy losses in Pomerania, and the 3d Company was nearly destroyed east of Berlin during late April 1945. Pehrsson had become *Nordland*'s Intelligence Officer (Ic) in Pomerania, but in Berlin at the end of April, he reassumed command of the 3d Company. Its last few armored personnel carriers became a divisional reserve, and Pehrsson's command vehicle was knocked out on 1 May. His driver, Swedish Army and *Wiking* veteran Ragnar Johansson, was killed. Pehrsson and Erik "Jerka" Wallin first hid in the Swedish embassy, and then in an apartment, and were fortunate to be able to escape to Sweden two months later. Almost all of the other Swedes still with the battalion were killed in action or went into Soviet captivity.

An additional 15 to 20 Swedes served with *Wiking* after the spring of 1943. They were assigned randomly to various sub-units and most became casualties by the end of the war. A few more Swedes served elsewhere, such as Sven Erik Olsson (who had a Swedish father, but was raised as a Baltic-German in Estonia), who was the personal radioman for Frundsberg Division commanding general Heinz Harmel during 1944. Olsson was proposed for the German Cross in Gold, which Harmel later claimed was approved. Per Sigurd Baecklund graduated from Bad Tölz and became the adjutant to *SS*-Panzer Battalion 11 "Hermann von Salza" commander Paul-Albert "Peter" Kausch. He later served with *Nordland*'s training and replacement battalion in Austria, and was able to go into American captivity at the end of the war.

Many Swedish and Estonian-Swedish volunteers were badly wounded during the war. Those unfit for further service were sent home to Sweden. As mentioned above, others deserted or otherwise made their way home. Those such as Baecklund who were able to avoid Soviet captivity were sent back to Sweden during the summer of 1945. There, only those who had deserted from the Swedish military were punished. The rest were reintegrated into Swedish society, including a few soldiers who had joined the German military with permission.

The surviving Swedish *Waffen-SS* volunteers were bitter that their sacrifices, which had often begun in 1939, had been in vain. The Estonian ethnic Swedes were naturally sad at the loss of their homes, but thankful for the survival of their families. With the Allies victorious, the Europe of 1945 seemed unpleasant to many Swedish *SS* veterans, and a number followed Hans-Caspar Krüger to South America, where they could again experience "Germanic camaraderie" with other Waffen-*SS* veterans who had fled there. Erik Wallin initially remained in Sweden, where he related his experiences during the last months of the war to Thorolf Hillblad. Wallin's account, as told to Hillblad, was published in Sweden before the end of 1945 as *"Ragnarök,"* which in Norse mythology is the end of the human and divine worlds, preceded by a massive battle between the forces of good and evil. This work became an important research tool for the study of the Swedish *Waffen-SS* volunteers.

Swedish researchers estimate that 250 Swedish citizens served in the *Waffen-SS* during World War II, with 45 dying from combat or in Soviet captivity. They believe that 10 to 15 times that number might have joined had Finland not accepted volunteers into its army. Those that did join the *Waffen-SS* were primarily the most devoted National Socialists, who believed they were shaping the future of Europe. In the end, they amounted to merely a footnote in history.

Switzerland and Liechtenstein

Switzerland has a predominantly German-speaking population, and Liechtenstein an entirely German-speaking one, and this has led to traditionally strong cultural ties with Germany. The French-speaking Swiss community maintained similar ties with France. Thousands of Swiss and Liechtensteiners lived in Germany and France as students or permanent residents. The National Socialist rise to power in Germany led many Swiss and Liechtensteiners to join similar parties in their countries, and to seek to have the Swiss military become a German ally. The largest Swiss fascist party was the National Front, which the Swiss government closely monitored, since it was seen as more pro-German than pro-Swiss. Its adherents in the Swiss Army were known as "Frontish" officers or men, and as it became clear by 1940 that Switzerland would steer a course of neutrality, dozens of Swiss professional soldiers of various ranks illegally crossed the border into Germany or France to offer their services to Germany.

Other Swiss joined the German military while legally in Germany. The earliest had come forward before the war. The most prominent was the Luzerne-born Dr. Franz Riedweg, who had studied in Germany and later married a daughter of former German War Mininster Field Marshal

The influential Swiss volunteer, Dr. Franz Riedweg, who headed the Germanic Office in the *SS*-High Command before becoming the head surgeon for III (Germanic) *SS*-Panzer Corps. He is still alive at the time of writing. (H.T. Nielsen)

Werner von Blomberg. Riedweg joined the *Waffen-SS* on 1 July 1938, becoming a surgeon for several elements of the *SS-V*. Swiss law specifically forbade military service in foreign armies, so a man who joined the *Waffen-SS* (as did the majority of Swiss volunteers) or other branches of the German forces became a criminal and a traitor, regardless of whether he left Switzerland illegally or already dwelled in Germany and sought German citizenship.

The *Waffen-SS* considered Swiss volunteers, as well as the few dozen Liechtensteiners, as essentially German. While they were recognized as Germanics in the same manner as, for example, the Dutch, they were not concentrated in any national units. Instead, the Swiss were dispersed as randomly as German nationals, to every element of the *Waffen-SS*.

Riedweg initially was able to develop a good relationship with Himmler. From 1941, he headed the newly-formed Department "D" in the *SS*-High Command. This was otherwise known as the Germanic Coordination Office, and was designed to see to the needs of the thousands of Germanic volunteers in the *Waffen-SS*. It maintained sections for most of the nationalities, with native officers who served as liaisons for the volunteers with their homelands and aided recruiting drives. During the spring of 1943, Riedweg delivered a speech to the Germanic cadets at the *SS*-Officer Training School at Bad Tölz, in which he promised autonomy for the Germanic nations in a future German-dominated European confederation of Germanic nations. This was the program of the political Germanic-*SS*, particularly in Norway, but it was not recognized by Himmler and the *SS* leadership. Riedweg was removed from Department D, and reassigned to the forming III (Germanic) *SS*-Panzer Corps as Chief Surgeon. As an *SS-Obersturmbannführer*, he then served as one of the three highest-ranking Swiss *Waffen-SS* officers.

The other two highest-ranking Swiss joined the *Waffen-SS* during 1941 after the German invasion of the Soviet Union. Militia-Major Eugen Corrodi deserted his border guard battalion command to cross into France on 24 June. He joined the *Waffen-SS* and was given the pseudonym "von Elfenau" to throw Swiss authorities off of his trail. Late in the year, cavalry *Major* Heinrich Hersche also enlisted in the *Waffen-SS*, while legally in Germany.

Also joining the *Waffen-SS* during 1941 was the active Frontist and journalist from Zurich, Benno Schäppi, who was quickly put in charge of overseeing pro-Germanic propaganda. Another coming forward that summer was the German-resident Peter Renold, who enlisted weeks after his seventeenth birthday. He was a member of the Hitler Youth.

As far as can be determined, *SS-Das Reich* had the greatest number of Swiss volunteers during 1941, while thereafter, most new Swiss volunteers were sent *SS-Nord* (which had 62 Swiss pass through the 2d Company of its reconnaissance battalion, among other elements). As indicated previously, however, this is only a generalization, and Swiss were found throughout the *Waffen-SS*. Dr. Alfred Koebel, for example, was assigned to the *Frikorps Danmark*, and was fatally wounded on 2 June 1942 in the same action in which Christian Fredrik von Schalburg lost his life. Liechtensteiners seem to have first been concentrated in *SS-Wiking*, but after 1942, records disappear. It is likely that nearly all the Liechtensteiners inclined to join the *Waffen-SS* did so during 1941.

From mid-1943, even as Swiss enlisted men remained scattered, many Swiss *Waffen-SS* officers were assigned to the forming III (Germanic) *SS*-Panzer Corps, to offset the shortage of native officers with non-Germans. The case of Riedweg has already been mentioned, and after attending Bad Tölz, Schäppi also joined the corps as the head of its war correspondents. Among others, Theo Läser commanded a platoon in the 1st Company of *SS*-DeRuyter, while former police officer Otto Löliger commanded the 10th Company of *SS-Norge*. Cavalry officer Günther Greer, whose father had been a German officer in the First World War, became the Intelligence Officer (Ic) of *SS-Nordland*, while "P. D." served as a *Haupsturmführer* in *SS*-Artillery Regiment 54.

Renold became a radio specialist, and jumped with *SS*-Parachute Battalion 500 onto Tito's headquarters at Drvar, Bosnia, on 25 May 1944. He survived the operation to attend officers' training.

By this time, a handful of French-speaking Swiss had joined the French *Waffen-SS*, serving with *SS*-Charlemagne, including Jean-Marie Stehli, who also attended officer training. The training and replacement battalion of the unit came to be commanded by Hersche, who was able to put to use his abilities at German and French. By 1945, his command was expanded to a regiment to train the many French exiles who lacked military experience, and he consequently received his ultimate promtion, to *SS*-Colonel.

Corrodi-von Elfenau commanded *SS*-Cavalry Regiment 3 during early 1943. After the Italian armistice, he became the Chief of Staff to Karl Wolff in the latter's office as Highest *SS* and Police Leader for Italy. Corrodi-von Elfenau's main task was to oversee the creation and training of the Italian *Waffen-SS*. A number of other Swiss volunteers with Italian speaking ability served with the Italian *Waffen-SS* as interpreters, including Bruno Tissi. Corrodi-von Elfenau ended the war as an *SS-Oberführer* and was recommended for the German Cross in Gold.

Renold was assigned to the 2d Battalion of *SS*-Panzer-Grenadier Regiment 5 *Totenkopf* after his commissioning. He earned a reputation as a tank-killer, which brought him the nickname "Panzer-Bubi" since he was still only 20 years old. For his repeated bravery, he was recommended for the Knight's Cross, and this may have been approved on

6 May 1945, though the documentation is missing. Renold spent three years in Soviet captivity before being sent to western Europe. He was one of many former *Waffen-SS* men (including a few fellow Swiss) to avoid the harsh conditions of French captivity by joining the French Foreign Legion, where he served in an airborne unit in Indochina. He survived this, and after his Legion discharge, he returned to Germany, where he eventually gained German citizenship.

Most Swiss volunteers were returned to Switzerland in the months immediately after the war, including those who considered themselves Germans, but had not gained German citizenship. As traitors, and in some cases, deserters, they were given prison sentences. These were as little as a few months for German residents who had only served as enlisted men, but were progressively longer for the more notorious and higher-ranking volunteers. Riedweg and Schäppi, in particular, were considered anti-Swiss political activists. Riedweg received a 16-year prison sentence, while Schäppi was jailed until 1956. Both moved to Germany after their release. The fate of Liechtenstein volunteers is not recorded.

On 8 September 1944, the *SS*-High Command noted that 755 Swiss volunteers had been recorded to that point, with 617 then in service. A few more joined after this date, so that a figure of approximately 800 Swiss volunteers in the *Waffen-SS* is reasonable. About 40 served as officers, either from the start of their service or after attending a training course. The number of Liechtenstein volunteers is unknown, but not believed to exceed 50. In the case of the Swiss volunteers, at least, they proved to be a useful, if small, source of competent professional soldiers for the *Waffen-SS*.

Wallonia

The story of Walloon collaboration, military and otherwise, is really the story of Leon Degrelle, a lawyer and Catholic activist of French ancestry born in 1906. As was common in Wallonia, and all of Belgium, he was raised as a devout Catholic, and from his teens was active in publishing. His outspoken opinions and notoriety led in due course to a political career, though also to a break with the Catholic leadership in Belgium.

Degrelle founded his own political party during 1935, naming it "Chistus Rex" (Christ the King) to show his continued Catholic belief and as a carry-over from the Catholic publishing house with which he had begun his public life. The party was commonly known simply as "Rex," and a year after its founding, captured many parliamentary seats in the 1936 elections. The pre-war Belgian government was well known for its corruption, and Rex sought to "clean up" the political climate, while maintaining the integrity of the Belgian state. This was in opposition to the Flemish *VNV* goal of an independent Flanders, and Rex gained only a small membership there.

The Walloon-dominated Belgian establishment reacted swiftly to the Rexist success of 1936. The Catholic Church demanded that its followers vote against Rex, and the media began to stress the Rexist sympathy toward New Order and Fascist ideologies, such as support for the Falangists in Spain. Communism was becoming strong in Wallonia, and the Communists were, of course, also opposed to Degrelle and Rex. As a result, the promising debut of Rex could not be sustained, and the party fell into decline, becoming almost a footnote by the beginning of the war.

Degrelle was arrested immediately after the German invasion of Belgium on 10 May 1940. Taken to France, he was fortunate not to be executed in captivity, as happened to *Verdinaso* leader Joris van Severen. Freed by the Germans, Degrelle returned to Belgium and reestablished Rex, setting up a militia known as the "Combat Formation" to parallel the Black Brigade of the *VNV*. The former Communist and *Verdinaso* member John Hagemans created a Rexist youth movement known simply as the Rexist Youth (later the National Socialist Youth).

Rex could only attract a few tens of thousands of supporters, since the German occupation of Wallonia met with very little of the goodwill it found in Flanders. The precise number of Rexists is unclear, since the figure was small enough that the party never published it, for fear of embarassment. Still, Rex represented the only support that Germany received in Wallonia, and so it was granted a political monopoly in May 1941. "Rex" really represented Degrelle; its leadership was a sort of clique that owed personal loyalty to him, rather than to a political goal.

Perhaps Degrelle's greatest quality was his ambition—he was determined to be an important man. He had risen to become a player in Belgian politics by the age of 30, and after the German occupation, he sought any means to become the chief executive of Belgium, or at least Wallonia. An aspect of his determination was his ruthlessness in purging Rex of any potential rivals to his cult of personality.

Not surprisingly, Degrelle made many enemies throughout his career. Another political party did form in Wallonia during 1941, known as the Friends of the Greater German *Reich (AGRA)*. This was allowed to exist because ostensibly it was, as with *DeVlag*, a "cultural" movement that sought closer ties with Germany. In fact, again in similar form to *DeVlag*, it sought the outright incorporation of Wallonia into Germany. With a platform much more extreme than Rex's collaboration, *AGRA* never gained more than a few thousand supporters, though these members were highly dedicated. *AGRA* claimed Germanic descent for the Walloons, and pursued the same Pan-Germanic agenda as did the Germanic-*SS* in Norway.

The German invasion of the USSR on 22 June 1941 presented Rex with the opportunity of strengthening its ties with Germany. Fernand Rouleau, one of Degrelle's deputies and head of the Combat Formation, arranged with the German occupation authorities for the creation of a Walloon Free Corps to fight on the Eastern Front. This would show Rexist support of the European New Order, and counter the influence of the separatist *VNV*, which had already enrolled volunteers in the Regiment *Nordwest* and the off-shoot Flemish Legion.

Rouleau's idea was followed, and he began to organize what became the battalion-sized Walloon Legion. While most of the Rexist leadership had at least reservist training because of compulsory Belgian Army service, Degrelle had been exempt because of his status as the eldest son of a large family. He lacked any sort of military experience, and initially had no intention of joining the Walloon Legion. He soon perceived a threat in Rouleau's growing stature, and decided to enlist after all. He sought a commission, as Flemish figures such as Jef Francois and Reimond Tollenaere obtained, but the Germans would not grant it to a man who lacked any military credentials. Thus, Degrelle began his military career as a private.

The Walloon Legion took shape as an infantry battalion organized by the German Army. Despite the claims of *AGRA*, the *SS* did not consider the Walloons to be Germanic, but rather Gallic. Thus, in a fashion similar to the French, the Walloons were initially outside of the scope of the *Waffen-SS*. Degrelle assured his followers that the war in the east would be over by Christmas 1941, and that he had been promised by the Germans that the Walloons would only have to serve in the rear areas. This proved attractive to many Rexists, including older family men, as well as to Russian *emigrés* who had settled in Belgium after the Russian Civil War, and who were not otherwise Rexist members.

The reality proved different. The Walloon Legion, formally known as the German Army's Infantry Battalion 373, arrived in Ukraine during November 1941 and found itself holding positions south of Kharkov in bitter weather well after Christmas. It saw heavy combat and sustained serious casualties at Gromovaja-Balka during late February 1942. Degrelle had been lightly wounded, but had proven himself to his men. He was willing to fight and suffer beside them, and was promoted to noncommissioned rank.

In fact, his authority was far greater, and Degrelle was able to use his influence as head of Rex to have his potential rivals removed from the legion. Rouleau had been cast out long before the first combat, as were two of the first commanders of the legion. The men were fortunate that sufficient Belgian Army officers were Rexist members that the unit could always be commanded by Walloon officers, and didn't need to rely on German officers and NCOs as did the Flemings and Dutch.

After further heavy fighting during the spring of 1942, the oldest members of the Walloon Legion were allowed to return home. Back in Belgium, Hagemans collected 150 volunteers from his youth movement (aged 16 to 18), and after training, they and other Rexist volunteers joined the legion in Ukraine during June. One of Hagemans' men was the 17-year-old Jacques Leroy. The Walloon Legion was back up to strength, but it would be the last time Rexists represented the majority of its personnel.

Before the summer 1942 campaign, command of the legion finally rested with Belgian Army artillery officer, Lucien Lippert. This proved acceptable to all. A professional soldier who provided solid leadership, he got along well with Degrelle, and he was not overtly political, so he was acceptable to the circles in the Belgian government and (it is speculated) royal family that were secretly supportive of the legion. Aside from Lippert, the leadership positions were now held by established Degrelle supporters with Belgian Army experience who had proven themselves during the previous fighting. This included men such as Jules Mathieu, Georges Ruelle, Marcel Bonniver, and Marcel Lamproye. Hagemans' arrival created quite a stir because he was dynamic. Despite poor health that forced him to serve in the rear, had more prewar military experience than Degrelle, who was now an officer. Before Hagemans could become a rival, however, he was killed in action in a skirmish on 26 August 1942 as the legion advanced towards the Caucasus.

By this stage, despite their non-Germanic "Gallic" classification, many other Walloons were serving nearby in the *Wiking* Division. *AGRA* members were not welcome in the Walloon Legion, nor did they wish to serve there. Instead, 300 eventually enlisted in the *Waffen-SS*, where as Pan-Germanics they fit in well in *Wiking*. Hundreds of additional *AGRA* members joined a section of the *NSKK* set up for them (Rex had its own, separate, *NSKK* section).

It was in the Caucasus that Degrelle met *Wiking* commander, Felix Steiner. Degrelle developed an appreciation of the multi-national nature of the *Waffen-SS*, and realized that *Waffen-SS* membership offered a greater opportunity for prestige than did being a German Army member.

The Walloon battalion fought well in the Caucasus. It was withdrawn in December 1942 to return to Belgium to rest. Soon after arriving, on 17 January 1943, Degrelle announced his "discovery" that the Walloons were in fact of Germanic descent, even though they spoke French. The way had been paved for the transfer of the Legion to the *Waffen-SS*.

Himmler and his recruiting chief Gottlob Berger constantly explored ways to expand the *Waffen-SS*. The Walloon Legion had proven to be of worth, and the Flemish Legion had particularly distinguished itself. As the Flemings were to be expanded into an armored combat group as the Langemarck Brigade, Himmler was eager to create a matching unit out of the Walloons, who to this point had belonged to the German Army. After negotiations into the spring, the transfer became official on 27 June 1943. The Walloon volunteers no longer were the French-named *"Legion Wallonie."* As de-facto Germanics and *Waffen-SS* men, they instead became the 5th *SS*-Assault Brigade *"Wallonien."*

As with the Flemings, the previous infantry battalion became a fully motorized, and partially armored, force based around an infantry battalion supported by five companies of heavy weapons (anti-tank, anti-aircraft, and so on). The legion had numbered roughly 900 men at full strength, and even with recovered wounded returning, extensive recruiting was required to fill the brigade to its intended number of 2,000 men. The reservoir of dedicated Rexists in Wallonia had run dry, so efforts instead turned to Walloon PWs in German camps and Walloon workers in German industry.

Already during 1941, Degrelle had attempted to recruit Belgian Army officers from PW camps. Over 50 agreed to join the legion, but almost all withdrew when they understood that with their release would come membership in Rex. A few officers did arrive from other sources, such as Henri Derriks, who had been stationed in the Congo during the 1940 campaign. Now, attention turned to offering Walloon enlisted men release from PW camps in return for joining the *Wallonien*. Factory workers were also asked to volunteer for the new unit, and many did, particularly to escape escalating Allied air attacks on German industry.

The *AGRA* volunteers still in *Wiking* were also sent to the Walloon brigade, and a handful of Soviet PWs were added to White Russian emigres still serving with the Walloons. Through these various efforts, the *Wallonien* reached its intended strength, and with Lippert still in command, the unit spent the summer of 1943 in training.

The German officer, Paul Wegener, who had earned the German Cross in Gold as the commander of the reconnaissance battalion of the *SS-Polizei* Division, became the liasion officer of the brigade. He outranked Lippert, and sought to have command influence over the unit, but Degrelle was able to deflect this. Degrelle had already long made a practice of always acting as if he was in charge of the Walloon unit when in the presence of senior German officials. He continued this after *Wallonien* arrived in Ukraine, along the Dnieper River south of Kiev, and joined *Wiking*. Commander Herbert Otto Gille and other *Wiking* officers were convinced that Degrelle actually commanded the brigade, though they recognized that Lippert made the military decisions.

Wiking was worn out after bloody fighting along the Dnieper the previous month, and welcomed this reinforcement. With the Walloons came an assault gun battery from the *SS-Polizei* Division, which stood in for the brigade's own unavailable battery. The Walloons and their armored support were quickly put to use destroying partisan strongholds in the swamps of the region. The strongest partisan enclave lay in the Teklino forest, and strong attacks by *Wiking* elements had failed to destroy it. Degrelle boldly declared to Gille that the Walloons could take the position, despite being inferior in numbers to the forces that had already tried. The Walloon attack commenced on 13 and 14 January 1944, and managed to capture the partisan camp with a minimum of casualties. The operation likely succeeded because the Walloons were much fresher than the tired *Wiking* troops, and it elevated their stock in German eyes.

From late January, *Wallonien* and *Wiking* were caught, along with several German Army infantry divisions, in the Cherkassy pocket. As the area of the pocket was reduced, the Walloons were forced to the west in heavy fighting. On 13 February, the surviving Walloons dug in at Novo Buda, at the southernmost point of the pocket. The town had to be held to keep the pocket from collapsing before the breakout attempt planned for 16 February could be carried out. Degrelle had been lightly wounded, and was with the supply services west of Novo Buda when Lippert was killed in action on 13 February. Jules Mathieu took command of the Walloons in the town, as the senior Belgian Army veteran persent, and he directed the successful defense of the Walloon positions for the next four days. The Walloons became the rear guard for the entire breakout effort, and finally withdrew from Novo Buda on 17 February. Despite what was sometimes later claimed, Lippert's body had to be left behind.

The Walloon combat elements rejoined their trains, and were able to join the breakout in good order. The remnants of the brigade were extremely fortunate that Mathieu located a small bridge that enabled them to safely cross the Gniloy Tikitsch River, an obstacle that claimed the lives of hundreds of German soldiers at other spots. Once safely out of the Cherkassy pocket, 632 Walloons were left of the 2,000 from the previous autumn.

Degrelle was immediately flown to Hitler's headquarters in the company of Gille for propaganda photos, to show the world that these men were still alive, despite Soviet claims to the contrary. Degrelle was spontaneously awarded the Knight's Cross on 20 February 1944 as a reward for the performance of the *Wallonien* and as a propaganda stunt. He did nothing to discourage the notion that he had indeed commanded the Walloons at Cherkassy. Lucien Lippert was remembered through a posthumous award of the German Cross in Gold on the same day.

Wegener had been killed in action during the Cherkassy campaign, and Degrelle now sought command of *SS-Wallonien*. He was rebuffed by Himmler, and was made to understand that a German would be appointed if a suitably high-ranking Belgian professional officer failed to step forward. The only officers Degrelle managed to recruit from PW camps during the spring of 1944 were Captain Hugo Lakaie and Major *BEM* Frans Hellebaut ("*BEM*" indicated a graduate of the Belgian Military College, and thus a trained staff officer). The latter was the mentor and friend of Lippert, and volunteered to maintain in *SS-Wallonien* the sort of professional, apolitical atmosphere that Lippert had cultivated. Hellebaut exercised the day-to-day command of the unit for the rest of the war. Degrelle tolerated Hellebaut and Derricks, though sharing mutual antipathy with the latter, because he needed their military abilities to keep up the efficiency of the brigade.

On 21 June 1944, Karl Burk was appointed commander of *SS-Wallonien*. Degrelle was ordered to avoid combat, as his death in action would be a propaganda blow. Thus, when the brigade was ordered to send a small battalion-sized combat group to Estonia during July 1944, Georges Ruelle was assigned to command it. Degrelle secretly made his way to Estonia and met up with his men, with Ruelle not hesitating to turn command over to him. Most of the combat group consisted of newly-recruited men who had not finished training, so they had been promised some time for exercises before going into battle. Thus, because the Flemish combat group was nearly destroyed on the Tannenberg line, the Walloons did not see action.

Degrelle arrived on 8 August, and soon had a conference with his old acquaintance, Felix Steiner. Degrelle assured Steiner that his men were ready for action, so the 386-man Walloon combat group was assigned to Combat Group Wagner, the detached elements of the III (Germanic) *SS-Panzer Corps* that fought around Tartu to hold off the Soviet advance around the south end of Lake Peipus. The Walloons suffered serious casualties twice on 19 August; in the first instance, a 30-man patrol was nearly all killed or captured. Later, 65 men became casualties while seizing Patska from the Soviets, and the survivors were soon forced out of the strongpoint. Leon Gillis, who had volunteered for the Legion *Wallonie* in 1941, assumed temporary command of a company and led it for the next few days in heavy defensive fighting. He returned to command of his anti-tank gun platoon on 22 August, and deployed his three guns to cover a crucial bridge before dawn the next day. Soviet tanks bypassed his position, so Gillis led his men in a running skirmish until he could set up the two remaining guns to again block the Soviet advance. This goal was achieved at the cost of both guns, and Gillis was seriously wounded while personally manning one. Degrelle recommended him for the Knight's Cross, which was awarded on 30 September.

Later that day, Degrelle, with a handful of Walloons, rallied a combination of Germans and Estonian border guards, leading them in a defensive stand against an unexpected breakthrough. For this, he was recommended for the Oakleaves to his Knight's Cross, and they were quickly approved on 27 August. The Walloons saw further heavy combat during the following days until they were at last evacuated in early September. During the brief spell of combat in Estonia, half of the Walloons became casualties, and many were awarded the Iron Cross 1st class.

As *SS-Wallonien* continued to rebuild and the Estonian survivors returned, Belgium was liberated by Allied forces during September 1944. Thousands of Walloon collaborators fled to Germany, and in parallel fashion to the situation with the Flemings, the *Waffen-SS* decided to expand the Walloon brigade into an infantry division. Hellebaut, who became the 1st General Staff Officer, was well aware that even by incorporating former *Organization Todt* and *NSKK* men, Rexist paramilitary functionaries, and Walloon factory workers in German industry, the manpower for a division was lacking. Degrelle insisted the title of division was necessary for maintaining prestige in comparison with the Flemings, and sought to attain the divisional command himself. His stock had improved, thanks to his leadership in Estonia, but the experienced *SS-Polizei* officer, Nikolaus Heilmann, who had recently won the Knight's Cross commanding the Latvian 15th *Waffen*-Grenadier Division, was named to command the formation staff of *SS-Wallonien* on 12 December 1944.

Degrelle always had an eye on political goals, and he was appointed by the Germans as the head of the Walloon exile community. He then attempted to extend his influence to the French exile community, which was divided into several factions. While Degrelle failed to gain political power with the French, about a hundred French *Waffen-SS* decided to join him in *SS-Wallonien*, deserting *SS*-Charlemagne. Degrelle also sought to exert a political role in reconquered Wallonia, after the initial German successes in the December 1944 Ardennes Offensive.

While Degrelle pursued political goals, Hellebaut and Heilmann brought the embryonic *SS-Wallonien* Division to the greatest possible state of readiness. Over 4,300 men were available, but many of these men were not militarily fit, and others were demoralized by the extent of the German defeat in western Europe during the summer of 1944. What developed was a combat group based around two regimental headquarters, three infantry battalions, single anti-tank and anti-aircraft batteries, two in-training companies of combat engineers, and an in-training artillery battalion.

Heilmann moved on to another assignment, and it was Degrelle who led the combat-ready portion of *SS-Wallonien* to Pomerania at the end of January 1945. Hellebaut exercised the main military command of the 2,000-man combat group, while Jules Mathieu commanded the two infantry battalions of *SS*-Volunteer Grenadier Regiment 69. Under him were Derriks and Lakaie as battalion commanders, with combat veterans as company and platoon leaders.

The Walloons fought delaying actions from 5 to 12 February, screening the deployment zone for the III (Germanic) *SS*-Panzer Corps as it prepared for the SONNENWENDE offensive. On 16 February, *SS-Wallonien* launched diversionary attacks to the west of the main German drive toward Arneswalde. Jacques Capelle, a young officer, but a veteran of long experience, including Estonia, led his 3d Company of *SS*-Volunteer Grenadier Regiment 69 in the seizing of a strongpoint at Lindenberg. He and his men were wiped out the next day in hand-to-hand combat, and Capelle was recommended for the Knight's Cross. The award was under consideration when the war ended.

The Walloons saw further heavy combat, with accompanying serious casualties, during the withdrawal of the III (Germanic) *SS*-Panzer Corps from the Ihna River back to the Altdamm bridgehead. On 12 March, the Walloons reorganized their scattered, depleted companies into a single strong infantry battalion. Many survivors wanted no more part of fighting in a lost war, and Hellebaut refused to force them to do so. Derriks commanded the battalion, which consisted of 23 officers and 625 NCOs and men. Degrelle took little role in combat operations, as he planned for his post-war career in which he hoped to wield some sort of political role.

The Walloons, now referred to as "Battalion Derriks," served as the rear guard for the German withdrawal from the Altdamm bridgehead, and were the last unit to cross the Oder River on 19 March. Derriks was recommended for the German Cross in Gold for his leadership during that action. Jacques Leroy, who had lost an arm and an eye at Teklino, assumed command of a platoon during the March fighting, and for his reckless bravery Degrelle recommended him for the Knight's Cross. While documentation is lacking, the Association of Knight's Cross Recipients' accepts that Leroy's award was approved on 20 April.

West of the Oder, the Walloons reorganized once again in early April 1945. The men of the artillery (without guns) and combat engineers arrived from training camps, along with hundreds of men who had just completed infantry training in the replacement battalion. Mathieu rejoined the unit, with the 1,000 men who had declined the previous month to continue fighting. Out of all of these elements, Hellebaut assembled a small regiment, with Derriks and Marcel Bonniver as the commanders of the two weak battalions.

From April 20, the Walloons began to counterattack Soviet advances across the Oder. During the ensuing fighting, the Walloons were intermingled with the last combat-ready elements of the Flemish *SS*-Langemarck. The offensive mission quickly changed to a defensive one, and the combined Belgian forces gradually retreated west toward the Elbe

River. Degrelle made his last appearance among his men on 24 April, passing out decorations, often in posthumous remembrance. Four days later, he abandoned his men, without informing Hellebaut or Mathieu of his intentions. Hellebaut never forgave Degrelle for this. Hellebaut, with Derriks and Bonniver, surrendered a handful of the most disciplined men to American forces on 3 May. The mass of the Walloons scattered, and with phony papers attempted to pass themselves off as impressed forced laborers. To the US Army, Derriks offered to lead his remaining men against the Japanese, as a way to avoid repatriation to Belgium. Degrelle, in the meantime, made his way through Denmark to Norway, from whence he flew to Spain and a life in exile. His political deputies had disbanded the Rexist party with no fanfare weeks earlier. Walloon collaboration had come to an end. Degrelle, Gillis, and Bonniver were the only three men who had participated in all of the campaigns from late 1941 through 1945 (claims that only three men of the 1941 volunteers survived the war are mistranslations).

Surviving Rexist political figures were harshly punished after the war, particularly those who had joined the Germans in operations against the Belgian resistance and innocent civilians. A few individuals guilty of only military collaboration were indiscriminately executed shortly after the war, in common with arbitrarily-selected Flemish veterans. The Walloon military collaborationist leadership got by with long prison sentences, however, while the lower ranks received shorter terms. Hellebaut was jailed until 1960, as he refused to sign a statement condemning his wartime service. Fernand Rouleau, ironically, eventually made his way to Spain where he became a fellow exile with one-time rival Degrelle.

While Flemish *Waffen-SS* veterans could live openly in Belgium by the 1960s, published magazines and books, and were considered heroes by part of the population of Flanders, the Walloon veterans were pariahs in Wallonia. They were unable to form an effective veterans' group or embark on a publishing campaign.

Hellebaut and Mathieu were able to record the military history of the Walloon Legion/Brigade/Division in detail for the benefit of historians, but it remained to Degrelle to make the the Walloon *Waffen-SS* well known to researchers. His memoirs were published in Germany in 1950, and translations in many languages followed. He wrote these without the benefit of access to documents, and it is human nature that he put himself in the best possible light. The book remains colorful, if unreliable reading. Degrelle also emerged as an international spokesman for the Germanic *Waffen-SS* veterans. From the safety of Spain, he assisted many historians, and became the mentor to many young Europeans who sought to reevaluate the wartime service of Germanic volunteers in the *Waffen-SS*. Thanks to Degrelle's writings, it is well known that over

10,000 Walloons served with the German military during World War II, although in their homeland they were among the most despised veterans in post-war Europe.

Conclusions

The creation of the Germanic-*SS* in the Waffen-*SS*, and the related Germanic political *SS* branches, was an event unique in history. Their racial aspects and implications were especially unique. Men from many nations, sometimes only tenuously or belatedly classified as being racially related to Germans, joined together in the military establishment of a foreign country, which in most cases occupied their homeland. Most were volunteers, and they risked their lives in a conflict which the majority of their countrymen did not endorse. The survivors were usually punished for their actions, and were left with bitter feelings.

Some veterans considered themselves dupes of the Germans, and renounced their former service. Few, outside of the Swiss, thought highly of Second World War Germany, or of its Nazi leadership. Yet many retained great pride in their wartime service. The opinions of tens of thousands of men can only be generalized, but in their post-war writings, most veterans express satisfaction at having acted. They offered their lives and service in the name of anti-Communism instead of merely chanting slogans or passing out leaflets. And they feel that in the ranks of the *Waffen-SS* they became accepted members of an elite; some of the best soldiers in the war. Additionally, many Germanic *Waffen-SS* veterans felt vindicated by the creation of NATO. They recognized the differences between independent states bound by treaty and their own service in units run by the military of one dictator-led country, yet they believe they set an example of international cooperation. And finally, the veterans are confident that their battlefield record, as a whole, can stand with that of any army in history.

Others are not so generous in their assessment. While Sweden and Finland did not punish *Waffen-SS* veterans, the remaining countries saw the Germanic *Waffen-SS* volunteers as dangerous traitors, men whose allegiance lay with Germany instead of at home. The existence of volunteers in the *Waffen-SS* is often an embarrassment that is officially covered up and minimized.

As the preceding pages have shown, the subject of Germanic volunteers in the *Waffen-SS* is one with many subtexts. Each country must be examined separately, and even then, the motives and details of individual volunteers vary greatly. Nothing is gained by either blanket praise for the Germanic volunteers as heroes, or by universal condemnation of them as mercenary traitors. Instead, they must be seen as products of their time, acting for very human reasons, which include opportunism, patriotism, and many more. Furthermore, the story is only complete when seen in a broader context. The Russian Civil War and related Baltic wars of independence from 1917–1921 made many Europeans aware of the aggressiveness of Soviet Communism and directly involved men who would fight again during the Second World War. This was also true to a greater extent of the Spanish Civil War which, between 1936 and 1939, involved thousands of foreign volunteers on both sides. Finally, the Soviet invasion of Finland in November 1939 gave anti-Communists another cause to which to rally.

It is this broad view of history that allows the events associated with the Germanic *Waffen-SS* to become comprehensible. Over 60,000 men from the Germanic nations joined the *Waffen-SS*, usually as volunteers, and often as an act of conscience. For the survivors, it was a small, but appreciated act of thanks when, in the 1990s, Finland and newly-independent Estonia issued memorial medals to foreigners who had fought against Communism in those two countries during the Second World War. It was a measure of closure to an era that began in 1917.

Non-Germans and Non-Germanics in the *Waffen-SS*

"The *SS* was conceived by *Reichsführer-SS* Heinrich Himmler as an organization for Germans (German citizens and from abroad) and racially related Nordic peoples (known to the *SS* as "Germanics"). Although racial ("Aryan") pedigrees were originally de rigeur for members of the Waffen-*SS*, ironically, the massive requirements of German belligerent activities eventually caused him to decide to employ non-Germans and non-Germanics on a scale unknown by the Heer, which never concerned itself with racial "standards" at all. Oddly, even after *SS* "race experts" proclaimed Slavs and others to be inferior human material, the Waffen-*SS* integrated tens of thousands of them into its ranks. Ultimately, Himmler employed over four times as many non-Germanics of all types than he did Germanics-primarily in areas other than the front lines, to free German and Germanic units for employment there. The following section briefly describes the contribution of foreign, non-Germanic nations to the Waffen-*SS*.

Albania

The *Waffen-SS* began to recruit Albanians of various tribes for service in during the formation of the 21st *Waffen*-Mountain Division of the *SS*-Skanderbeg from 17 April 1944. By 25 September of that year, 9,275 had volunteered or been conscripted, and 6,500 had been accepted. Most of these men were Ghegs who came from Kosovo. The majority of the Albanians deserted during the autumn and summer of 1944, and only a hard core of 500 were incorporated into *SS*-Combat Group Skanderbeg, which fought alongside *SS-Prinz Eugen* for the remainder of the war.

Armenia

With their homeland split between the Russian (later Soviet) Empire and Turkey, the Armenians were one of the most repressed peoples in the world in the late nineteenth and early twentieth centuries. Thousands of Armenians from the Armenian S.S.R. joined the German military establishment, either during the autumn 1942 German advance into the Caucasus, or after becoming prisoners of war. During February 1945, the *Heer* Armenian Legion was transferred to the Caucasian *Waffen-Verband* of the *SS*, becoming the *Waffen*-Group of the *SS*-"*Armenien.*" Between 2,000 and 3,000 Armenians served with this force in northern Italy until the end of the war.

Azerbaijan

Conquered by the Russian Empire in the early nineteenth century, Azerbaijan declared its independence as a republic in 1917. It was reconquered by the Soviet Army in 1920, and was part of the Soviet Empire at the time of Barbarossa. In common with Armenians, thousands of Azerbaijanis joined the Germans, and in December 1944, the *Heer* Azerbaijani Legion was assigned to the Caucasian *Waffen-Verband* of the *SS*. Over 1,000 Azerbaijanis served with this force in northern Italy.

Bosnia

Bosnian Muslims had formed regiments of the Austro-Hungarian Army through the First World War. After the spring 1941 German occupation of Yugoslavia, the Bosnian Muslim community largely refused to support the Communist partisans. They suffered severe losses from partisan and royalist-Chetnik raids, and sought German assistance. The *Waffen-SS* decided to create a Bosnian division as the sister unit to *SS-Prinz Eugen*, with formation beginning on 1 March 1943.

The division, first known as "Croatian," attracted many volunteers, including ethnic Croats (Catholics), and quickly attained a strength of over 20,000 men (including German cadre). The 13th *Waffen*-Mountain

Division *Handschar* fought well defending its homeland during the spring and summer of 1944, which led the *Waffen-SS* to order the creation of a second Bosnian division on 17 June.

This became the 23d *Waffen*-Mountain Division *Kama* which only acquired a few thousand men before the German withdrawal from Bosnia necessitated disbanding it. Most of the Bosnian Muslims from both divisions remained in their homeland to protect their people from partisan attacks, with only a few hundred remaining with the *SS-Combat Group Handschar* until the end of the war. Between them, *SS-Handschar* and *SS-Kama* totalled perhaps 18,000 non-Germans, with possibly 20 percent being ethnic Croatians instead of Muslims.

Bulgaria

The *Waffen-SS* first proposed a Bulgarian *SS*-Legion in December 1942 as a way of drawing Bulgaria into the Axis campaign against the Soviet Union. Nothing came of this, as Bulgaria was determined to stay out of the conflict. When the country declared war on Germany during September 1944, hundreds of pro-German Bulgarians retreated with the Germans or made their way to German-held territory. Some of these men were combined with Bulgarians already in Germany on 13 November 1944 to form the Bulgarian *Waffen*-Grenadier Regiment of the *SS*, which was to be expanded to a full division if conditions allowed. The regiment was at only battalion strength, with fewer than 600 men, and never saw combat. A few dozen Bulgarians did see active duty duing the last months of the war with *SS-Jagdverbände "Südost"* ("Southeast")

Belorussia

Several thousand Belorussians were among the *Schuma* units combined into the 30th *Waffen*-Grenadier Division of the *SS*, which was initially classified as "Russian," but later reclassified as "Belorussian," though its manpower came primarily from Russians.

Czechia

Individual Czechs enlisted in the *Waffen-SS* throughout the German occupation of 1938–1945. They possibly totalled 100 men, though no precise figure is known.

Estonia

The Estonians are related to the Finns and Karelians, and as Finns, had been taken into the *Waffen-SS* during 1941. Estonians were considered acceptable, too, after the German occupation of Estonia. An Estonian *Waffen-SS* Legion was set up on 28 August 1942, based around former Estonian Army personnel and veterans of *Heer* and police volunteer battalions. The first battalion of the legion fought with *SS-Wiking* between July 1943 and February 1944 as *SS*-Volunteer-Panzer-Grenadier Battalion "Narwa." The rest of the legion, reorganized as the 3d *SS*-Volunteer Brigade, fought in northern Russia from November 1943 to early February 1944. This was changed during 1944, because conscription was used to replace losses as it expanded into the 20th *Waffen*-Grenadier Division of the *SS*.

On 4 February 1944, the Germans began raising six Estonian Border Guard Regiments, along with a seventh replacement regiment. While the 20th Division fought at Narva and on the Tannenberg Line from February through September 1944, these regiments, retitled as *SS*-Border Guard Regiments, defended quieter sections of the front in southeastern Estonia. They were largely destroyed during the September 1944 German evacuation of Estonia, while the 20th Division was sent to Germany to reform. The 20th Division then rebuilt with survivors of the Border Guard Regiments and all available male

NCOs and enlisted men of the *SS*-Estonian Legion, circa 1943 (note the sign in the background). The only name recorded from this group is that of the man second from left, Kristoving. The *SS-Oberscharführer* third from the right wears the breast badge of a graduate of the pre-war Estonian Army's platoon commander's course. (Rundkvist)

Hando Ruus in *Heer* uniform. He was one of the first Estonians in the Estonian *Waffen-SS* Legion, and became a company commander in the SS-Volunteer Panzergrenadier Battalion "Narwa." His bravery and leadership made him a legend in the unit, and he was decorated with the German Cross in Gold on 30 December 1944. By that time, he was in Soviet captivity, and he was executed in Moscow during the spring of 1945. (Tammiksaar)

Estonians over age 16 from the refugee community in Germany. It fought in Silesia from late January 1945, and gradually retreated to the Prague area by the end of the war. Thousands of young Estonians were undergoing training at the same time with the divisional replacement regiment in Denmark.

The *SS*-Border Guard Regiments were not considered *Waffen-SS*, but the men did become part of it when reassigned to the 20th Division. The division suffered frequent heavy casualties and had over 15,000 men at full strength, so the number of Estonians in the *Waffen-SS* can be estimated at almost 30,000, with over 25,000 participating in combat.

France

France possessed several fascist political parties before and during the war. These joined together during 1941 to promote a French Volunteer Anti-Bolshevik Legion (*LVF*), which fought with the *Heer* from late 1941 until the summer of 1944 as an infantry regiment. Individual Frenchmen (up to 300) enlisted in the *Waffen-SS* from the summer of 1941, usually passing themselves off as Flemings (which some of them were, ethnically) or Walloons.

Hitler authorized French volunteers to enlist in the *Waffen-SS* on 30 January 1943. In theory, candidates were to be of Aryan descent, but in practice, any man who met height and health requirements was accepted, as long as his background wasn't Jewish. Later that year, on 22 July, the Vichy French government authorized the service of French citizens in the *Waffen-SS*, as an addition to already-approved service in the *LVF.* Soon after, on 18 August, the hundreds of volunteers were collected into the French *SS*-Volunteer Grenadier Regiment. During the spring of 1944, this was retitled as the 8th *SS*-Volunteer Assault Brigade. One battalion of the brigade fought in Galicia during August 1944, attached to *SS*-Panzer-Grenadier Regiment 40 from *SS*-Horst Wessel.

While part of the French assault brigade was in combat, on 10 August 1944, the *Waffen-SS* gained control of the *LVF,* and announced its merger with the French *Waffen-SS*. This resulted in the *Waffen*-Grenadier Brigade of the *SS* "Charlemagne," which did not have "volunteer" status, probably because members of the *LVF* had not been screened for Aryan ancestry. French *Organization Todt*, *NSKK*, and Germany Navy volunteers, along with former members of the *Milice Français* police, were forcibly added to the brigade, which on 10 February 1945 became the 33d *Waffen*-Grenadier Division "Charlemagne."

SS-Charlemagne fought in Pomerania from February 1945, and during April, the survivors who wanted to continue fighting formed a small battalion of 300 men. This was destroyed in Berlin during the last days of the war. The divisional training regiment surrendered to American forces in Bavaria about the same time. A few French served with the *SS-Jagdverbände* from the autumn of 1944.

All of the French in the *Waffen-SS*, from 1941 enlistees to those sent against their will late in 1944, totalled perhaps 11,000 men. This does not take into account thousands of 1940 French citizens who volunteered or were drafted into the *Wehrmacht* and *Waffen-SS* after the provinces of Alsace and Lorraine were annexed by Germany and declared *Reichsländer*, that is, integral parts of Germany. Alsatians most notably were numerous among the replacements that rebuilt *SS-Das Reich* in the spring of 1944.

Georgia

Conquered by Russia from the Ottoman Empire in the 1870s, an independent Georgia briefly existed in 1918. However, the Soviets seized Georgia and incorporated it into the Soviet Empire in 1920. Although some of Georgia's minorities (such as the Ossetians, the group to which Stalin belonged) welcomed Bolshevik rule, most Georgians did not. Georgians in the German military formed the *Waffen*-Group "Georgian" from December 1944 in the North Caucasian *Waffen-Verband* of the *SS*. They numbered up to 2,000 men.

Hungary

Ethnic Magyars individually enlisted in the *Waffen-SS* from 1940 because of pro-German sentiment or to be a member of a better-quality armed force than the Hungarian *Honved*. Hundreds of ethnic Magyars were caught up in the conscription of Hungarian ethnic Germans during 1943 and 1944, and ended up serving with *SS*-Horst Wessel, *SS*-Maria Theresia, and the 31st *SS*-Volunteer Grenadier Division.

After the pro-German Arrow Cross party came to power in Hungary during October 1944, negotiations began for the establishment of four ethnic Magyar *Waffen-SS* divisions. This led to the establishment of *SS*-Hunyadi during November 1944, and *SS-Hungaria* the next month. As the third and fourth divisions never began formation, excess men went into the first two, which organized around *Honved* tranfers, the most recent classes of conscripts, and Levante Youths (a force somewhat similar to the Hitler Youth that provided pre-military training). These were considered "*Waffen*-Grenadier" units, as much of the manpower was not volunteer.

Separate Hungarian regiments and battalions were also taken into the *Waffen-SS*, with the most elite such as the *SS*-Regiment "Ney" and 1st Hungarian *SS*-Ski Battalion (which actually consisted of three battalions) being granted "full" *Waffen-SS* status equal to that of German units. These formations saw heavy combat during the last four months of the war.

The two Hungarian *Waffen-SS* divisions never finished their formation because of shortages of equipment and training disruptions from Soviet advances. Emergency combat groups from them covered withdrawals, briefly seeing heavy combat. The men of the Hungarian *Waffen-SS* divisions dispersed among the Hungarian refugee community in Germany at the end of the war, with most eventually going into American captivity. Between these divisions and the independent regiments and battalions, up to 50,000 ethnic Magyars served in the *Waffen-SS*, along with tens of thousands of Hungarian ethnic Germans.

India

The 2,500 men of the Free India Legion, raised in German prisoner of war camps, were transferred to the *Waffen-SS* on 8 August 1944. This was purely an administrative move, and the men continued to wear *Heer* uniforms. They were kept as a propaganda tool, and did not see combat.

Ireland

Individual Irish served with the *SS-Jagdverbände* during the last phases of the war. They were recruited from the Irish Republican Army and from Irish national prisoners of war captured with British Army units.

Italy

Even after Italy surrendered to the Allies in late September 1943, many Italians continued to support Fascism and Germany. The best of the pro-Axis volunteers were collected into the Italian *Waffen-Verband* of the *SS*, with an initial strength of 15,000 men. They were organized into battalions, and because of the worsening war situation of the Axis, this number declined to 9,000 men by February 1944.

Two reinforced Italian *Waffen-SS* battalions fought in the front lines at Anzi-Nettuno between March and May 1944, while the majority of the volunteers were forming the Italian *Waffen*-Grenadier Brigade of the *SS* from 27 April. The infantry battalions and supporting units fought separately in anti-partisan operations from the spring of 1944 through the end of the war. On 10 February 1945, the brigade was retitled as the 29th *Waffen*-Grenadier Division, which included 5,000 of the 6,200 men in the Italian *Waffen-Verband* of the *Waffen-SS*. All together, perhaps 10,000 men saw active duty with the Italian *Waffen-SS*.

Latvia

After receiving what they considered to be poor training and weapons in Heer and police volunteer battalions, Latvian soldiers wanted access to full military training and modern weapons. After the Estonians were granted a *Waffen-SS* volunteer legion, Latvian politicians and Army veterans requested a similar force for their nation. Two Latvian *Schuma* battalions were serving with the 2d *SS*-Infantry Brigade on the Leningrad siege lines when, on 23 January 1943, Himmler announced that the brigade would be converted into a purely Latvian unit, incorporating other German-raised Latvian battalions and new volunteers.

This occurred during the spring of 1943, and a separate full division began to form in Latvia at the same time. Most of the manpower was now provided through Latvian-aided conscription, and the units were gradually redesignated from "volunteer" to "*Waffen*-Grenadier." The brigade fought on the front into the spring of 1944, when it expanded into the 19th *Waffen*-Grenadier Division. The second unit was a division from the start, and thus became the lower numbered 15th *Waffen*-Grenadier Division, which fought at the front from late 1943. The divisions together formed the VI *Waffen*-Army Corps of the *SS*.

Similar to the situation with Estonia, six Latvian *SS*-Border Guard Regiments were raised in early 1944, along with three Latvian Police Regiments. The first two border guard regiments were quickly broken up to reinforce the VI *Waffen*-Army Corps. The others reinforced the 19th *Waffen*-Grenadier Division in Kurland after the September–October 1944 retreat from the main portion of the country. The police regiments were merged into the first regiment after heavy losses, and after reconstitution, the first and second regiments were used to help rebuild the 15th *Waffen*-Grenadier Division in Germany.

The 19th *Waffen*-Grenadier Division finished the war in Kurland, where many local men were inducted as replacements during the last months of the war. The 15th *Waffen*-Grenadier Division absorbed all available Latvian manpower in Germany before returning to combat in January 1945. Both divisions had suffered very heavy losses throughout their existence, making estimates of the Latvian contribution to the *Waffen-SS* difficult to calculate. An educated guess is that over 60,000 Latvians served in the 15th and 19th *Waffen*-Grenadier Divisions and their supporting elements.

Lithuania

Attempts to form a Lithuanian *Waffen-SS* Legion similar to those of Estonia and Latvia failed because of German mishandling of Lithuanian manpower and general reluctance among the Lithuanian population to be associated with the *SS*. Only individual Lithuanians joined the *Waffen-SS*, usually after becoming attched to various *Waffen-SS* or police combat groups while serving with *Heer* and Lithuanian volunteer police battalions.

North Caucasus

Chechens, Ingushens, and neighboring peoples served together in the German military, and from December 1944, formed the *Waffen*-Group "*Nordkaukasus*" in the Caucasian *Waffen-Verband* of the *SS*. This numbered between 1,000 and 2,000 men.

Poland

Individual Poles ended up in the *Waffen-SS*, though usually as nominal ethnic Germans or ethnic Ukrainians. Thousands of ethnic Polish families declared themselves of German descent to obtain better living conditions, and this subsequently exposed the men to German military conscription. These men served in every branch of the *Wehrmacht* and *Waffen-SS*.

Galicia was part of pre-war Poland, and ethnic Poles were mixed with the predominantly Ukrainian population. Some of the volunteers for the 14th *Waffen*-Grenadier Division were almost certainly ethnic Poles, though, as with those in the German formations, no figures are available.

Romania

Much of the leadership of the Romanian Legion of the Archangel Michael (popularly known as the Iron Guard) went into exile in Germany after the failure of their attempt to seize power during January 1941. When Romania declared war on Germany in late August 1944, these men were freed from protective custody, and most enlisted in the *Waffen-SS*. The 4th Infantry Division of the Romanian Army was captured intact by the Germans, and much of its manpower then volunteered for German military service. Iron Guardists and other politicians set up a government in exile, and Iron Guardists combined with Romanian Army professional soldiers to establish the nucleus of an ethnic Romanian *Waffen*-Grenadier Division of the *SS*. Additional men deserted from the Romanian forces fighting alongside the Soviets in Hungary.

The available men were organized into an infantry regiment and the cadre of a second regiment. The full regiment became known as *Waffen*-Grenadier Regiment 103, and joined the III (Germanic) *SS*-Panzer Corps on the Oder River front during March 1945. It was destroyed in the Soviet Berlin offensive the following month.

The second Romanian *Waffen-SS* regiment never completed formation, and a third regiment was created in name only. It collected the fragments that would have become the cadre of the supporting elements for the Romanian *Waffen-SS* division, had time and conditions allowed. Up to 100 Romanian volunteers did fight with *SS-Jagdverbände* Southeast the spring of 1945. Between the first regiment, the cadres, and the commandos, over 6,000 Romanians served with the *Waffen-SS*, not including tens of thousands of Romanian ethnic Germans.

Russia

Tens of thousands of Russians served in *Heer* and police volunteer battalions. Others joined locally-raised units that were separate from normal German command channels, and had a degree of political autonomy. The best known of these was the Lokot Republic, which was based around the private army of Bronislav Kaminski in the Bryansk region southwest of Moscow. This force became known as the Russian Army of National Liberation, and it joined the Germans on anti-partisan operations between 1942 and the summer of 1944. After the autumn 1943 evacuation of Lokot, the unit was known as the "Kaminski" Brigade.

Part of the unit fought in Warsaw in August 1944 and became notorious for their atrocities. Kaminski was murdered by the Germans. Himmler had planned to incorporate the brigade into the *Waffen-SS* as the 29th *Waffen*-Grenadier Division, but difficulties in the summer of 1944 led to the 5,000 survivors instead being assigned to the Vlasov Army.

The Germans were forced out of all parts of the Soviet Union by the late summer of 1944, and no longer needed Russian volunteers for service against Soviet partisans. The various *Schuma* battalions, therefore, were collected into the 30th *Waffen*-Grenadier Division and used in eastern France against the French resistance. During October and November 1944, the division was forced to fight American and Free French forces on an emergency basis, and was largely destroyed. It had the strength of a regiment for the rest of the war and did not see combat.

Individual ethnic Russians joined the Estonian and Latvian *Waffen-SS* units as citizens of those countries. Others, no doubt, ended up in other *Waffen-SS* formations after their units were destroyed during the course of various assigments. The Russian contribution to the *Waffen-SS* is not known with certainty, but probably is under 20,000 men. To these can be added the 15,000 men of the Cossack Cavalry Corps, who were assigned to the *Waffen-SS* for administrative purposes late in the war. These men were largely ethnic Russians, though considered distinct culturally.

Slovakia

The Tiso regime that took over leadership of independent Slovakia in 1939 maintained a militia known as the Hlinka Guard. The most loyal and elite portion was Tiso's personal bodyguard, which helped the Germans suppress the autumn 1944 Slovak Revolt. This force retreated from Slovakia with the German evacuation, and during April 1945, the last few hundred survivors were taken into the *Waffen-SS* and used in *SS*-Combat Group/Division Böhmen-Mähren. Several thousand Slovak ethnic Germans served in the *Waffen-SS* as volunteers or conscripts.

Spain

In gratitude for German aid during the Spanish Civil War, Spain sent the manpower for an infantry division to join the Germans on the Eastern Front. After being equipped from German stocks, the division fought from the late summer of 1941 through the autumn of 1943. It was then withdrawn under Allied pressure, and a few months later, its successor, the regimental-sized Spanish Legion, was withdrawn as well. A few dozen Spaniards were determined to remain in German service, and they were supplemented by adventure seekers who crossed into France from Spain and workers in German industry. All of these men faced the loss of Spanish citizenship, since Spain was no longer aiding the Axis.

The *Waffen-SS* was handling virtually all foreigners by early 1944, and decided to add these men to the Flemish *Waffen-SS*. This was because the Spanish division had fought alongside the Flemish *SS*-Legion near Leningrad, and the two units developed a good relationship. The man first assigned to recruit Spaniards for continued German service had a Flemish name, but was actually a Walloon, and so he brought the men he collected to a Walloon recruiting post. He met a Walloon comrade with whom he had fought in the Spanish Civil War, and the latter suggested to Walloon leader Leon Degrelle that the Spanish in the *Waffen-SS* join *SS-Wallonien*.

This transpired between December 1944 and February 1945, groups of Spanish volunteers joined the Walloon combat group in Pomerania. They formed the 3d Company of *SS*-Volunteer Grenadier Regiment 70, with a strength of 240 men, and most became casualties during the fighting through mid-March 1945. The survivors were reassigned to the staff of the III (Germanic) *SS*-Panzer Corps, where they formed *SS*-Volunteer Company 101, which was destroyed in Berlin in the last days of the war.

A small number of Spaniards were in the Bandenburger units that became *SS-Jagdverbände Südwest* from the autumn of 1944. With them, there may have been 300 Spaniards in the *Waffen-SS*. The "Spanish" volunteers in German service always included individual Portugese who were counted as Spaniards.

Turkics

During December 1943 and January 1944, Turkic volunteers in the German military, primarily ex-Soviet prisoners of war, were collected into a projected *"Ostmuselmanische SS-Division Neu Turkistan"* ("Turkistani Eastern Muslim Division of the *SS*," with "Turkestani" understood to include men from Turkestan and neighboring regions such as Uzbekistan).

By the spring of 1944, the first regiment, known simply as the Eastern Muslim Regiment of the *SS*, was involved in anti-partisan operations in Belorussia. The division was given low priority, and made little progress. It slowly developed into the loosely-organized Eastern Turkic *Waffen-Verband* of the *SS*. This included the *Waffen*-Groups "Idel-Ural," "Turkistan," and "Azerbaijan." The latter properly belonged with other Caucasians, and transferred to the newly-formed Caucasian *Waffen-Verband* of the *Waffen-SS* during December 1944. In its place during February 1945 came the *Waffen*-Group *"Krim,"* formed from Crimean Tatars. These men had formerly been the cadre of the *Waffen*-Mountain Brigade of the *SS* (*tatarische* no. 1), which never fully formed.

Numerous Turkic volunteers saw action from 1941 into 1944, but very few saw any combat after assignment to the *Waffen-SS*. Perhaps 10,000 men were involved in this step, far fewer than the total in German service.

Ukraine

German rule in western Ukraine was much less harsh than in the eastern portion, and the occupiers were on fairly good terms with the population. The German administration decided during April 1943 to create a Ukrainian *Waffen-SS* infantry division, though under the label "Galician" to discourage Ukrainian nationalist feeling.

The western Ukrainian population was highly receptive to German recruiting, since it allowed their men to receive military training for future use, whether for defense of Ukraine against the return of Communism, or possibly against the Germans. Many of the volunteers were secretly members of the anti-Communist and anti-German UPA partisan force.

Tens of thousands of Ukrainians volunteered, so the best 10,000 were combined with a German cadre to form the 14th *Waffen*-Grenadier Division. The remaining men were formed into police regiments. The division was almost destroyed during the summer of 1944, and was then rebuilt from the men diverted from police regiments.

During April 1945, the 14th Division was reassigned to the Ukrainian National Army. Ukrainians essentially provided the manpower for two divisions, and likely contributed over 18,000 volunteers to the *Waffen-SS* for the 14th Division alone. Additional Ukrainians no doubt served in the "Russian" 30th *Waffen*-Grenadier Division, and from 1942 to 1944, Ukrainians formed the largest portion of the Dirlewanger Brigade.

When these men are included, the Ukrainian tally reaches over 20,000 men for the *Waffen-SS*.

Conclusion

If these various nationalities are added together, they contributed over 250,000 men to the ranks of the Waffen-SS, though their contributions were usually of far less significance than those of the German and Germanic units. Still, as previously mentioned, many of these formations did free up Germans for frontline service, and they contributed to the pride that Baltic Waffen-SS veterans in particular felt at having belonged to a multi-national army.

Leading Personalities of the *Waffen-SS*

As previously discussed, the *Waffen-SS* originated in the Political Readiness Detachments of the *SS*, which used Imperial Army, *Freikorps*, *Reichswehr*, and police veterans as the officer cadre. To these men were added younger men who joined the *SS* without military or paramilitary experience, and still-younger men who volunteered specifically for service as professional soldiers from August 1934. Dozens of men from the latter categories distinguished themselves during the war, earning promotions and high decorations. To cover all of the important officers of the *Waffen-SS* is outside the scope of this work, but a representative selection of influential and significant *Waffen-SS* commanders follows.

Paul Hausser

Paul Hausser was born to a military family in Brandenburg an der Havel on 7 October 1880. As was common in military circles at the time, he joined the Prussian Cadet Corps in 1892. He graduated on 18 March 1899 from the Gross-Lichterfelde cadet academy, the future home barracks of the *Leibstandarte* Adolf Hitler.

Hausser first demonstrated his great military abilities as a young *Leutnant* with infantry units, and he was selected for General Staff training. Accepted for the prestigious German General Staff, Hausser was promoted to *Hauptmann* several months before the First World War began.

Paul Hausser stands over Fritz Vogt during the September 1940 parade that honored Vogt as the first junior officer of the *Waffen-SS* to earn the Knight's Cross.

During the war, Hausser was promoted to *Major* and received numerous German and Austrian decorations while serving as a staff officer with various infantry units, and on the staff of Crown Prince Rupprecht of Bavaria.

Shortly after the war, Hausser commanded *Füsilier Regiment "Generalfeldmarschall Graf von Moltke,"* as well as border defense units in eastern Germany. Taken into the 100,000-man *Reichswehr*, he spent the ensuing years typically alternating between staff postings and field commands, gradually advancing in rank until promotion to *Generalmajor* on 1 February 1931. On 31 January 1932, he retired with a *Generalleutnant's* pension. A year later, Hausser joined the *Stahlhelm* ("Steel Helmet") veterans' association, and his leadership position brought him an *SA* commission when the *Stahlhelm* was merged with the *SA* during 1934. *SA-Standartenführer* Paul Hausser was out of his element, and soon accepted Heinrich Himmler's invitation to switch to the *SS* as an *SS-Standartenführer*, receiving that rank on 15 November 1934.

Hausser came to the *SS* specifically to oversee training in the newly-forming military units of the *SS-V*. He founded the *SS*-Officer Training

Paul Hausser, "the Senior," the man who ensured that the *SS-V* became a professional elite. This photo was taken after his award of the Knight's Cross on August 8, 1941, but before the wounds suffered weeks later on 14 October that cost him his right eye.

School at Braunschweig, and set the curriculum for that establishment and the sister school at Bad Tölz. In the following years, Hausser served as Inspector of the officer schools and Inspector of the entire *SS-V*. His talents, his humor, and his concern for his men, along with his advanced age, quickly brought him the nickname "Papa Hausser," one which he kept throughout his life.

Most of the *SS-V* fought in Poland during September 1939 and Hausser was on hand as an observer. The next month, he began to organize the *SS-V* Division from the subunits of the *SS-V* (aside from the *SS-LAH*), with the division officially activated during November 1939.

Hausser excelled as a first-time division commander, leading his elite soldiers in France during 1940, and in Yugoslavia and the Soviet Union the next year. As a long time professional army officer with wide experience, he had very good relations with his *Heer* counterparts, particularly his corps commander, Heinrich von Vietinghoff-Scheel, who recommended Hausser for the Knight's Cross for superior leadership during the Western European campaign and the summer 1941 advance to the Dnieper River. The award was approved on 8 August 1941.

Hausser was badly wounded by shrapnel on 14 October 1941, losing sight in his right eye. Following his recovery, he began to organize the headquarters for the first *SS* army corps during May 1942. Initially known as the *SS*-Panzer Corps, it consisted of his previous command (renamed *Das Reich*) and the *SS-LAH* and *SS-Totenkopf* Divisions. These units trained and rebuilt during 1942.

The *SS*-Panzer Corps, at first with just *SS-LAH* and *SS-Das Reich*, arrived in the Kharkov sector during January 1943, in the midst of the Stalingrad-Caucasus disaster. The corps, including the elite *Heer* Panzer-Grenadier Division *Grossdeutchland*, were almost surrounded in Kharkov by the middle of February. Hitler ordered the defense of the city, but Hausser courageously ignored the command and directed a breakout from near-encirclement on 15 February. In later years, Hausser shrugged off the potential consequences of his action, stating that he wasn't punished because of the obvious correctness of his decision.

The *SS*-Panzer Corps was joined by *SS-Totenkopf* for the successful counteroffensive that began in late February 1943 and which recaptured Kharkov the next month. In light of his official disobediance, Hausser could not be decorated for his decisive leadership during the campaign.

The *SS*-Panzer Corps fought very well at Kursk during early July 1943, and again along the Mius River later that month. Hausser was now recommended for the Oakleaves to his Knight's Cross by 4th Panzer Army commander Hermann Hoth, with the award granted on 28 July 1943.

Hausser's corps was retitled II *SS*-Panzer Corps and by the time it returned to combat in March 1944, it controlled the *SS*-Hohenstaufen and *SS*-Frundsberg Divisions. Hausser directed his corps in the successful relief of the encircled 1st Panzer Army, and then in further heavy fighting in Galicia.

The II *SS*-Panzer Corps was sent to Normandy during June 1944, and went into action on 28 June, counterattacking the British "Epsom" offensive across the Odon River. The 7th Army commander, Friedrich Dollmann, committed suicide that day, and Hausser was named to succeed him, becoming the first *Waffen-SS* officer to assume army-level command. Hausser personally led his men out of the Falaise encirclement until he was wounded by mortar fragments on 20 August 1944. He was driven out of the pocket in an armored personnel carrier of the *SS-Hitlerjugend* Division.

Hausser was awarded the Swords to his Knight's Cross with Oakleaves days later on 26 August 1944, for his short tenure as 7th Army commander. He spent the rest of the year convalescing, and then replaced Himmler as the commander of Army Group Upper Rhine on 23 January 1945. Five days later, the command was dissolved, and Hausser took over Army Group G, becoming the only *Waffen-SS* officer to hold army-group-level command. He was dismissed from the post on 3 April

1945, after arguing with Hitler, and finished the war at an unimportant staff position.

Hausser's army service and his later influence of a generation of *Waffen-SS* officers lent a degree of legitimacy to the early *Waffen-SS*, setting a professional standard without which the *Heer* might not have allowed supplying the *SS-V* with modern weapons and equipment. Thanks to his efforts, the "classic" units fulfilled his vision of a new guards force that excelled on the battlefield.

Hausser testified at Nuremburg on behalf of the *Waffen-SS* as a defense witness. He then wrote the first basic military history of his mens' campaigns, *Waffen-SS im Einsatz* (The *Waffen-SS* in Action), published in 1953. He was recognized as "the Senior" by the *Waffen-SS* veterans, and he continued to look out for the welfare of his men for the rest of his life. As increased documentary material became available, he expanded his book into *Soldaten wie andere Auch* (Soldiers Also Like the Others), published during 1968, the year he turned 88. A man of remarkable vitality, he remained in control of his facilities until his death at age 92 on 21 December 1972, months after he had contributed the introduction to the massive *Waffen-SS* photo book, *Wenn alle Brüder schweigen* (When All Brothers Are Silent).

Paul Hausser was the spiritual founder of the *Waffen-SS*, and his efforts before, during, and after the war always set an example for his men. Hausser ensured that the *SS-V* maintained a military bearing, despite Himmler's political police intentions; he provided first-class leadership in the field, and his books established a tone of objectivity that was followed by *Waffen-SS* veterans as they wrote histories of their units. It was thanks to Hausser, above all, that many *Waffen-SS* officers and men comported themselves with decency and honor, despite the negative influences present in Nazi Germany and the *SS* organization.

Felix Steiner

Felix Martin Julius Steiner, born on 23 May 1896 in East Prussia, of distant Austrian ancestry. His service life was marked by strong opinions and an acceptance of new ideas.

Steiner's military career began shortly before the First World War, when he joined the Prussian Army. He was quickly promoted to NCO, and then commissioned on 27 January 1915, less than a year after entering service. His potential was rated highly, so Steiner received staff training, after which he commanded machine gun units that were utilized in the new *Stosstrupp* ("shock troop") formations that broke the deadlock on the Eastern Front during the 1917 Riga campaign. He then

Steiner in the field with *SS-Wiking*, near Dniepropetrovsk, Ukraine, during September 1941. In the foreground is Finnish general Harald Öqvist, who was on a visit to *SS-Wiking* to meet with Finnish volunteers. Second from left is Herbert Otto Gille. (Brenden)

participated in similar actions on the Western Front during the spring of 1918. He came away from the war convinced that he had witnessed the future of warfare.

After service in *Freikorps* in Lithuania, Steiner found a place in the *Reichswehr*, but retired as a *Hauptmann* at the end of 1933. He was frustrated by what he considered a lack of innovation, and sought a platform for his concept of an elite soldier-athlete. He first sought this through joining the *SA*, but on 24 April 1935, he switched to the *SS*, assuming command of the 3d Battalion of the still-forming *SS-Deutschland* Regiment. Here, with superb men under his leadership, he at last was able to demonstrate the validity of his ideas. The impressive performance of his battalion led to Steiner, as an *SS-Standartenführer*, becoming the first commander of *SS-Deutschland* on 1 July 1936. The continued success of his training methods earned the approval of Paul Hausser, who spread them through the *SS-V*, and later to the *SS-LAH*. Steiner also popularized the use of the camouflage smock, developed by his subordinate, Dr. Wim Brandt. Camouflage clothing later spread to the rest of the *SS-V* and then to armies around the world.

SS-Deutschland fought admirably in the Polish and Western campaigns, and Steiner became one of the first *Waffen-SS* recipients of the Knight's Cross on 17 June 1940, based on a recommendation by Hausser. He became an *SS-Brigadeführer* on 9 November 1940, and on 1 December assumed command of the newly-formed *SS-Wiking* Division. Here he discovered a phenomenon that became a personal cause for the rest of his life.

SS-Wiking, based around the *SS-V Germania* Regiment, included the recently raised *SS-Nordland* and *SS-Westland* Regiments. The former

Felix Steiner, the innovator who brought his tactical insights to the *SS-V* and *Waffen-SS*. He later embraced the Germanic volunteer movement, and helped to make it a success. This is a photo originally shot in color at Hitler's headquarters by Walter Frentz, on the occasion of Steiner receiving his Oak-leaves. Under his Knight's Cross is the Finnish Freedom Cross.

included volunteers from Norway and Denmark, while the latter had men from Flanders and the Netherlands. While many Prussians were skeptical of the value of foreign volunteers, Steiner embraced the idea with an enthusiam more typical of culturally-tolerant Austrians. Some claim that his awareness of his Austrian ancestry was influential in this regard.

The European volunteers, including Finns, Swiss, Swedes, and others, returned Steiner's goodwill. They came to admire him for his firm, caring leadership. He became known for shaking hands with every man in formations drawn up for inspection, and for emphasizing military efficiency over politics. Steiner was reprimanded by Himmler on several occasions for downplaying *SS* and Nazi ideology, and also for never abandoning his Christian faith, but he kept his commands because of his military abilities. His influence extended to the officer corps of *SS-Wiking*, so that the foreign volunteers were always respected and well treated, even as those officers were reassigned to the off-shoot *SS-Nordland* and *SS-Nederland* Divisions.

During the Caucasus campaign, Steiner assumed temporary command of the *Heer*'s III Panzer Corps from November 1942 through January 1943. This was an unusual step, but he had earned the respect and cooperation of his *Heer* colleagues, including General Staff officer Joachim Ziegler. Steiner earned the Oakleaves to his Knight's Cross on 23 December 1942. He was marked for a permanent corps command, and this became official during May 1943, when he became the first commander of the III (Germanic) *SS*-Panzer Corps, which collected most of the available Western European volunteers. Ziegler transferred to become the corps chief of staff, and he and Steiner worked closely together for the rest of the war, even after Ziegler took command of the *SS-Nordland* Division. Ziegler's staff training became the perfect complement to Steiner's leadership.

The III (Germanic) *SS*-Panzer Corps fought very well during 1944 against heavy odds in the retreat from the Oranienbaum front, back to the Narva bridgehead, and finally on the Tannenberg defense line. Steiner received the Swords to his Knight's Cross with Oakleaves in recognition of this on 10 August 1944, based on a recommendation submitted by Narva area commander Anton Grasser. Steiner continued to lead his corps until late January 1945, when he preceded it to Pomerania to organize an offensive. The scattered units available were given the grandiose title "11th *SS*-Panzer Army," though they were below conventional army strength.

Steiner resumed command of the III (Germanic) *SS*-Panzer Corps west of the Oder River during April 1945, and soon after defied Hitler's order to launch a hopeless relief attack on Berlin. The decision spared the lives of many of his men, even though Ziegler was forced to bring much of *SS-Nordland* into the city, where he was killed in action and the division destroyed. Steiner and Ziegler intended to surrender all of the remaining Western European volunteers to the Western Allies, under the faintest of hopes that they might be used against the Communists in a post-war struggle.

In captivity, Steiner refused to testify against British volunteers who had joined the *Waffen-SS*. He later helped organize the *Hilfsgemeinschaft auf Gegenseitigkeit der Soldaten der ehemaligen Waffen-SS* (Mutual Aid Society for Former Members of the *Waffen-SS*, or *HIAG*), a veterans' self-help organization, and then devoted his time to writing studies of military history. He defended his and Hausser's concept of the *Waffen-SS* in the book, *Die Armee der Geächteten* (The Army of Outlaws), and he also defended the European volunteers in his work, *Die Freiwilligen der Waffen-SS: Idee und Opfergang* (The Volunteers of the *Waffen-SS*: Concept and Self-Sacrifice).

Felix Steiner died on 17 May 1966, and his former soldiers honored him by naming the veterans' association for the Germanic volunteers

Felix Steiner, right, dines with *SS-Deutschland* during the autumn of 1940. In the middle, between the hands and face of the clapping man, is Erwin Reichel, who joined Steiner as a staff officer with *Wiking*, and who was killed in action commanding *SS-Westland*, receiving the Knight's Cross posthumously. At left is Hermann Buch who became a leading post-war historian of the *Waffen-SS*, and helped publish the veterans' magazine *Der Freiwillige*.

(and their German and ethnic German comrades) *"Korps Steiner."* In unit histories written during the following years, the men of his commands further preserved his memory by always stressing his decisive influence on the high military quality of *Wiking* and its sister formations.

"If Hausser shaped the overall character of the *Waffen-SS*, it was Steiner who profoundly influenced *Waffen-SS* training through his substitution of athletics and tactical skills for rote drill, and for his emphasis on initiative and flexible leadership."

Sepp Dietrich

Josef "Sepp" Dietrich was born in southern Germany on 28 May 1892. He briefly joined the Bavarian branch of the German Army before the First World War, and returned to service in August 1914, fighting with several artillery units. During the spring of 1918, he served in one of the only German units equipped with German-made A7V tanks, before finishing the war as a crewman with captured British tanks. Dietrich earned the rare First World War Tank Combat Badge, and was one of the few recipients to fight in the Second World War.

An experienced NCO, Dietrich rose rapidly in the Bavarian police, from the spring of 1919. He gained additional military experience by

Dietrich in Normandy with senior officers of I SS-Panzer Corps. They are celebrating the presentation of the Knight's Cross (approved on 11 July 1944) to Karl-Heinz Prinz, right, a long-time SS-LAH officer who commanded 2d Battalion, SS-Panzer Regiment 12. Next to him is SS-Hitlerjugend Division commander Kurt Meyer, commonly known as "Panzermeyer." At left is Dietrich's former adjutant, SS-Panzer Regiment 12 commander Max Wünsche.

simultaneously joining the *Freikorps* "*Oberland.*" He took leave from his police duties at various times to join the *Freikorps* on campaigns, including fighting the Poles in Upper Silesia. Dietrich was with the *Freikorps* when it participated in the 9 November 1923, "Beer Hall Putsch" in Munich, and this doesn't seem to have damaged his civil career, as he was promoted to police captain the next year.

From this early start, Dietrich became aquainted with many leading Nazi party personalities, although he didn't join the NSDAP until 1 May 1928, becoming an *SS* member four days later. He had left the police during 1927, and forged a new career as an *SS* leader and National Socialist politician (gaining a seat in the *Reichstag* from 1932–1945). In his free time, he indulged his passions of hunting and auto racing, earning a reputation as a sportsman.

Even as he immersed himself in politics, soldiering was Dietrich's goal, and he was able to attain a semi-military status by heading Hitler's bodyguard detachment from 1929 onward. With the National Socialist ascension to power on 30 January 1933, this force was reorganized on 17 March, with 117 carefully selected volunteers forming the *SS*-Staff Guard "Berlin." This was the origin of the unit which expanded throughout 1933, and on 13 April 1934, received the title "*Leibstandarte* Adolf Hitler" (*LAH*). Later that year, the force was ordered to take part in the murder of *SA* leaders during the "Night of the Long Knives. Dietrich had gained first-hand experience of the darker side of Nazi politics.

The *SS-LAH* developed into a motorized infantry regiment, but it was soon apparent that Dietrich's leadership qualities far exceeded his tactical abilities. He was a proud man, and it took into 1938 before he accepted the outside influence of Hausser to bring the parade-perfect *SS-LAH* to a state of combat competence. Highly-experienced professional officers were assigned to assist Dietrich for the remainder of the war, beginning with Willi Bittrich and Wilhelm Keilhaus. This arrangement, later involving younger officers such as Max Wünsche and Rudolf Lehmann, proved highly successful. While Dietrich served as a public figure, and often personally intervened in combat at crisis spots, his staff officers quietly directed the military operations of the unit.

Dietrich, seemingly a flawed leader from an outside point of view, always received the highest admiration and respect from the men of the *SS-LAH*, with many of his subordinate commanders having served in the unit since 1933. They recognized his limitations but never questioned his personal courage, demonstrated in both wars, and appreciated the constant concern he showed for the welfare of his men. His admirers were quick to point out that Dietrich was the living embodiment of the traditional Prussian system in which a revered commander such as Blücher or Hindenburg owed his success to his chief of staff.

Dietrich commanded the *SS-LAH* as a reinforced regiment in Poland and France. It was small division by the time it fought in Greece and then the Soviet Union during 1941. He won the Knight's Cross on 5 July

Josef "Sepp" Dietrich, here in black Panzer uniform, befitting his role as one of the most experienced tank veterans in the German military. He wears his Knight's Cross with Oakleaves and Swords, and, seen in profile, is his First World War Tank Combat Badge, next to his Iron Cross 1st class.

1940, and the Oakleaves to it on the last day of 1941. During 1942, *SS-LAH* expanded into a full armored division, and Dietrich won the Swords to his Knight's Cross with Oakleaves on 16 March 1943, for his unit's distinguished role in the Kharkov campaign.

After this, during the late spring of 1943, Dietrich left his division to begin forming the headquarters of the I *SS*-Panzer Corps *"Leibstandarte,"* which was to include the *SS-LAH* and its new sister division, *SS-Hitlerjugend*. *Heer* staff officer Fritz Kraemer transferred to the *Waffen-SS* to become the corps chief of staff, and he and Dietrich developed a fine working relationship. The corps fought in Normandy from June 1944, and Dietrich was awarded the Diamonds to his Knight's Cross with Swords and Oakleaves on 6 August 1944. This was the second and final such decoration within the *Waffen-SS*. Days earlier, on 1 August, he had joined Hausser as the second *Waffen-SS* man to attain the rank of *SS*-(Four-Star) General (*SS-Oberstgruppenführer*). In recognition of his lengthy experience in armored warfare, his military *SS* rank was honorarily listed as *"Panzer-Generaloberst der Waffen-SS."*

Dietrich took command of the *Heer* 5th Panzer Army in Normandy on 9 August 1944. A month later, on 14 September, he was ordered to form the 6th Panzer Army, based around the I and II *SS*-Panzer Corps. Kraemer joined him again as chief of staff for the rest of the war, as the army, retitled the 6th *SS*-Panzer Army, fought in the Ardennes and then in Hungary. Dietrich seems to have lost faith in Hitler and the Nazi leadership by 1943 at the latest, and he considered Hitler to have broken faith once and for all when the order came to 6th *SS*-Panzer Army in Hungary in 1945 demanding that its divisions remove their cuff-titles for supposed failure to fulfill their duty.

After the war, Dietrich was tried for allegedly giving the orders that resulted in the Malmedy massacre during December 1944. After his release from prison, he was again tried for his role in the execution of the *SA* leadership, and only was able to live freely after early 1959. He had never lost contact with his men, and became active in the *HIAG*. Thousands of *Waffen-SS* veterans attended Dietrich's funeral after his death on 21 April 1966.

Theodor Eicke

Theodor Eicke was born in Alsace on 17 October 1892, and began his adult life by joining the Bavarian military at age 17. During a modest career that lasted until after the First World War, he specialized as a paymaster, and developed a hatred for the traditional Prussian military class that lasted for the rest of his life.

Theodor Eicke, the head of the guard units of the concentration camp system, which were the cadre for the *SS-Totenkopf* Division. This is another Frentz color photo from Hitler's headquarters, taken when Eicke received his Oakleaves.

Eicke seems to have been the sort with an innate need to go against authority. His anti-Weimar Republic views cost him several opportunities to forge a police career. His ruthless determination at last found an outlet when he became an anti-sabotage and security specialist with I.G. Farben in 1923. This also brought him into contact with the Nazi party, which he joined, along with the *SA*, on 1 December 1928.

Two years later, Eicke switched to the *SS*, where he rose rapidly to senior rank because of his ability to get things done. He continued to rankle those with authority over him, however, and Himmler had to protect and rebuke him on several occasions.

Eicke finally found a position suitable for his talents when he became commandant of the Dachau concentration camp during mid-1933. A year later, he was made Inspector of all concentration camps, and of the associated guard units. Days previously, he and his assistant, Michael Lippert, had murdered *SA* Chief Ernst Röhm during the "Night of Long Knives" aftermath.

As the uncontested head of the *Totenkopfverbände* from 1936, Eicke devoted his energies to forming the *SS-TV* into a new sort of elite. He

Heinrich Himmler, second from left, and his adjutant Karl Wolff, left, meet with *SS-Totenkopf* in France, summer 1940. Theodor Eicke is second from right, and at right is *SS-Totenkopf* Infantry Regiment 3 commander Matthias Kleinheisterkamp. Kleinheisterkamp can be seen wearing a "*SS-Heimwehr Danzig*" cufftitle, probably to honor his predecessor, despite never having belonged to this formation that no longer existed!

trained his men to be fanatical political soldiers, who rejected conservative *Junker* values and were determined to destroy the enemies of the Nazi state. With Himmler's compliance, Eicke recruited far more men than were necessary for camp guard duties, as a way of circumventing the *Wehrmacht*'s limitations on the size of the *SS-V*, although it must be realized that the men of the *SS-TV* had to meet lower standards upon enlistment, and were far less well trained.

During and after the September 1939 Polish campaign, Eicke and some of the *SS-TV* carried out "pacification" duties in Poland, involving extensive killings and deportations. Soon after, on 14 November 1939, the *SS-Totenkopf* Division was formed around a cadre of 6,500 *SS-TV* men, with Eicke as commander.

After intensive training, the motorized division generally fought well in the Western Campaign, although Eicke clashed with his anti-Nazi corps commander, Erich Hoepner, who wished to have him removed. Hoepner tried to use the Le Paradis incident as grounds for Eicke's dismissal.

By the time *SS-Totenkopf* fought in the advance on Leningrad during 1941, Eicke had come to develop an appreciation of soldiering. While his leadership continued to emphasize blunt power over finesse, he began to recognize the efforts of such apolitical subordinates as Matthias Kleinheisterkamp, where previously those officers from outside the *SS-TV* had been subject to bad treatment.

Eicke was seriously wounded in the foot on 6 July 1941, not returning to command until 21 September. His energetic leadership in the ensuing battles was recognized through the award of the Knight's Cross on 26 December 1941. From early 1942 until October of that year, *Totenkopf* was involved in the Demyansk fighting, during which the division played a major role in preventing the initially-encircled German forces from being destroyed. The price was enormous casualties, and Eicke went through tremendous grief watching his men suffer. He was awarded the Oakleaves to his Knight's Cross on 20 April 1942, but again had very poor relations with his corps commander. If Eicke was becoming more soldierly in bearing, he still could not see eye to eye with noblemen such as the *Graf* von Brockdorff-Ahlefeldt.

The situation didn't improve when Eicke was sent back to Germany to restore his health. Eicke's deputy, Max Simon, commanded the remnants of *SS-Totenkopf* in his stead, and he and Eicke continually complained that *SS-Totenkopf* was being worn away at Demyansk. As Simon led the remnants of the old division in Russia, Eicke oversaw the creation of a new *Totenkopf* Division in France. Although the new version was joined by cadres of the old division, the camp guard and *Allegemeine-SS* character was almost gone, since the manpower and junior officer corps came from the same sources that supplied replacements to *SS-LAH*, *SS-Das Reich*, and *SS-Wiking*.

Eicke barely had a chance to lead the new *SS-Panzer-Grenadier* Division *Totenkopf* in action. The unit detrained in Ukraine during February 1943, and joined the *SS-Panzer Corps* in the counteroffensive to recapture Kharkov. On 26 February, Eicke was flying north of Pavlograd in his personal aircraft, seeking to pass along an order to his Panzer Regiment, which had lost communications with divisional headquarters. He died when the plane was shot down by Soviet anti-aircraft fire, and was buried at Orelka. When the Kharkov area was abandoned six months later, his body was evacuated and reburied at Zhitomir, west of Kiev. It had to be abandoned there soon after. The former *SS-Totenkopf* Infantry Regiment 3, which became the *SS*-Panzer-Grenadier Regiment 6, received the honor title "Theodor Eicke" in his memory.

Eicke's death was probably the best result for all concerned. He died as a hero to his men, instead of through suicide or execution after the war. While his protegés Simon and Hellmuth Becker had leadership roles with the division after his death, most important command positions passed into the hands of professional *SS-V* officers, including such distinguished soldiers as Hermann Priess, Otto Baum, Karl Ullrich, and Josef Swientek. They fostered a degree of professionalism previously unknown in the division, which went on to fight with great local success in losing campaigns for the rest of the war.

Of Eicke, the best that can be said is that he was personally courageous, and that after becoming a division commander, he worked hard to improve his tactical abilities. His charisma as a troop commander led his men to nickname him "Papa Eicke," and he seems to have cared deeply for his enlisted men. On the other hand, he also showed little hesitation in issuing orders certain to cause high casualties, in situations where a more experienced commander might have suffered fewer losses. Considering Theodor Eicke's pre-war career, it is no wonder that *Waffen-SS* veterans tend to downplay his name, in favor of other men with less notorious backgrounds.

Herbert Otto Gille

Born on 8 March 1897, Herbert Otto Gille initially followed a career path similar to that of Paul Hausser. He became a Prussian cadet at age twelve, and later attended the Cadet Academy at Gross Lichterfelde. As a cadet, he specialized in artillery, and was commissioned on 27 January 1915. Serving throughout the First World War with Baden units, he left the army during April 1919. Gille then pursued a civilian career into 1931, when he joined the Nazi Party and the *SS*.

On 20 May 1934, he joined the fledgling *SS-V* as a company commander in the Political Readiness Detachment Württemburg, which later became the 3d Battalion of the *SS-Deutschland* Regiment. It was here he first made the acquaintance of Felix Steiner.

Late in 1936, Gille transferred into *SS-Germania*, where he remained into 1939. During this time, he participated in training courses with the *Heer* in preparation for his future artillery role. He then became the first commander of the 1st Battalion of the newly-formed *SS-V* Artillery Regiment on 1 May 1939, and led his unit in action in Poland and France.

On 1 December 1940, he joined Steiner in *SS-Wiking*, becoming the first commander of what developed into *SS*-Armored Artillery Regiment 5, with his former battalion as cadre. This began a fruitful period of cooperation, as Steiner frequently entrusted Gille with the leadership of special combat groups during *Wiking*'s advance to the Mius River, and then to the Caucasus. In recognition of his abilities, Gille was awarded the Knight's Cross on 8 October 1942, after already receiving the German Cross in Gold months earlier on 28 February.

While Steiner led the German Army's III Panzer Corps between November 1942 and January 1943, Gille replaced him as *SS-Wiking* commander. He finally became Steiner's full successor on 1 May 1943, when the latter transferred to form the III (Germanic) *SS*-Panzer Corps. Gille led *SS-Wiking* successfully through heavy fighting in the Kharkov

Herbert Otto Gille, the most highly decorated member of the *Waffen-SS*. Yet another Frentz photo, this was taken during the autumn of 1943 when Gille received his Oakleaves from Hitler.

area during the summer of 1943, and then through incredibly intense combat along the Dnieper River that autumn. He was awarded the Oakleaves to his Knight's Cross on 1 November 1943, for his division's defense of Foxtail Island the previous month.

SS-Wiking badly needed rest and replenishment, but its intended quiet zone along the Dnieper around Korsun became encircled during January 1944. On 16 February, a depleted *SS-Wiking* spearheaded the breakout from the called Cherkassy pocket. For his steadying influence on the operation, Gille received the Swords to his Knight's Cross with Oakleaves personally from Hitler on 18 February 1944.

SS-Wiking still received little rest. Just after beginning its reformation, it was ordered to the Kovel zone, on the fringe of the Pripet Marshes, where a Soviet advance threatened to turn the southern flank of Army Group Center. On 16 March, Gille flew into Kovel ahead of his division, to organize the defense of what was both an island in a swamp and a surrounded German strongpoint. Gille rallied the dejected, makeshift garrison, and energized them sufficiently to hold out until

The leading personalities to escape from Cherkassy were honored at Hitler's headquarters on 18 February 1944, and photographed to prove to the world that they were still alive. From the left are *SS-Wiking* commander Herbert Otto Gille, *Heer* general Theobold Lieb, and Walloon Rexist leader Leon Degrelle. With them is German Press Chief Otto Dietrich. Degrelle has just been presented with the Knight's Cross, and Gille the Swords to his Knight's Cross with Oakleaves.

SS-Wiking and *Heer* armored units finally relieved the city on 5 April. For again turning a potential disaster into a defensive victory, Gille became the first soldier of the *Waffen-SS* to earn the Diamonds to the Knight's Cross with Oakleaves and Swords on 19 April 1944.

On 20 July 1944, Gille became the first field commander of the IV *SS*-Panzer Corps, which controlled *SS-Wiking* and *SS-Totenkopf* (with brief exceptions) for the rest of the war. Under his direction, the corps fought well north of Warsaw, and then in Hungary during the three KONRAD offensives of January 1945. That latter campaign was mismanaged by Hermann Balck, who unfairly blamed Gille for not attaining unrealistic objectives. Bad blood had first formed between members of Balck's staff and Gille and his staff at Cherkassy, and in Hungary; this almost cost Gille his command. Fortunately, he was able to retain his post, and he led the IV *SS*-Panzer Corps with the best possible results until the end of the war.

After the war, Gille remained in close contact with his men, and founded the *SS-Wiking* veterans' magazine *Wiking Ruf* (Viking Battle Cry). This merged with another publication during 1954 to become the monthly *Waffen-SS* magazine *Der Freiwillige* (The Volunteer) which remained in publication until the end of 1999 (and today is continued in non-veteran hands). Gille was also active in the *HIAG* until his death on 26 December 1966.

His award of the German Cross in Gold in addition to the Diamonds put Herbert Otto Gille ahead of Sepp Dietrich as the most highly-decorated man in the *Waffen-SS*. In his case, however, his tactical abilities matched his leadership qualities, and his battlefield successes helped stave off Germany's defeat, for which he was rightly rewarded. Gille was also noted for his apolitical attitude, despite his early Nazi membership. He advanced the soldierly, professional mindset advocated by Hausser and Steiner, and was also admired for his personal bravery. His positive qualities have rarely received proper credit, because of Balck's view of the Hungarian fighting being widely quoted. In any examination of the Second World War era, however, Gille must rank as one of the best soldiers in any army, not just the *Waffen-SS*.

Willi Bittrich

One of the best-known *Waffen-SS* commanders, Wilhelm "Willi" Bittrich was born on 26 February 1894. After specializing in athletics and gymnastics, he joined the Prussian Army days before the beginning of the First World War. He quickly became a pilot, and was commissioned while with the Flying Service. After the war, he fought with the *Freikorps* before joining the *Reichswehr*. He served in the Soviet Union during the period of secret German-Soviet military cooperation that was facilitated by the Rapallo accords, secretly training pilots for future employment.

Bittrich joined the Nazi Party late in 1932, after serving for several months with the *SA* and then the *SS*. With the *SS*, he led a flight training staff until March 1934. As the German armed forces began to expand, Bittrich could have joined the embryonic *Luftwaffe*, but instead became the first commander of the Political Readiness Detachment Hamburg on 25 August 1934. The next spring, he took command of the Austrian 2d Battalion of the forming *SS-Deutschland*. During 1938, Bittrich's unit was sent to Vienna as the 1st Battalion and cadre of the new *SS-Der Führer*.

On 1 June 1939, Bittrich was transferred to *SS-LAH* as a steadying influence on Sepp Dietrich, serving until early 1940, when he transferred into the *SS*-High Command to help oversee the supply of replacements for the *SS-V* and *SS-Totenkopf*. He then succeeded Felix Steiner as *SS-Deutschland* commander, leading the regiment in the Barbarossa campaign until Paul Hausser was wounded on 14 October 1941. Bittrich replaced Hausser as *SS-Reich* commander, and earned the Knight's Cross on 14 December 1941 for his regimental command, from a recommendation Hausser filed while convalescing.

Wilhelm "Willi" Bittrich, the First World War pilot, who became a successful corps commander. He is seen here during the summer of 1942 as commander of the SS-Cavalry Division.

Bittrich's tenure as a division commander was brief, as he left *SS-Reich* because of illness in early January 1942, but he had proven his abilities. During May 1942, he assumed command of the *SS*-Cavalry Brigade to oversee its conversion the next month into the *SS*-Cavalry Division. He led this division until the end of the year, after which he was prepared for a new assignment.

Beginning on 15 February 1943, Bittrich formed and commanded the 9th *SS*-Panzer(-Grenadier Division) "Hohenstaufen," in which he was able to instill something of the old *SS-V* spirit to the young conscripts and *RAD* volunteers. He led the new division with great success in Galicia during March and April 1944, and then went to Normandy with it during that June. Just as *SS*-Hohenstaufen began to counterattack the British EPSOM offensive across the Odon River, Hausser had to take command of the 7th Army, and Bittrich succeeded him as II *SS*-Panzer Corps commander, a post he held until the end of the war. For his divisions' role in rescuing thousands of men from the Falaise pocket, he was awarded the Oakleaves to his Knight's Cross on 28 August 1944.

The next month, Bittrich and his corps were refitting near Arnhem when Operation MARKET literally dropped on their heads. His quick decisionmaking sent *SS*-Hohenstaufen and *SS*-Frundsberg to the decisive spots, so that the Allied offensive could be contained by the badly-depleted German formations. Bittrich's name has since always been associated with this German victory.

During October 1944, Bittrich again became a subordinate of Sepp Dietrich when the II *SS*-Panzer Corps came under the command of the 6th Panzer Army. In that formation, Bittrich led his corps in the Ardennes and then in Hungary. Dietrich recognized Bittrich's efforts by awarding him the Swords to his Knight's Cross with Oakleaves on 6 May 1945.

After the war, Bittrich was tried by the French for alleged atrocities committed by his men. Acquitted, he wasn't released until 1954. He joined the *HIAG*, and was the senior member after Hausser passed away, until his own death on 19 April 1979. Though Bittrich was critical of Dietrich during post-war interrogations, he gave the eulogy at Dietrich's funeral.

Wilhelm Bittrich was a man of wide military experience before assisting the formation of the *SS-V*. This, and his background in athletics, helped turn the concepts of Felix Steiner into reality. Though a highly-ranked, longtime member of the *SS*, Bittrich did not get along well with Himmler, in part because of his insistence on allowing Christian religious services for his men. When Himmler removed Bittrich from command of the II *SS*-Panzer Corps after Arnhem, Army Group B commander Walter Model, under whom Bittrich had served as far back as 1941, intervened, and ordered Bittrich to remain, since he was too valuable to replace. Never flashy or dynamic, Bittrich was simply steady and professional, enabling the men of his commands to fight hard and well.

Matthias Kleinheisterkamp

Perhaps the least-known of the important *Waffen-SS* leaders, troubleshooter Matthias Kleinheisterkamp was born on 22 June 1893. He joined the army as an officer candidate at the start of the First World War, and after commissioning, served with infantry units as a platoon commander and as adjutant for larger units. He fought with a *Freikorps* during 1919, and later joined the *Reichswehr*, in which he became a company commander.

Kleinheisterkamp left the *Reichswehr* as a *Hauptmann* in early 1934, joining the *SS* as a training advisor. From March 1935 to April 1936, he taught infantry tactics at the *SS*-Officer Training School Braunschweig,

Matthias Kleinheisterkamp, the unrecognized tactics instructor. This shot was probably taken in Finland during the summer of 1942 after he assumed command of *SS-Nord*.

influencing dozens of future *Waffen-SS* officers. He then spent over two years as Paul Hausser's chief of staff with the Inspectorate of the *SS-V*, helping to implement the programs of Hausser and Steiner.

Kleinheisterkamp commanded the 3d Battalion of *SS-Deutschland* in Poland and the first weeks of the Western campaign. Hausser recommended him for the Knight's Cross for capturing the Scheldt Estuary, which protected Antwerp, but the award was not approved. On 3 June 1940, Kleinheisterkamp replaced the fallen Hans-Friedmann Götze as the commander of *SS-Totenkopf* Infantry Regiment 3. He and Theodor Eicke disliked each other personally, the latter probably seeing him as an unnecessary extension of Hausser's influence onto *SS-Totenkopf*. This didn't prevent Eicke from coming to appreciate the apolitical Kleinheisterkamp's soldierly abilities the next summer, when he recommended him for the Knight's Cross.

Kleinheisterkamp was next to have assumed command of the troubled *SS-Nord* in Finland, but was redirected to *SS-Reich*, where he replaced the ill Willi Bittrich in early January 1942. For his leadership of the division in desperate defensive fighting, Kleinheisterkamp was recommended for the Knight's Cross for a third time, and it was approved on 31 March 1942.

Days later, Kleinheisterkamp assumed command of the new elements of *SS-Nord* forming in Germany. He then commanded the united division in north Karelia from June 1942 until 15 December 1943. His next assignment was as Felix Steiner's deputy commander of the III (Germanic) *SS*-Panzer Corps at Narva from 25 February to 16 April 1944 while the latter was on sick leave.

Kleinheisterkamp then organized the headquarters of VII *SS*-Panzer Corps between May and July 1944, before that unit took the field as the IV *SS*-Panzer Corps under Herbert Otto Gille. The next month, Kleinheisterkamp organized the headquarters of the XI *SS*-Army Corps, which he quickly led into action in Poland as a *Heer* infantry formation. During February 1945, the corps redeployed to the Oder River front as XI *SS*-Panzer Corps. During the last week of April 1945, Kleinheisterkamp and his corps spearheaded the breakout of the 9th Army from the Halbe pocket. He was awarded the Oakleaves to his Knight's Cross on 9 May 1945 for the efforts of his men, which allowed tens of thousands of soldiers and civilians to escape the Soviets.

Matthias Kleinheisterkamp did not make it out of the Halbe pocket. Differing accounts have him killed in action amongst his men, or committing suicide in Soviet captivity. He died sometime between 30 April and 9 May 1945, and his final resting place is unknown. His soldierly qualities and professionalism were highly regarded by Hausser and by various *Heer* commanders, but his apolitical attitude retarded his advancement. He was almost expelled from the *SS*, and from 1942 had to accept less than prime assigments. His lack of political zeal may also have contributed to the delay in his receving the Knight's Cross, and to his not being awarded the Oakleaves far sooner. However, from a military standpoint, Kleinheisterkamp was one of the best higher commanders in the *Waffen-SS*.

Otto Kumm

At this writing, the last surviving *Waffen-SS* general and division commander, Otto Kumm was born on 1 October 1909, in Hamburg. He was part of the in-between generation, too young to serve in the First World War, but old enough to join the *SS* and be commissioned before the *SS-V* and its associated officer training schools were created. Kumm first enlisted in the *SA* during 1930, but the next year transferred to the *SS*, and became an officer in early 1934. During August of that year, he became a founding member of the Political Readiness Detachment

Hamburg, which developed into the 1st Battalion of *SS-Germania*. Here his military education began under two future corps commanders, Willi Bittrich and Matthias Kleinheisterkamp.

Kumm commanded various companies in *SS-Germania*, then *SS-Deutschland*, and finally with the newly-formed *SS-Der Führer* from its foundation in May 1938. Three days into the Western Campaign, on 13 May 1940, he assumed command of his regiment's 3d Battalion after his predecessor was wounded. He distinguished himself at his new position, to the extent that when *SS-Der Führer* commander Georg Keppler transferred to *SS-Totenkopf* to replace the wounded Theodor Eicke, Kumm succeeded him on 11 July 1941. The very junior *SS-Sturmbannführer* received an accelerated promotion to *SS-Obersturmbannführer*, and was recommended for the Knight's Cross by his former commander, Bittrich. This was denied, but Kumm instead became one of the first recipients of the German Cross in Gold on 3 December 1941.

During the first weeks of 1942, *SS-Der Führer* was nearly destroyed in desperate defensive fighting in the Voga River bend near Rzhev.

Otto Kumm, right, poses during the summer of 1943 with his new commander, Transylvanian ethnic German Artur Phleps. The latter had just begun forming the V *SS*-Mountain Corps, after creating and leading the 7th *SS*-Volunteer Mountain Division *"Prinz Eugen."*

Otto Kumm, who rose from company to division commander, and founded the *HIAG*. He is seen during the Kharkov campaign in February or March 1943.

Kumm inspired his men to make a successful stand, during which the 9th Army was saved, but the regiment was reduced to only 35 men fit for combat. This sacrifice was recognized through the award of the Knight's Cross to Kumm on 16 February 1942.

Kumm oversaw the reconstitution of *SS-Der Führer* during the rest of 1942, before leading his regiment to Ukraine for the Kharkov campaign. For his role in the dramatic campaign, he became the first recipient of the Oakleaves to the Knight's Cross in *SS-Das Reich* on 6 April 1943. Soon after, on 1 May, he became the Chief of Staff of the newly-formed V *SS*-Mountain Corps, despite lacking any staff training.

After several months with the corps in Yugoslavia, Kumm assumed command of the main component, the *SS*-Volunteer Mountain Division *Prinz Eugen* in early February 1944. The division's previous anti-partisan mission became a front line one that autumn, as Soviet and Bulgarian troops attempted to cut off the retreat of hundreds of thousands of German soldiers from the Balkans. During October and November 1944, *SS-Prinz Eugen* held a bridgehead across the Morava River at Nish, and then another at Kraljevo, in screening operations that allowed the German evacuation to be completed successfully. Kumm then led his greatly weakened division in an overland march through the mountains in oppressive winter conditions, salvaging it from what could have been a suicide mission. In recognition of this, Kumm was recommended for the Swords to his Knight's Cross with Oakleaves.

Kumm had been promoted to *SS-Brigadeführer* on 9 November 1944. He left *SS-Prinz Eugen* in late January 1945, and early the next month assumed command of *SS-LAH* for the fighting in Hungary, beginning with the destruction of the Gran bridgehead. While with *SS-LAH*, Kumm's Swords were approved on 17 March. He led the remnants of the division until the end of the war, going with it into American captivity.

His escape from a PW camp spared Kumm from extradition to Yugoslavia, where he certainly would have been executed. He had trained as a typesetter before joining the *SA*, and made a post-war career in Hamburg in the printing industry. Relatively well-to-do, and in sound health, Kumm was dismayed over the suffering of disabled *Waffen-SS* veterans and the families of the those who were dead or incapacitated. During a meeting with old comrades during 1950, he established the *HIAG*. Since the German government wouldn't provide many services to Waffen-*SS* veterans, Kumm's organization took over this function. Thousands of men and their families were helped by the *HIAG*, which soon developed branches all over Germany.

After his 1975 retirement, Kumm wrote the history of his former division, *Vorwärts Prinz Eugen!* (Forward, *Prinz Eugen!*), followed by a photo book, *7. SS-Freiwilligen-Gebirgs Division Prinz Eugen im Bild* (7th *SS*-Volunteer Mountain Division *Prinz Eugen* in Pictures). He also authored a section of the history of *Regiment Der Führer*, *Kameraden bis zum Ende* (Comrades to the End), and served as the honorary head of the veterans' associations for his former commands. As late as 1999, he addressed the reunion of the I (*SS*-)Panzer Corps Association. His legacy is secure as one of the the two best *Waffen-SS* generals among those without First World War experience.

Heinz Harmel

Heinz Harmel was born in Metz in the then-German province of Lorraine on 29 June 1906. He received his first taste of soldiering with the youth organization of a *Freikorps*, and decided to become a professional soldier. The first step to this was joining the *Reichswehr* during May 1926, but he left four months later because of an injury. After his recovery, he became a reserve NCO, and took a refresher course with the *Heer* during 1935. He then joined the *SS-V* as an NCO on 2 October of that year, assuming command of a platoon in the 1st Company of *SS-Germania*. Later Harmel was commissioned and commanded a platoon in *SS-Deutschland*, and was with the cadre that formed *SS-Der Führer* during March 1938. The next year, he took command of the 9th Company of *SS-Der Führer*, and led it in the Western campaign.

On 14 November 1940, Harmel assumed command of the 2d Battalion of his regiment, and for his leadership during the summer of 1941, was awarded the German Cross in Gold on 29 November of that year. This was the same day that his regimental commander Otto Kumm received the decoration, and these were two of the first such awards in the entire German military establishment. Days later, on 4 December, Harmel took command of *SS-Deutschland*, which he led in extremely heavy combat into the spring of 1942. As with Kumm, he was still a junior *SS-Sturmbannführer* when he assumed the post, but was soon promoted to *SS-Obersturmbannführer* when the assignment became permanent. By this time, he had begun to develop his reputation from always leading from the front, even as a regimental commander.

Harmel then led *SS-Deutschland* in the Kharkov campaign during February and March 1943, in the course of which he personally knocked out a Soviet tank. He was awarded the Knight's Cross on 31 March 1943 for the success of his regiment. After further successful fighting in the

Heinz Harmel, "the old Frundsberger," and one of the most recognized *Waffen-SS* commandesr due to his role in defeating MARKET-GARDEN. This photo dates from the autumn of 1944, prior to his December 15 award of the Swords. Harmel wears a black Panzer uniform.

Kursk offensive, Harmel personally led the foremost elements of *SS-Deutschland* in the decisive attack on Hill 203.9 and Stepanovka on 31 July 1943. The hill and town were taken after desperate fighting, freeing the Panzer Group (combat group based around the Panzer Regiment) of *SS-Das Reich* to penetrate the Soviet bridgehead across the Mius River. This allowed the destruction of the bridgehead after some of the most intense combat ever experienced by *SS-Das Reich* and *SS-Totenkopf*. For his role in the victory, Harmel was awarded the Oakleaves to his Knight's Cross on 7 September 1943.

A month later, Harmel suffered a head wound, and after his recovery, attended a course for division commanders, the first time in his career he received specialized instruction prior to assuming a post. He then assumed "full" command of *SS-Frundsberg* in Galicia on 27 April 1944, as an *SS-Standartenführer*. This was an unusual step, as officers junior in rank compared to their assignment usually spent time proving themselves as temporary commanders before being confirmed as full commander.

Harmel next led *SS*-Frundsberg in costly fighting in the Odon valley in Normandy during the summer of 1944. The division remained on the defensive when most of the other *Waffen-SS* units launched Operation LIEGE at Mortain, and thus was in a better position to attack to the east beginning on 19 August, when the 7th Army tried to break out of the Falaise pocket. Harmel and his men set an example for several demoralized units, which he rallied and directly led in successful assaults that linked up two days later with elements of the II *SS*-Panzer Corps attacking west into the pocket. This freed the way for the escape of much of the 7th Army, and allowed the evacuation of two severely wounded higher officers, Paul Hausser and *SS-LAH* commander Theodor "Teddy" Wisch.

Willi Bittrich recommended Harmel for the Swords to his Knight's Cross with Oakleaves, with the award approved on 15 December 1944.

Harmel, who had only become an *SS-Unterturmführer* on 30 January 1937, completed his meteoric rise on 7 September 1944 when he was promoted to *SS-Brigadeführer*. He commanded *SS*-Frundsberg at Nijmegen later that month, and like Bittrich, was associated with Operation MARKET-GARDEN for the rest of his life. His division played a vital role in preventing the Allied ground forces with linking up with the British airborne troops near Arnhem. Harmel continued to lead his men with relative success in 1945, during Operation *NORDWIND* in Alsace and then in Operation *SONNENWENDE* in Pomerania. After heavy defensive combat near Dresden, Harmel was dismissed from command of *SS*-Frundsberg on 27 April 1945, for retreating against orders.

Reassigned to the *SS*-Officer Training School at Klagenfurt, he commanded a combat group from the school in northern Italy during the last days of the war. His unit continued fighting after the official ceasefire in Italy, allowing tens of thousands of German soldiers and civilians to reach Austria and escape captivity at the hands of the Yugoslav partisans.

After the war, Harmel remained in close contact with the men of his former commands, who called him "the old Frundsberger." He also frequently attended reunions for the participants of the MARKET-GARDEN campaign, and shared his views with many historians. He was one of the few *SS* generals to never join the Nazi party, but this didn't hinder his career advancement because of his outstanding battlefield record. Heinz Harmel ranks with Kumm as one of the two best *Waffen-SS* generals without First World War experience. He joined Kumm as the last surviving *Waffen-SS* generals and division commanders until his death on 2 September 2000.

Dr. Oskar Dirlewanger

The most notorious man in the *Waffen-SS*, even more infamous than Theodor Eicke, was Oskar Dirlewanger, born on 26 September 1895. He began his military career in 1913, and found his calling in life when the First World War began the next year. He excelled as an enlisted soldier, was commissioned, and received numerous decorations for bravery. He also demonstrated leadership, taking charge of the remnants of his battalion in Ukraine at the end of the war, and leading them back to Germany to avoid Soviet captivity. He was classified as 40 percent disabled because of the numerous wounds he suffered during the war.

These positive traits initially concealed Dirlewanger's darker ones, but in the post-war years, in common with many traumatized veterans, he developed a reputation as an alcoholic. He continued to fight, this time in various *Freikorps*, seeing extensive action against Communists and again sustaining a wound. He also pursued a university degree, receiving a doctorate in political science during 1922. As happened with many others, his *Freikorps* service brought him into contact with the fledgling Nazi party and the *SA*, both of which he eventually joined.

Dirlewanger seems to have had an innate need to clash with those in authority over him, and this frequently got him into trouble as civil strife ended in Germany and the Nazis gradually consolidated their power. With no real enemy available, he instead entered power struggles with his superiors, who eventually brought Dirlewanger's fondness for alcohol and allegations of a sexual liaison with an adolescent girl to the attention of the appropriate authorities. For the latter activity, he was

Dr. Oskar Dirlewanger, the most notorious member of the *Waffen-SS*. Here he wears the Spanish Cross for his service with the Condor Legion, and also the Slovak War Victory Cross under his Knight's Cross.

tried, convicted, stripped of many of his honors, and spent most of 1935 and 1936 in prison.

After Dirlewanger's release, his old Freikorps comrade Gottlob Berger, now with the SS, arranged a posting for him with the Condor Legion in Spain. Back in the familiar role of soldier, Dirlewanger again distinguished himself during two tours of duty, winning high praise as a company commander in one of the camps that trained Falangist personnel. Once back in Germany, he had his child molestation case reopened. After investigation by SS officials, the conviction was overturned.

Berger became head of recruiting for the *Waffen-SS*, and during early 1940, followed up Hitler's idea of creating a unit of convicted game poachers for security duty in Poland. He arranged for his newly rehabilitated friend to be placed in command of this formation, which initially was at company strength. During 1941, the "Special Unit Dr. Dirlewanger" dug fortifications and guarded labor camps, while also fighting partisans. Dirlewanger was considered an excellent leader of his unit, but lost a power struggle with his superiors, and was reassigned with his men to Belorussia.

Here the Dirlewanger unit developed into a battalion, and later a regiment, as it fought partisans and murdered civilians. It took on military convicts from the *Waffen-SS* and every branch of the *Wehrmacht*, and recruited Russian and Ukrainian volunteers. Dirlewanger was usually at the head of his men when they were in combat, displaying his proven bravery, but away from action he became known for cruelty and unruliness. Nevertheless, for his many acts of valor, Dirlewanger was awarded the German Cross in Gold on 5 December 1943.

Through late June 1944, the Dirlewanger unit fought as a police formation, but late that month, the front reached its zone near Minsk. Dirlewanger then led his men in front line combat against the Soviets as the police units of Combat Group von Gottberg covered the German withdrawal from Belorussia. After this, the weakened unit was deployed between August and October 1944 in savage, no-quarter fighting in Warsaw against the Polish Home Army.

While the Dirlewanger unit reinforced its reputation for atrocity, it also absorbed enormous casualties. From a beginning strength of under 900 men, fewer than 650 remained two months later, and it must be taken into account that the unit took on 2,500 replacements during the course of the fighting. Dirlewanger was again frequently at the head of his men during the elimination of Polish strongpoints, and for this, along with actions against partisans and the Red Army in the preceding months, was awarded the Knight's Cross on 30 September 1944. He had recently received his final promotion, to *SS-Oberführer*, and this was the high point of his life.

The Dirlewanger unit was expanded into a brigade, with most of the new manpower consisting of political prisoner volunteers (usually Communists) released from concentration camps. The unit became more unreliable than ever, as it fought against the Slovak uprising, and then in Hungary. It redeployed to the Oder front during February 1945, and Dirlewanger was wounded on 15 February while leading a counterattack. He never commanded the division which bore his name, the 36th *Waffen*-Grenadier Division of the *SS*. During his convalescence, he made his way to Altshausen, in southwest Germany. He was murdered there while in Allied captivity on 7 June 1945, though rumors frequently had him serving as an advisor the post-war Egyptian Army.

Dr. Oskar Dirlewanger remains a paradox. He was a brave man, but otherwise gave in to his base instincts and regularly acted in a thoroughly immoral manner. His service in the First World War and immediately after was similar to that of many men who went on to form the the German military of the Second World War. During the latter conflict, he fought primarily as a rear area police leader, in a manner far removed from what Hausser and Steiner had conceived for the *SS-V*. In the crisis of 1944–1945, the Dirlewanger Brigade and Division did fight as part of the *Waffen-SS*, to the horror of many more honorable *Waffen-SS* veterans who to this day do everything in their power to stress the tenuousness of the links between the *Waffen-SS* and the Special Unit Dr. Dirlewanger. The history of Dirlewanger and his unit will always remain complicated, and no easy answer does justice to the case.

Otto Weidinger

A prime example of a disciple of Paul Hausser, Otto Weidinger was born on 27 May 1914. He joined the *SS* while still in school during 1933, and the next year passed his *Abitur*. He became an *SS*-? on 20 March 1935, and was earmarked for an officer career. The next month, he became part of the first class to attend Hausser's newly-founded *SS*-Officer Training School at Braunschweig. After graduation, Weidinger assumed command of a platoon in the 9th Company of *SS-Deutschland*, and received his commission on 20 April 1936. A few months later, *SS-Deutschland* came under the command of Felix Steiner, and Hausser and Steiner together were the prime influences on Weidinger early in his service. From them, he learned professionalism and flexibility.

Weidinger served as adjutant to *SS-V* Reconnaissance Battalion commander Dr. Wim Brandt (the inventor of modern camouflage clothing) during the Polish campaign, and then commanded the battalion's armored car company in the Western campaign. Brandt recommended that Weidinger receive General Staff training, and so Hausser took him onto his staff as Intelligence Officer (Ic) and then division adjutant (IIa) for the *SS-V* Division (renamed *SS-Reich*).

Weidinger worked closely with Hausser during the Yugoslavian campaign, and in the opening weeks of BARBAROSSA. Then, during the summer and autumn of 1941, he commanded various companies in the motorcycle battalion of *SS-Reich*, earning a reputation for bravery in hand-to-hand combat. After twice sustaining wounds, Weidinger was reassigned on 1 November 1941, becoming a tactics instructor at his *alma mater*, the Braunschweig officers' school. He remained there until May 1943, aside from spending January 1943 attending a course for battalion commanders.

Prior to Kursk, Weidinger rejoined *SS-Reich*, now retitled *SS-Das Reich*, and took command of the 1st Battalion of *SS-Deutschland*. He led it at Kursk and in the destruction of the Mius bridgehead, before assuming command of *SS-Das Reich*'s *SS*-Armored Reconnaissance Battalion 2. He particularly distinguished himself at the head of this unit during the Fourth Battle of Kharkov, and then in the retreat to the Dnieper and the fighting west of Kiev. For this time, as well as for his performance during the summer of 1941, Weidinger was awarded the German Cross in Gold on 26 November 1943. Days earlier, he had

Otto Weidinger, the historian, in a photo shot after his 21 April 1944 award of the Knight's Cross.

successfully defended a bridgehead at Negrebovka with his depleted battalion, making possible a decisive counterattack by other units.

When *SS-Das Reich* was transferred to France to refit during December 1943, it left behind a combat group of combat-capable units. Weidinger commanded the infantry regiment of *SS*-Combat Group *Das Reich*, which consisted of two weak battalions. Elements of the combat group gradually joined the main body of the division in France, until Weidinger was left in command of the last 800 men still in Ukraine. This small *SS*-Combat Group, Weidinger finally departed for France on 20 April 1944. The next day, Weidinger was awarded the Knight's Cross for his achievement at Negrebovka the previous autumn.

During June 1944, Weidinger commanded the lead elements of *SS-Das Reich* that arrived in Normandy ahead of the main body. He had assumed command of *SS-Der Führer* from Sylvester Stadler on 14 June, and led the regiment in costly fighting. From 19 to 21 August, *SS-Der Führer* was part of the II *SS*-Panzer Corps attack that linked up with

SS-Frundsberg and other units inside the Falaise pocket, allowing part of the 7th Army (including commander Paul Hausser) to escape. For this, Weidinger was awarded the Oakleaves to his Knight's Cross on 27 December 1944.

Weidinger received his final promotion, to *SS-Obersturmbannführer*, on 9 November 1944, and continued to lead *SS-Der Führer* until the end of the war. After the defensive fighting in Vienna in mid-April 1945, the regiment was forced away from the main body of *SS-Das Reich*. On May 1, Weidinger was ordered to Prague, where he and his men supervised the evacuation of the German population of the city. Without the efforts of *SS-Der Führer*, hundreds of civilians would have faced captivity or worse at the hands of the vengeful Czechs. Weidinger then led his regiment into American captivity.

During 1947, Weidinger was turned over to the French because of the role of *SS-Der Führer* in the Oradour-sur-Glane affair. He wasn't tried until 1951, when he was acquitted after proving he had nothing to do with the incident. On 24 June of that year, he was released, and learned from old comrades that he had been awarded the Swords to his Knight's Cross with Oakleaves on 6 May 1945.

As Weidinger made a career as a pharmacist, he renewed his friendship with his wartime comrades, and worked closely with Paul Hausser in creating a written history of the *Waffen-SS*. His initial efforts resulted in the 1962 book, *Kameraden bis zum Ende* (Comrades to the End), a history of *SS-Der Führer* compiled with the assistance of fellow former commanders Georg Keppler, Otto Kumm, and Sylvester Stadler. Weidinger then began the long work of writing the history of *SS-Das Reich* from the creation of the Political Readiness Detachments to the end of the war. The first of five volumes appeared during 1967, with the final not released until 1982. After this, he assisted various researchers outside of Germany, always seeking to have accurate, detailed information about the *SS-V* and *Waffen-SS* be made available to posterity. Otto Weidinger died on 10 January 1990, and is remembered for his contributions both as a soldier and as a historian.

Hans Dorr

Hans Dorr was born on 7 April 1912, as the son of a farmer. He joined the newly formed *SS-V* during 1934, and became an NCO in the 2d Company of *SS-Deutschland*. After graduating from Bad Tölz, he was commissioned late in 1938, and then commanded a platoon in the 10th Company of *SS-Germania*. Dorr commanded his regiment's 4th Company when *SS-Germania* became the cadre of *SS-Wiking* during

December 1940. Felix Steiner entrusted Dorr with the leadership of a special training course for the first Germanic volunteers to arrive at the division, the first step on Dorr's rise to prominence.

Dorr proved himself as a company commander during BARBAROSSA, becoming an early recipient of the German Cross in Gold on 19 December 1941. The following summer, his company was the vanguard of the German advance toward the Caucasus. With other elements, it seized a bridgehead across the Kuban River at Grigoripolnskaya on 3 August, with Dorr becoming bridgehead commandant. He led a successful defense for several days until German infantry forces could arrive, ensuring a springboard for the continued advance. For this, Dorr was awarded the Knight's Cross on 27 September 1942.

On 22 January 1943, Leopold Krocza was killed in action, and Dorr replaced him as commander of *SS-Germania*'s 1st Battalion. Dorr had developed a reputation as a quick thinker who led his men from the front, and this continued during his tenure as a battalion commander. At the beginning of October, as *SS-Wiking* settled into positions on the west bank of the Dnieper River, a crisis developed in the sector of the 3d Panzer Division at Silischische. Dorr gathered 34 men, and led them

Gille, left, poses with Hans Dorr during a break in the fighting, summer 1944. Gille now wears the Diamonds to his Knight's Cross with Oakleaves and Swords, earned at Kovel. Dorr has not yet added his Swords, but has attained his final rank of *Obersturmbannführer*.

Hans Dorr, who rose from officer cadet to regimental commander with *SS-Germania*. This portrait was taken after his award of the Swords on 9 July 1944.

in the containment of a Soviet bridgehead until forces of the 3d Panzer Division could arrive and take care of the situation. This brought Dorr the Oakleaves to his Knight's Cross on 13 November 1943.

During the Cherkassy breakout, 15–16 February 1944, Dorr and his 1st Battalion served as the rear-guard for the surrounded German forces. Afterward, he succeeded Fritz Ehrath as commander of the entire *SS-Germania*, which was in action again just over a month later. The regiment played a leading role in the eventual relief of Kovel in early April, and as a result, Dorr was awarded the Swords to his Knight's Cross with Oakleaves on 9 July 1944. Soon after, on 18 August, he received his final promotion, to *SS-Obersturmbannführer*.

Dorr continued to lead *SS-Germania* during the summer and autumn 1944 fighting near Warsaw, and then in the KONRAD offensives in Hungary beginning in early January 1945. On 21 January, as KONRAD III made good progress toward the Vali River, Dorr called a commanders' meeting at his headquarters. An artillery shell struck nearby during the

In Ukraine during the late spring of 1943, Dorr stands at left, observing as *SS-Germania* commander Jürgen Wagner speaks with an officer. Wagner would earn the Knight's Cross a few months later, and leave his regiment to assume command of the Dutch brigade/division *SS-Nederland*. At center, with eyes shut, is Dietrich Ziemssen, who joined Wagener with *SS-Nederland* as his chief of staff, and earned the German Cross in Gold.

conference, and Dorr was evacuated with serious wounds, his sixteenth wounding during the war. Initially, his recovery went well, but by early April 1945, his health deteriorated. He passed away on 17 April, and was buried in Judenburg, Styria (Austria).

Hans Dorr was the sort of man who likely could not have forged an officer career in the *Reichswehr* because of his lower-class background. He had to prove himself at every level, and with *SS-Germania* was able to rise from platoon leader to regimental commander in just over five years, while earning some of his country's highest decorations. His career was proof of the validity of the concepts of Hausser and Steiner, which were to give promising men the education and opportunity they needed. Sadly, Dorr rarely receives the attention he deserves because he didn't fight in the West after 1940, and because he didn't survive the war.

Walter Schmidt

Walter Schmidt was born on 28 January 1917, and joined the *SS-V* during 1935, serving with *SS-Germania*'s 3d Battalion. He was Hans Dorr's classmate at Bad Tölz, graduating in 1938 and becoming a platoon commander.

Schmidt was badly wounded during the campaign in Western Europe, and retrained on artillery, taking command of the 13th (Light Infantry

Gun) Company of the newly-formed *SS-Nordland* after his recovery. Later, on 1 August 1942, he became the adjutant of the 2d Battalion of *SS-Westland*.

During January 1943, Dietrich Ziemssen was transferred for General Staff training. Schmidt succeeded him as commander of *SS-Westland*'s 2d Battalion. For his leadership during the following months, he was awarded the German Cross in Gold on 9 April 1943.

SS-Wiking rested during the first part of the summer of 1943, but returned to action south of Kharkov in late July. *SS-Westland* was heavily assaulted during the last days of the month, suffering heavy casualties, but successfully holding, thanks to the efforts of Schmidt in rallying the men of his battalion and neighboring units. One strongpoint was successfully defended because of the efforts of the anti-tank gun platoon of *SS-Westland*'s 4th Company, led by Albert "*Pak*" Müller. Schmidt and Müller were both awarded the Knight's Cross on 4 August 1943, and received their decorations in a combined ceremony shortly thereafter.

During the Cherkassy breakout on 16 February 1944, Schmidt's 2d Battalion formed one of the spearheads. It followed the lead element, but in the face of growing resistance, Schmidt scouted out a new route. He led his men in overcoming eight successive Soviet positions, clearing the way for the main body of the encircled troops to escape from the pocket. For this success, Schmidt was awarded the Oakleaves to his Knight's Cross on 14 May 1944.

Schmidt was shot through the chest on 31 October 1944, while commanding his battalion in the "Wet Triangle" north of Warsaw. This was his eighth wound of the war. He was promoted to *SS-Sturmbannführer* days later, on 9 November. As part of his convalescence, he joined the faculty at his *alma mater*, Bad Tölz, in early 1945 (and may have been promoted to *SS-Obersturmbannführer* during the spring). The courses were suspended shortly afterward, and the staff and officer cadets became the cadre for the *SS-Nibelungen* Division. Schmidt assumed command of one of the regiments, which eventually received the designation *SS*-Panzer-Grenadier Regiment 96. He led it in action against American forces in the Danube Valley during the last weeks of the war, and then took to the hills with many of his men. The men of his regiment were primarily teenage students of the Sonthofen Adolf Hitler School. They had received pre-military training in the Hitler Youth, and were experienced hikers and campers. Schmidt had them build shelters, and they lived for several weeks in the wild before gradually dispersing to return to their homes. This spared several hundred of these underage soldiers from becoming prisoners of war.

Schmidt evaded captivity, and under an assumed identity found employment with an American occupation unit. He later opened a successful furniture business, and after the establishment of the

Walter Schmidt, "the old *Westlander*," after his 9 November 1944 promotion to *SS-Sturmbannführer*. He wears the Oakleaves he received on 14 May of that year.

Bundeswehr, became a reserve *Oberstleutnant*. He stayed in close contact with the men of his wartime commands, and was known to them as "our Walter" and "the Old Westlander." Walter Schmidt died on 28 July 2000, after several weeks in a coma, following a car accident.

Weapons of the *Waffen-SS*

With a few exceptions, the *Waffen-SS* used the same weapons as the *Heer*. The following section will list the weapons used within the *Waffen-SS*, beginning with infantry weapons and progressing to artillery and armor. In most cases, only the main models will be listed, but the occasional special interest weapon will also be mentioned. **For detailed weapons data, see the Appendix.**

Infantry Weapons

The principal weapon of the junior enlisted man was the Kar-98 bolt action rifle, in 7.92mm. This was used by infantrymen, mountain troopers, cavalry, and others who did not see most of their service within enclosed armored vehicles. It was supplemented in small numbers by *Gewehr 43* semi-automatic rifles from early 1943 onward.

During the last year of the war, the *Sturmgewehr 44* assault rifle was widely issued to the infantry companies of the *Waffen-SS* panzer and panzer-grenadier divisions, often equipping entire platoons. The improvised emergency units formed during the last six months of the war often were issued rifles and ammunition from stocks captured in France, the Soviet Union, and elsewhere. The Italian 29th *Waffen-*Grenadier Division made use of Italian Carcano bolt-action rifles.

From 1938, squad leaders and platoon commanders were issued MP38 and MP40 9mm submachine guns, and the crews of armored vehicles often received these as well. The less-elite elements of the *Waffen-*

SS, such as the cavalry brigade/division, used the MP41, along with the MP28 and similar older-model wooden-stocked submachine guns, though most of these were out of service by 1943. Emergency units of the final stages of the war received captured British Sten submachine guns and the German MP3008 copy.

Captured Soviet PPSh and similar 7.62mm model submachine guns were widely used by all German combat units on the Easten Front because of their reliability and large magazines. They could be kept supplied with ammunition by scouring battlefields, even during the last year of the war. The Finnish *Waffen-SS* Volunteer Battalion used Finnish Suomi submachine guns specially shipped from Finland.

The principal machine gun of all German infantry was the MG-34, a 7.92mm aircooled, multi-purpose machine gun. It was capable of firing from a bipod or, for greater accuracy at longer ranges, using a traversing and elevating mechanism with at telescope from a tripod. The MG-34s issued at the squad level were equipped with the bipod only, but those issued to heavy weapons platoons had the tripod and associated equipment. From the summer of 1942, the 7.92mm MG-42 supplemented, and then gradually replaced the MG-34. It had a much higher rate of fire than the already high rate of the MG-34, so it was less popular with some Waffen-*SS* machine gunners, who felt it consumed too much ammunition too fast—an especial problem with ammunition becoming harder to come by in the closing months of the war.

Captured examples of practically every model of machine gun in Europe were issued to lower priority and emergency units. *SS-Totenkopf* and the *SS*-Cavalry Brigade/Division in particular used Czech pieces into 1942, while French Hotchkiss guns were issued to the Germanic Legions. First World War vintage Maxim machine guns, found in every armory in Europe, found extensive use in fixed defenses and during training.

The *Waffen-SS* used standard German stick and egg hand grenades, and the rifle grenade dischargers for the Kar 98 and *Sturmgewehr* 44.

Czech ZB 30 Light Machine Gun (NA)

Teller mine

For personal defense, the main pistols used were the famous Luger P08, the Walther P38, and the Browning Hi-Power, license built in Belgium by FN and kept in production during the occupation.

Infantry companies began the war with the 50mm *GrW-36*. Heavy weapons companies used the 81mm *GrW-34*, which was heavier than necessary. It was supplanted, and the 50mm replaced entirely, by the lighter 81mm *GrW-42* from 1942 to the end of the war. The first Soviet 120mm mortars were captured during 1941, and these were so impressive that the German copy 120 mm *GrW-42* was introduced the next year to supplement the many Soviet booty examples in service at regimental level.

50mm mortar (NA)

Combat engineers received standard infantry weapons, along with quantities and types of mines, particularly Model 35 and 42 Teller mines, and hollow charges for the destruction of armor and strongpoints. They also employed the Model 35 and 41 flamethrowers.

Anti-Tank Weapons (Including Tank-Destroying Vehicles)

Regimental anti-tank companies began the war with the *Pak 36* 37mm anti-tank gun. This was supplemented during 1941 by the *sPzB 41* taper-bored heavy anti-tank rifle, which was quickly phased out of service because of a shortage of tungsten for the ammunition. However, *SS-LAH*, almost alone in the German military, continued to use a few of these pieces through early 1944.

The 50mm *Pak 38* was introduced during 1940, and gradually replaced the *Pak 36*. While it remained in use to the end of the war, from the spring of 1942 it was itself supplanted by the 75mm *Pak 40*, which remained the standard anti-tank gun for the rest of the war. Due to the shortage of the *Pak 40* during 1942, the substitute 75 mm *Pak 97/38* was issued to lower priority troops such as the Germanic *Waffen-SS* legions. This was a pre-First World War French barrel mounted on a *Pak 38* carriage and, while crude, was far superior to the *Pak 36* these units had used previously.

50 mm Pak 38 (NA)

75mm Pak 40 (NA)

Divisional anti-tank battalions usually employed the heaviest anti-tank guns available, and from 1943 had 88mm pieces in their towed sections. This was the *Pak 43* and its variant, the *Pak 43/41*. The *Waffen-SS* armored divisions (panzer and panzer-grenadier) also received self-propelled guns for their anti-tank battalions from 1942. These were initially the various *Marder II* and *Marder III* models, which used the *Pak 40* or captured Soviet 76mm cannon on the turretless hulls of Czech 38(t) tanks. From the spring of 1944, these were replaced with fully

75mm Pak 97/38

Marder III (NA)

armored *Jagdpanzer IVs*. Some of the *Waffen-SS* infantry and mountain divisions received *Sturmgschütz III* assault guns and *Hetzer* tank destroyers beginning in mid-1944, though most had to rely on towed pieces.

Waffen-SS units at every level received generous supplies of single shot *Panzerfaust* anti-tank rocket launchers from the late spring of 1944. Also introduced that year was the *RPGr 54*, which replaced the rare earlier *RPGr 43*. Both were 88mm rocket launching tubes, based on the American bazooka. As well as being general issue to infantry units, the *RPGr 54* was issued to regimental anti-tank companies in cases where the *Pak 40* was not available, from late 1944, and to specially formed tank hunting squads. It and the much more numerous *Panzerfaust* were both very effective at close range.

Armored Vehicles

The first tanks to see service with the *Waffen-SS* were three Czech 38(t) models, which formed a platoon in the reconnaissance battalion of *SS-Totenkopf* from formation through the Western Campaign.

SS-LAH received a battery of *Sturmgeschütz III* assault guns during 1940, and *SS-Das Reich* obtained a battery the next year. Batteries were also raised for *SS-Totenkopf*, *SS-Wiking*, and *SS-Nord*, but before they could see service, they were sent to *SS-LAH* to form a full battalion. There, they replaced the Panzer I hulls mounted with Austrian 47mm

Skoda Panzer 38(t) (NA)

A *Sturmgeschütz* III of the Assault Gun Battalion of *SS-LAH* at Taganrog during early 1942.

anti-tank guns, a vehicle which *SS-LAH* was the only *Waffen-SS* element to use.

SS-Das Reich and *SS-Totenkopf* received *Sturmgeschütz* III battalions during 1942, and with *SS-LAH*, kept them until the spring of 1944. *Sturmgeschütz* III were issued in place of tanks to *SS*-Panzer Regiment 5 during 1943, and to *SS*-Panzer Regiments 9 and 10 the next year. From 1943 on, *Sturmgeschütz* III also formed the main component of the panzer battalions of *SS-Polizei*, *SS-Nordland*, *SS-Reichsführer-SS*, *SS*-Götz von Berlichingen, and *SS*-Horst Wessel.

Self-propelled 47mm AT gun on Panzer I chassis (NA)

The panzer regiments for *SS-LAH*, *SS-Das Reich*, *SS-Totenkopf*, and *SS-Wiking* were established during 1942, and at first received mainly Panzer IIIs of the J-M models. These were supplemented by Panzer IVs of the G-J models, which by 1944 were to be the entire strength of one battalion. The other battalion of the regiment was then to have Panzer V "Panther" tanks of the D, A, and G models. Panthers were also used in small numbers by *SS*-Panzer Battalion 11 "Hermann von Salza."

SS-Panzer Regiments 1, 2, and 3 each received a company of Panzer VI "Tigers" during 1942, and these remained in service with the first two units into the spring of 1944. *SS*-Panzer Regiment 3 kept its company until the end of the war. Tigers were used in Heavy *SS*-Panzer Battalions 101 and 102 during the summer of 1944. They were then replaced in those battalions (renumbered 501 and 502) by Tiger II "King Tigers" from the autumn of 1944, which were also then issued to heavy *SS*-Panzer Battalion 503. Several of the King Tiger-derived "*Jagdtiger*" tank destroyers were issued to *SS*-Panzer Regiment 1 during the last week of the war.

The *SS-V* regiments *SS-Deutschland*, *SS-Germania*, and *SS-Der Führer*, along with *SS-LAH*, each contained a platoon of armored cars. Those of the first three were combined into the *SS-V* Reconnaissance Battalion during 1940, and that of *SS-LAH* became part of its own reconnaissance battalion. From 1940 onward, each motorized, later armored *SS* division included a company of armored cars in its reconnaissance battalion.

Panzer III/L (NA)

SS-LAH veteran Gerhard Stiller stands alongside a late-model Panzer III while with a tank training unit at Bitsch during 1943. Soon after, he became a platoon commander in the 7th Company of *SS*-Panzer Regiment 1, before taking over the 5th Company in Normandy. After the war, Stiller contributed substantial accounts to several books about *SS-LAH* and *SS*-Panzer Regiment 1. (Månsson)

Panzer IV (NA)

These Panzer IVs of SS-Panzer Regt 1 carry the short-lived version of the divisional insignia next to the Balkan Cross on the left rear, with oak leaves forming a full wreath around the shield and key. This design, honoring Dietrich's award of the Oakleaves to his Knight's Cross, was soon changed to simply a set of leaves under the shield. Paris, July 1942.

Panzer V "Panther" (NA)

Initially, these were *SdKfz* (*Sonderkraftfahrzeug*, or Special Motor Vehicle) *221-223* light four-wheel models (including *260-261* radio versions) and *SdKfz 231* heavy eight-wheel models (including *263* radio versions). The light cars were phased out from 1942, and the heavy ones replaced by the improved *SdKfz 234* series.

In the seven *SS* panzer divisions, armored halftracks were used from the summer of 1942 for one of six panzer-grenadier battalions, as well as in the divisional armored combat engineer and armored reconnaissance battalions. The *SS* panzer-grenadier divisions had armored halftracks solely in the divisional armored reconnaissance battalion. For both types of divisions, the vehicles were of the one-ton *SdKfz 250* and

Sdkfz. 251 half-track/armored personnel carrier (NA)

Sdkfz. 231 (eight-wheel version) heavy armored car (NA)

the 3-ton *SdKfz 251* classes. The panzer-grenadier and reconnaissance battalions provided platoon and company commanders with the *SdKfz 251/10* modification, which mounted a *Pak 36*. The heavy companies included a platoon of *SdKfz 251/9* "*Stummel*" models, which were equipped with a short-barrelled 75mm gun. During the last year of the war, a few units such as *SS-LAH* received the *SdKfz 251/21*, which carried triple mounted 15mm machine guns or automatic 20mm cannon also carried in aircraft.

Artillery

The lightest artillery was employed by the heavy weapons companies of infantry battalions. These had a platoon of the low velocity 75mm lIG (*leichtes Infanteriegeschütz*, or light infantry gun) 18. Each infantry regiment was supposed to have a company of 150mm sIG 33 (*schweres Infanteriegeschütz*, or heavy infantry gun), though these were sometimes replaced by 120mm mortars. From the summer of 1943, "Bison" self-propelled guns (the *sIG 33* mounted on a 38(t) chassis) replaced the towed pieces in the heavy infantry gun company of one panzergrenadier regiment in the seven *SS* panzer divisions (the same regiment that had an infantry battalion mounted aboard armored personnel carriers). Captured Soviet 76mm model 1927 infantry guns were widely used for training, to free *lIG 18s* for the front.

The standard 105mm piece was the *leFH 18* (*leichte Feldhaubitze*, or light field howitzer Model 1918) while the standard 150mm piece was

75mm lIG 18 (NA)

the *sFH 18* (*schwere Feldhaubitze* Model 1918). The panzer and panzergrenadier divisions typically had an additional battery with the 105mm K 18 field gun (a field gun has a longer barrel than a howitzer, and is built for firing on a much shallower trajectory). In the seven panzer divisions, one artillery battalion would be equipped with two batteries of "*Wespe*" self-propelled 105mm howitzers and one of "*Hummel*" self-propelled 150mm howitzers.

SS-Totenkopf during 1939–1940, and *SS-Prinz Eugen* throughout its existence, utilized captured Czech artillery such as the 105mm M35 and the 150mm M37. Heavy *SS*-Artillery Battalion 101 used the 170mm K18 cannon and the 210mm *Mrs18* ("Mörser" was the German term for a heavy howitzer of low velocity; it was not a term for a mortar, which was a "*Granatewerfer*," or "grenade thrower"). Other anomalies included various models of multi-barrel rocket launchers, towed and mounted on halftracks, that served with *SS*-Artillery Regiment 1, the rocket launcher battalions of selected panzer divisions and specialized detachments.

K. 18 105mm field gun (NA)

Wespe (NA)

Hummel (NA)

170 mm field gun (NA)

For air defense, the standard light weapons at the start of the war were automatic cannon, including the 20mm *Flak 30* (*Fliegerabwehrkanone*, or Anti-Aircraft Gun) and *Flak 38*, and the 37mm *Flak 36* and *Flak 37*. These remained in use for the entire war, and from 1940 were supplemented by the four-barrelled 20mm *Flakvierling 38*. All of these weapons were frequently mounted on trucks or halftracks within the anti-aircraft battalions of *Waffen-SS* divisions, and the anti-aircraft companies of *SS*-panzer-grenadier regiments.

150mm Nebelwerfer
41 (NA)

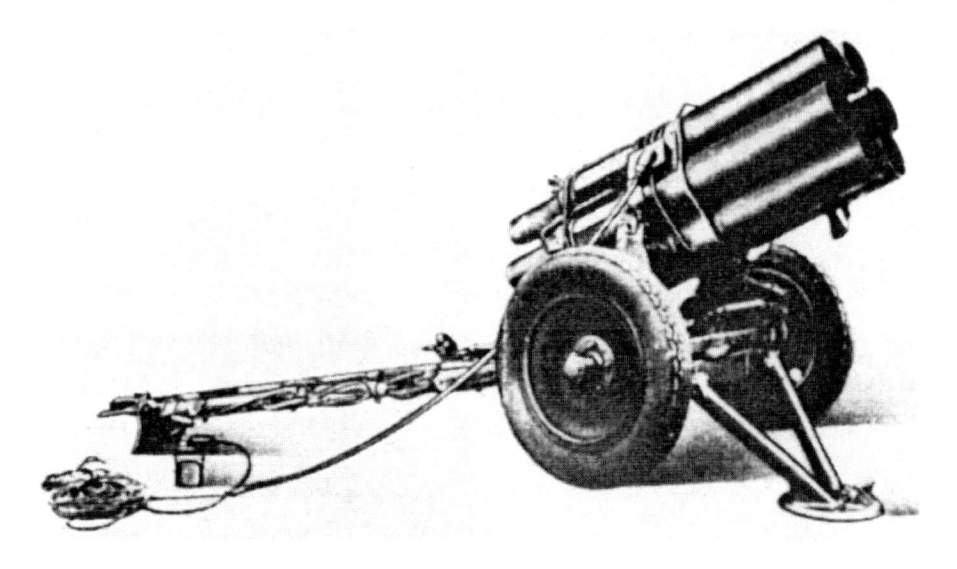

The heavy air defense was provided by the famous 88mm *Flak 18* and *Flak 36* pieces, and these were expected to also provide anti-tank defense when needed. They were only found in divisional anti-aircraft battalions, and not in regimental companies. The light anti-aircraft guns were also frequently used for ground combat, particularly from 1944, when they were mounted on 38(t) and Panzer IV chassis for use in the seven *SS* panzer regiments.

Misconceptions and Controversies About the *Waffen-SS*

The history of the *Waffen-SS* began to be recorded before and during the Second World War, and many accounts were understandably biased, as they were written by pro-Nazi sources or wartime enemies. After the war, some German veterans of other branches of service made statements against the *Waffen-SS*, based on their experiences or to distract attention from their own service. The atrocities committed by certain *Waffen-SS* units made investigators ready to believe the worst about the entire *Waffen-SS*. And *Waffen-SS* veterans attempted to portray themselves in the best possible light in their post-war writings.

All of these factors contributed to many incorrect concepts being taken into historiography as accepted truths. It is only with the opening of archives and the cooling of passions that continued research has been able to present a more balanced view of the following issues, among many others. Further study will no doubt further clarify many aspects of Second World War history.

The *Waffen-SS* Were the "Asphalt Soldiers"

It was long believed that "Asphalt Soldiers" was a *Heer* nickname for the *Waffen-SS*, based on the latter's black uniforms. In fact, from 1935, the *SS-V* and *SS-LAH* wore field grey uniforms of the same material as the *Heer*, and uniforms had nothing to do with the term. Rather, the *SS-V* was contemptuous, and perhaps a bit jealous, of *SS-LAH*, which functioned as a palace guard for Adolf Hitler. So, while the men of the *SS-V*

An officer of *SS-Germania*, seen circa 1940, displays the field grey uniform that became standard for the *Waffen-SS*.

were engaged in rigorous military training during the years 1934–1938, the *SS-LAH* men developed a reputation for participating in parades and standing at sentry duty outside Hitler's residences. In consequence, the *SS-V* referred to their *SS-LAH* colleagues as "Asphalt Soldiers."

The *Waffen-SS* Was Atheistic

The official religious doctrine of the Nazi Party and the *SS* was a sort of deism, an undefined belief in God separate from any organized religion. The *SS*, in particular, encouraged the belief in Nordic paganism, and urged its members to abandon any Christian denomination. Before the war, over 60 percent of the members of *SS-TV* did so, as did half of the *Allegemeine-SS*, while in the *SS-V*, only 40 percent made this choice.

The *SS-V*, *SS-LAH*, *SS-TV* and subsequent German wartime *Waffen-SS* units did not have military chaplains, unlike the *Wehrmacht*. As mentioned, however, a majority of men in the *Waffen-SS* maintained their faith, and they were joined in this by various senior officers such as Wilhelm Bittrich and Felix Steiner, who both came under pressure from Heinrich Himmler for their decisions. Bittrich, who throughout the war made chaplains available to the men of his commands (see his biography), was sacked for this by Himmler during the autumn of 1944. His military abilities ensured that his *Heer* superiors refused to allow his removal.

While Himmler wanted German *Waffen-SS* men to be free of Judeo-Christian influence, he had no qualms about allowing clerics to units formed around foreigners (other than ethnic Germans). This meant that Muslim *imams* were found in the Bosnian *SS-Handschar* and *SS-Kama* Divisions, and in the Albanian *SS*-Skanderbeg. Catholic priests administered to the Belgian *SS*-Langemarck and *SS-Wallonien*, and to the French *SS*-Charlemagne. Lutheran pastors saw to the needs of the Latvian and Estonian *Waffens-SS*. The Ukrainian 14th *Waffen*-Grenadier Division had many priests from the Galician Greek-Catholic church. Finally, III (Germanic) *SS*-Panzer Corps had Catholic and Protestant chaplains, for its diversity of European nationalities.

So while the *SS-V* was intended to be a non-religious force, this was never fully implemented, and as the *Waffen-SS* developed, religious services were provided to non-Germans. German cadre in foreign units were able to take advantage of this, and those in primarily German formations could seek out chaplains from neighboring *Heer* units. This allowed Himmler's desire to keep his men free of Christianity to be circumvented in practice, if not on paper.

The *Waffen-SS* Suffered Unnecessarily High Casualties in Battle

It is an often-asserted generality that the *Waffen-SS* suffered higher losses in combat than units of the *Heer*, although numbers in support of this are not produced. The casualties are attributed to fanaticism, poor leadership, and, sometimes, inferior training.

This is a very complicated subject to judge, and although it is beyond the scope of this book to present a complete or valid study, an appreciation of the scale and complexity can help readers understand why the current state of scholarship on the subject does not validate any generalization.

The *Waffen-SS* consisted primarily of combat formations and training units/schools. By comparison, the *Heer* included many more higher headquarters staffs, combat support (signal, military police, construction engineer, and so on) and service units (supply, maintenance, transportation—including the world's most extensive military railway system—medical, and so on) that also provided their services to the *Waffen-SS*, along with far larger administrative staffs and training commands than comparable *Waffen-SS* elements. This means that the *Waffen-SS* consisted of a higher percentage of combat troops, the men most likely to see action.

Clearly, if all other things are equal, one would expect casualties to be proportionately higher among such organizations.

Further, the *SS-V*, *SS-LAH*, and *SS-TV* were created to act as elite formations for use at the decisive points of the front. This became true of the first six *Waffen-SS* divisions, as well as the later-formed panzer and panzer-grenadier divisions. They were normally employed in the areas of the heaviest fighting, whether engaged in offensive or defensive operations. The remaining *Waffen-SS* divisions also saw intense combat at various points during the last two years of the war, in the same circumstances as the front line units of the *Heer*. By that stage, casualties were severe for most units from any branch of the German armed forces that saw ground combat.

An interesting trend sometimes pointed out by *Waffen-SS* advocates can be discerned from from figures released by the *WASt* (German government agency for tracing the fate of wartime casualties) during 1972 are examined. Approximately 950,000 men passed through the *Waffen-SS* up to the end of the war, and 253,000 were listed as killed or missing in action. This equals just less than 27 percent.

There were 11 million men in the *Heer*, which sustained 3,280,000 dead and missing; this represents just under 30 percent of the force. It would appear that, given the far higher proportion of non-combat formations in the *Heer*, that its 30 percent loss rate means that the combat units of the *Heer* suffered significantly higher casualties than those sustained by the *Waffen-SS*, with its intrinsically much higher "tooth to tail" ratio.

However, this, too, is misleading. To analyze the comparative loss rates between the *Heer* and *Waffen-SS*, a study would have to account for the following:

1. It is pointless to compare casualties of units operating under dissimilar circumstances. Using gross numbers cannot account for different conditions present on the battlefield, such as mission; enemy capabilities and circumstances; terrain; and comparative enemy-friendly combat power ratios. To conduct an accurate comparison, for example, one would have to acquire casualty data on Army panzer divisions committed against prepared positions in 1942 and compare them to data on *Waffen-SS* panzer divisions committed against similar defenses in the same year. Otherwise, one is only proving that dissimilar things are not the same.
2. Whether due to political influence, operational considerations, or other factors, the fact is that *Waffen-SS* units were not allowed to remain with doomed units, such as the 6th Army at Stalingrad (or the 6th Army in Romania the following year, for that matter, when the new field army bearing that name was destroyed again!) Similarly,

An *SS-Unterscharführer* listens to *Generalfeldmarschall* Model (NA)

there were no major *Waffen-SS* formations committed in Africa or Sicily, where *Heer* units also suffered wholesale destruction. Thus, *Heer* units suffered disproportionately in such operations, and this, too, distorts any analytical attempt using only gross casualty statistics.

3. Over the duration of the Second World War, the combat exposure of *Waffen-SS* units was significantly less than that of most units of the *Heer*. Only a handful of *Waffen-SS* units saw action in Poland in 1939 or Western Europe in 1940, and none of them were larger than regiments. Three were divisions: *SS-V, SS-TK, SS-Polizei*. In contrast, hundreds of *Heer* divisions participated. Only six *Waffen-SS* divisions saw front line action on the Eastern Front in the second half of 1941 while there were 136 *Heer* divisions in constant combat during those first six months of the war in the East. In all of 1942, there were only six *Waffen-SS* divisions and three brigades in combat in the East, while there were over 200 *Heer* divisions in combat during the year. Some *Waffen-SS* divisions were deployed solely on anti-partisan operations for most of their existence (nasty, but less costly employment than combat against the Soviet Army), and only saw front line combat in the last six months of the war. Thus, any accurate assessment of relative casualties would have to account for this phenomenon of reduced "combat exposure" as well.
4. No *Waffen-SS* units were used in coastal defense or defense of fixed fortifications, roles in which *Heer* units (especially those in the West)

sometimes suffered enormously from encirclement, as well as concentrated air, naval, and artillery bombardment.
5. No *Waffen-SS* formations were reorganized as *Volks-Grenadier* divisions (although Himmler did attempt to gain control of them in his capacity as Commander in Chief of the Reserve Army in 1944). Some of these *Heer VGD*s were built around the demoralized cadres of utterly devastated units, and were filled out with *Luftwaffe* and Navy enlisted men with no infantry experience or training. In every case, they were sent into combat with six weeks or less of unit training, and were organized in a fashion inconsistent with the doctrine by which they were expected to fight. Commencing in the summer of 1944, there were 76 *Heer* divisions reorganized and committed to combat as *Volks-Grenadier* Divisions; coincidentally, this is exactly twice as many divisions as the *Waffen-SS* ever fielded, in the entire war!

Overall, then, like so many myths and misunderstandings, the idea that the *Waffen-SS* suffered disproportionately higher casualties is at best a gross and currently unsubstantiable generalization. At worst—when this generalization is further attributed to vague and amorphous causes such as "political fanaticism" and incompetent leadership—it is irresponsible as well. Clearly, this is a field that remains wide open for scholars to explore in the future.

The *Waffen-SS* Had Inferior Leadership

As mentioned above, one of the reasons advanced for alleged excessive casualties in the *Waffen-SS* is that its leadership was inferior to that of the *Heer*. This argument asserts that *Waffen-SS* officers possessed more political zeal than military knowledge. This isn't born out by a study of the origins of the *SS-V*, *SS-LAH*, and *SS-TV*. As the sections on Germans in the *Waffen-SS* and biographies of significant *Waffen-SS* officers indicate, the senior leadership of these formations all possessed First World War experience, usually at officer rank. Only a minority had served continuously in military units since the end of the war, yet this was equally true for the *Heer*, which grew from the 100,000-man *Reichswehr*.

The senior leadership of what developed into the *Waffen-SS* came primarily from the *Reichswehr* and the police, and just as with the *Heer*, these long-serving men passed the lessons of their experience on to younger men. This included the students of the two *SS* officer schools established in 1934 and 1935. That the abilities of the original cadre officers, and also those commissioned from 1934 onward, was considered more than adequate by the *Heer* is reflected in the numerous positive evaluations made by *Heer* commanders of their *Waffen-SS* subordinates, and through the many decorations for which they recommended them.

It has also been said that Paul Hausser was the sole significant high-ranking commander to emerge from the *Waffen-SS*. This ignores the numerous highly-regarded corps commanders that served during the war. At the least Wilhelm Bittrich (II *SS*-Panzer Corps), Felix Steiner [III (Germanic) *SS*-Panzer Corps], Herbert Otto Gille (IV *SS*-Panzer Corps), Artur Phleps (V *SS*-Volunteer Mountain Corps), Walter Krüger (VI *SS*-Volunteer Army Corps), and Matthias Kleinheisterkamp (XI *SS*-Panzer Corps) distinguished themselves at their positions, as rated by their non-*SS* superiors.

Additionally, by the same standard, numerous *Waffen-SS* men who only attained junior officer rank during the 1930s became effective division commanders during the war, including Theodor Wisch, Werner Ostendorff, Hermann Priess, Karl Ullrich, Otto Kumm, Sylvester Stadler, Heinz Harmel, Fritz von Scholz, Fritz Witt, Georg Bochmann, Bruno Streckenbach, Franz Augsberger, and Jürgen Wagner. Augsberger earned the Knight's Cross, and all of the others attained the Oakleaves or higher to that decoration, almost always through the recommendation of impressed *Heer* corps and army commanders.

The notion that the *Waffen-SS* possessed inferior leadership probably endured because of a lack of research in the wartime files of the *Waffen-SS* leadership, files that contain the service records and evaluations of these men.

The *Waffen-SS* Possessed Superior Weaponry to the *Heer*

German veterans often state, "The *Waffen-SS* got the best weapons, and more of them." This is true for some elements of the *Waffen-SS*, but definitely not all. As in most armies of WWII, different units received weapons in accordance with availability, missions (expected or in progress), and their reputation for using them.

The original *SS-V* and *SS-LAH* were recognized by the *Heer* as possessing the human material and training to qualify as an elite. As a consequence, early on, they were made fully motorized and given artillery and other specialized weapons such as armored cars. The weapons and equipment were almost wholly German. The *SS-TV* was not rated as highly, and when the *SS-Totenkopf* Division was formed during the winter of 1939–40, it had to make due with largely-captured Czech heavy weapons. The *SS-Polizei* Division, formed at the same time, was organized and equipped in the manner of a *Heer* infantry division, with horse-drawn artillery and conveyances.

So the *SS-V* and *SS-LAH* Divisions were better equipped than the majority of the *Heer* infantry units, but also in comparison to the *SS-Polizei*, and even *SS-Totenkopf*.

During 1942, *SS-LAH*, *SS-Das Reich*, *SS-Totenkopf*, and *SS-Wiking* all received tanks. At the same time, *SS-Prinz Eugen* was forming, and it was equipped primarily with captured weapons from French and Yugoslav sources, and was not as well equipped as *Heer* mountain divisions, or even the other *SS* mountain division formed to that point, *SS-Nord*.

As the war progressed, *SS-LAH*, *SS-Das Reich*, *SS-Totenkopf*, and *SS-Wiking* were joined by *SS*-Hohenstauffen, *SS*-Frundsberg, and *SS-Hitlerjugend* as full panzer divisions, with two battalions of tanks in a panzer regiment, and one of six infantry battalions in armored personnel carriers. In this regard, their organization matched those of *Heer* panzer divisions. *SS*-Panzer battalions, however, were authorized four, rather than three, tank companies in each battalion, giving them more (although not better) combat power. In fact, by 1945, some *SS*-Panzer divisions, such as *SS-LAH* and *SS-Hitlerjugend*, stood apart from the others in that they were authorized an additional tank platoon per company, as well as the extra company per battalion. These divisions were also authorized their own *Nebelwerfer* multi-barrelled rocket launcher battalions, which no other *SS*-Panzer divisions possessed. All, however, were frequently used to spearhead attacks on both the Eastern and Western Fronts, and so were organized according to especially robust lines.

It must be remembered that there were also inconsistencies within the *Heer*. By the summer of 1943, the *Heer*'s exceptional Panzer-Grenadier Division *Grossdeutschland* possessed three tank battalions in its panzer regiment, and eight infantry battalions. The Army's *Panzer Lehr* Division, organized the following spring, only possessed four infantry battalions, but all of them rode in armored half-tracks. Both of these divisions were allotted especially challenging missions as well.

As this demonstrates, equipment levels were highly variable, and *Heer* infantrymen were likely to be equally jealous of the soldiers of *SS-LAH* and *Grossdeutschland*. As the *Waffen-SS* grew during the war, the greatest part of its new formations were infantry divisions, and these were equipped to the level of *Heer* infantry divisions, with *Waffen-SS* and *Heer* infantry units both lower in priority for the best weapons than the armored formations.

The 29th *Waffen*-Grenadier Division, with Italian personnel and weapons, was part of the *Waffen-SS*, yet equipped to nowhere close to the level of, for example, *SS-LAH*, and no one claims that it received special treatment. Among the mountain infantry divisions, *SS-Nord* actually grew during its lengthy defensive missions in its impossibly long sector in northern Karelia, retaining a motorized infantry (later Panzer-Grenadier) battalion and receiving the attachment of a Norwegian *SS* ski battalion in late 1943. Meanwhile, the other *SS* mountain divisions were organized differently, in recognition of their missions, meaning that some may have exceeded *Heer* standards in some regards, and been inferior in others. The infantry regiments of *SS-Prinz Eugen*, for example, each were authorized an additional battalion (which were highly useful in the heavily wooded, deeply compartmented terrain in which it fought partisans), but its light and medium artillery battalions were only authorized two batteries each, probably in recognition of the paucity of artillery with which its partisan opponents were armed.

All this further shows that the issue of the *Waffen-SS* receiving special treatment has no simple answer. It is always necessary to compare the types of units involved, their missions, and their commanders' expectations. When this is done, it appears that, as a rule, *Waffen-SS* panzer divisions were better off than most of their *Heer* counterparts, but that even within the *Waffen-SS*, some panzer units were more lavishly equipped than others. *Waffen-SS* mountain infantry divisions ran the gamut from better-equipped than their *Heer* counterparts, to stronger in some ways but weaker in others. Finally, some of the infantry divisions of the *Waffen-SS* were clearly weaker and less well equipped than most of those in the *Heer*, probably reflecting their late war origins and second-line missions.

The *Waffen-SS, Einsatzgruppen,* and Concentration Camp Guards

Contrary to Hausser's and Steiner's original conception, *Reichsführer-SS* Himmler assigned numerous units to the *Waffen-SS* that had purposes other than combat. These included *Einsatzgruppe* murder squads and wartime concentration camp guards (*Totenkopfwachbataillone*). These men carried *Waffen-SS* paybooks, and the *Einsatzgruppen* included numbers of *Waffen-SS* soldiers, along with soldiers from *Heer* military police units, *SD* (*SS* security service) men, and foreigners, but had more in common with the political *Allegemeine-SS* than with members of combat units of the *Waffen-SS*. These executioners and guards were not expected to serve in a military role, and did not do so. *Waffen-SS* veterans point out that they themselves had no say in the matter of these men being assigned to the *Waffen-SS*, and in many cases, had no idea that they were organizationally linked to such groups.

In the minds of the *SS-V* survivors, they and their Germanic comrades were "the" *Waffen-SS*, the others being elements forced upon them by wartime necessity. In their written histories, the veterans stress those details that were important to them. They saw themselves as an elite; they had fought well in many battles and had usually served honorably as soldiers. They claimed to have been employed as "soldiers like the others [in the *Heer*]" and the *SS-V* men, at least, were justified in this claim.

What complicates the picture is that the *Waffen-SS* came to include so many other elements, as described above. To make matters even more complex, there were varying degrees of personnel exchange between the *Einsatzgruppen*, *Totenkopfwachbataillone*, and combat units. Historians often dwell on negatives and point to various units that came to be associated with the *Waffen-SS* that committed frequent dishonorable acts. This was not what Hausser and Steiner had had in mind during the 1930s, and the conflict in vision that existed from the beginnings of the *Waffen-SS* doomed the *SS-V* and *SS-LAH*—along with hundreds of thousands of German non-volunteers and highly-motivated foreigners—to condemnation that extends into the new millenium.

The *Waffen-SS* and War Crimes

If issues such as the service of Germanics in the *Waffen-SS* are complex matters that are easily misunderstood (See pages 84–180), this is no less true when studying the war crimes and atrocities associated with that body. Both are subjects on which much is sometimes presumed, often in the absence of solid facts. Wartime and post-war propaganda has also clouded the issue, and with this has come the desire of many, including many Germans, to identify the *Waffen-SS* with the commission of war crimes, to the exclusion, or near-exclusion, of other branches of the German armed forces.

There is a widespread assumption that the men of the *Waffen-SS* were indoctrinated political soldiers of one sort or another, with the precise meaning of this term varying with the outlook of the user. This outlook, in turn, is assumed to account for the greater proportion of war crimes attributed to the *Waffen-SS*. Surviving records, however, support *Waffen-SS* veterans' claims that political indoctrination was at most a minor part of their training. Instead, indoctrination on political, ethnic, and historical matters was handled by National Socialist youth groups such as the German Youth and the Hitler Youth. Membership in the

Hitler Youth and its various subgroups became mandatory in 1936, and was accompanied by state efforts to shape the curriculum of schools and universities according to National Socialist teachings. These processes combined to influence a generation of German young people, including the age groups born through 1928 who were called upon to perform military service in the Second World War.

The youth influenced in this way primarily served in the *Wehrmacht*, which during the course of the war increasingly meant the German Army (*das Heer*) in particular. Throughout the Third *Reich*, the German Army consisted overwhelmingly of German men, with ethnic Germans and foreigners contributing only a small percentage of its manpower. By comparison, between 33 and 50 percent of the *Waffen-SS* consisted of ethnic Germans raised outside of Germany and Germanic or non-Germanic foreigners. These were young men who had not been raised in the atmosphere of National Socialist indoctrination, and had not been subjected to the racial and other poisonous theories of National Socialism. While some had been subjected to fascist or other chauvinistic indoctrination, few had been exposed to, much less professed, the course of propaganda delivered by the Nazi organizations in Germany.

Thus, as an organization, the *Waffen-SS* possessed a smaller percentage of young men who had grown up under the teachings of National Socialism than did the *Wehrmacht*, especially the German Army. Countering this, it may also be theorized that those German citizens who did serve with the *Waffen-SS* tended to be volunteers, and that these volunteers were likely to hold a greater belief in the validity of National Socialist teachings. Of course, there was a high percentage of young volunteers in the German Army, Navy, and *Luftwaffe*, too. Thus, the *Waffen-SS* cannot fairly be characterized as being comprised mainly of Nazi fanatics, or of having soldiers who had been exposed to more (or, on the average, even as much!) Nazi hatemongering than the soldiers of the German Army.

To explain the bad reputation of the *Waffen-SS*, it is more useful to consider the impact of political opportunism and the nature of anti-partisan warfare. The elite *SS* armored divisions in particular were a compact, easily recognized target even during the war, when they were singled out for blame by the Western Allies and Soviets if military reverses ensued. Sometimes, they were even blamed by German Army commanders if operations did not produce the desired results. Afterward, these units and others in the *Waffen-SS* were identified as being culpable for war crimes, with few corresponding accusations being made against German Army units, even when such accusations may have been justified. Interestingly, separate crimes were found for each of the first eight *Waffen-SS* divisions, and for the sister divisions of three of these. These incidents have sometimes received little study, but are taken at face value and their few particulars are repeated in countless works that rehash one another's content.

Specifically, the 1st *SS*-Panzer Division is associated with the Malmedy Massacre; the 2nd *SS*-Panzer Division with Tulle-Oradour; the 3rd *SS*-Panzer Division with Le Paradis; the 4th *SS-Polizei*-Panzergrenadier Division with Larissa; the 5th *SS*-Panzer Division with the murder of 600 Galician Jews just after Barbarossa; the 6th *SS*-Mountain Division with the destruction of Rovaniemi, Finland; the 7th *SS*-Volunteer-Mountain Division and 8th *SS*-Cavalry Division with massacres in their respective areas of operations; the 12th *SS*-Panzer Division with the murder of Canadian prisoners of war in Normandy; the 13th Waffen-Mountain Division of the *SS* with, again, massacres in its area of operations; and the 16th *SS*-Panzergrenadier Division with the massacre at Marzabotto, Italy.

It is not the purpose of this piece to examine each case. It is essential, however, to realize that most cases result from some previous atrocity committed in violation of the laws and customs of war and were often of an exceptionally heinous nature. In other words, they were often a part of the pernicious cycle of cruelty that stem from other, similar acts. Each must be examined individually and closely before any opinion on the general nature of the *Waffen-SS* can be considered to be well informed. Detailed study reveals many interesting subplots to the various storylines. For example, Fritz Knöchlein became a martyr in certain circles following his execution for the commission of murders at Le Paradis, because evidence exists that he had simply reacted to earlier British war crimes. When Knöchlein is then given heroic stature, however, the matter has been carried too far, as the testimony of veterans and records in his file indicate that by late 1944 he was considered a poor regimental commander and an officer of unsavory character.

In another case demonstrating the value of continuing research—the burning of the town of Rovaniemi, Finland—a late war memoir by a Finnish commando has revealed that the town burned down not as a result of a deliberate "scorched earth" tactic, but as a consequence of the actions by his leader who blew up a German ammunition train parked at the railway station. The killing in and around Marzabotto in the autumn of 1944 is normally labelled an "*SS* crime," yet the anti-partisan operation in that area was not the sort of police action that was typically organized by German police and/or security forces. It was actually a military operation directed by the headquarters of the *Luftwaffe* I Parachute Corps, which sought to remove threats to its rear area supply lines. The extent and character of the killing in and around this mountain village remains unclear to this day. Somewhere between 700 and 1,000 civilians died there, depending on the account one reads. However, which deaths were the result of combat (plain-clothed partisans and collateral civilian casualties), which were the targets of organized reprisals, and which may have been simply murdered outright remain clouded in controversy. Further, the situation is complicated by the fact that the Emilia-Romagna region in which Marzabotto lies was controlled by Communists at the time and for over 50 years afterward. Clearly, no more venomous political enmity existed than that between National Socialists and Communists, and as in so many similar situations, truth is often one of the first casualties. Investigations of allegations against eight members of the *Reichsführer-SS* Division allegedly involved in the killing at Marzabotto are actually still going on in Germany as of the time this book was written!

"Anti-partisan" becomes the key term in so many of these cases, such as the incidents involving the "*Das Reich*," "*Prinz Eugen*," "*Florian Geyer*," and "*Reichsführer-SS*" divisions. Before casting judgment, it is worth remembering that before and during WWII, reprisals involving the civilian population in occupied lands were tolerated as a last resort by the Customary Law of Nations, including the principles of the so-called Martens' Clause in the preamble to the Convention, that is, "the usages established among the civilized peoples," "the laws of humanity," and "the dictates of the public conscience." The right to take reprisals against civilian hostages at that time was explicitly acknowledged by the court of the seventh follow-up trial of the International Military Tribunal in Nuremberg (1948). It was only in 1949 that the Hague Convention Relative to the Protection of Civilian Persons in Time of War of 12 August that collective penalties, measures of intimidation or terrorism against civilians, as well as reprisals against persons and taking of hostages were prohibited (Article 33).

According to the Customs of War on Land at that time, then, not every killing of a civilian by men of the *Waffen-SS* was a crime, even before the question is raised about the killing of unarmed civilians compared with those who had taken up weapons. In short, true massacres, such as the executions at and the razing of Lidice in the wake of Reinhard Heydrich's assassination (an incident perpetrated not by the *Waffen-SS* but by *Gestapo*, *SD*, and German and Czech police units), were never allowed under international law, but *some* reprisals against civilians were. Since the post-war Allied revision of the international conventions governing this distasteful aspect of warfare, modern people generally find such actions inconceivably reprehensible, but such was not the law or the outlook during World War II. Even the wartime (1940) US Army's Field Manual 27-10, *The Rules of Land Warfare*, allowed hostage taking and reprisals against civilians under some circumstances to "induce the enemy to desist from illegitimate practices" (pp. 89–90).

To get to the bottom on those incidents, the nature of partisan warfare must be considered. Such activity took place long before the

Second World War, and it has continued up to the time of writing, not least in places like Vietnam, Somalia, Iraq, and Afghanistan. When Axis forces operated in Yugoslavia between 1941 and 1945, they became involved in a style of warfare that had existed there for centuries, and which resumed five decades later in the same regions. "Ethnic cleansing" had been practiced in the Balkans at intervals for centuries before the Germans' arrival, and has been continuing until very recently. The *Waffen-SS*, with its associations to the German police and security forces, had a substantial proportion of its units involved in anti-partisan warfare, not only in southeastern Europe, but in the Soviet Union, Italy, and elsewhere. These formations became caught up in an unusually cruel and merciless cycle of warfare characteristic of partisan activities as have some elements of the armies of the wartime Allies in the years since. The results are often disturbing and sometimes inexcusable, but not entirely unique to the *Waffen-SS*.

It is within the realm of anti-partisan operations that the bulk of *Waffen-SS* atrocities can be found. With this understood, it is important to form judgments based on contemporary, not modern, requirements of the rules of land warfare, and on the study of policies which involved German military forces, and elements of the *Waffen-SS* in particular, in counterinsurgency roles.

Appendix: Weapons Tables

Small Arms, Rifles, Machine Guns, & Anti-Tank Rifles

	Caliber (mm)	Weight (lbs)	Magazine (rds)	Cyclic Rate (rds/min)	Range (eff./max.)
Pistols					
P08 "Luger"	9x19	2	8	Toggle	50/—
Walther P-38	9x19	2.3	8	SA	50/—
Submachine Guns					
MP28	9x19	8.8	20/32/50	500	100/—
MP38	9x19	9	32	500	100/—
MP40	9x19	9	32	500	100/—
MP41	9x19	8.14	32	600	100/—
Suomi	9x19	11.3	25/50/70	850	100/—
Rifles and Carbines					
Mauser 98 Carbine	7.92x57	9	5	Bolt	600/—
Carcano M1891	6.5x52	8.5	6	Bolt	500/—
MP43 Assault Rifle	7.92x33	11	30	600	400/—
MP44 Assault Rifle	7.92x33	11	30	600	400/—
G43 rifle	7.92x57	10	10	SA	600/—
Machine Guns					
MG34 LMG	7.92x57	26.5	Belt	900	800/3,500
MG42 LMG	7.92x57	23.75	Belt	1,400	800/3,500
MG34 w/tripod (HMG)*	7.92x57	68.5	Belt	900	2,500/3,500
MG42 w/tripod (HMG)*	7.92x57	65.75	Belt	1,400	2,500/3,500
Czech ZB 30	7.92x57	20.02	20	600	800/—
Hotchkiss	8x50R	52	Belt	600	1,100/—
Maxim 08	7.92x57	53	Belt	450	1,100/—

Mortars	Weight	Weight of Projectile	Effective Range
50mm Leichter Granatenwerfer 36	31	2.2	521
81mm Schwerer Grantenwerfer 34	124	7.7	2,400
120mm Granatenwerfer 42	616	35	6,035

*Including telescope and tables for overhead firing
SA=Semi-automatic; Bolt=bolt action; Toggle=toggle action; xx/xx/xx=optional magazine capacities

Artillery & Rocket Launchers

	System Weight (lbs)	Shell Weight (lbs)	Range (m)
Guns and Howitzers			
75mm le I. G. 18	880	13.2	3,566
75mm le I. G. 37	1,124	13.2	5,148
75mm Geb. G. 36	1,650	12.6	9,235
105mm Geb H. 40	3,660	32.6	12,628
105mm leFH 18	4,320	32.7	12,326
Wespe SP 105mm	24,200	32.7	12,326
Czech 105mm	3,700	39.4	11,100
150mm s. I. G. 33	3,360	85	4,700
150mm s. F. H. 18	12,096	95.7	13,378
Hummel SP 150mm	50,800	95.7	13,378
Czech 150mm (149.1mm)	11,572	92.4	13,716
105mm s. 10 cm K. 18	11,424	31.3-34.6	19,065
150mm K. 18	28,440	94.6-95.7	24,725
170mm K. im Mörser Lafette	38,080	138	29,600
210mm Mörser	36,740	249	16,734
Rocket Launchers			
150mm Nebelwerfer 41	1,195	75.3	6,703
Nebelwerfer 42	approx. 1,200	248	7,864

Anti-Aircraft Guns

	Weight (lbs)	Muzzle Velocity (m/sec)	Range (Vertical) (meters)	Elevation (Min/Max) (degrees)	Rate of Fire (Rds/min)
20mm Flak 30	1,021	900	2,200	-12 /+90	120/280
20mm Flak 38	896	900	2,200	-20/+90	220/450
20mm Flakvierling 38	3,360	900	2,200	-10/+100	720–1800
37mm Flak 18, 36, 37	3,858	820	2,000	-5/+85	80
88mm Flak 18, 36	10,980	830	10,600	-3/+85	15–20

Armored Vehicles

Weapon	Weight (tons)	Crew	Main Gun/ Rds. on board	MGs/ Rds on board	Armor Turret/ Body (inches)	Speed (mi/hr)	Combat Radius (mi)
Tanks							
Skoda 38t	10.4	4	37mm L/47.8 72	2 x 7.92mm 2,400	.6–1/ .4–1	26	155
Panzer III/L	25.4	5	50mm L/60 78	2 x 7.92mm 4,960	1.2–2.3/ 1.2–2.8	28	90
Panzer IV/H	27.6	5	75mm L/48 87	2 x 7.92mm 3,159	1.2–2/ 1.2–3.4	25	124
Panzer V/G "Panther"	50.2	5	75mm L/70 79	2 x 7.92mm 4,500	1.8–4.3/ 2–3.2@55°	29	124
Panzer VI/E "Tiger"	62.8	5	88mm L/56 92	2 x 7.92mm 3,920	3.2–4/ 3.15–4	23	73
Panzer VI "Königstiger"	76.9	5	88mm L/71 84	2 x 7.92mm 4,800	3.2–7.3/ 3.2–5.9@50°	26	106
Tank Destroyers							
47mm AT Gun on Pz I Chassis	8.4	3	47mm L/43 86 NA	None .5	NA	25	87
Marder II	11.9	3	76mm L/51 30	1 x 7.92mm 1,500	NA .79–2	26	155
Marder III	11.6	4	75mm L/46 41	None NA	.3–2	29	124
Hetzer	17.6	4	75mm L/48 41	1 x 7.92mm 600	NA .8@45°- 2.4@60°	24	111
Jagdpanzer IV 70(V)	26.9	5	75mm L/70 55	1 x 7.92mm —	NA/ 1.6@30°- 3.2@45°	25	124
Jagdpanzer V "Jagdpanther"	51.3	5	88mm L/71 60	1 x 7.92mm 3,000	NA 2@35°- 3.2@55°	29	124
Jagdpanzer VI "Jagdtiger"	79	6	128mm L/55 38	1 x 7.92mm 3,000	3.2–9.9/ 3.2–5.9@50°	22	106

Anti-Tank Weapons

Weapon	Ammo Types	Muzzle Veloc (AP, m/sec)	Armor Penetration
Anti-Tank Guns			
28mm s. Pz. B 41	HE AP	1,400	53mm/366m/30°
37mm Pak 36	HE AP	2,625	36mm/500m/90°
50mm Pak 38	HE AP	930	95mm/500m/60°
75mm Pak 40	HE AP	2,530	154mm/500m/90°
75mm Pak 97/38	HE AP	1,870	60mm/818m/30°
76.2mm Pak 36	HE AP	3,520	83mm/914m/30°
88mm Pak 43	HE AP	3,280	205mm/1,000m/60°
88mm Pak 43/41	HE AP	3,280	205mm/1,000m/60°

Weapon	Range (m)	Armor Penetration
Anti-Tank Rocket Launchers		
Panzerfaust 30	30	200mm
Panzerfaust 60	60	200mm
Panzerfaust 100	100	200mm
Panzerfaust 150	150	at least 200mm
88mm Panzerschreck 43	150	211mm
88mm Panzerschreck 54	200	211mm

Annotated Bibliography

Abbott, Peter, and Nigel Thomas. *Germany's Eastern Front Allies, 1941–45* (Men at Arms 131). London: Osprey, 1982.
Puts Finnish, Hungarian, Italian, and Romanian contributions to the Axis in perspective.

Agte, Patrick. *Europas Freiwillige der Waffen-SS.* Pluwig, Germany: Munin Verlag, 2000.
Biographies of non-German high-award recipients, with very rare photos.

_____. *Jochen Peiper: Commander, Panzer Regiment Leibstandarte.* Winnipeg, Canada: J.J. Fedorowicz, 1999.
Similar in tone to Agte's Wittmann book, another translation with exhaustive detail on Peiper and a history of the units he commanded, especially *SS-Panzer Regiment 1*.

_____. *Michael Wittmann and the Tiger Commanders of the Leibstandarte.* Winnipeg: Fedorowicz, 1996.
A translation of the best book on Wittmann, and also a history of 13th Company of *SS*-Panzer Regiment 1, and its successor, heavy *SS*-Panzer Battalion 501, written by the post-war head of the veterans' association for *SS-LAH* and *SS-Hitlerjugend*.

Angolia, John R. and Stan Cook. *Cloth Insignia of the SS.* 2d ed. San Jose: Bender, 1989.
Helps make sense of a confusing subject with many interesting photos.

_____. *For Führer and Fatherland: Military Awards of the Third Reich.* 3d ed. San Jose: Bender, 1987.
A solid, basic reference.

Bayer, Hanns. *Kavallerie-Divisionen der Waffen-SS im Bild.* Osnabrück: Munin, 1982.
One of the least interesting of the Munin photo books. In German and English.

Bender, Roger James, and Hugh Page Taylor. *Uniforms, Organization, and History of the Waffen-SS.* Vol. 1. San Jose: Bender, 1969.
Interesting as a reflection of what was state-of-the-art research at the time.

_____. *Uniforms, Organization, and History of the Waffen-SS.* Vol. 3. San Jose: Bender, 1972.
Out of date, but pioneering in its approach to dealing with the *Waffen-SS*.

Bernage, Georges, and Hubert Meyer. *12. SS-Panzer-Division "Hitlerjugend."* Bayeux: Editions Heimdal, 1991.
A French translation of Meyer's text volume, but with additional photos not found in the German and English editions.

Bernage, Georges, et al. *Leibstandarte Adolf Hitler: la Garde personnelle d'Adolf Hitler au combat.* Bayeux: Editions Heimdal, 1996.
Essentially a one-volume compendium of the photos found in the Lehmann and Walther photo books on the division. In German and French.

Bernage, Georges, and Francois de Lannoy. *La Luftwaffe La Waffen-SS 1939–1945.* Bayeux: Editions Heimdal, 1998.
Many unpublished photos supplement short histories of the major formations of both arms of service. In French only.

Bernau, Günter. *SS-Panzer-Artillerie-Regiment 5 in der Panzer-Division Wiking.* privately published, 1990.
A very detailed history of this regiment, with photos not found elsewhere. Written by a highly-decorated battalion commander in the unit.

Biddiscombe, Perry. *Werwolf!: The History of the National Socialist Guerila Movement 1944–1946.* Toronto: Univ. of Toronto Press, 1998.

Proves that this movement, largely organized by the *SS*, amounted to more than previously believed, and was especially active against the Soviets.

Blandford, Edmund L. *Hitler's Second Army: The Waffen-SS*. Osceola, WI: Motorbooks, 1994.

Some historical inaccuracies, but interesting philosophical discussions on the place of the *Waffen-SS* in history.

Bradley, Ken. *International Brigades in Spain 1936–39* (Elite Series 53). London: Osprey, 1994.

A good introduction to to the anti-fascists of the Second World War era, men and women who were to some degree the opposites of the Germanic *Waffen-SS*.

Brant, Allen. *The Last Knight of Flanders: Remy Schrijnen and his SS-Legion "Flandern"/Sturmbrigade "Langemarck" Comrades on the Eastern Front, 1941–1945*. Atglen, PA: Schiffer, 1998.

The best book available in English on the Flemish *Waffen-SS*; gripping detail on the Tannenberg Line fighting, summer of 1944.

Breyette, Thomas W., and Roger James Bender. *Tank Killers: History of the Tank Destruction Badge*. San Jose: Bender, 2000.

Includes brief biographies of many successful German tank killers, including *Waffen-SS* soldiers.

Bundesverband der Soldaten der ehemaligen *Waffen-SS* e.V. *Befehl des Gewissens: Charkow Winter 1943*. Osnabrück: Munin, 1976.

Reprinted war diaries which recount the role of the *SS*-Panzer Corps in the Kharkov campaign of January–March 1943.

_____.V. *Wenn alle Brüder schweigen: Grosser Bildband über die Waffen-SS*. 5th ed. Coburg: Nation Europa 1992.

The first large photo book on the *Waffen-SS*, interesting for sheer volume, but badly organized and captioned. In German and English.

Carell, Paul. *Hitler Moves East, 1941–1943*. Winnipeg: Fedorowicz, 1991.

Does for the first two years of the Eastern Front what Carell's *Invasion* did for Normandy.

_____. *Invasion—They're Coming!* New York: Bantam, 1964.

Exciting reading, and gives a feel for the German experience in Normandy during the summer of 1944, but full of inaccuracies.

_____. Paul. *Scorched Earth: The Russian-German War, 1943–1944*. Atglen, PA: Schiffer, 1994.

Continues the narrative thread from *Hitler Moves East*,with extensive details on the *Waffen-SS* at Kharkov and Kursk.

Carius, Otto. *Tigers in the Mud*. Winnipeg: Fedorowicz, 1992.

Translation of the memoirs of a Tiger tank officer with includes much detail on Carius' support of the III (Germanic) *SS*-Panzer Corps at Narva.

Conway, Martin. *Collaboration in Belgium: Leon Degrelle and the Rexist Movement*. New Haven, CT: Yale, 1993.

The best English language background on the politics of Rex.

Cook, Stan, and R. James Bender. *Uniforms, Organization, and History of the Leibstandarte SS Adolf Hitler*. Vol. 1. San Jose: Bender, 1994.

Some interesting photos, but the historical and uniform details are also found in other books.

Cuppens, Gerd. *Massacre a Malmedy? Ardennes: 17 decembre 1944*. Bayeux: Editions Heimdal, 1989.

The best research in print on what actually occurred at Baugnez crossroads.

Davis, Brian L. *Flags of the Third Reich 2: Waffen-SS* (Men at Arms 274). London: Osprey, 1994.

A good introduction, but the material can be found elsewhere.

_____. *Waffen-SS*. Poole, UK: Blandford, 1986.

A basic collection of photos, mostly taken by war reporters.

De Bruyne, Eddy. *Dans L'Etau de Degrelle: Le Service du Travail Obligatoire ou de l'Usine a la Waffen-SS*. Jalhay, Belgium: Foxmaster, 1994.

A groundbreaking study of how Degrelle attempted to force Walloon workers in Germany into military service during the last months of the war.

_____. *La Collaboration Francophone en Exil Septembre 1944–Mai 1945*. Housse, Belgium: privately published, 1997.

A very detailed examination of the Walloons who went into exile in Germany after the September 1944 liberation of Belgium, with most of the space devoted to the Walloons in the *Waffen-SS*.

De Gruyter, Bert. *Beknopte Geschiedenis van de 3. Kompanie van Debica 1941 tot Narva 1944*. Belgium: privately published, n.d.

A veterans' history of the 3d Company of the Flemish *SS*-Legion and the *SS*-Assault Brigade "Langemarck," with unique photos.

Degrelle, Leon. *Campaign in Russia: The Waffen SS on the Eastern Front*. Torrance, CA: Institute for Historical Review, 1985.

The English version of Degrelle's memoirs, which, while inaccurate, make very exciting reading.

Dobrich, Momcilo, with Antonio J. Muñoz. "Chetnik: The Story of the Royal Yugoslav Army of the Homeland, 1941–1945" *Axis Europa Magazine* 16 (1998).
A very good background to the conflict which led to the creation of several *Waffen-SS* divisions.

Dörr, Manfred. *Die Träger der Nahkampfspange in Gold: Heer, Luftwaffe, Waffen-SS, 1943–1945*. 2d ed. Osnabrück: Biblio Verlag, 1988.
Details, often with photos, of all of the known recipients of the Close Combat Clasp in Gold, including many from the *Waffen-SS*. In German, but easy to figure out.

Duffy, Christopher. *Red Storm on the Reich: The Soviet March on Germany, 1945*. New York: Da Capo, 1993.
Helps set the context of the 1945 combat of the *Waffen-SS* units on the Eastern Front.

Edwards, Robert J., Jr., and Michael H. Pruett. *Field Uniforms of Germany's Panzer Elite*. Winnipeg: Fedorowicz, 1998.
Includes many previously unpublished *Waffen-SS* photos.

Ertel, Karl-Heinz, and Richard Schulze-Kossens. *Europäische Freiwillige im Bild*. Osnabrück: Munin, 1986.
Fascinating photos of the foreign *Waffen-SS* combined with poor captions and worse editing. In German and English.

Escuadra Sanchez, Alfonso. *Feldherrnhalle: Forgotten Elite—The Panzerkorps Feldherrnhalle and Antecedent Formations, Eastern and Other Fronts, 1939–1945*. Bradford, UK: Shelf, 1996.
A translation of the best existing history of the military contributions of the SA, which makes an interesting comparison between political soldiers of the SA and SS.

Fey, Will. *Armor Battles of the Waffen-SS, 1943–45*. Winnipeg: Fedorowicz, 1990.
Much of the material is now available in other books, but this translation remains a good introduction to the subject.

Fleischer, Wolfgang, and Richard Eiermann. *Das letze Jahr der Waffen-SS, Mai 1944–Mai 1945*. Wölfersheim-Berstadt, Germany: Podzun-Pallas, 1997.
Many photos and details not found elsewhere.

Forbes, Robert. *Pour l'Europe: The French Volunteers of the Waffen-SS*. Privately published, 2000.

The best work ever on the French *Waffen-SS*, uses oral history to compare accounts from other books.

Fürbringer, Herbert. *9. SS-Panzer-Division "Hohenstaufen."* Bayeux: Editions Heimdal, 1985.
A detailed history of the division combined with good private photos and superb maps. In German and French.

Gailit, Karl. *Eesti Sõdur Sõjatules*. Tallinn: Eesti Riigikaitse Akadeemia kirjastus, 1995.
The memoirs of an Estonian *Waffen-SS* war reporter.

Glantz, David M., and Jonathan M. House. *The Battle of Kursk*. Lawrence: Univ. Press of Kansas, 1999.
The first study of this campaign to be based on archival material.

Hakanpää, Mika and Hannu Varrio. *Suomalaisten Waffen-SS Vapaaehtoisten Matrikkeli 1941–1943*. Helsinki: Wiking-Divisioona Oy, 1999.
Brief details on every known Finnish *Waffen-SS* volunteer, with facial photos for over 1,000. In Finnish, but easy to figure out.

Halcomb, Jill. *The SA: A Historical Perspective*. Overland Park, Kansas: Crown/Agincourt, 1985.
A good introduction the subject, including details on the Night of the Long Knives.

Hammer, Karl. *SS War Stories*. Privately published, 1988.
Translated propaganda accounts from German wartime publications.

_____. *SS War Stories*. Vol. 2. Privately published, 1991.
More translations from German wartime publications.

Harms, Norman. *Waffen-SS in Action*. Carrollton, TX: Squadron/Signal, 1973.
One of the first English-language photo booklets on the *Waffen-SS*.

Hastings, Max. *Das Reich: The March of the 2d SS Panzer Division Through France*. New York: Henry Holt, 1981.
An account based largely on interviews with veterans of the French resistance.

_____. *Overlord: D-Day and the Battle for Normandy*. New York: Simon & Schuster, 1985.
Based primarily on interviews with German and Allied veterans, and very objective. Several *Waffen-SS* veterans contributed their views.

Holzträger, Hans. *In a Raging Inferno: Combat Units of the Hitler Youth, 1944–45*. Solihull, UK: Helion, 2000.

A translation full of very rare accounts and photos, which sometimes involve the *Waffen-SS*.

How, J. J. *Hill 112: Cornerstone of the Normandy Campaign*. London: William Kimber, 1984.
The author participated in the campaign, and is very respectful to his German former opponents.

Hunt, Roger. *Death's Head: Combat Record of the SS Totenkopf Division in France 1940*. Madison, WI: Roger Hunt, 1979.
Translated from a wartime publication based on interesting war reporter photos.

Husemann, Friedrich. *Die guten Glaubens waren: Geschichte der SS-Polizei-Division Band II, 1943–1945*. 2d ed. Osnabrück: Munin, 1986.
The veterans' history, which has extensive detail on the little-known fighting in Romania 1944 and around Danzig 1945.

Iltal, Georg. *Kohustus Kutsub: Eesti Leegioni suurtükiväelasena II maailmasõjas*. Tallinn: Eesti Riigikaitse Akadeemia kirjastus, 1997.
The memoirs of an Estonian *Waffen-SS* officer, relating his wartime experiences.

Jentz, Thomas L. *Panzertruppen: The Complete Guide to the Creation and Combat Employment of Germany's Tank Force, 1933–1942*. Atglen, PA: Schiffer, 1996.
Includes accurate information on the first *Waffen-SS* armored units.

———. *Panzertruppen: The Complete Guide to the Creation and Combat Employment of Germany's Tank Force, 1943–1945*. Atglen, PA: Schiffer, 1996.
Includes accurate strength reports for *Waffen-SS* armored units.

Jokipii, Mauno. *Pantti-Pataljoona: Suomalaisen SS-Pataljoonan historia*. Helsinki: Veljesapu, R.Y., 1996.
The standard, highly detailed, Finnish language history of the Finnish *Waffen-SS* volunteer battalion available in an updated version.

Jones, Gregory T. *Panzerheld: The Story of Hauptsturmfuhrer Michael Wittmann, The Greatest Tank Commander of World War Two*. Privately published, 1993.
A good study of Wittmann's life, though not nearly as in depth as Agte's book.

Jurado, Carlos Caballero. *Foreign Volunteers of the Wehrmacht, 1941–45* (Men at Arms 147), London: Osprey, 1983.
Includes units which later went into the *Waffen-SS*, especially the Walloons.

Jurs, August, et al. *Estonian Freedom Fighters in World War Two*. Canada: The Voitleja Relief Foundation Book Committee, n.d.
The best English-language study of the Estonian Axis forces, compiled by veterans.

Keegen, John. *Waffen SS: The Asphalt Soldiers*. New York: Ballantine, 1970.
One of Keegen's earliest books. He offered corrections to many details in his later works.

Kershaw, Robert J. *"It Never Snows in September": The German View of Market Garden and The Battle of Arnhem, September 1944*. New York: Hippocrene, 1994.
Extensive information on the *Waffen-SS* role in this campaign.

———. *War Without Garlands: Operation Barbarossa, 1941/42*. New York: Sarpedon, 2000.
Helps set the background of the ideological conflict and conditions of the Eastern Front.

Kessler, Leo (Charles Whiting). *SS Peiper: The Life and Death of SS Colonel Jochen Peiper*. Philomont, VA: Eastern Front/Warfield Books, 1996.
Concentrates on the events of the Battle of the Bulge and the Malmedy trial.

Klapdor, Ewald. *Die Entscheidung: Invasion 1944*. Siek: Ewald Klapdor, 1984.
Covers the II *SS*-Panzer Corps in Galicia and Normandy.

———. *Mit dem Panzer Regiment 5 Wiking im Osten*. Siek: Ewald Klapdor, 1981.
A detailed history of the regiment by an officer veteran.

Kleine, Egon, and Volkmar Kühn (Franz Kurowski). *Tiger: The History of a Legendary Weapon, 1942–1945*. Winnipeg: Fedorowicz, 1989.
Groundbreaking translated study of all of the Tiger tank battalions, including those of *Waffen-SS*, with good photos.

Kocevar, Monika Kokalj. *Gestapo Volunteers: The Upper Carniola Home Defense Force, 1943–1945*. Bayside, NY: Axis Europa, 1999.
Explores an aspect of collaboration run by another branch of the *SS*.

Krabbe, Oluf (von). *Danske soldaten i kamp pa Östfronten 1941–1945*. 2d ed. Lynge, Denmark: Bogan's Forlag, 1998.
A basic account of the Danish *Waffen-SS*, by an officer veteran.

Krätschmer, Ernst-Günther. *Die Ritterkreuzträger der Waffen-SS*. 3d ed. Preussisch Oldendorf, Germany: Verlag K. W. Schütz, 1982.

Outdated, but highly-detailed study of all of the Knight's Cross recipients of the *Waffen-SS*.

Krag, Ernst August. *An der Spitze im Bild: Späher-Aufklärer-Kradschützen in den Divisionen der Waffen-SS*. Osnabrück: Munin, 1988.

One of the best Munin photo books, with good photos and captions on the reconnaissance troops of the *Waffen-SS*. In German and English.

Kumm, Otto. *The History of the 7. SS-Mountain Division "Prinz Eugen."* Winnipeg: Fedorowicz, 1995.

The translation of the best available history of the unit, though with less detail than many other divisional histories.

_____. *7. SS-Gebrigsdivision "Prinz Eugen" im Bild*. Osnabrück: Munin, 1983.

Another of the best Munin books, the photos make clear the difficult circumstances under which the division operated. In German and English.

Kunzmann, Adolf, and Siegfried Milius. *Fallschirmjäger der Waffen-SS im Bild*. Osnabrück: Munin, 1986.

A small photo collection prepared by the unit's war reporter photographer and its last commander. In German and English.

Kurowski, Franz. *Infanterie Aces*. Winnipeg: Fedorowicz, 1994.

Does for infantry combat what Kurowski's *Panzer Aces* did for armor. Includes Josef "Sepp" Leiner (*SS-Der Führer*) and Alfred Schneidereit (*SS-LAH*), along with *Heer* and *Luftwaffe* soldiers.

_____. *Panzer Aces*. Winnipeg: Fedorowicz, 1993.

Slightly fictionalized biographies that give a feel for armored combat, this volume includes Michael Wittmann and Rudolf von Ribbentrop (both *SS-LAH*), along with several *Heer* soldiers.

_____. *Panzer Aces 2*. Winnipeg: Fedorowicz, 2000.

Includes an especially long chapter on Karl Nicolussi-Leck from *SS*-Panzer Regiment 5.

Kursietis, Andris J. *The Hungarian Army and Its Military Leadership in World War II*. 3d ed. Bayside, NY: Axis Europa, 1999.

Biographies of high-ranking Hungarian officers, several of whom joined the *Waffen-SS*, combined with an introduction to the organization and history of the Hungarian *Waffen-SS*.

Kuusela, Kari, and Olli Wikberg. *Wikingin suomalaiset*. Helsinki: Wiking-Divisioona Oy, 1996.

Hundreds of private photos provided by Finnish *Waffen-SS* veterans; Finnish and English captions.

Laar, Mart. *Isamaa ilu hoieldes*. Stockholm: VälisEesti & EMP, 1997.

An Estonian study of the 1944 Narva and Tannenberg campaigns.

_____. *War in the Woods: Estonia's Struggle for Survival, 1944–1956*. Washington, DC: Compass, 1992.

The translation of a detailed study of the anti-Soviet partisan war in Estonia that involved many former *Waffen-SS* men.

Landau, Sigmund Heinz. *Goodbye Transylvania*. Derby, UK: Breeden, 1985.

The experiences of an ethnic German, including *Waffen-SS* service.

Landwehr, Richard. *Britisches Freikorps: British Volunteers of the Waffen-SS, 1943–1945*. Brookings, OR: Siegrunen, 1992.

A good summary of the available information on the subject.

_____. *Charlemagne's Legionnaires: French Volunteers of the Waffen-SS, 1943–1945*. Silver Spring, MD: Bibliophile Legion, 1989.

Slightly out of date because of the new information in Forbes' book, but a good introduction to the subject, and includes a detailed supplement on the 1945 fighting of the III (Germanic) *SS*-Panzer Corps.

_____. *Estonian Vikings: Estnisches SS-Freiwilligen Bataillon Narwa and Subsequent Units, Eastern Front, 1943–1944*. Halifax, UK: Shelf Books, 1999.

Very rare photos, otherwise found only in the Narwa Battalion's Estonian-language histories.

_____. *V. SS Mountain Corps and 32d SS Panzer Grenadier Division "30 Januar" on the Oder Front, 1945*. Brookings, OR: Siegrunen, 1991.

The only available English account of this division and campaign.

_____. *Fighting for Freedom: The Ukrainian Volunteer Division of the Waffen-SS*. 3d ed. Silver Spring, MD: Bibliophile Legion, 1993.

A good account of this division, though somewhat superceded by the Logusz book.

_____. *Frontfighters: The Norwegian Volunteer Legion of the Waffen-SS, 1941–1943*. Madison, WI: Roger Hunt, 1986.

Primarily the translation of a wartime photo history of the Norwegian *SS* Legion, with a supplement on the Norwegian *SS*-Ski Battalion.

_____. *Hungarian Volunteers of the Waffen-SS.* Brookings, OR: Siegrunen, 1988.

A brief, but highly detailed, introduction to the subject.

_____. *Italian Volunteers of the Waffen-SS.* Glendale, OR: Siegrunen, 1987.

A good, short introduction to the subject.

_____. *Lions of Flanders: Flemish Volunteers of the Waffen-SS, 1941–1945.* Silver Spring, MD: Bibliophile Legion, 1983.

Inaccurate in spots, but significant as the first English-language work on the subject.

_____. *Narva 1944: The Waffen-SS and the Battle for Europe.* Silver Spring, MD: Bibliophile Legion, 1981.

Essentially a translation of part of Tieke's book on the III (Germanic) *SS*-Panzer Corps, and without the updating which that volume has received.

_____. *Romanian Volunteers of the Waffen-SS, 1944–45.* Brookings, OR: Siegrunen, 1991.

The only detailed account of the service of the Romanians in the *Waffen-SS*, with information and many very rare photos provided by Romanian veteran sources.

_____. *The "Wallonien": The History of the 5th SS-Sturmbrigade and 28th SS Volunteer Panzer-Grenadier Division.* Brookings, OR: Siegrunen, 1992.

A good, brief introduction to the subject.

Landwehr, Richard, and Holger Thor Nielsen. *Nordic Warriors: SS-Panzer-Grenadier Regiment 24 Danmark, Eastern Front, 1943– 1945.* Halifax, UK: Shelf Books, 1999.

Based on the previous Narva 1944 book, but with many private photos from Danish veterans.

Lannoy, Francois de. *Pannwitz Cossacks, 1942–1945.* Bayeux: Editions Heimdal, 2000.

A fantastic collection of unpublished war reporter photos from French archives, combined with an up-to-date text. In French and English.

Ledwoch, Janusz. *Waffen SS.* Warsaw: Militaria, 1993.

A brief introduction to the *Waffen-SS* with photos from Polish archives.

_____. *Waffen SS Czesc 2.* Warsaw: Militaria, 1994.

A continuation of the previous work.

Lefevre, Eric. *Panzers in Normandy Then and Now.* London: After the Battle. 2d ed. 1990.

Out of date, but a good introduction to the *Waffen-SS* and *Heer* armored units that fought in Normandy during 1944.

Lehmann, Rudolf. *Die Leibstandarte im Bild.* 3d ed. Osnabrück: Munin, 1988.

One of the better Munin photo books with good coverage from 1933 through Normandy. The author was a longtime member of the unit. In German and English.

_____. *The Leibstandarte I.* Winnipeg: Fedorowicz, 1987.

The translation of the highly-detailed veterans' history of the unit, covering through the Greek campaign.

_____. *The Leibstandarte II.* Winnipeg: Fedorowicz, 1988.

Continues the history from Barbarossa to the end of 1942.

_____. *The Leibstandarte III.* Winnipeg: Fedorowicz, 1990.

Covers the year 1943 in extensive detail.

Lehmann, Rudolf, and Ralf Tiemann. *The Leibstandarte IV/1.* Winnipeg: Fedorowicz, 1993.

Covers the spring 1944 and Normandy fighting, but in less detail than the previous volumes, as Tiemann finished the book from Lehmann's notes after the latter passed away.

Leleu, Jean-Luc. *10. SS-Panzer-Division "Frundsberg": Normandie, 1944.* Bayeux: Editions Heimdal, 1999.

Good information in French; some new photos.

Lepre, George. *Himmler's Bosnian Division: The SS-Handschar Division, 1943–1945.* Atglen, PA: Schiffer, 1996.

One of the best works ever on the *Waffen-SS*, its research in Yugoslavian archives makes everything previously written on this unit obsolete.

Littlejohn, David. *Foreign Legions of the Third Reich. Vol. 1: Norway, Denmark, France.* San Jose: Bender, 1979.

A good introduction to the uniforms and insignia of the collaborators, though the military history details are often in error.

_____. *Foreign Legions of the Third Reich. Vol. 2: Belgium, Great Britain, Holland, Italy, and Spain.* San Jose: Bender, 1981.

Especially good coverage of Belgium and the Netherlands.

_____. *Foreign Legions of the Third Reich. Vol. 3: Albania, Czechoslovakia, Greece, Hungary, and Yugoslavia.* San Jose: Bender, 1985.

Includes some of the rarest material in this series.

_____. *Foreign Legions of the Third Reich. Vol. 4: Poland, the Ukraine, Bulgaria, Romania, Free*

India, Estonia, Latvia, Lithuania, Finland, and Russia. San Jose: Bender, 1987.
More rare material, the culmination to a very useful set of books.

Logusz, Michael O. *Galicia Division: The Waffen-SS 14th Grenadier Division, 1943–1945.* Atglen, PA: Schiffer, 1997.
Includes much material that veterans had never revealed previously; a necessary work for understanding the Eastern Front.

Lucas, James. *Alpine Elite: German Mountain Troops of World War II.* London: Jane's, 1980.
A basic introduction to the subject, including *Waffen-SS* mountain units.

_____. *Battle Group!: German Kampfgruppen Action of World War Two.* London: Arms and Armour, 1993.
Cannibalized from previous books, with some *Waffen-SS* coverage.

_____. *Das Reich: The Military Role of the 2d SS Division.* London: Arms & Armour, 1991.
A very good introductory history of the *SS-V* and *SS-Das Reich* based on material collected by Mark Yerger for his works.

_____. *Hitler's Mountain Troops.* London. Arms and Armour, 1992.
Includes more extensive detail than his previous book on the same subject, with enhanced *Waffen-SS* coverage.

_____. *SS-Kampfgruppe Peiper.* Bradford, UK: Shelf, 1997.
A novel, but based on solid research on Peiper's role in the Kharkov campaign, especially the rescue of the 320th Infantry Division.

_____. *War on the Eastern Front, 1941–1945.* New York: Bonanza, 1982.
A very good first work for understanding the Eastern Front, includes some *Waffen-SS* coverage.

Lumsden, Robin. *A Collector's Guide to the Waffen-SS.* New York: Hippocrene, 1994.
A good introduction to the study of the *Waffen-SS* for more than just collectors.

Luther, Craig W. H. *Blood and Honor: The History of the 12th SS Panzer Division "Hitler Youth," 1943–1945.* San Jose: Bender, 1987.
Actually only covers the formation and Normandy campaign.

Mabire, Jean. *Division de Choc Wallonie: Lutte a mort en Pomeranie.* Paris: Jacques Grancher, 1996.
Continues the oral history of the Walloon veterans in his *Legion Wallonie* book.

_____. *Legion Wallonie au front de l'Est, 1941–1944.* Paris: Presses de la Cite, 1987.
An oral history with many veterans' anecdotes.

Mabire, Jean, and Eric Lefevre. *Leon Degrelle et la Legion Wallonie, 1941–1945.* Paris, Art et Histoire d'Europe, 1988.
A fabulous large collection of photos on Degrelle and his men, one of the best books ever published on the Germanic *Waffen-SS*.

MacLean, French L. *The Cruel Hunters: SS-Sonder-Kommando Dirlewanger, Hitler's Most Notorious Anti-Partisan Unit.* Atglen, PA: Schiffer, 1998.
A good study of the history of this unit, although not always fully objective.

Madisso, Voldemar. *Nii nagu see oli: Sõduri märkmekaust.* Tallinn: SE & JS, 1997.
The memoirs of an Estonian *Waffen-SS* enlisted man.

Malaparte, Curzio. *The Volga Rises in Europe.* Edinburgh: Birlinn, 2000.
A classic translated account by an Italian journalist, with valuable details about conditions on the Eastern Front and Finnish involvement in the war.

McKee, Alexander. *Last Round Against Rommel: Battle of the Normandy Beachhead* (also published as *Caen: Anvil of Victory*). New York: Signet, 1966.
A balanced examination of the campaign, including accounts of atrocities committed by both sides.

McKee, Alexander. *The Race for the Rhine.* New York: Zebra, 1979.
Includes some of the only English mentions of *SS-Landstorm Nederland* in action.

Mehner, Kurt. *Die Waffen-SS und Polizei, 1939–1945.* Norderstedt, Germany: Militair-Verlag Klaus D. Patzwall, 1995.
A valuable collection of orders of battle and commander lists, despite many minor inaccuracies.

Messenger, Charles. *Hitler's Gladiator: The Life and Times of Obergruppenführer and Panzergeneral-Oberst der Waffen-SS Sepp Dietrich.* New York: Brassey's, 1988.
A very sympathetic biography, with much useful information.

Meyer, Hubert. *The History of the 12. SS-Panzerdivision Hitlerjugend.* Winnipeg: Fedorowicz, 1994.

An English translation of the tremendously detailed veterans' history, written by the chief of staff of the division.

Meyer, Kurt. *Grenadiers*. Winnipeg: Fedorowicz, 1994.

"Panzermeyer's" memoirs in translation, with many small unit actions examined in detail. He recounts his experiences with *SS-LAH* and *SS-Hitlerjugend* in one of the most exciting books ever written.

Michulec, Robert, and Ronald Volstad. *Waffen-SS: Forging an Army, 1934–1943*. Hong Kong: Concord, 1997.

A small book of well-captioned, mostly unpublished war reporter photos from the Polish archives.

———. *Waffen-SS: From Glory to Defeat, 1943-1945*. Hong Kong: Concord, 1998.

Continues the previous work to the end of the war.

———. *Waffen-SS in Combat*. Hong Kong: Concord, 1999.

Additional photos as a supplement to the two previous titles.

Mitcham, Samuel W., Jr. *Hitler's Legions: The German Army Order of Battle. World War II*. New York: Stein and Day, 1985.

Actually only covers divisions, pioneering for an English-language work, but often inaccurate, since it is based primarily on wartime US intelligence reports.

Moore, John P. *Signal Officers of the Waffen-SS*. 3d ed. Portland, OR: J. P. Moore, 1996.

Noteworthy for demonstrating that many of these men were both outstanding soldiers and then distinguished citizens after the war. Prepared with information from wartime files and contributions from the subjects.

Muñoz, Antonio J. *The Druzhina SS Brigade: A History, 1941–1943*. Bayside, NY: Axis Europa, 2000.

Briefly covers a little-known Russian collaborationist unit, and helps in comprehending the partisan war behind the Eastern Front.

———. *Forgotten Legions: Obscure Combat Formations of the Waffen-SS*. Boulder, CO: Paladin, 1991.

A good introduction to various units that normally receive little attention in any language, including *SS*-Parachute Battalion 500/600, the 23d and 24th *Waffen*-Mountain Divisions, and the 30th *Waffen*-Grenadier Division. Most information from wartime documents.

———. *Forgotten Legions Companion Book: Additional Data for the Classic Study*. Bayside, NY: Axis Europa, nd.

Supplemental details to the previous work, a useful complement.

———. *The German Police*. Bayside, NY: Axis Europa, 1997.

A reprint of a highly-detailed 1945 Allied intelligence report, with good German wartime material added. Includes some *Waffen-SS* information.

———. *For Czar and Country: A History of the Russian Guard Corps, 1941–1945*. Bayside, NY: Axis Europa, 1999.

A brief account of this unit that fought the same enemy as the *Waffen-SS* units in Yugoslavia.

———. *Hitler's Eastern Legions, Volume 1: The Baltic Schutzmannschaft, 1941–1945*. 2d ed. Bayside, NY: Axis Europa, n.d.

Brief coverage of units that were transferred into the *Waffen-SS*.

———. *Iron Fist: A Combat History of the 17. SS Panzer-Grenadier Division "Götz von Berlichingen."* Bayside, NY: Axis Europa, 1999.

Briefly covers the division between the summer of 1944 and early 1945; useful as an introduction to the division and its battles.

———. *The Kaminski Brigade: A History, 1941–1945*. Bayside, NY: Axis Europa, n.d.

Collects the available information on a notorious unit, and aids in comprehending the partisan war behind the Eastern Front.

Montyn, Jan, and Dirk Ayelt Kooiman. *A Lamb to Slaughter*. New York: Viking, 1985.

Translation of the life story of a Dutch volunteer in the German Navy, useful for understanding the German occupation and the motives of collaboration.

Newland, Samuel J. *Cossacks in the German Army, 1941–1945*. London: Frank Cass, 1991.

A valuable, short introduction to the subject.

Niehorster, Leo W. G. *The Royal Hungarian Army, 1920–1945*. Bayside, NY: Axis Europa, 1998.

The first detailed work in English on the subject includes a brief summary of the Hungarian *Waffen-SS* units. Researched from Hungarian sources.

Nipe, George M., Jr. *Decision in the Ukraine: Summer 1943*. II. *SS* and III. Panzerkorps. Winnipeg: Fedorowicz, 1996.

A very detailed account of the destruction of the Mius bridgehead and the subsequent Fourth Battle of Kharkov.

_____. *Last Victory in Russia: The SS-Panzerkorps and Manstein's Kharkov Counteroffensive, February–March 1943*. Atglen, PA: Schiffer, 2000.
A tremendously detailed history of the Kharkov campaign. One of the best studies of its type ever written because it is based on wartime war diaries and post-war veterans' histories.

Norling, S. Erik. *Raza de Vikingos: La division SS Nordland, 1943–1945*. Granada, Spain: Garcia Hispan, n.d.
A very good history of the division, using primarily Norwegian veteran sources to cover points not found in Tieke's book on the III (Germanic) SS-Panzer Corps. Some of the material has appeared in modified form in English in *Siegrunen*.

_____. *Sangre en la Nieve: Voluntarios europeos en el Ejercito finlandes y las Waffen SS en el Frente de Finlandia, 1939–1945*. Granada, Spain: Garcia Hispan, 1996.
A detailed look at foreign volunteers who fought in Finland, including the Norwegian SS-Ski Battalion. Some material on that unit has appeared in modified form in English in *Siegrunen*.

Oertle, Vincenz. *"Solte ich aus Russland nicht zurückkeheren . . .": Schweizer Freiwillige an deutscher Seite, 1939–1945*. Zurich: Thesis Verlag, 1997.
An extremely detailed, thorough account of the Swiss volunteers in the German military; numerous personal accounts, documents, and photos.

Ojamaa, Arved. *Capful of Wind*. Tallinn: Privately published, 1999.
The memoirs of a medic in the Estonian *Waffen-SS* who emigrated to the United States after the war and wrote his account in English.

Pallud, Jean Paul. *Ardennes 1944: Peiper and Skorzeny* (Elite Series 11). London: Osprey, 1987.
An offshoot booklet of Pallud's *Battle of the Bulge*, it explores its two subjects in increased detail and is a good preview of the entire work.

_____. *Battle of the Bulge, Then and Now*. 2d ed. London: After the Battle, 1986.
The best single book ever written on the Ardennes offensive, with outstanding photo coverage complementing a good text.

Perret, Bryan. *Knights of the Black Cross: Hitler's Panzerwaffe and Its Leaders*. New York: St. Martin's, 1988.
The best English-language introduction to the campaigns of the German armored forces ever written. Helps put the accounts of individual divisions into perspective.

Perro, Oskars. *Fortress Cholm*. Toronto: Privately published, 1992.
The first of several memoirs by the Latvian author that cover his wartime experiences in a *Schuma* battalion and then in the *Waffen-SS*. This is the only one translated into English, and tells of his pre-*Waffen-SS* involvement in the siege of Cholm in early 1942.

Pierik, Perry. *From Leningrad to Berlin: Dutch Volunteers in the Service of the German Waffen-SS, 1941–1945*. Soesterberg, Netherlands: Aspekt, 2001.
A translation of a book that has less military historical details than the title would suggest. It deals more with the campaigns of the Eastern Front and the nature of the SS than with the specific experiences of Dutch *Waffen-SS* men.

_____. *Hungary 1944–1945 The Forgotten Tragedy: Germany's Final Offensives During World War II and The Destruction of Europe's Last Remaining Jewish Community*. Nieuwegein, Netherlands: Aspekt, 1996.
A translation that provides a good English summary of the three Operations KONRAD and FRÜHLINGSERWACHEN.

Piin, Voldemar. *Kolonel Alfons Rebane*. Pärnu, Estonia: Privately published, 1997.
A short, but detailed, biography of Estonian Oakleaves recipient Alfons Rebane.

_____. *Rüütliristi-Kandja Harald Nugiseks*. Pärnu, Estonia: Privately published, 1995.
A short, but detailed, biography of Estonian Knight's Cross recipient Harald Nugiseks.

_____. *Rüütliristi-kandja Kolonelleitnant Harald Riipalu*. Pärnu, Estonia: Privately published, 1999.
Final book in the series. A short, but detailed, biography of Estonian Knight's Cross recipient, Harald Riipalu.

_____. *Rüütliristi-kandja Major Paul Maitla*. Pärnu, Estonia: Privately published, 1998.
These books are scheduled for eventual translation into English, as is Riipalu's memoir of the 1944 fighting. Continues the series with Estonian Knight's Cross recipient, Paul Maitla.

Pionierkameradschaft Dresden. *Pioniere der Waffen-SS im Bild*. Osnabrück: Munin, 1985.

One of the better Munin photo books, with many photos not found elsewhere. In German and English.

Proschek, Rolf. *Verweht sind die Spuren: Bilddokumentation 5. SS-Panzerregiment "Wiking."* Osnabrück: Munin, 1979.

Many very good armor and armored halftrack photos, but one of the shorter Munin photo books, and in German only.

Puntigam, Josef Paul. *Vom Plattensee bis zur Mur: Die Kämpfe 1945 im Dreiländereck.* 2d ed. Feldbach, Austria: Hannes Krois, 1993.

This is actually the veterans' history of the 16th SS-Panzer-Grenadier Division from February 1945 until the end of the war, with extensive detail and many good documents and maps on the fighting in Hungary.

Quarrie, Bruce. *Hitler's Samurai: The Waffen-SS in Action.* 3d ed. Wellingborough, UK: Patrick Stephens, 1986.

An expanded version of Quarrie's previous work, *The Waffen SS in Russia*, with many of the same photos and a text that shows a lack of archival research.

_____. *Hitler's Teutonic Knights: SS Panzers in Action.* 2d ed. Wellingborough, UK: Patrick Stephens, 1986.

A continuation of his two previous works and, as with them, a nice collection of war reporter photos, but of little use as a reference source.

_____. *Waffen SS in Russia.* Cambridge: Patrick Stephens, 1978.

A small collection of interesting war reporter photos from the German archives. Many are actually from other fronts.

_____. *Weapons of the Waffen-SS: From Small Arms to Tanks.* New York: Sterling, 1990.

In the same vein as his other books, though most of the photos are not of the *Waffen-SS*.

Ready. J. Lee. *The Forgotten Axis: Germany's Partners and Foreign Volunteers in World War II.* Jefferson, NC: McFarland, 1987.

Despite many minor inaccuracies, this is a vital work for understanding that the Eastern front involved every nation in Europe on one or both sides.

_____. *World War Two Nation by Nation.* London, Arms & Armour, 1995.

Useful for demonstrating the role that "minor" countries played in the war, including contributions to the *Waffen-SS*. This book has some of the same errors as his previous work.

Regimentskameradschaft "Deutschland." *Das Regiment "Deutschland" 1934–1945.* 2d ed. Germany: Privately published, 1988.

The veterans' history of this unit, with good detail through Normandy. Recent reprints have been retitled *Hart wie Stahl.*

Regimentskameradschaft des ehemaligen SS-Panzer-Grenadier-Regiments Nr. 10 "Westland." *Panzer-Grenadiere der Panzerdivision "Wiking" im Bild.* 2d ed. Osnabrück: Munin, 1987.

One of the best Munin photo books, includes good photos on most elements of *SS-Wiking* and substantial text on *SS-Westland.* In German and English.

Restayn, Jean. *The Battle of Kharkov: Winter 1942–1943.* Winnipeg: Fedorowicz, 2000.

Hundreds of war reporter photos from various archives, this is the perfect complement to Nipe's text study of the Kharkov campaign. Author concentrates on the SS-Panzer Corps.

Reynolds, Michael. *The Devil's Adjutant: Jochen Peiper, Panzer Leader.* New York: Sarpedon, 1995.

A useful retracing of Peiper's activities in the Ardennes by an expert on the battle.

_____. *Men of Steel: I SS Panzer Corps in the Ardennes and on the Eastern Front, 1944–45.* New York: Sarpedon, 1999.

Continues his previous work, *Steel Inferno*; the Eastern Front portion is almost entirely based on the veterans' histories.

_____. *Steel Inferno: I SS Panzer Corps in Normandy.* New York: Sarpedon, 1997.

Essentially a summary of the information in the veterans' histories of *SS-LAH* and *SS-Hitlerjugend*, though supplemented by comparison with Allied accounts.

Richter, Klaus Christian. *Kavallerie der Wehrmacht.* Wölfersheim-Berstadt, Germany: Podzun-Pallas, 1994.

A photo study of WWII-era German cavalry, including the *Waffen-SS* cavalry units. Also available in an English translation.

Rikmenspoel, Marc. *Soldiers of the Waffen-SS: Many Nations, One Motto.* Winnipeg: Fedorowicz, 1999.

The best book ever written, bar none. A collection of private and war reporter photos assembled by the present author.

Roolaine, Kalju. *Skaudipoisina Elu Miiniväljadel.* Valga, Estonia: Privately published, 1999.

A short study of the Estonian *Waffen-SS* prepared by a veteran.

Sawicki, Robert, et al. *4 Panzer Division.* Vol. 3, *1943–1944.* Warsaw: Militaria, 2000.

Part of a set of booklets on the 4th Panzer Division of the *Heer*, based on the photos shot by divisional photographers that ended up in a Polish archive after the war. This and the following two titles include nice photos of Panther tanks of the 2d Battalion of *SS*-Panzer Regiment 5, which fought alongside the 4th Panzer Division near Kovel during March and April 1944.

_____. *4 Panzer Division.* Vol. 4, *1944–1945.* Warsaw: Militaria, 2000.

_____. *4 Panzer Division.* Vol. 5, *1941–1945.* Warsaw: Militaria, 2000.

Schadewitz, Michael. *The Meuse First and Then Antwerp: Some Aspects of Hitler's Offensive in the Ardennes.* Winnipeg: Fedorowicz, 1999.

A translated in-depth study of the history of Skorzeny's 150th Panzer Brigade, which included many *Waffen-SS* elements. The best book on the subject.

Scheibert, Horst. *Die Träger des Deutschen Kreuzes in Gold—Das Heer.* Friedberg, Germany: Podzun-Pallas, 1992.

A listing of all known German Army recipients of the German Cross in Gold; some of these men later transferred to the *Waffen-SS*.

_____. *Die Träger des Deutschen Kreuzes in Gold—Kriegsmarine, Luftwaffe, Waffen-SS und Deutschen Kreuzes in Silber—Heer, Kriegsmarine, Luftwaffe, Waffen-SS.* Friedberg, Germany: Podzun-Pallas, 1992.

The companion to the previous title, listing recipients of the German Cross in Gold from other branches of service, and all known recipients of the German Cross in Silver. Both volumes leave out a number of individuals.

Schmitz, Peter, et al. *Die Deutschen Divisionen, 1939–1945.* Vol. 1, *Die Divisionen 1–5.* Osnabrück: Biblio, 1993.

Examines the structure, assignments, and high-award recipients of all German divisions numbered 1 to 5, including the first five *Waffen-SS* ones. Also has many good maps.

_____. *Die Deutschen Divisionen, 1939–1945.* Vol. 2, *Die Divisionen 6–10.* Osnabrück: Biblio, 1994.

Continues the previous book with all divisions numbered 6 to 10, including *Waffen-SS*.

Schneider, Jost W. *Their Honor was Loyalty!: An Illustrated and Documentary History of the Knight's Cross Holders of the Waffen-SS and Police, 1940–1945.* 2d ed. San Jose: Bender, 1993.

Brief details and a photo or two for all Knight's Cross holders of the *Waffen-SS* and police. Less detailed but more accessible than Kräschmer's book, and in German and English.

Schneider, Russ. *Götterdammerung 1945: Germany's Last Stand in the East.* Philomont, VA: Eastern Front/Warfield Books, 1998.

Translations of bits and pieces from various German books that are mostly out of print and hard to find. Some of the material involves the *Waffen-SS*.

Schneider, Wolfgang. *Tigers in Combat I.* Winnipeg: Fedorowicz, 1994.

A fabulous collection of private and war reporter photos of the *Heer* Tiger tank battalions, with brief histories of each unit. These battalions often directly supported *Waffen-SS* units.

_____. *Tigers in Combat II.* Winnipeg: Fedorowicz, 1998.

The sequel to the previous book, covering the other Tiger units, especially the *Waffen-SS* companies and battalions. Most of this material is not available elswhere.

Schulze-Kossens, Richard. *Die Junkerschulen: Militärischer Führernachwuchs der Waffen-SS.* 2d ed. Osnabrück: Munin, 1987.

A very detailed text and photo history of the *SS* officer training schools, focusing on Bad Tölz, and written by the last commander of that academy. Full of important information on almost all aspects on the *Waffen-SS*.

Siegrunen: The Waffen-SS in Historical Perspective, Issues 1–71, 1976–2001.

The earlier issues are out of date, but for the past 15 years, it has included numerous articles on the foreign *Waffen-SS* with information not found elewhere. The tone is very favorable to the *Waffen-SS* and Germany.

Silgailis, Arthur. *Latvian Legion.* San Jose: Bender, 1986.

The only detailed English-language history of the two Latvian *Waffen-SS* divisions, written by a staff officer who helped to organize them.

Simpson, Gary L. *Tiger Ace: The Life Story of Panzer Commander Michael Wittmann.* Atglen, PA: Schiffer, 1994.

More a work of fiction than of history, and one of the most poorly edited books ever published. It takes the reader into Wittmann's head during his numerous armored engagements.

Skorzeny, Otto. *My Commando Operations: The Memoirs of Hitler's Most Daring Commando.* Atglen, PA: Schiffer, 1995.

The translation of Skorzeny's own version of the historic events in which he participated. While he exaggerates and distorts many facts, he also includes interesting observations on various aspects of the Third Reich.

Smith, Roland, et al. *Das Kreuz: Autographs and Photographs of Knight's Cross Recipients.* Privately printed, 1994.

Includes many rare autographed photos of personalities (not only Knight's Cross recipients) from all branches of the German military of the Second World War era.

SS-Personalhauptamt. *Dienstalterliste der Schutzstaffel der NSDAP (SS-Oberst-Gruppenführer-SS-Standartenführer) Stand vom 9. November 1944* (facsimile ed.). Winnipeg: Fedorowicz, 1986.

A valuable source of details about senior SS officers, including *Waffen-SS* ones.

Strassner, Peter. *European Volunteers: 5th SS-Panzer Division Wiking.* Winnipeg: Fedorowicz, 1988.

The translation of the one of the first Munin veterans' text histories. Interesting, but far less detailed than similar books on *SS-LAH*, *SS-Das Reich*, and *SS-Totenkopf*. Fortunately, the many other books by *SS-Wiking* veterans supplement this one.

Stein, George H. *The Waffen-SS: Hitler's Elite Guard at War.* Ithaca: Cornell University Press, 1966.

A groundbreaking study in its time, now badly outdated. Its research in documents from Himmler's headquarters isn't extended to the situation in the field, which often differed from what was believed at higher levels.

Stern, Robert C. *SS Armor: A Pictorial History of the Armored Formations of the Waffen-SS.* Carrollton, TX: Squadron/Signal, 1978.

A nice, small collection of war reporter photos, though the text and captions are hghly inaccurate.

Steurich, Alfred. *Gebirgsjäger im Bild: 6. SS-Gebirgsdivision Nord 1940–1945.* Osnabrück: Munin, 1976.

A good collection of photos of this unit by an officer veteran. One of the first, and smallest, Munin photo books, recent reprints have included a supplement of English caption translations.

Steven, Andrew, and Peter Amodio. *Waffen-SS Uniforms in Colour Photos.* London: Windrow & Greene, 1990.

Modern photos of wartime uniforms worn by reenactors, useful for showing how camouflage uniforms actually appeared in the field.

Stoves, Rolf. *Die Gepanzerten und Motorisierten deutschen Grossverbände, 1935–1945.* Friedberg, Germany: Podzun-Pallas, 1986.

Brief histories and organizational charts for all independent German armored and motorized formations, including those of the *Waffen-SS*.

Swirin, M., et al. *Budapeszt Balaton 1945.* Warsaw: Militaria, 2000.

Soviet photos of knocked out Axis armor in Hungary during 1945, most of the photos show *Waffen-SS* vehicles, with useful details of camouflage and markings not available in German photos from the era.

Sydnor, Charles W., Jr. *Soldiers of Destruction: The SS Death's Head Division, 1933–1945.* 2d ed. Princeton, NJ: Princeton Univ. Press, 1990.

Groundbreaking study of the introduction of concentration camp elements into the framework of the *SS-V*. Exaggerates its point, and its post-1942 history of the division is sometimes inaccurate.

Tammiksaar, Leo. *Eesti Diviisi Struktuur ja Ohvitseride Koosseis ii Maailmasõjas.* Tallinn: Eesti Riigikaitse Akadeemia kirjastus, 1998.

A listing of all known Estonian *Waffen-SS* officers combined with organizational charts for the Estonian *Waffen-SS* Legion, Brigade, and Division.

Taylor, Blaine. *Guarding the Führer: Sepp Dietrich, Johann Rattenhuber, and the Protection of Adolf Hitler.* Missoula, MT: Pictorial Histories, 1993.

A nice collection of photos from the US National Archives that chronicle the early history of *SS-LAH* and related units. The text is based largely on secondary sources.

Taylor, Hugh Page, and Roger James Bender. *Uniforms, Organization, and History of the Waffen-SS.* Vol. 5. San Jose: Bender, 1982.

The best volume in this series; the detail on the 19th and 20th *Waffen*-Grenadier Divisions is still highly useful.

Thomas, Franz. *Sturmartillerie im Bild, 1940–1945.* Osnabrück: Biblio, 1986.

Many unpublished photos of German assault guns, with some about the *Waffen-SS*.

Thomas, Nigel. *Foreign Volunteers of the Allied Forces, 1939–45* (Men at Arms 238). London: Osprey, 1991.

A good introduction to the subject, which makes an interesting counterpoint to the study of those who volunteered for the German military.

_____. *Partisan Warfare, 1941–45* (Men at Arms 142). London: Osprey, 1983.

Good for background on the Eastern Front and the anti-partisan war that involved various *Waffen-SS* units.

Thomas, Nigel, and Carlos Caballero Jurado. *Wehrmacht Auxiliary Forces* (Men at Arms 254). London: Osprey, 1992.
A very good introduction to various paramilitary formations, which often included non-Germans who later joined the *Waffen-SS*.

Thomas, Nigel, and Krunoslav Mikulan. *Axis Forces in Yugoslavia 1941–45* (Men at Arms 282). London: Osprey, 1995.
A useful introduction to the complex civil war in Yugoslavia, which involved various *Waffen-SS* divisions.

Tieke, Wilhelm. *The Caucasus and the Oil: The German-Soviet War in the Caucasus, 1942/43*. Winnipeg: Fedorowicz, 1995.
A translation of the best single work on this subject, with much detail on *SS-Wiking* in particular. Written by a *Waffen-SS* veteran of that campaign.

———. *In the Firestorm of the Last Years of the War: II. SS-Panzerkorps with the 9. and 10. SS-Divisions "Hohenstaufen" and "Frundsberg."* Winnipeg: Fedorowicz, 1999.
A translation of the highly-detailed veterans' history of these two divisions. The Fürbringer book makes a good supplement because of its maps and photos.

———. *Tragedy of the Faithful: A History of the III. (germanisches) SS-Panzer-Korps*. Winnipeg: Fedorowicz, 2001.
The best English source on *SS-Nordland* and *SS-Nederland*, a combined translation of two German veterans' histories with unpublished photos added.

Tiemann, Ralf. *Chronicle of the 7. Panzer-Kompanie, 1. SS-Panzer Division "Leibstandarte."* Atglen, PA: Schiffer, 1998.
The translation of the veterans' history of this tank company, includes accounts not found in the main divisional history. Written by the former company commander.

———. *Der Malmedyprozess: Ein Ringen um Gerechtigkeit.* 2d ed. Coburg: Nation Europa, 1993.
German version of the Malmedy trial, which criticizes the methods of the American prosecution.

———. *The Leibstandarte IV/2*. Winnipeg: Fedorowicz, 1998.
The final volume of the veterans' history, assembled and written by Tiemann after Lehmann's death. He had more time for this than for volume IV/1, and the result is a more thorough study, which runs to the end of the war.

Tinits, Arvi. *Välgumärgi Kasvandikud*. Toronto: Lennuväepoiste Klubi Torontos kirjastus, 1982.
The account of an Estonian youth of how he and his comrades became *Luftwaffe* anti-aircraft gunners, before being reassigned to the replacement regiment of the 20th *Waffen*-Grenadier Division, and then came to Canada after the war.

Tout, Ken. *The Bloody Battle for Tilly, Normandy, 1944*. Phoenix Mill, UK: Sutton, 2000.
A British veteran's study of this battle that involved the *SS-LAH*. Interesting for the British perspective as a counterpoint to Tiemann's 7th Panzer Company book in particular.

Trang, Charles. *The "Florian Geyer" Division*. Bayeux: Editions Heimdal, 2000.
A short, but detailed, history of the 8th *SS* cavalry division, with very good war reporter photos from the French archives. In French and English.

Truppenkameradschaft 5. SS-Panzer-Division *Wiking* ("Veterans' Association of the 5th *SS*-Panzer Division 'Viking'"). *Unser Wiking-Ruf*. Germany: Privately published, 1996.
The veterans' association yearbook, published at the end of 1996. Includes many death notices and anecdotes of wartime experiences.

Truppenkameradschaft der 16. SS-Panzer-Grenadier-Division "Reichsführer-SS." *"Im gleichen Schritt und Tritt": Dokumentation der 16. SS-Panzer-Grenadierdivision "Reichsführer-SS."* Munich: Schild, 1998.
The extremely detailed veterans' history of this division, from formation through February 1945. Produced in exceptionally high quality, it includes many photos and color maps. The history is continued in Puntigam's book.

Truppenkameradschaft der *SS-Polizei*-Division. *Die guten Glaubens waren—Bildband*. Osnabrück: Munin, 1977.
The photo book supplement to the veterans' history. Not one of the more exciting Munin titles, but the material is not found elsewhere. In German only.

Truppenkameradschaft Flak-Abteilung Leibstandarte. *Gefärten unsrer Jugend: Die Flak-Abteilung der Leibstandarte, Geschichte, und Geschichten*. Preussisch Oldendorf, Germany: K. W. Schütz, 1984.
Detailed veterans' history of the anti-aircraft battalion of *SS-LAH*; many private photos.

Tulp, Harry, et al. *Pataljon "Narva" Ajalugu*. Tartu, Estonia: Greif, 1995.

The first volume of the detailed veterans' history of the Panzer-Grenadier Battalion "Narva." Many of the photos were used in *Landwehr*'s book on the unit.

_____. *Terasest Tugevamad: Pataljon "Narva" Ajalugu II*. Tartu, Estonia: Greif, 1997.

Continues the veterans' history with length personal accounts. Few photos, but a useful English summary of the battalion's history.

_____. *Visadus Võitis: Pataljon "Narva" Ajalugu III*. Tartu, Estonia: Greif, 1999.

Finishes the veterans' history with additional accounts and portrayals of the battalion in the Estonian media.

Ullrich, Karl. *Wie ein Fels im Meer: 3. SS-Panzerdivision "Totenkopf" im Bild*. Osnabrück: Munin, 1984.

One of the best Munin photo books, by a former regimental commander in the division.

_____. *Wie ein Fels im Meer: Kriegsgeschichte der 3. SS-Panzerdivision "Totenkopf."* Osnabrück: Munin, 1987.

The text complement to the previous book, with the entire history of the division in one volume. For more detail, see the Vopersal series.

Ulric of England with Otto Spronk. *Deutschland Erwache: The History and Development of the Nazi Party and the "Germany Awake" Standards*. San Jose: Bender, 1997.

An excellent collection of pre-war photos and a sympathetic introduction to the history of the Nazi party. Includes coverage of the SS-V's flags.

Vickers, Philip. *Das Reich: 2d SS Panzer Division Das Reich—Drive to Normandy, June 1944* (Battleground Europe series). Conshohocken, UK: Combined Pub., 2000.

A good account of the operations of the French resistance in the Dordogne, but not objective in dealing with the Germans.

Vincx, Jan. *Vlaanderen in Uniform, 1940–1945*. Part 5. Antwerp: Etnika, 1983.

Part of an exhaustive, well-illustrated series that covers all aspects of the Flemish collaboration. This volume gives an overview of the entire *Waffen-SS* in the context of the Flemish volunteers. The author was a highly-decorated *Waffen-SS* veteran.

_____. *Vlaanderen in Uniform, 1940–1945*. Part 6. Antwerp: Etnika, 1983.

Continues the previous book's exploration of the *Waffen-SS* by examining *SS-Wiking*, the officer schools, and other elements that included substantial Flemings.

_____. *Vlaanderen in Uniform, 1940–1945*. Part 7. Antwerp: Etnika, 1984.

Finishes the series by setting out the history of the Flemish *SS*-Legion, and its successor Langemarck Brigade and Division.

Vincx, Jan, and Viktor Schotanius. *Nederlandse vrijwilligers in Europese krijgsdienst, 1940–1945*. Part 1, *De Landstorm*. Antwerp: Etnika, 1988.

The only detailed history available on the *SS-Landstorm Nederland*, prepared largely from wartime documents.

_____. *Nederlandse vrijwilligers in Europese krijgsdienst, 1940–1945*. Part 2, *Vrijwilligers Legioen "Nederland."* Antwerp: Etnika, 1988.

The history of the Dutch *SS*-Legion told mainly through war diaries.

_____. *Nederlandse vrijwilligers in Europese krijgsdienst, 1940–1945*. Part 3, *Vrijwilligers Panzergrenadier Brigade "Nederland" and 23e Pantsergrenadier Divisie "Nederland."* Antwerp: Etnika, 1989.

A fascinating history of the *SS-Nederland* Brigade and Division, told mainly through war diaries. Much of this information is not found elsewhere in studies of the III (Germanic) *SS*-Panzer Corps.

_____. *Nederlandse vrijwilligers in Europese krijgsdienst, 1940–1945*. Parts 4, 5. *SS-Pantserdivisie "Wiking" & Alsmede Diverse Militaire Formaties*. Antwerp: Etnika, 1991.

The history of *SS-Wiking* from the perspective of its Dutch volunteers, with supplemental information on its Flemings that was unavailable when Vincx wrote Vlaanderen in Uniform, Part 6.

Vopersal, Wolfgang. *Soldaten Kämpfer Kameraden: Marsch und Kämpfe der SS-Totenkopf-Division*. Vol. 1. Osnabrück: Biblio, 1983.

The first volume of a minutely-detailed veterans' history of *SS-Totenkopf*, covering the division from formation until early 1941. The entire series is full of personal accounts and wartime documents.

_____. *Soldaten Kämpfer Kameraden: Marsch und Kämpfe der SS-Totenkopf-Division*. Vol. 2a. Osnabrück: Biblio, 1984.

Covers the division during BARBAROSSA and the first stage of the Demyansk fighting. Includes many photos.

_____. *Soldaten Kämpfer Kameraden: Marsch und Kämpfe der SS-Totenkopf-Division.* Vol. 2b. Osnabrück: Biblio, 1984.

Finishes the Demyansk campaign coverage.

_____. *Soldaten Kämpfer Kameraden: Marsch und Kämpfe der SS-Totenkopf-Division.* Vol. 3. Osnabrück: Biblio, 1987.

Begins with the reforming of *SS-Totenkopf* in France during 1942, and then covers the 1943 combat at Kharkov, Kursk, the Mius, and again near Kharkov, finishing at the end of September 1943.

_____. *Soldaten Kämpfer Kameraden: Marsch und Kämpfe der SS-Totenkopf-Division.* Vol. 4a. Osnabrück: Biblio, 1988.

Follows the division in the retreat to the Dnieper River, and then west of the river through February 1944. Fewer photos than previous volumes.

_____. *Soldaten Kämpfer Kameraden: Marsch und Kämpfe der SS-Totenkopf-Division.* Vol. 4b. Osnabrück: Biblio, 1988.

Covers the division in Romania through the June 1944 rebuild.

_____. *Soldaten Kämpfer Kameraden: Marsch und Kämpfe der SS-Totenkopf-Division.* Vol. 5a. Osnabrück: Biblio, 1990.

Devoted to the fighting around Warsaw during the summer of 1944.

_____. *Soldaten Kämpfer Kameraden: Marsch und Kämpfe der SS-Totenkopf-Division.* Vol. 5b. Osnabrück: Biblio, 1991.

A massive book which follows *SS-Totenkopf* to the end of the war, with enormous detail on the operations of the entire IV *SS*-Panzer Corps in Hungary during 1945. Perhaps the best volume in the most impressive veterans' history of any Second World War division.

Wachter, Hans-Otto. *Wir Funkten: Geschichte der Funkkompanie Nachrichten Abteilung 8 "Florian Geyer."* Germany: Privately published, 1980.

A veterans' history of the *SS*-Cavalry Division, from the viewpoint signal battalion's radio companym with many interesting anecdotes and photos from other elements of the division. This began Wachter's series of self-published of photos and accounts from veterans of the *SS* cavalry units.

Walter, Hannes. *Eesti Teenetemärgid: Estonian Orders and Decorations.* Tallinn: Miniplast Pluss, 1998.

A beautiful book with many illustrations, some in color. Many of the personalities included served with the Estonian *Waffen-SS*. In Estonian and English.

Walther, Herbert. *Divisionen der Waffen-SS im Einsatz, 1940–1945: Fotos der Kriegsberichter.* Freidberg, Germany: Podzun-Pallas, 1985.

Additional war reporter photos, the sequel to Walther's *Waffen-SS*. Many of the photos appear elsewhere.

_____. *The 1st SS Panzer Division.* West Chester, PA: Schiffer, 1989.

A nice, small collection of photos, though the translation is rough.

_____. *The 12th SS Panzer Division.* West Chester, PA: Schiffer, 1989.

A good complement to the previous title.

_____. *The Waffen-SS.* West Chester, PA: Schiffer, 1990.

A translation of one of the first collections of war reporter photos assembled by a veteran. The captions have little detail, and have had a mediocre translation, but the photos remain interesting.

Weidinger, Otto. *Comrades to the End: The 4th SS-Panzer-Grenadier Regiment "Der Führer," 1938–1945.* Atglen, PA: Schiffer, 1998.

The translation of the history of this regiment as prepared by its former commanders (Weidinger, Keppler, Kumm, & Stadler), with new photos not in the German version.

_____. *Das Reich I, 1934–1939.* Winnipeg: Fedorowicz, 1990.

The translation of the first of Weidinger's five-volume set, with vital information on the origins of the *Waffen-SS* in the Political Readiness Detachments and *SS-V*. Covers the *SS-V* units through the end of the Polish campaign.

_____. *Das Reich II, 1940–1941.* Winnipeg: Fedorowicz, 1995.

Covers the *SS-V* Division from creation through the Yugoslavian campaign. The remaining volumes await translation, but are kept in print in German.

_____. *Division Das Reich im Bild.* Osnabrück: Munin, 1981.

Has good photo coverage of the *SS-V* and *SS-Das Reich* through the end of 1941, but relatively few photos from the rest of the war.

_____. *Tulle and Oradour: A Franco-German Tragedy.* n.p., n.d.

A translation of Weidinger's summary of the German version of the events in the Dordogne during June 1944.

Weingartner, James J. *Hitler's Guard: The Story of the Leibstandarte SS Adolf Hitler, 1933–1945*. Nashville: Battery Press, n.d.
A pioneering study which is quite basic, and has been superceded by later, more in-depth works.

Wikberg, Olli. *Dritte Nordland*. Helsinki: Wiking-Divisioona Oy, 2001.
The follow up to *Meine Ehre heißt Treue!*, with hundreds of unpublished veterans' photos of the Finnish *SS*-Volunteer Battalion and detailed captions. In Finnish and English.

_____. *Meine Ehre heißt Treue!* Helsinki: Wiking-Divisioona Oy, 1999.
The sequel to *Wikingin suomalaiset*, focusing on the uniforms of the Finnish *Waffen-SS* volunteers, with many additional photos. In Finnish and English.

Williamson, Gordon. *Aces of the Reich*. London: Arms and Armour, 1989.
Short biographies of highly decorated armor, fighter, and submarine specialists, with many of the armor soldiers belonging to the *Waffen-SS*.

_____. *German Military Police Units, 1939–45* (Men at Arms 213). London: Osprey, 1989.
Includes a lot on *Waffen-SS* units.

_____. *Infantry Aces of the Reich*. London: Arms and Armour, 1991.
Extends previous book's theme to infantry specialists, including several *Waffen-SS* men.

_____. *The Iron Cross: A History, 1813–1957*. Poole, UK: Blandford, 1984.
Focuses on the Second World War, with short biographies of various award recipients, including *Waffen-SS* soldiers.

_____. *Knights of the Iron Cross: A History, 1939–1945*. London: Blandford, 1987.
Continues the theme of the previous book, again with several *Waffen-SS* soldiers.

_____. *Loyalty Is My Honor: Personal Accounts from the Waffen-SS*. Osceola, WI: Motorbooks, 1995.
A collection of good, but overly brief, personal accounts from *Waffen-SS* veterans, with some unpublished private photos.

_____. *SS—The Bloodsoaked Soil: The Battles of the Waffen-SS*. Osceola, WI: Motorbooks, 1995.
A history of the role of the *Waffen-SS* in various campaigns, though lacking material from unit histories.

_____. *The SS: Hitler's Instrument of Terror*. Osceola, WI: Motorbooks, 1994.
After a number of books that were respectful to German soldiers, this one sensationalizes its topic.

Windrow, Martin. *Waffen SS* (Men at Arms series). London: Osprey, 1971.
Interesting as a historical artifact: research and publishing have made enormous strides over the past 30 years.

_____. *The Waffen-SS*. Rev. Ed. (Men at Arms 34). London: Osprey, 1982.
A redone version of the previous title, and itself out of date. Includes brief summaries on the formation and service of each *Waffen-SS* division.

Winter, George. *Ernst August Krag: Knight's Cross with Oakleaves*. Atglen, PA: Schiffer, 1996.
Less detailed and less interesting than his Weidinger and Kumm biographies, but still an interesting study of an important officer.

_____. *Freineux and Lamormenil, the Ardennes*. Winnipeg: Fedorowicz, 1994.
A sequel to the next title, exploring a related battle in the same format. Includes good unpublished photos.

_____. *Manhay, the Ardennes, Christmas 1944*. Winnipeg: Fedorowicz, 1990.
A nice account of one of the little-known turning points of the Battle of the Bulge, written using American and German veteran accounts, the latter stemming from *SS-Das Reich*.

Yerger, Mark C. *Images of the Waffen-SS: A Photo Chronicle of Germany's Elite Troops*. Atglen, PA: Schiffer, 1996.
A collection of very nice rare photos, though poorly organized and captioned.

_____. *Knights of Steel: The Structure, Development, and Personalities of the 2. SS-Panzer Division*, Vol. 1. Hershey, PA: Michael Horetsky, 1989.
The beginning of a unique study of *SS-Das Reich*, with organizational charts and biographies of leading personalities and high-award recipients. This volumes covers the panzer and artillery regiments, and the divisional staff. Many unpublished photos and documents.

_____. *Knights of Steel: The Structure, Development, and Personalities of the 2. SS-Panzer Division*, Vol. 2. Lancaster, PA: Mark C. Yerger, 1994.
The last published volume of this set, though two more were planned. It includes the assault gun,

motorcycle, and combat engineer battalions, and the 1944 *SS*-Combat Group *"Das Reich."* More good photos and documents.

_____. *Otto Kumm: Knight's Cross with Oakleaves and Swords*. Winnipeg: Fedorowicz, 1989.

The follow up to the next book, establishing Kumm's historical importance, with many rare photos.

_____. *Otto Weidinger: Knight's Cross with Oakleaves and Swords*. 2d ed. Atglen, PA: Schiffer, 2000.

Adds many unpublished photos to the previous edition, including fascinating group shots with important personalities.

_____. *Otto Weidinger: Knight's Cross with Oakleaves and Swords*. Winnipeg: Fedorowicz, 1987.

This began Yerger's long career in publishing documentary material provided by *Waffen-SS* veterans. A good biography of an important officer.

_____. *Riding East: The SS Cavalry Brigade in Poland and Russia 1939–1942*. Atglen, PA: Schiffer, 1996.

A very well done history of this unit, which doesn't hide the crimes it committed. Includes rare photos and documents.

_____. *Waffen-SS Commanders: The Army, Corps and Divisional Leaders of a Legend Augsberger to Kreutz*. Atglen, PA: Schiffer, 1997.

The first part of one of the most important works ever published on the *Waffen-SS*. It sets out once and for all the military credentials and successes of the higher *Waffen-SS* officers, and includes numerous unpublished photos. The information was collected from wartime official files and also provided by *Waffen-SS* veterans.

_____. *Waffen-SS Commanders: The Army, Corps and Divisional Leaders of a Legend Krüger to Zimmermann*. Atglen, PA: Schiffer, 1999.

Finishes the set begun in the previous volume, maintaining the high standard, and with supplementary information to the first part. Many more good photos.

Zetterling, Niklas. *Normandy 1944: German Military Organization, Combat Power, and Organizational Effectiveness*. Winnipeg: Fedorowicz, 2000.

A useful supplement to other works on Normandy, with a section on orders of battle that includes *Waffen-SS* units. The information comes from wartime documents.

Zoepf, Wolf T. *Seven Days in January: With the 6th SS-Mountain Division in Operation NORDWIND*. Bedford, PA: Aberjona, 2001.

The best English language book on *SS-Nord*, with the impressive detail on its role in the combat in the Vosges Mountains taken from wartime German and American documents.

Zwarts, Marcel. *German Armored Units at Arnhem, September 1944*. Hong Kong: Concord, 2001.

A mix of rare and more common photos with very good captions that identify the units and places. Much of the coverage focuses on II *SS*-Panzer Corps.

Other Titles by The Aberjona Press...

Victory Was Beyond Their Grasp: With the 272nd Volks-Grenadier Division from the Hürtgen Forest to the Heart of the Reich by *Douglas E. Nash*
412 pages. 22 Maps. 88 Photos and Drawings.
Paperbound. ISBN 13: 978-0-9777563-2-2.
$24.95 plus $4.00 US shipping

Victims, Victors: From Nazi Occupation to the Conquest of Germany as Seen by a Red Army Soldier
by *Roman Kravchenko-Berezhnoy*;
foreword by *David M. Glantz*
310 pages. 6 Maps. 26 Photos.
Paperbound. ISBN 13: 978-0-9717650-6-1.
$19.95 plus $4.00 US shipping

To the Flag! A Selection of Patriotic & Military Verse
by *Steven C. Myers*
148 pages. Photos. Paperbound. ISBN 13: 978-0-9777563-3-9.
$14.95 plus $4.00 US shipping

Slaughterhouse: The Encyclopedia of the Eastern Front
by *Keith E. Bonn, ed., et al.*
520 pages. Maps. Photos. Paperbound.
ISBN 13: 978-0-9717650-9-2.
$29.95; plus $4.50 US shipping

Seven Days in January: With the 6th SS-Mountain Division in Operation Nordwind
by *Wolf T. Zoepf*
304 pages. Maps. Photos. Index.
Paperbound. ISBN 13: 978-0-9666389-6-7.
$12.95 plus $4.00 US shipping

Five Years, Four Fronts: The War Years of Georg Grossjohann, Major, German Army (Retired)
by *Georg Grossjohann*
218 pages. Maps. Photos. Index.
Paperbound. ISBN 13: 978-0-9666389-3-6.
$14.95 plus $4.00 US shipping

Sledgehammers: Strengths and Flaws of Tiger Tank Battalions in World War II
by *Christopher Wilbeck*
272 pages. 35 Maps. 42 Photos.
Paperbound. ISBN 13: 978-0-9717650-2-3.
$19.95 plus $4.00 US shipping

Black Edelweiss: A Memoir of Combat and Conscience by a Soldier of the Waffen-SS
by *Johann Voss*
224 pages. Maps. Photos.
Paperbound. ISBN 13: 978-0-9666389-8-1.
$19.95 plus $4.00 US shipping

The Final Crisis: Combat in Northern Alsace, January 1945
by *Richard Engler*
362 pages. Maps. Photos. Index.
Paperbound. ISBN 13: 978-0-9666389-1-2.
$29.95 plus $4.00 US shipping

The Good Soldier: From Austrian Social Democracy to Communist Captivity with a Soldier of Panzer-Grenadier Division "Grossdeutschland"
by *Alfred Novotny*
160 pages. 62 Photos.
Paperbound. ISBN 13: 978-0-9666389-9-8.
$14.95 plus $4.00 US shipping
Audiobook on 6 CDs. ISBN 13: 978-0-9777563-0-8.
$29.95 plus $4.00 US shipping

Odyssey of a Philippine Scout: Fighting, Escaping and Evading the Japanese, 1941–1944
by *Arthur K. Whitehead*
304 pages. Maps. Photos.
Paperbound. ISBN 13: 978-0-9717650-4-7.
$19.95 plus $4.00 US shipping

Forthcoming from The Aberjona Press

Swedes at War: Willing Warriors of a Neutral Nation, 1914–1945 by *Lars Gyllenhaal and Lennart Westberg*
Approximately 300 pages. Maps. Photos.
Paperbound. ISBN 13: 978-0-9777563-1-5.
$19.95 (t) plus $4.00 US shipping

Defending Fortress Europe: The War Diary of the German 7th Army, June–August 1944
by *Mark Reardon*
Approximately 300 pages. Maps. Photos.
Paperbound. ISBN 13: 978-0-9717650-3-0.
$19.95 (t) plus $4.00 US shipping

For more information, visit our website at:
www.aberjonapress.com

THE ABERJONA PRESS Setting the highest standards... in *History*
P.O. Box 629, Bedford, PA 15522; **toll free: (866) 265-9063**; aegis@bedford.net

What the reviewers are saying about books by The Aberjona Press…

Victory Was Beyond Their Grasp

"While small-unit histories of World War Two's Allied forces abound, there are few counterparts that tell the story from the German side. The *Wehrmacht*'s long retreat and the utter destruction of so many combat units erased the history of its fighting forces. Using a trove of recently discovered materials, Douglas Nash has pulled together the remarkable story of one German unit that was almost continuously engaged in a futile effort to stop the Allied advance across western Europe. Here is the war we rarely see—close combat from the German side. Nash has done a great service to general readers and future historians."
—Ed Ruggero, author of *The First Men In: US Paratroopers and the Fight to Save D-Day*

"This study is unique in that it focuses on a small unit, an infantry company, when most books describe warfare on the divisional level, or an even larger scale."
—George Nipe, author of *Decision in the Ukraine, Summer 1943, II. SS and III Panzerkorps*

"As told through the eyes of German soldiers, Nash gives the first full accounting and range of experience of a Volks-Grenadier division. In detailing the experience of one such division in the Hürtgen Forest, Nash has opened a new window into the bloody fighting at the end of World War II. He also helps to explain why it was that the western allies failed to exploit their successes of the summer and autumn of 1944 and lost their momentum amid the cold, sodden, dreary forests that ranged along the German border. The Volks-Grenadier divisions, even at this late stage of the war, could call on skilled commanders, outstanding small-arms weaponry, and a pool of determined soldiers."
—Stephen G. Fritz, author of *Frontsoldaten*

Victims, Victors

"A remarkable document, casting light on events little understood. . . . Required reading for students of World War II and modern Russian history."
—Walter Dunn, *Journal of Military History*

The Good Soldier

"[Novotny's] wartime experiences . . . come vividly to life . . . [His] sharply-etched memories . . . are compelling in their detail."
—*Peoria Journal-Star*

Sledgehammers

"[*Sledgehammers*] takes a refreshing approach to the topic of Tiger tanks, the author does his homework, he writes well enough, and he remains very even-handed in his descriptions of Tiger battalions in action and in his assessment of their effectiveness. Overall, this book should favorably impress most readers, and it's probably the sort of obscure classic that will remain very much in demand over the years by armor enthusiasts in general and Tiger buffs in particular. Recommended."
—Stone and Stone Second World War Books,
the main online clearing house for information about
books about all aspects of WWII military history.

"Well written, reasonably priced, and offers an insightful professional assessment for military historians. . . . ."
—*The Journal of Military History*

"Excellent. . . . The description of the performance and the technical weaknesses of the Tiger is, in my opinion, entirely correct."
—Fritz Langanke, former Panther company commander
2nd *SS*-Panzer Division; recipient of the Knight's Cross

Black Edelweiss

"At a moment in history when the nexus between extremist ideology, individual fanaticism, and highly motivated military elites once again dominates the security and military planning of the world's democracies, the author provides a thoughtful, insightful, and highly-readable account of how a seemingly ordinary, well-educated young man can be manipulated by the values of an absolutist, all-embracing belief system, allied with longstanding familial values, into willingly going out to do righteous battle against a particular concept of 'barbarism'. . . .

"The author vividly describes the dangers, discomforts, camaraderie, and intense isolation, indeed myopia, of combat. He perfectly captures the reality of a situation where life and death are experienced at the level of the section or platoon; identification is with the company or battalion; and where interest and knowledge only rarely expand to embrace any wider setting. . . .

"A fascinating and unique contribution to our knowledge of the motivations of the men who comprised not only the *Waffen-SS*, but much of the rest of the German armed forces in the Second World War. . . . It is highly recommended."
—*The Journal of Military History*

"Highly recommended . . . complements *The Good Soldier* and *Into the Mountains Dark*."
—*Armchair General* magazine

"A strong description of a young man's burning idealism to serve his country and how this idealism is later shattered."
—Swedish State Institute for Living History

"Highly valuable because of its grass-roots perspective of the war and the Third Reich."
—*Svenska Dagbladet* (Swedish Daily Newspaper)

"[This book possesses] an authenticity lacking in works written and also adjusted long after the war."
—*Gefle Dagblad* (Gefle [Sweden] Daily Newspaper)

Seven Days in January

"Zoepf tells a great story . . . [drawing] heavily on German and American accounts. . . . The balanced, integrated account of American and German experience is exemplary. . . . The evolving German perception of their American foe is fascinating. . . . And the maps are perfect. . . . Anyone with any interest in the European campaign will find this a compelling, valuable read."
—*World War II* magazine

"A fine story by someone who tells all the nitty-gritty of this desperate action."
—Stone and Stone Second World War Books

"An engaging first-person account . . . a fine book that provides an exciting story . . . with expert analysis about small unit tactics. . . . "
—*The Journal of Military History*

"I am sure that it is a valuable contribution to the history of small unit warfare. . . . [Modern soldiers] will learn much from the daily battle analysis provided by the author, who summarizes the actions, the governing factors, and the lessons learned from each day's activities. . . ."
—General Frederick J. Kroesen, Former CG, Seventh Army, *Army* magazine

"A literary masterpiece. . . . Aberjona Press continues to find gold nuggets of history."
—*Military Heritage* magazine

The Final Crisis

"Quite remarkable. . . . Superbly researched and well written. . . . What emerges is a clear sense of just how important the individual American soldier was in winning the war in Europe and just how effectively he generally performed in combat."
—*Military Heritage* magazine

"Excellent editing and a broad purpose make this book a model for memoirs."
—*The Journal of Military History*

Five Years, Four Fronts

"This is not an *All Quiet on the Western Front* or another *The Forgotten Soldier*. In my opinion, it is a better book."
—*The Journal of Military History*

"[Grossjohann] undeniably tells it like it was."
—*Military Heritage* magazine

To the Flag!

"Captain Myers captures the emotions of the sailor and the lure of the sea in his works: *To the Flag!* A true tribute that paints in words the adventures and disappointments of veterans of the sea. Best read on a quiet, warm, breeze-stirred night while sitting on the deck. A must for the nautical library."
--Captain David E. Meadows, US Navy (Ret.),
and author of the *Sixth Fleet* series of books